Nonlinear Control Systems with Discontinuity: Theory and Practice

Tsinghua University Press

NEW AGE

Nonlinear Control Systems with Discontinuity: Theory and Practice

Edited by

Tielong Shen • Yuanzhang Sun
Yu Yao • Yasuhiko Mutou

PUBLISHING FOR ONE WORLD

NEW AGE INTERNATIONAL (P) LIMITED, PUBLISHERS
New Delhi • Bangalore • Chennai • Cochin • Guwahati • Hyderabad
Jalandhar • Kolkata • Lucknow • Mumbai • Ranchi
Visit us at **www.newagepublishers.com**

First Indian Sub-Continent Edition : 2010
by New Age International (P) Ltd., Publishers

Branches:

- 37/10, 8th Cross (Near Hanuman Temple), Azad Nagar, Chamrajpet, **Bangalore**-560 018. Tel.: (080) 2675 6823, Telefax: 2675 6820, E-mail: bangalore@newagepublishers.com
- 26, Damodaran Street, T. Nagar, **Chennai**-600 017. Tel.: (044) 24353401, Telefax: 24351463, E-mail: chennai@newagepublishers.com
- CC-39/1016, Carrier Station Road, Ernakulam South, **Cochin**-682 016. Tel.: (0484) 2377004, Telefax: 4051303. E-mail: cochin@newagepublishers.com
- Hemsen Complex, Mohd. Shah Road, Paltan Bazar, Near Starline Hotel, **Guwahati**-781 008. Tel.: (0361) 2513881. Telefax: 2543669, E-mail: guwahati@newagepublishers.com
- 105, 1st Floor, Madhiray Kaveri Tower, 3-2-19, Azam Jahi Road, Nimboliadda, **Hyderabad**-500 027. Tel.: (040) 24652456, Telefax: 24652457, E-mail:hyderabad@newagepublishers.com
- RDB Chambers (Formerly Lotus Cinema)106A, 1st Floor, S.N. Banerjee Road, **Kolkata**-700 014. Tel.: (033) 22273773, Telefax: 22275247, E-mail:kolkata@newagepublishers.com
- 16-A, Jopling Road, **Lucknow**-226 001. Tel.: (0522) 2209578, 4045297, Telefax: 2204098, E-mail: lucknow@newagepublishers.com
- 142C, Victor House, Ground Floor, N.M. Joshi Marg, Lower Parel, **Mumbai**-400 013. Tel.: (022) 24927869. Telefax: 24915415, E-mail: mumbai@newagepublishers.com
- 22, Golden House, Daryaganj, **New Delhi**-110 002. Tel.: (011) 23262370, 23262368, Telefax: 43551305. E-mail: sales@newagepublishers.com

Printed in India at Glorious Printers, Delhi.
C-10-05-4582

ISBN: 978-81-224-3059-2
Indian Edition Price: Rs. 495.00

PUBLISHING FOR ONE WORLD
NEW AGE INTERNATIONAL (P) LIMITED, PUBLISHERS
4835/24, Ansari Road, Daryaganj, New Delhi-110002
Visit us at **www.newagepublishers.com**

Preface

Discontinuity in dynamic systems is a tough property for analysis and control of the system. However, in practical engineering, we are often faced with the discontinuity in control system design. In dynamical systems, the discontinuity is usually caused by natural phenomenon such as static friction, stroke changes etc., in mechanical systems or control actions engineered by controller design such as variable structure control, switching control, etc. For this kind of systems, the conventional framework for analysis and synthesis is not sufficient to provide a solution in exact theoretical sense. The field of control theory for dynamical systems with discontinuity is widely open for future research and development.

The aim of the second China-Japan joint workshop on control theory and technology is to provide a forum for scientists on automatic control from both China and Japan to exchange contemporary research results on this issue and to promote the applications of advanced control theory to practical engineering problems, and as a result to enhance the development and spread new results of control theory on the dynamical systems with discontinuities. The papers included in this book are selected from the workshop, and this selection is focused on the papers dealing with the closely related topics of *nonsmooth, switching and hybrid systems* and its applications in self driven hybrid systems such as the power systems, aircraft, land vehicles, mechanical and electrical systems.

This book is organized as three parts: the first part contains 7 papers that addressed theoretical problems in design of nonlinear control systems with discontinuity and time-delay. The second part contains 6 papers with physical application of mechanical and electrical system, and the last part collects 4 papers that focus on the control problem in vehicular systems including railway, automotive engine, etc.

The editors appreciate the Control and Simulation Center, Harbin Institute of Technology. The second China-Japan joint workshop on control theory and technology was hosted by the center as oneday event in Victoria Hotel, Harbin, at 6th of August, 2006. The workshop was sponsored technically by Technical Committee on Control Theory, CAA(China), Committee of Electric Mathematics, CALC(China), Committee on Adaptive Learning Control, SICE(Japan). Moreover, it should be noted that this book is the second book published by Tsinghua University Press for the China-Japan joint workshop on this topic. The first one was published in May of 2005 that contains the selected papers from the first China-Japan joint workshop on control theory and applications held in Fragrant Hill Hotel Beijing, 22-26, Sep., 2004, under financial support from Natural Science Foundation of China (NSFC) and Japan Science Promotion Society (JSPS).

Finally, we would like to express our thanks to Dr. Fenghua He for helping in organizing the workshop, and the PhD Candidate, Mr. Kai Zheng for technical helping in editing the book.

Tielong Shen Sophia University, Tokyo, Japan
Yuanzhang Sun Tsinghua University, Beijing, China
Yu Yao Harbin Institute of Technology, Harbin, China
Yasuhiko Mutou Sophia University, Tokyo, Japan

Beijing, 30 June, 2007

Contents

Part I

Design Method of Nonlinear Systems

Design of Decentralized Robust Full-MRACS Based on Sliding Mode Control

Yazdan Bavafa-Toosi[1] and Hiromitsu Ohmori[2]

[1] Y. Bavafa-Toosi is with the Graduate School of Science and Technology, School of Integrated Design Engineering, Keio University, Yokohama, Kanagawa 223-8522, Japan (phone: +81-35-566-1727; fax: +81-35-566-1720)
[2] H. Ohmori is with the School of Integrated Design Engineering, Keio University, Yokohama, Kanagawa 223-8522, Japan
ohm@sd.keio.ac.jp

1 Introduction

Mathematical theory of networks and systems has been significantly enriched in the last few decades due partly to the injection of new blood from different backgrounds. The contributions of past and present investigators span a vast body of theory and applications. Of particular importance in this arena is the field of decentralized adaptive control, whose relevant results are teeming in the literature [1].

In the broad sense, the existing results on decentralized adaptive control can be categorized as in the following, where due to lack of space not are all of the pertinent works cited:

- Decentralized linear adaptive control [12~16];
- Decentralized intelligent adaptive control [17~20];
- Decentralized optimal adaptive control [21];
- Decentralized robust adaptive control [22~26];
- Decentralized nonlinear adaptive control [27~30].

It is noted that it is possible to have different categorizations (e.g. vs. linear/nonlinear systems, or delay-free/delay systems) or to further ramify each category and/or to have their integrations. Actually, many of the existing results present an integrated approach and do not fully belong to one of the above categories. Here, in particular, (in some sense) from the integration of the last two we single out the sequel branch,

- *Decentralized adaptive variable-structure (or sliding-mode) control (VSC or SMC)* [31~42][3], since it will be conceptually used in this work.

To the best of our knowledge, and broadly speaking, all the existing decentralized MRAC methods suffer from two major drawbacks, see [1] for details:

[3] It should be noted that the results of [34] and [37] are erroneous, as reported in [42].

- accommodation of reference models for subsystems only, i.e., not for interconnections;
- necessity for the so-called matching conditions.

In the spirit of a recursive nonlinear design methodology - the so-called integrator back stepping - developed in the early 1990s [43], which alleviated the necessity for matching conditions in centralized adaptive control, the second drawback was partially solved in the mid 1990s [44]. More precisely, for the special class of large-scale systems transformable to decentralized strict feedback form, the aforementioned necessity was relaxed in [44]. Later, it has been tackled by a few other works as well, see [1] for details.

As for the first problem, the situation is worse. In fact, it seems to be folk knowledge that it is irrelevant or rather impossible to consider a full reference model whose interconnection parts are not identical with those of the system, since the system has no adjustable parameters in those parts. Nevertheless, this argument, though appealing, is no mathematical proof.

On the other hand, incorporation of a desirable reference model for interconnections, i.e., a full model reference whose interconnection parts are not identical with those of the system, will result in performance enhancement, since the overall system will behave like a reference model whose interconnections, as well as subsystems, are desirable. Inspired by this, the aforementioned folk knowledge is examined in this work and this long-standing stereotype is shown to be wrong. More precisely, for systems satisfying the matching conditions, a *full*-MRAC with non-identical interconnections is proposed in this paper.

Before embarking on the main result, a general picture of the status quo of MRAC is drawn in the following.

In both centralized and decentralized MRAC, the subsequent assumptions are standard [43,45~52], where in the decentralized case the plant refers to each of the isolated subsystems:

- The plant is single-input single output (SISO);
- The plant is minimum phase;
- The relative degree of the plant is known, usually one or two;
- The sign of the high-frequency gain is known;
- There is no nonlinearity, disturbance, perturbation;
- There is no delay in interconnections.

It is of course well known that in the realm of centralized MRAC there are *many* results alleviating any one or more of the above assumptions or rather shortcomings [43,45~52], but, to the best of our knowledge, not all of them together. In the realm of decentralized MRAC the situation is poorer: there are only *afew* works addressing some of them. In particular, to our best knowledge, only some VSC-based schemes have been able to relax the first and/or second of the aforementioned defects. Also, the relative degree of the plant can be larger than two, but an upper bound of it should be known a priori [11], the sign of the high-frequency gain can be unknown [12], and perturbations, disturbances, nonlinearities, and delays can be handled, e.g., [22~26]. In addition, it should be mentioned that the case of unknown time-delay interconnections has been tackled only by few works like [25, 26, 40].

On the other hand, in both centralized and decentralized cases, adaptation and control laws depend on whether the plant (each isolated subsystem) is known or unknown. That is, to our best knowledge, there is no universal MRAC scheme treating known and unknown systems in a unified framework with the same adaptation and control laws.

What is presented in this work is a full-MRAC with non-identical interconnections that rectifies *all* the above-mentioned shortcomings as well. More precisely, without any of the aforementioned standard assumptions, we consider a class of *known* systems with unknown time-varying interconnection delays and unknown time-varying perturbations (model uncertainties, nonlinearities, or external disturbances), upper bounds of the latter being unknown. The accommodation of this kind of perturbations - along with a *reformulation* of the problem - enables us to consider *unknown* systems in the same framework, as will be explained in the next section. For this class a decentralized robust full-MRAC with non-identical interconnections is presented. To this end, conceptually similar to [31 ~ 42] in particular [40][4], a stable decentralized full-model-reference adaptive sliding-mode control is proposed. The controller has two parts: the adaptive part which compensates for the perturbations whose upper bounds are unknown, and the linear part, together enforcing the sliding motion and global asymptotic exact tracking. Moreover, as will be seen, the proposed controller does not suffer from the inherent shortcomings of standard VSC, namely, need for a priori knowledge of the upper bound of perturbations (as mentioned above), and the notorious chattering phenomenon.

The organization of this work is as follows. In Section II the system is described and the problem is formulated. Controller design is presented in Section III, where the stability of the system is proven using an improved Lyapunov function. Finally, conclusions are drawn in Section IV. This work presents part of [1] in continuation of [53, 54].

2 System Description

Consider a large-scale system consisting of N interconnected subsystems whose ith one is represented by,

$$\begin{aligned} \dot{x}_i &= A_i x_i + B_i u_i + v_i + \sum_{j \neq i}^{N} A_{ij} x_j (t - \tau_{ij}) \\ x_i &= \varphi_i, t \in [-T, 0], \end{aligned} \tag{1}$$

[4] This work can also be seen as an extension of [40] to full-MRAC and also to the case of unknown systems, see Remark 3.4 and 3.5 for details.

in which $x_i(t) \in \mathbb{R}^{n_i}$, $u_i(t) \in \mathbb{R}^{m_i}$, and $v_i(x_i, u_i, x_j, t) \in \mathbb{R}^{n_i}$ are the state, input, and uncertain nonlinear time-varying parameter perturbation of the ith subsystem. More precisely, v_i denotes *any* unknown time-varying perturbation in the form of model uncertainty ($\Delta A_i x_i$, $\Delta B_i x_i$, $\sum_{j\neq i}^{N} \Delta A_{ij} x_j$), external disturbance, or nonlinearity. The scalar function $0 \leqslant \tau_{ij}(t) \leqslant T < \infty$ represents the unknown nonnegative continuous bounded time-varying delay, where T is a known positive constant. The continuous function $\varphi_i(t) \in \mathbb{R}^{n_i}$ denotes the arbitrary initial condition. Moreover, all the matrices A_i, B_i, A_{ij} are known, of appropriate dimensions, with obvious meanings, and (A_i, B_i) is a controllable pair. The terms $\sum_{j\neq i}^{N} \Delta A_{ij} x_j$ denote the interconnections with other subsystems. In case of unknown systems, the matrices A_i, B_i, A_{ij} are chosen arbitrarily up to the assumptions to follow shortly. The rest of the unknown parts are lumped and denoted by v_i. This reformulation enables us to treat both known and unknown systems in the same framework with the same adaptation and laws.

$$\dot{x}_{mi} = A_{mi} x_{mi} + B_{mi} r_i + \sum_{j\neq i}^{N} A_{mij} x_{mj} \tag{2}$$

in which the involved terms have obvious meanings. In addition, A_{mi} is chosen such that (A_{mi}, B_i) is a controllable pair. Defining the tracking error vector as,

$$e_i = x_i - x_{mi}, \quad i = 1, \cdots, N \tag{3}$$

the error dynamics is given by $i = 1, \cdots, N$,

$$\dot{e}_i = A_{mi} e_i + (A_i - A_{mi}) x_i + B_i u_i + \sum_{j\neq i}^{N} A_{ij} x_j (t - \tau_{ij}) - B_{mi} r_i - \sum_{j\neq i}^{N} A_{mij} x_{mj} + v_i \tag{4}$$

As stated before, as in the majority of the literature, we consider the class of systems satisfying the matching conditions. As such, there exist continuous matrix and vector functions M, H, J, G, and f (in general, non-unique) of appropriate dimensions such that,

$$\begin{aligned} A_i - A_{mi} &= B_i M_i \\ A_{ij} &= B_i H_{ij} \\ A_{mij} &= B_i J_{ij} \\ B_{mi} &= B_i G_i \\ v_i &= B_i f_i \end{aligned} \tag{5}$$

It should be noted that although this class does not cover all systems, it is still fairly large and embodies a huge body of real-world systems like many mechanical ones [1~52]. Besides, it is clear that the above conditions are satisfied, based on the theory of generalized inverse [55], iff $\text{rank}(X; B) = \text{rank}(B)$, where $X = BY$.

For this class the following assumptions are made, as in the literature, where the first two are clearly feasible and natural in practice:
A1) Local controllability and availability of all states for measurement in all time;
A2) Continuous differentiability and piecewise continuity in time;
A3) Existence of unknown positive scalar constants α_i and β_i such that [56],

$$||f_i|| \leqslant \alpha_i + \beta_i||x_i|| \tag{6}$$

for all time. This assumption will be used in the stability proof.

Remark 2.1 *For the aforementioned large class of real-world systems we are concerned with actual signals, systems, and quantities. The assumption A3 is thus natural and does not impose any restriction on the class of systems considered, since it is actually equivalent to the Lipschitz boundedness of the perturbations. For the sake of completeness, on the other hand, the following mathematical argument can be made. If an upper bound on $||f_i||$ is given in terms of higher orders of $||x_i||$, e.g., a polynomial of high order, still the first order given bound is valid, because we are concerned with actual signals and quantities, which are all bounded, not with abstract mathematical quantities. However, in this case, due to conservatism, the control effort will be in general larger.*

Under the aforementioned assumptions A1~A3 and (5), the error dynamics is reduced to,

$$\dot{e}_i = A_{mi}e_i + B_iM_ix_i + B_iu_i + \sum_{j\neq i}^{N} B_iH_{ij}x_j(t-\tau_{ij}) - B_iG_ir_i - \sum_{j\neq i}^{N} B_iJ_{ij}x_{mj} + B_if_i \tag{7}$$

In the proceeding section a decentralized full-model-reference adaptive sliding-mode controller will be proposed by which the global stability of the error dynamics is guaranteed. Prior to this, one of the merits of the advocated methodology is restated.

Remark 2.2 *The above unified analysis has a nice interpretation and is worth paraphrasing. For both known and unknown systems, the system can be perturbed, disturbed, nonlinear, and/or time varying. All the designer needs to do is to choose the system parameters (A_i, B_i, A_{ij}) some constant matrices satisfying (5) with (A_i, B_i) controllable (and to pursue the proposed synthesis approach of the next section). Needless to say, in general, the closer these parameters to their true values, the smaller the v_i, and hence the smaller and smoother the control action and the transient error.*

3 Controller Design

The majority of the existing MRAC methods fall in three main categories: Lyapunov function method, hyperstability method, and SMC (or VSC) method. The advantages and disadvantages of each category have been extensively studied in the literature. The adaptive SMC strategy is adopted in this work.

3.1 Conventional SMC Schemes

The principle of the conventional SMC method is to employ a discontinuous control law to drive the system to the origin along a user-specified trajectory, the so-called sliding mode [57~62]. Broadly speaking, the design procedure can be divided into two steps. In the first step, some discontinuous surfaces (i.e., sliding hyperplanes) are designed in such a way that not only the sliding motion can take place on them, but also some desired performance is achieved. In the second step, a discontinuous control law is derived by which the sliding motion is guaranteed.

It is well-known that VSC exhibits well transient response and is a powerful tool for handling uncertain perturbations, nonlinearities, and disturbances. Two major disadvantages, nevertheless, are associated with it. The first one is the notorious chattering phenomenon, which is not only detrimental to the control object, but also excites the high frequency unmodeled plant dynamics. The second one is that, in general, upper bounds of perturbations (model uncertainties, nonlinearities, or disturbances) are needed to be known a priori, whilst in practice it is often difficult or impossible to have a (non-conservative) measure of them.

These shortcomings are rectified in the ensuing development.

3.2 The Proposed Controller

To compensate for the inherent, undesirable chattering problem, apart from quick fixes like the variable sliding surface [31], boundary-layer technique [59], and filtering and variable step-size implementation [60], there has been a fundamental modification in the traditional SMC scheme in that the discontinuous control law is replaced by a continuous one [62], while preserving all the other features of the approach. As will be seen, our proposed controller is also continuous and thus does not suffer from the chattering problem (see also Remarks 3.4 and 3.5). The sliding surface is defined as,

$$s_i = C_i e_i - \int_0^t C_i(A_{mi} + B_i K_i) e_i \, \mathrm{d}\tau \qquad i = 1, \cdots, N \tag{8}$$

where $C_i \in \mathbb{R}^{n_i \times n_i}$ is of full rank and chosen such that $C_i B_i$ is invertible. The matrix $K_i \in \mathbb{R}^{m_i \times n_i}$ is designed such that $A_{mi} + B_i K_i$ is Hurwitz, see Remark 3.1.

As for the unknown upper bounds of perturbations, similar to the method of [56], later used in [40], the following strategy is adopted. It is assumed that the earlier-mentioned assumption A3, namely, $||f_i|| \leqslant \alpha_i + \beta_i ||x_i||$ holds. Then, some adaptation laws are proposed for the unknown upper bounds, and an adaptive sliding-mode controller is designed accordingly. More precisely, the scalars $\hat{\alpha}_i$ and $\widehat{\beta}_i$ are used to adapt the unknown constants α_i and β_i, respectively. The adaptation errors are defined by $\Delta\alpha_i \stackrel{\text{def}}{=} \hat{\alpha}_i - \alpha_i$ and $\Delta\beta_i \stackrel{\text{def}}{=} \widehat{\beta}_i - \beta_i$. The controller is proposed as,

$$u_i = u_i^{lin} + u_i^{adp} \tag{9}$$

where the linear and adaptive parts are respectively given by,

$$\begin{aligned} u_i^{lin} &= -M_i x_i + G_i r_i + K_i e_i - (C_i B_i)^{-1}\lambda_i s_i \\ &\quad -(C_i B_i)^{-1} s_i ||s_i||^{-1} \Big(\sum_{j\neq i}^{N} ||C_j B_j|| ||H_{ji}|| x_i^{\text{sup}}(t)\Big) \\ &\quad -(C_i B_i)^{-1} s_i ||s_i||^{-1} \Big(\sum_{j\neq i}^{N} ||C_j B_j|| ||J_{ji}|| ||x_{mi}||\Big) \\ u_i^{adp} &= -B_i^{\mathrm{T}} C_i^{\mathrm{T}} s_i ||s_i^{\mathrm{T}} C_i B_i||^{-1} (\widehat{\alpha}_i + \widehat{\beta}_i ||x_i||) \end{aligned} \tag{10}$$

in which λ_i is a user-specified positive constant and $x_i^{\text{sup}}(t) \stackrel{\text{def}}{=} \sup_{t-T \leqslant h \leqslant t} ||x_i(h)||$.

The adaptation parameters are updated by,

$$\begin{aligned} \dot{\widehat{\alpha}}_i &= \rho_i \left(\frac{||s_i^{\mathrm{T}} C_i B_i||}{||s_i||} \right) \\ \dot{\widehat{\beta}}_i &= \mu_i \left(\frac{||s_i^{\mathrm{T}} C_i B_i|| ||x_i||}{||s_i||} \right) \end{aligned} \tag{11}$$

in which the positive scalars ρ_i, μ_i denote the adaptation gains. In theory, the higher the adaptation gains, the higher the adaptation rates. In practice, this of course has an upper bound due to actuator limitations and other practical considerations including the safe operation region of the plant.

The main result of this work is presented in the sequel theorem.

Theorem 3.1 *Given the large-scale system (1), the full reference model (2), and all the earlier-mentioned assumptions. Using the sliding hyperplanes (8), if the sub-controllers $u_i (i = 1, \cdots, N)$ are designed by (9),(10) and adapted by (11), then the error dynamics (7) is globally asymptotically stable.*

Proof: Consider the improved Lyapunov function,

$$V = \sum_{i=1}^{N} ||s_i|| + \sum_{i=1}^{N} \frac{1}{2} \left(\rho_i^{-1} \tilde{\alpha}_i^2 + \mu_i^{-1} \tilde{\beta}_i^2 \right) \tag{12}$$

The derivative of V is,

$$\dot{V} = \sum_{i=1}^{N} \frac{s_i^{\mathrm{T}} \dot{s}_i}{||s_i||} + \sum_{i=1}^{N} \left(\rho_i^{-1} \tilde{\alpha}_i \dot{\tilde{\alpha}}_i + \mu_i^{-1} \tilde{\beta}_i \dot{\tilde{\beta}}_i \right) \tag{13}$$

Similar to [40], it is easy to show that $\dot{V} \leqslant -\sum_{i=1}^{N} \lambda_i ||s_i||$ and conclude that $\lim_{t\to\infty} s_i \to 0$. In other words, the sliding motion will eventually be obtained. When the system is in the sliding mode $s_i = 0$, $\dot{s}_i = 0$, where the latter is obtained by the equivalent control,

$$u_i^{equ} = -M_i x_i - \sum_{j\neq i}^{N} H_{ij} x_j(t-\tau_{ij}) - f_i + G_i r_i + \sum_{j\neq i}^{N} J_{ij} x_{mj} + K_i e_i \quad (14)$$

yielding $\dot{e}_i = (A_{mi} + B_i K_i)e_i$, guaranteeing the global asymptotic stability of the error dynamics. □

Some remarks are in order.

Remark 3.1 *The above theorem implies that the system state and the adaptive parameters are all bounded.*

Remark 3.2 *Among* [53, 54], *eigenstructure assignment can be employed as a powerful technique to design K_i so that some desired error dynamics is achieved. Due to lack of space, and because it is not the objective of this paper, it is not further followed inhere. However, the following trade-off is noted as a rule of thumb: the larger K_i, the faster the error convergence to zero, but the larger the control effort in the transient phase.*

Remark 3.3 *The difference between this work and that of* [40] *is remarkable: a) incorporation of a full reference model with non-identical interconnections, which is novel, b) applying the same method in the same framework without any modifications in adaptation and control laws to unknown systems (the above-cited paper considers only known systems) by the way of reformulation of the problem, which is a remarkable distinction of this work, not existing even in centralized adaptive control results* [43,45~52], *and c) giving more insight to the details of the approach. On the other hand, formulation wise, the differences are not considerable: the presence of the reference model for interconnections, A_{mij}, resulting in the modifications of the matching assumptions (5) and u_i^{lin}.*

Remark 3.4 *A mistake in* [40, page 1217] *is pointed out, or rather, the following explanation is added: Contrary to what they say, their controller - similar to ours - is continuous and thus does not suffer from the chattering problem, for multi-input multi-output (MIMO) subsystems. However, it is clear that if the ith subsystem is SISO, then s_i and $C_i B_i$ will be scalars, and thus $s_i||s_i||^{-1}$ and $B_i^{\mathrm{T}} C_i^{\mathrm{T}} s_i||s_i^{\mathrm{T}} C_i B_i||^{-1}$ will be sign functions (of their arguments), making the ith control input discontinuous. In this case, any of the previously-mentioned quick fixes can be used for that subsystem.*

Remark 3.5 *Another mistake in* [40, page 1215] *is pointed out: They argue that since in finite time s_i will not be exactly equal to zero, in practice the adaptive parameters (11) will increase until $s_i = 0$, and thus they propose the dead-zone technique as a remedy. In their statement the conclusion (i.e., unbounded growth of the adaptive parameters, and the use of the dead-zone technique as* *a remedy) is correct, but the reason (i.e., because in finite time s_i will not be exactly equal to zero) is wrong. In fact, it is easy to show that independently of s_i the adaptive parameters in (11) will unboundedly increase. To show this, suppose the ith subsystem is SISO. Then,*

$$\begin{aligned} \widehat{\alpha}_i &= \widehat{\alpha}_i(0) + \int_0^t \rho_i \left(\frac{\|s_i^{\mathrm{T}} C_i B_i\|}{\|s_i\|} \right) \, \mathrm{d}t \\ &= \widehat{\alpha}_i(0) + \rho_i |C_i B_i| t \,, \end{aligned} \tag{15}$$

which will grow unboundedly independently of s_i. In the MIMO case, note that at any time the integrand is positive, and through time that s_i decreases and tends to zero, $\frac{\|s_i^{\mathrm{T}} C_i B_i\|}{\|s_i\|}$ increases and tends to its maximum, which is the largest singular value of C_iB_i, a constant positive scalar. That is, again the adaptive parameter will grow unboundedly independently of s_i. For the sake of completeness it is added, though it is clear, that in the MIMO case the adaptive parameter does depend on s_i, but no matter s_i becomes zero or not, the adaptive parameter will increase unboundedly. Moreover, because we have a tracking not a regulation problem, x_i will not be regulated to zero, and thus a similar argument applies to $\widehat{\beta}_i$. (In case of a regulation problem that x_i is regulated to zero, although $\widehat{\beta}_i$ will be bounded, it may be unacceptably large.) Consequently, in order to avoid these problems, the dead-zone technique is used as a remedy, which is pervasive in the VSC literature,

$$\dot{\widehat{\alpha}}_i = \begin{cases} \rho_i \left(\frac{\|s_i^{\mathrm{T}} C_i B_i\|}{\|s_i\|} \right) &, \|s_i\| \geqslant d \\ 0 &, \|s_i\| < d \end{cases} \tag{16a}$$

$$\dot{\widehat{\beta}}_i = \begin{cases} \mu_i \left(\frac{\|s_i^{\mathrm{T}} C_i B_i\| \|x_i\|}{\|s_i\|} \right) &, \|s_i\| \geqslant d \\ 0 &, \|s_i\| < d \end{cases} \tag{16b}$$

in which the small positive constant d denotes the border of the dead zone.

Remark 3.6 *No simulation results are offered since the present work is in principle similar to* [40], *as explained above, which provides some. In other words, the applicability and effectiveness of the advocated methodology are already verified.*

Remark 3.7 *It is noteworthy that in the matching assumptions on the interconnections, i.e., $A_{ij} = B_i H_{ij}$, $A_{mij} = B_i J_{ij}$, there is no assumption on H_{ij}, J_{ij}. Thus, the interconnection parts of the system and model are non-identical. On the other hand, still there remains the fact that this rebuttal is for the class of systems considered in this work, which, though fairly large, does not include all systems, see Section 4.*

Remark 3.8 *It was first proven in* [63] *and* [31] *that the matching conditions (5) are sufficient for solving the centralized and decentralized MRAC problems for the class of systems described by (1), respectively. Here we established the same result for the decentralized full-MRAC problem and the same class of systems corrupted by unknown delays and perturbations.*

4 Concluding Remarks

Inspired by performance considerations, the long-standing stereotype that decentralized MRAC methods can consider reference models only for subsystems, and not for interconnections, has been shown to be wrong. Performance enhancement can thus be achieved by enforcing the system to behave like a full reference model whose interconnections, as well as subsystems, are desirable. To this end, for a class of known/unknown large-scale systems with unknown time-varying interconnection delays and unknown time-varying perturbations whose upper bounds are unknown, a decentralized full-model-reference adaptive sliding-mode control has been proposed. Each subcontroller has a composite structure, the adaptive part which compensates for the perturbations whose upper bounds are unknown, and the linear part, together globally asymptotically stabilizing the error dynamics.

The advocated approach has the sequel distinctive merits: a) applicability to both known and unknown systems in a unified framework with the same adaptation and control laws, b) removal of all the standard assumptions in MRAC (except the knowledge of the order of the system), and c) resolution of the inherent problems of standard SMC. In particular, a), put simply, means that for both known and unknown systems, the system can be perturbed, disturbed, nonlinear, and/or time varying. All the designer needs to do is to *adopt* the parameters of the system some constant matrices satisfying conditions (5) and A1, which is always possible, and to follow the proposed synthesis methodology. In general, the more exact this adoption, the better the result; that is, the closer these parameters to their true values, the smaller and smoother the control effort and the transient error.

Among the topics for future research are the extension of the idea of decentralized (robust) full-MRAC to larger classes of systems [64],[65] (including those not satisfying the matching conditions (5) and those not in the input-output decentralized form) and to the output feedback case, as well as the use of flexible neural networks [66~70] in subcontrollers.

Acknowledgement

This work was supported in part by a Grant in Aid for the 21st Century Center of Excellence for "System Design: Paradigm Shift from Intelligence to Life" from The Ministry of Education, Culture, Sport and Technology of Japan.

References

1. Y. Bavafa-Toosi, Decentralized adaptive control of large-scale system, *PhD Dissertation, School of Integrated Design Engineering, Keio University, Yokohama, Japan*, 2006 (in preparation).
2. M. Sundareshan, A condition for decentralization in model reference adaptive systems, *IEEE Trans. Automatic Control*, vol. 21, no. 6, pp. 880-881, 1976.

3. P. A. Ioannou, Decentralized adaptive control of interconnected systems, *IEEE Trans. Automatic Control*, vol. 31, no. 4, pp. 291-298, 1986.
4. D. T. Gavel and D. D. Siljak, Decentralized adaptive control: Structural conditions for stability, *IEEE Trans. Automatic Control*, vol. 34, no. 4, pp. 413-426, 1989.
5. K. A. Ossman, Indirect adaptive control for interconnected systems, *IEEE Trans. Automatic Control*, vol. 34, no. 8, pp. 908-911, 1989.
6. H. Seraji, Decentralized adaptive control of manipulators: Theory, simulation, and experimentation, *IEEE Trans. Robotics and Automation*, vol. 5, no. 2, pp. 183-201, 1989.
7. L. Shi and S. K. Singh, Decentralized adaptive controller design for large-scale systems with higher order interconnections, *IEEE Trans. Automatic Control*, vol. 37, no. 8, pp. 1106-1118, 1992.
8. A. Karakasoglu, S. I. Sudharsanan, and M. K. Sundareshan, Identification and decentralized adaptive control using dynamical neural networks with application to robotic manipulators, *IEEE Trans. Neural Networks*, vol. 4, no. 6, pp. 919-930, 1993.
9. A. Datta, Performance improvement in decentralized adaptive control: a modified model reference scheme, *IEEE Trans. Automatic Control*, vol. 38, no. 11, pp. 1717-1722, 1993.
10. R. Ortega, An energy amplification condition for decentralized adaptive stabilization, *IEEE Trans. Automatic Control*, vol. 41, no. 2, pp. 285-288, 1996.
11. C. Wen and Y. C. Soh, Decentralized model reference adaptive control without restriction on subsystem relative degrees, *IEEE Trans. Automatic Control*, vol. 44, no. 7, pp. 1464-1469, 1999.
12. X. Ye, Decentralized adaptive regulation with unknown high-frequency-gain signs, *IEEE Trans. Automatic Control*, vol. 44, no. 11, pp. 2072-2076, 1999.
13. K. S. Narendra and N. O. Oleng, Exact output tracking in decentralized adaptive control systems, *IEEE Trans. Automatic Control*, vol. 47, no. 2, pp. 390-395, 2002.
14. X. Ye and H. Jie, Decentralized adaptive output regulation for a class of large-scale nonlinear systems, *IEEE Trans. Automatic Control*, vol. 48, no. 2, pp. 276-281, 2003.
15. B. M. Mirkin, Comment on "Decentralized adaptive output regulation for a class of large-scale nonlinear systems", *IEEE Trans. Automatic Control*, vol. 48, no. 2, pp. 348-350, 2003.
16. N. Hovakimyan, E. Lavretsky, B.J. Yang, and A. J. Calise, Coordinated decentralized adaptive output feedback control of interconnected systems, *IEEE Trans. Neural Networks*, vol. 16, no. 1, pp. 184-194, 2005.
17. Y. Jin, Decentralized adaptive fuzzy control of robot manipulators, *IEEE Trans. Systems, Man and Cybernetics-B*, vol. 8, no. 1, pp. 47-57, 1998.
18. F. Da, Decentralized sliding mode adaptive controller design based on fuzzy neural networks for interconnected uncertain nonlinear systems, *IEEE Trans. Neural Networks*, vol. 11, no. 6, pp. 1471-1480, 2000.
19. K. Y. Lian, C. S. Chiu, and P. Liu, Semi-decentralized adaptive fuzzy control for cooperative multirobot systems with Hinf motion/internal force tracking performance, *IEEE Trans. Systems, Man and Cybernetics B*, vol. 32, no. 3, pp. 269-280, 2002.
20. S. Tong, H. X. Li and G. Chen, Adaptive fuzzy decentralized control for a class of large-scale nonlinear systems, *IEEE Trans. Systems, Man and Cybernetics-B*, vol. 34, no. 1, pp. 770-775, 2004.
21. C. M. Lagoa, C. Hao, and B. A. Movsichoff, Adaptive control algorithms for decentralized optimal traffic engineering in the Internet, *IEEE Trans. Networking*, vol. 12, no. 2, pp. 415-428, 2004.

22. D. J Hill, C. Wen, and G. C. Goodwin, Stability analysis of decentralized robust adaptive control, *Systems & Control Letters*, vol. 11, no. 4, pp. 277-285, 1988.
23. W. Changyun, Indirect robust totally decentralized adaptive control of continuous-time interconnected systems, *IEEE Trans. Automatic Control*, vol. 40, no. 6, pp. 1122-1126, 1995.
24. Y. Liu and X. Y. Li, Decentralized robust adaptive control of nonlinear systems with unmodeled dynamics, *IEEE Trans. Automatic Control*, vol. 47, no. 5, pp. 848-856, 2002.
25. H. Wu, Decentralized adaptive robust control for a class of large-scale systems including delayed state perturbations in the interconnections, *IEEE Trans. Automatic Control*, vol. 47, no. 10, pp. 1745-1751, 2002.
26. C. Hua, X. Guan, and P. Shi, Decentralized robust model reference adaptive control for interconnected time-delay systems, *in Proceedings of the American Control Conf.*, vol. 5, pp. 4285-4289, Boston, MA, July 2004.
27. A. Hmammed, and L. Radouane, Decentralized nonlinear adaptive feedback stabilization of large scale interconnected systems, *IEE Proceedings-Control Theory and Applications*, vol. 130, no. 1, pp. 57-62, 1983.
28. Z. P. Jiang, Decentralized and adaptive nonlinear tracking of large-scale systems via output feedback, *IEEE Trans. Automatic Control*, vol. 45, no. 11, pp. 2122-2128, 2000.
29. H. Zhang and C. Lilong, Decentralized nonlinear adaptive control of an HVAC system, *IEEE Trans. Systems, Man and Cybernetics-C*, vol. 32, no. 4, pp. 493-498, 2002.
30. L. Jiang, Q. H. Wu, and J. Y. Wen, Decentralized nonlinear adaptive control for multimachine power systems via high-gain perturbation observer, *IEEE Trans. Circuits and Systems I*, vol. 51, no.10, pp. 2052-2059, 2004.
31. F. Al-Abbass and U. Ozguner, Decentralized model reference adaptive system using variable structure control, *in Proceedings of the 24th IEEE Conf. Decision and Control*, pp. 1473-1478, 1985.
32. H. Khurana, S. I. Ahson, and S. S. Lamba, On stabilization of large-scale control systems using variable structure system theory, *IEEE Trans. Automatic Control*, vol. 31, pp. 176-178, 1986.
33. G. P. Mathews and R. A. DeCarlo, Decentralized tracking for a class of interconnected nonlinear systems using variable structure control, *Automatica*, vol. 24, pp. 187-193, 1988.
34. X. Xiaohao, Y. Wu, and W. Huang, Variable-structure control approach of decentralized model reference adaptive systems, *IEE Proceedings-Control Theory and Applications*, vol. 147, no. 4, pp. 395-402, 1990.
35. W. J. Wang and J. L. Lee, Decentralized variable structure control design in perturbed nonlinear systems, *ASME Jr. Dynam. Syst. Measur. Control*, vol. 115, pp. 551-554, 1993.
36. G. Feng and Y. A. Jiang, Variable structure based decentralised adaptive control, *IEE Proceedings-Control Theory and Applications*, vol. 142, no. 5, pp. 439-443, 1995.
37. C. C. Chiang, Decentralized variable-structure model reference adaptive control of linear time-varying large-scale systems with bounded disturbances, *Int. Jr. Systems Science*, vol. 26, no. 10, pp. 1993-2003, 1995.
38. K. C. Hsu, Decentralized variable-structure control design for uncertain large-scale systems with series nonlinearities, *Int. Jr. Control*, vol. 68, no. 6, pp. 1231-1240, 1997.

39. K. C. Hsu, Decentralized sliding mode control for large-scale time-delayed systems with series nonlinearities, *ASME Jr. Dynamic Systems, Measurement and Control*, vol. 121, pp. 708-713, 1999.
40. C. H. Chou and C. C. Cheng, A decentralized model reference adaptive variable structure controller for large-scale time-varying delay systems, *IEEE Trans. Automatic Control*, vol. 48, no. 7, pp. 1213-1217, 2003.
41. Shyu, K. K., W. J. Liu, and K. C. Hsu, Design of large-scale time-delayed systems with dead-zone input via variable structure control, *Automatica*, vol. 41, no. 7, pp. 1239-1246, 2005.
42. Y. Bavafa-Toosi and H. Ohmori, Comment on Decentralized variable-structure model reference adaptive control of linear time-varying large-scale systems with bounded disturbances, *Int. Jr. Systems Science*, 2005 (under review).
43. M. Krstic, I. Kanellakopoulos, and P. V. Kokotovic, Nonlinear and adaptive control design. *NY: Wiley*, 1995.
44. S. Jain and F. Khorrami, Decentralized adaptive control of a class of large-scale interconnected nonlinear systems, *IEEE Trans. Automatic Control*, vol. 42, no. 2, pp. 136-154, 1997.
45. G. C. Goodwin and K. S. Sin, Adaptive filtering, prediction and control. *NJ: Prentice-Hall*, 1984.
46. K. S. Narendra and A. M. Annaswamy, Stable adaptive systems. *NJ: Prentice-Hall*, 1989.
47. S. S. Sastry and M. Bodson, Adaptive control: Stability, convergence, and robustness. *NJ: Prentice-Hall*, 1989.
48. K. S. Tsakalis and P. A. Ioannou, Linear time-varying systems: Control and adaptation. *NJ: Prentice-Hall*, 1993.
49. K. J. Astrom and B. Wittenmark, Adaptive control, 2nd ed. *Addison Wesley*, 1995.
50. R. Marino and P. Tomei, Nonlinear control design: Geometric, adaptive & robust. *NJ: Prentice-Hall*, 1995.
51. P. A. Ioannou and J. Sun, Robust adaptive control. *NJ: Prentice-Hall*, 1995.
52. G. Tao and P. V. Kokotovic, Adaptive control of systems with actuator and sensor nonlinearities. *John Wiley & Sons*, 1996.
53. Y. Bavafa-Toosi, On multivariable linear output feedback, *MEng Thesis, Department of Electrical Engineering, K. N. Toosi University of Technology, Tehran, Iran*, 2000.
54. A. Khaki-Sedigh, and Y. Bavafa-Toosi, Design of static linear multivariable output feedback controllers using random optimization techniques, *Jr. Intelligent & Fuzzy Systems*, vol. 10, nos. 3,4, pp. 185-195, 2001.
55. G. W. Stewart, Introduction to matrix computations. *NY: Academic Press*, 1973.
56. D. S. Yoo and M. J. Chung, A variable structure control with simple adaptation laws for upper bounds on the norm of the uncertainties, *IEEE Trans. Automatic Control*, vol. 37, no. 6, pp. 860-864, 1992.
57. S. V. Emelyfyanov, Automatic control systems of variable structure. *Moscow: Naruka.*
58. U. Itkis, Control systems of variable structure. *NY: John-Wiley*, 1976.
59. J. J. E. Slotine and S. S. Sastry, Tracking control of nonlinear systems using sliding surfaces, with applications to robot manipulators, *Int. Jr. Control*, vol. 68, pp. 465-492, 1983.
60. R. Morgan and U. Ozguner, Decentralized variable structure control algorithm for robotic manipulator, *IEEE Journal of Robotics*, vol. 1, no. 1, pp. 57-65, 1985.
61. V. I. Utkin, Sliding modes in control and optimization. *NY: Springer-Verlag*, 1992.

62. F. Zhou and D. G. Fisher, Continuous sliding mode control, *Int. Jr. Control*, vol. 55, pp. 313-327, 1992.
63. H. Erzberger, Analysis and design of model following systems by state space techniques, *in Proceedings of the Joint Automatic Control Conf.*, pp. 572-581, 1968.
64. Y. Bavafa-Toosi, H. Ohmori, and B. Labibi, Failure-tolerant performance stabilization of the generic large-scale system by decentralized linear output feedback, *ISA Transactions*, vol. 44, no. 4, pp. 501-513, 2005.
65. Y. Bavafa-Toosi, H. Ohmori, and B. Labibi, A generic approach to the design of linear output-feedback controllers, *Systems & Control Letters*, vol. 55, pp. 282-292, 2006.
66. M. Teshnehlab and K. Watanabe, Intelligent control based on flexible neural networks. *Dordrecht: Kluwer Academic Publishers*, 1999.
67. Y. Bavafa-Toosi, and H. Ohmori, Flexible neural networks: Some system-theoretic properties and a new class, *in Proceedings of the Joint IEEE Conf. Decision and Control & European Control Conf.*, pp. 2554-2562, Seville, Spain, 2005.
68. Y. Bavafa-Toosi, and H. Ohmori, On flexible neural networks: Some system-theoretic properties, *IEEE Trans. Neural Networks*, 2006 (under review).
69. Y. Bavafa-Toosi and H. Ohmori, Flexible neural network-based associative memories - Part I: Behavior, *in Proceedings of the 17th Symp. Mathematical Theory of Networks and Systems, Kyoto, Japan*, 2006.
70. Y. Bavafa-Toosi and H. Ohmori, Flexible neural network-based associative memories - Part II: Memory functionality, *in Proceedings of the 45th IEEE Conf. Decision and Control, San Diego, CA, Dec.* 2006 (under review).

Stabilization of Switched Systems via both Controls and Switches

Yahong Zhu and Daizhan Cheng

Institute of Systems Science, Chinese Academy of Sciences, Beijing 100080, China
yhzhu@amss.ac.cn,dcheng@iss03.iss.ac.cn

1 Introduction

In recent years, the control of switched systems has attracted more and more attractions. This is because it is not only practically important but also theoretically challenging. Some of its main topics and recent developments can be found in [16, 23] and the references therein.

A switched nonlinear control system is described as

$$\dot{x}(t) = f^{\sigma(t)}(x) + g^{\sigma(t)}(x)u(t), x(t) \in \mathbb{R}^n, u(t) \in \mathbb{R}^m \tag{1}$$

where the switching law $\sigma(t) : [0, \infty) \to \Lambda$ is a right-continuous piecewise constant mapping, $\Lambda = \{1, 2, \cdots, N\}$ for some integer $N \geqslant 2$, and $f^i(x)$, $g^ij(x)$, $j = 1, \cdots, m$, $i = 1, \cdots, N$ are C^∞ vector fields.

As a particular case, a switched linear system is

$$\dot{x}(t) = A^{\sigma(t)}x + B^{\sigma(t)}u(t), \quad x(t) \in \mathbb{R}^n, \ u(t) \in \mathbb{R}^m \tag{2}$$

One basic problem considered for switched control systems is the controllability. There are some fundamental works on controllability and controllable subspace of switched linear systems [22]. The controllability of the set out of the controllable subspace was discussed in [8]. The controllability of switched nonlinear systems is a hard topic. There is a recent result on switched bilinear systems in [25]. Relative stabilizability is another hot topic[24]. Unlike non-switched linear case, controllability doesn't mean (linear state feedback) stabilizability[24]. But, general speaking, controllability is closely related to stabilizability.

The stability of switched linear systems has been investigated via many advanced tools [1,2]. Among them common quadratic Lyapunov function has been shown to be an effective tool. But finding a common quadratic Lyapunov function for a given set of stable matrices, or equivalently, a set of linear stable switching modes, is a hard topic. Lie-algebra and/or Lie-group have been used to provide some useful results [5,19~21].

The importance of the common Lyapunov function is based on the converse Lyapunov theorem for switched systems [12,17]. Consider system (1).

Definition 1.1 *The system (1) with* $u = 0$ *is said to be globally uniformly asymptotically stable (GUAS), if the trajectory converges to zero:*

$$\lim_{t\to\infty} \phi_\sigma^t(x_0) = 0 \tag{3}$$

uniformly with respect to any switchings.

Equivalently, there exists an $\mathcal{KL}$ *function* $\beta(x,t)$*, such that*

$$\|\phi_\sigma^t(x_0)\| \leqslant \beta(x_0, t)$$

Definition 1.2 *The system (1) with* $u = 0$ *is said to have a common Lyapunov function* V*, if* $V : \mathbb{R}^n \to \mathbb{R}$ *is* C^1 *positive definite, and*

$$L_{f_\lambda} V(x) = -W_\lambda(x), \quad i \in \Lambda \tag{4}$$

where W_λ*,* $\lambda \in \Lambda$ *are positive definite.*

When $|\Lambda|$ is finite, (4) can be replaced by

$$L_{f_\lambda} V(x) < 0, \quad i \in \Lambda \tag{5}$$

The following two results show the equivalence.

Theorem 1.1 [18] *(Lyapunov Theorem) If there exists a common Lyapunov function* $V(x)$ *for the system (1) with* $u = 0$*, then the system with* $u = 0$ *is UAS. In addition, if the function* $V(x)$ *is radially unbounded, then the system is GUAS.*

Theorem 1.2 [17] *(Converse Lyapunov Theorem) If the system (1) with* $u = 0$ *is UAS, then there exists a common Lyapunov function* V*. Moreover, if the system is GUAS, then the common Lyapunov function is radially unbounded.*

This equivalence forces us to find a common Lyapunov function for stability and stabilization of switched systems.

Note that common quadratic Lyapunov function is not necessary for the stability of switched linear systems [12].

Based on stability results, stabilization problem has also been investigated a lot. When the switching strategy is not controllable, that is the switching is arbitrary, common quadratic Lyapunov function may be used to prove quadratic stabilization of switched linear system. A necessary and sufficient condition for planar systems is presented in [7] . Assume each linear switching mode is controllable, some stabilization results based on average dwell time have been obtained. We refer to [9] and the references therein. A related topic is the stabilization via switched control [3,26] . Basically, they are the same as stabilization of switched system because the resulted closed-loop system is a switched system. The stabilization of switched nonlinear control systems is another hard topic [17,18] .

For non-switched control system if the uncontrollable part is not stable then the system is not stabilizable. But switched linear systems are different. Because we know the following fact [2] : even if each switching mode is stable, a "bad" switching law may make the switched system unstable, and conversely, a "nice" switching law may stabilize a system with all unstable modes. This is one of the basic motivations of this paper.

Firstly, the paper provides a design technique to stabilize a class of switched linear system. The design process consists of two steps. First step, we design a switching law to stabilize the uncontrollable and usually unstable subsystem. Then use controls to stabilize the controllable part. Using the technique quadratic Lyapunov function to assure the stability of the closed-loop modes of the controllable sub-system. Then we consider nonlinear case. Two kinds of systems are considered: (i) From controllability subspace we get a normal form. Using Lyapunov function with homogeneous derivative (LFHD) we stabilize the controllable subsystem and use designed switches, we stabilize the uncontrollable subsystem. (ii)Using compared Byrnes-Isidori Normal form, we decompose switched system into three subsystems: linearizable subsystem, hyperbolic zero dynamics, and center zero dynamics. The first part is stabilized by quadratic Lyapunov function, second part is stabilized by LFHD, and the third part is stabilized by design switches. Then we prove that under certain condition the overall system can be stabilized.

The rest of this paper is organized as follows: In Section 2, we give a sufficient condition for exponential stabilization of switched linear system with unstable switching modes by using designed switching law. Section 3 presents the main result for stabilizing overall system. The technique of common quadratic Lyapunov function is implemented. The stabilization of switched nonlinear systems is considered in Section 4 and Section 5 for two normal forms respectively. Section 6 is the conclusion.

2 Stabilization via Switching Law

Consider a switched nonlinear system

$$\dot{z} = f^{\sigma(t)}(z) \tag{6}$$

where the switching $\sigma(t)$ is as in Section 1.

Definition 2.1 *System (1) is exponentially stabilizable if there exist a switching law $\sigma(t) : [0, \infty) \to \{1, 2, \cdots, N\}$, two constant numbers $M > 0$, and $\mu > 0$, such that under this switching law the trajectories of (1) satisfy*

$$\|z(t)\| \leqslant M\mathrm{e}^{-\mu t}\|z_0\|, \quad t > 0 \tag{7}$$

We first consider linear case:

$$\dot{z} = A^{\sigma(t)}z \tag{8}$$

We assume all the switching modes are unstable, i.e., A^{λ}, $\lambda \in \Lambda$ are unstable matrices. Since we assume the switching law is controllable. That is, it can be manipulated as we wish. Then if there is a stable mode, the problem becomes trivial. We give a simple sufficient condition for the exponential stabilizability of system (5). Further discussion can be found in [14].

Theorem 2.1 *Suppose all the matrices in (5) are diagonal ones, i.e.,*

$$A_i = \begin{pmatrix} \lambda_i^1 & 0 & \cdots & 0 \\ 0 & \lambda_i^2 & \cdots & 0 \\ \vdots & \vdots & & \vdots \\ 0 & 0 & \cdots & \lambda_i^n \end{pmatrix}$$

If there exist $\alpha_i \geqslant 0,\ 1 \leqslant i \leqslant N$, *such that*

$$\sum_{i=1}^{N} \Re(\lambda_i^j)\alpha_i < 0, \quad \text{for } 1 \leqslant j \leqslant n \tag{9}$$

then system (5) is exponentially stabilizable.

Suppose $A_i \in \mathbb{R}^{n\times n}$ is a simple matrix with eigenvalues $\lambda_1^i, \cdots, \lambda_n^i$, then A_i can be expressed as

$$A_i = \sum_{k=1}^{n} \lambda_k^i w_k^i (y_k^i)^{\mathrm{T}} \tag{10}$$

where $w_k^i, y_k^i \in \mathbb{R}^n$, $A_i w_k^i = \lambda_k^i w_k^i$, $\|w_k^i\| = 1$, $(y_k^i)^{\mathrm{T}} A_i = \lambda_k^i (y_k^i)^{\mathrm{T}}$, and $(y_k^i)^{\mathrm{T}} w_j^i = \delta_{kj}$, $1 \leqslant k, j \leqslant n$.

Then

$$\mathrm{e}^{A_i t} = \sum_{j=1}^{n} \mathrm{e}^{\lambda_j^i t} w_j^i (y_j^i)^{\mathrm{T}}, \quad 1 \leqslant i \leqslant N \tag{11}$$

Define a set of indexes as

$$\Xi = \left\{ (j_1, j_2, \cdots, j_N) \ \Big|\ \prod_{k=1}^{N} w_{j_k}^k (y_{j_k}^k)^{\mathrm{T}} \neq 0,\ 1 \leqslant j_1, j_2, \cdots, j_N \leqslant n \right\} \tag{12}$$

Theorem 2.2 *Suppose all the matrices in (5) are simple matrices with*

$$\sigma(A_i) = \{\lambda_i^1, \lambda_i^2, \cdots, \lambda_i^n\}, \ \ 1 \leqslant i \leqslant N$$

If there exist N *numbers* $\alpha_i \geqslant 0,\ 1 \leqslant i \leqslant N$, *such that*

$$\sum_{k=1}^{N} \Re(\lambda_k^{j_k})\alpha_k < 0, \ \ \textit{for } j_1, j_2, \cdots, j_N \in \Xi \tag{13}$$

then system (5) is exponentially stabilizable.

3 Stabilizer Design Based on Lyapunov Functions

In this section we consider stabilization of the switched linear system (2). We assume the switching strategy is controllable. First, denote

$$V = \langle A^1, \cdots, A^N | B^1, \cdots, B^N \rangle$$

Then V is the controllable subspace of system (2) [22,25]. Then the system (2) can be converted into the following form

$$\dot{x} = A_{11}^{\sigma(t)} x + A_{12}^{\sigma(t)} z + B^{\sigma(t)} u(t) \tag{14a}$$

$$\dot{z} = A_{21}^{\sigma(t)} z \tag{14b}$$

Definition 3.1 *System*

$$\dot{x} = A^{\sigma(t)} x + B^{\sigma(t)} u(t) \tag{15}$$

is quadratically stabilizable if there exists $P > 0$ and a set of feedback K_i, $i = 1, \cdots, N$, such that

$$P(A_i + B_i K_i) + (A_i + B_i K_i)^{\mathrm{T}} P < 0, \quad i = 1, \cdots, N \tag{16}$$

Roughly speaking, the stabilization technique developed in this section is as follows. First, we design a switched law, which stabilizes the uncontrollable sub-system (14b). Then we design controls to stabilize the controllable sub-system of (14a), which is obtained from (14a) be setting $z = 0$. It will be done by finding common quadratic Lyapunov function for closed-loop form of controllable sub-system. Finally, we prove that such a switching strategy plus control can stabilize the overall system.

Definition 3.2 *A switching sequence is defined as*

$$\pi \stackrel{\text{def}}{=} \{(i_1, h_1), (i_2, h_2), \cdots, (i_M, h_M)\} \tag{17}$$

or, briefly $\pi = \{(i_m, h_m)\}_{m=1}^{M}$, where $M < \infty$ is the length of π. Denote $T_{[\pi]} = \sum_{m=1}^{M} h_m$.

Given a switching sequence π, an associated switching signal $\sigma(t)$, $t \in (0, T_{[\pi]})$ can be determined as

$$\sigma(t) = i_m, \quad \text{if} \quad t \in (t_{m-1}, t_m] \tag{18}$$

where $t_0 = h_0 = 0$, $t_m = \sum_{l=0}^{m} h_l$, $m = 1, \cdots, M$.

In the sequel, the notion $\prod_{i=1}^{n} A_i$ stands for the matrix product $A_1 \cdot A_2 \cdots A_n$, and $\prod_{i=n}^{1} A_1$ stands for the matrix product $A_n \cdot A_{n-1} \cdots A_1$.

Our main result in this section is:

Theorem 3.1 *System (14)is globally asymptotically stabilizable via designed controls and switching strategy, if*

$$\dot{x} = A_{11}^{\sigma(t)} x + B^{\sigma(t)} u(t) \tag{19}$$

is quadratically stabilizable, and

$$\dot{z} = A_{21}^{\sigma(t)} z \tag{20}$$

is exponentially stabilizable.

Proof: Choose $u(t) = K^{\sigma(t)}x$, such that $\dot{x} = A_{11}^{\sigma(t)}x + B^{\sigma(t)}u(t)$ is quadratically stabilizable. So there exists a common quadratic Lyapunov function $V = x^{\mathrm{T}}Px$ and positive defined matrixes Q_i such that $P\tilde{A}_{11}^i + (\tilde{A}_{11}^i)^{\mathrm{T}}P < -Q_i$, where $\tilde{A}_{11}^i = A_{11}^i + B^iK^i$. Denote

$$D = \max\{\|A_{12}^i\| \quad | \quad 1 \leqslant i \leqslant N\}$$

$$d = min\{\lambda_i^j \quad | \quad \lambda_i^j \in \sigma(Q_i), i \in \Lambda\}$$

$$\begin{aligned}\dot{V}|_{(14a)} &= (\dot{x})^{\mathrm{T}}Px + x^{\mathrm{T}}P\dot{x} \\ &= x^{\mathrm{T}}(P\tilde{A}_{11}^i + (\tilde{A}_{11}^i)^{\mathrm{T}}P)x + z^{\mathrm{T}}PA_{12}^ix + x^{\mathrm{T}}(A_{12}^i)^{\mathrm{T}}Pz \\ &< -x^{\mathrm{T}}Q_ix + +z^{\mathrm{T}}PA_{12}^ix + x^{\mathrm{T}}(A_{12}^i)^{\mathrm{T}}Pz \\ &< -\|x\|(d\|x\| - 2D\|P\| \cdot \|z\|)\end{aligned} \tag{21}$$

Step1: Prove that for any $\varepsilon > 0$, there exists $T > 0$, such that $\|x(t)\| < \varepsilon$ when $t > T$.

Suppose $z(t)$ is exponentially stabilizable under the following switching sequence

$$\pi = \{(i_1, h_1), (i_2, h_2), \cdots\}$$

so when $\|z(t)\| < d\epsilon/(2D\|P\|)$, we can obtain $\dot{V}|_{(14a)} < 0$ if $\|x\| > \epsilon$, so $\|x\|$ can not always be big than ϵ, and once $\|x\| < \epsilon$ at $t = \bar{T}$, it will be small than ϵ for any $t > \bar{T}$.

Step2: Prove that for any $\varepsilon > 0$, there exists $\delta_1 > 0$, $\delta_2 > 0$, such that $\|x(t, x_0) - x(t, x)\| < \varepsilon$ for all $t > 0$, when $\|x - x_0\| < \delta_1$, $\|z - z_0\| < \delta_2$. where $x(t, x_0)$ is the solution of(14a) starting from x_0.

At Step 1, we know there exists $\mu > 0$, such that $\|x(t)\| < \frac{\varepsilon}{2}$ when $t > \sum_{i=1}^{\mu} h_i$, so $\|x(t, x_0) - x(t, x_1)\| < \varepsilon$ when $t > \sum_{i=1}^{\mu} h_i$.

When $t \in (\sum_{i=0}^{M-1} h_i, \sum_{i=0}^{M} h_i]$, $1 \leq M \leqslant \mu$, the solution of (14a) is

$$x(t, x_0) = \mathrm{e}^{\tilde{A}_{11}^{i_M}t} \prod_{m=M-1}^{1} \mathrm{e}^{\tilde{A}_{11}^{i_m}h_m}x_0 + \sum_{m=1}^{M-1}(\prod_{j=M}^{m+1} \mathrm{e}^{\tilde{A}_{11}^{i_j}h_j} \int_{t_{m-1}}^{t_m} \tilde{A}_{12}^{i_m}z(\tau)\mathrm{d}\tau) + \int_{t_{M-1}}^{t_M} \tilde{A}_{12}^{i_M}z(\tau)\mathrm{d}\tau \tag{22}$$

Denote by

$$R = \max_{1 \leqslant M \leqslant \mu} \left\{ \sup_{t \in [t_{M-1}, t_M]} \|\mathrm{e}^{\tilde{A}_{11}^{i_M}t} \prod_{m=M-1}^{1} \mathrm{e}^{\tilde{A}_{11}^{i_m}h_m}\| \right\} \tag{23}$$

$$s = \max_{\substack{1 \leqslant M \leqslant \mu-1 \\ 1 \leqslant m \leqslant M-1}} \{\| \prod_{j=M}^{m+1} \mathrm{e}^{\tilde{A}_{11}^{i_j}h_j}\|\} \tag{24}$$

$$b = \max_{1 \leqslant i_m \leqslant N} \{\|A_{12}^{i_m}\|\}, \quad h = \max_{1 \leqslant i \leqslant \mu} h_i \tag{25}$$

We choose $\delta_1 < \frac{\varepsilon}{3R}$ and because (20) is exponentially stabilizable, we can choose δ_2 such that $\|z(t,z_0) - z(t,z_1)\| < \min\{\frac{\varepsilon}{(\mu-1)shb}, \frac{\varepsilon}{bh}\}$ when $\|z_0 - z_1\| < \delta_2$. So when $\|x_0 - x_1\| < \delta_1$, $\|z_0 - z_1\| < \delta_2$, we have $\|x(t,x_0) - x(t,x_1)\| < \frac{\varepsilon}{3} + \frac{\varepsilon}{3} + \frac{\varepsilon}{3} = \varepsilon$. □

Example 3.1 Consider the following systems of the form (19)-(20), where:

$$A_{11}^1 = (3) \quad A_{12}^1 = (1\ 2) \quad B^1 = (1)$$

$$A_{11}^2 = (5) \quad A_{12}^2 = (4\ 8) \quad B^2 = (5)$$

$$A_{21}^1 = \begin{pmatrix} -6 & 14 \\ 0 & 8 \end{pmatrix} \quad A_{21}^2 = \begin{pmatrix} -1.5 & -6.5 \\ -6.5 & -1.5 \end{pmatrix}$$

We choose $u^1(t) = -6x$, $u^2(t) = -3x$, it is easy to verify that $\dot{x} = A_{11}^{\sigma(t)} x + B^{\sigma(t)} u^{\sigma(t)}(t)$ is quadratically stabilizable. Then we will prove that $\dot{z} = A_{21}^{\sigma(t)} z$ is exponentially stabilizable under some certain switching strategy.

A_{21}^1 and A_{21}^2 are simple matrices, and it is easy to figure out eigenvalues and eigenvectors of them, so

$$\mathrm{e}^{A_{21}^2 \alpha_2 t} \mathrm{e}^{A_{21}^1 \alpha_1 t} = \mathrm{e}^{5\alpha_2 t - 6\alpha_1 t} \begin{pmatrix} -1 \\ 1 \end{pmatrix} \left(-\tfrac{1}{2}\ \tfrac{1}{2}\right) +$$

$$\mathrm{e}^{-8\alpha_2 t + 8\alpha_1 t} \begin{pmatrix} 1 \\ 1 \end{pmatrix} (0\ 1) + \mathrm{e}^{-8\alpha_2 t - 6\alpha_1 t} \begin{pmatrix} 1 \\ 1 \end{pmatrix} \left(\tfrac{1}{2}\quad -\tfrac{1}{2}\right)$$

According to Theorem 3 and using the method in [14], we consider the following equations, where α_1, α_2 are positive.

$$\begin{cases} 5\alpha_2 - 6\alpha_1 < 0 \\ -8\alpha_2 + 8\alpha_1 < 0 \\ -8\alpha_2 - 6\alpha_1 < 0 \\ \alpha_1 + \alpha_2 = 1 \end{cases} \tag{26}$$

We can obtain a solution as

$$\begin{cases} \alpha_1 = \frac{10}{21} \\ \alpha_2 = \frac{11}{21} \end{cases} \tag{27}$$

and

$$\max\{5\alpha_2 - 6\alpha_1, -8\alpha_2 - 6\alpha_1, -8\alpha_2 + 8\alpha_1\} = -\frac{5}{21} \tag{28}$$

$$\left\| \begin{pmatrix} -1 \\ 1 \end{pmatrix} \left(-\tfrac{1}{2}\ \tfrac{1}{2}\right) \right\| \leqslant \left\| \begin{pmatrix} -1 \\ 1 \end{pmatrix} \right\| \cdot \left\| \left(-\tfrac{1}{2}\ \tfrac{1}{2}\right) \right\| = 1$$

$$\left\| \begin{pmatrix} 1 \\ 1 \end{pmatrix} \left(\tfrac{1}{2}\ -\tfrac{1}{2}\right) \right\| \leqslant \left\| \begin{pmatrix} 1 \\ 1 \end{pmatrix} \right\| \cdot \left\| \left(\tfrac{1}{2}\ -\tfrac{1}{2}\right) \right\| = 1$$

$$\left\| \begin{pmatrix} 1 \\ 1 \end{pmatrix} (0\ 1) \right\| \leqslant \left\| \begin{pmatrix} 1 \\ 1 \end{pmatrix} \right\| \cdot \|(0\ 1)\| = \sqrt{2}$$

Therefore,

$$\Omega(t) \stackrel{\text{def}}{=} \left\| \mathrm{e}^{A_{21}^2 \frac{11}{21} t} e^{A_{21}^1 \frac{10}{21} t} \right\| \leqslant 3\sqrt{2} e^{-\frac{5}{21} t} \tag{29}$$

Consider the algebraic equation

$$3\sqrt{2} e^{-\frac{5}{21} t} = \frac{1}{2} \tag{30}$$

we get

$$T = \frac{21}{5} \ln(6\sqrt{2}) \approx 9 \tag{31}$$

$$\mu = \max \left\{ \sup_{t \in (0, \alpha_1 T)} \left\| e^{A_{21}^1 t} \right\|, \sup_{t \in (0, \alpha_2 T)} \left\| e^{A_{21}^2 t} e^{A_{21}^1 \alpha_1 T} \right\| \right\} \tag{32}$$

Then under the following switching law,

$$\sigma(t) = \begin{cases} 1, & lT \leqslant t < lT + \alpha_1 T \\ 2, & lT + \alpha_1 T \leqslant t < lT + T \end{cases} \tag{33}$$

where $l = 0, 1, 2, \cdots$, we can obtain

$$\|z(t)\| \leqslant \mu (\frac{1}{2})^{[\frac{t}{9}]} \cdot \|z_0\| \tag{34}$$

So $\dot{z} = A_{21}^{\sigma(t)} z$ is exponentially stabilizable. Then according Theorem 3.1, the overall system is globally asymptotically stabilizable. □

4 Stabilization via Controllability Approach

Now consider the switched nonlinear system (1). Mimic to linear case, we can define a controllability distribution as

$$\mathcal{C}(x) = \langle f^1(x), \cdots, f^N(x) \,|\, g_j^i(x), \forall i, j \rangle \tag{35}$$

which is the smallest distribution containing g_j^i, $i = 1, \cdots, N$, $j = 1, \cdots, M$ and f^i, $i = 1, \cdots, N$, invariant. Assume $C(x)$ is non-singular at the origin. Then it is easy to prove that it is also involutive (We refer to [15] for a proof for non-switching case.).

Then it is easy to prove that locally (1) can be expressed as

$$\dot{x}_1 = f_1^{\sigma(t)}(x_1, x_2) + g_1^{\sigma(t)}(x_1, x_2) u \tag{36a}$$

$$\dot{x}_2 = f_2^{\sigma(t)}(x_2) \tag{36b}$$

Denote

$$A_{11}^{\lambda} = \left.\frac{\partial f_1^{\lambda}(x_1, x_2)}{\partial x_1}\right|_{x=0}; \quad A_{12}^{\lambda} = \left.\frac{\partial f_1^{\lambda}(x_1, x_2)}{\partial x_2}\right|_{x=0}, \quad \lambda \in \Lambda$$

and

$$B^{\lambda} = g^{\lambda}(0), \quad \lambda \in \Lambda$$

Then we have a linear approximation of the first sub-system of (36) as

$$\dot{x}_1 = A_{11}^{\sigma(t)} x_1 + A_{12}^{\sigma(t)} x_2 + B_1^{\sigma(t)} u \tag{37}$$

The following result is an immediate consequence of our linear result.

Proposition 4.1 *Assume*

$$\dot{x}_2 = f_2^{\sigma(t)}(x_2)$$

is exponentially stabilizable and

$$\dot{x}_1 = A_{11}^{\sigma(t)} x_1 + B_1^{\sigma(t)} u$$

is quadratically stabilizable. Then system (36) is asymptotically stabilizable.

Next, we consider more general case. We need some notations about Lyapunov function with homogeneous derivatiAccordive (LFHD). A brief survey is given is Appendix. We refer to [4, 6] for details, and [11] for some recent developments.

We define a new norm on the vector space $\mathbb{R}^n$ as

$$\|x\|_{2m} = \sqrt[2m]{\sum_{i=1}^{n} (x_i)^{2m}}, \quad m \geqslant 1 \tag{38}$$

According to the famous H.Minkowski inequality

$$\Big(\sum_{i=1}^{n} (x_i + y_i)^r\Big)^{\frac{1}{r}} \leqslant \Big(\sum_{i=1}^{n} x_i^r\Big)^{\frac{1}{r}} + \Big(\sum_{i=1}^{n} y_i^r\Big)^{\frac{1}{r}}, \quad r > 1 \tag{39}$$

It is easy to prove that $\|.\|_{2m}$ is a norm on $\mathbb{R}^n$.

Definition 4.1 *A1.The equilibrium state* $x = 0$ *is said to be stable if for any* $\epsilon > 0$ *there exists* $\delta > 0$*, such that if* $\|x_0\|_{2m} < \delta$*, then* $\|x(t, x_0)\|_{2m} < \epsilon$ *for all* $t > 0$.
A2.The equilibrium state $x = 0$ *is said to be asymptotically stable if it is stable and* $x(t, x_0) \to 0$ *as* $t \to 0$

Using Taylor series expansion with respect to x^2, the first sub-system of (36) can be expressed as

$$\dot{x}_1 = a^{\sigma(t)}(x_1) + (x_2)^{\mathrm{T}} c^{\sigma(t)}(x_1) + [b^{\sigma(t)}(x_1) + (x_2)^{\mathrm{T}} d^{\sigma(t)}(x_1)]u \tag{40}$$

Define an system as

$$\dot{x}_1 = a^{\sigma(t)}(x_1) + b^{\sigma(t)}(x_1)u \tag{41}$$

We seek a set of feedback controls as

$$u^\lambda = u^\lambda(x_1), \quad \lambda \in \Lambda \tag{42}$$

and the approximate system of closed-loop system (41)(42) is denoted by

$$\dot{x}_1 = \alpha^{\sigma(t)}(x_1) \tag{43}$$

Denote

$$\beta(x_1) = c^{\sigma(t)}(x_1) + d^{\sigma(t)}(x_1)u \tag{44}$$

Then the approximate system of the first sub-system of (36) can be expressed as

$$\dot{x}_1 = \alpha^{\sigma(t)}(x) + (x_2)^{\mathrm{T}}\beta(x_1) \tag{45}$$

Definition 4.2 *System (41) is called LFHD-stabilizable, if we can find feedback back $u = u^\lambda(x_1)$, such that the approximate system of the closed-loop system (43) share a common LFHD. That is, there exist a LFHD, $V(x)$, such that*

$$\left\langle \frac{\partial V}{\partial x}, \alpha^\lambda(x_1) \right\rangle < 0, \quad \lambda \in \Lambda \tag{46}$$

Then we have the following result:

Theorem 4.1 *System (36) is asymptotically stabilizable if (i) System (41) is LFHD stabilizable; (ii) its second sub-system is exponentially stabilizable; (iii) $\beta(x_1)$ and $\frac{\partial V}{\partial x}$ are locally bounded.*

Proof: Since $\beta(x_1)$ and $\frac{\partial V}{\partial x}$ are locally bounded, we can denote $\beta = sup\{\|\beta(x_1)\|_{2m}\}$, $\gamma = sup\{\|\frac{\partial V}{\partial x}\|_{2m}\}$. Since system (41) is LFHD stabilizable, so according to [4], there exists a LFHD, $V(x_1)$, such that

$$\dot{V}(x_1)|_{(43)} \leqslant -b\|x_1\|_{2m}^{2m} \tag{47}$$

where $b > 0$ and $m \geqslant 1$ are defined by the system itself and $V(x_1)$.

We can obtain

$$\dot{V}(x_1)|_{(45)} \leqslant -b\|x_1\|_{2m}^{2m} + \beta\gamma\|x_2\|_{2m} \tag{48}$$

Step1: We can prove that for any $\varepsilon > 0$, there exists $T > 0$, such that $\|x_1(t)\| < \varepsilon$ when $t > T$.

Suppose $x_2(t)$ is exponentially stabilizable under the following switching sequence

$$\pi = \{(i_1, h_1), (i_2, h_2), \cdots\}$$

so when $\|x_2(t)\| < b\epsilon^{2m}/(\beta\gamma)$, we can obtain $\dot{V}|_{(45)} < 0$ if $\|x_1\|_{2m} > \epsilon$, so $\|x_1\|_{2m}$ can't always be big than ϵ, and once $\|x_1\|_{2m} < \epsilon$ at $t = \bar{T}$, it will be small than ϵ for any $t > \bar{T}$.

Step2: we can prove that for any $\varepsilon > 0$, there exists $\delta_1 > 0$, $\delta_2 > 0$, such that $\|x_1(t, x_1^0)\| < \varepsilon$ for all $t > 0$, when $\|x_1^0\|_{2m} < \delta_1$, $\|x_2^0\|_{2m} < \delta_2$, where $x_1(t, x_1^0)$ is the solution of (45) starting from x_1^0.

Since $x_2(t)$ is exponentially stable, so there exists $\delta_2 > 0$, such that $\|x_2(t, x_2^0)\|_{2m} < b\epsilon^{2m}/(\beta\gamma)$ for all $t > 0$ when $\|x_2^0\|_{2m} < \delta_2$, so we can choose any $0 < \delta_1 < \epsilon$, then $\|x_1(t, x_1^0)\| < \varepsilon$ for all $t > 0$ when $\|x_1^0\|_{2m} < \delta_1$. □

Example 4.1 Consider the following systems of the form (36)

$$\Sigma_1 : \quad \begin{cases} \dot{x_1} = -x_1^3 - x_1 x_2 + (1 - x_2) u_1 \\ \dot{x_2} = -x_2 \end{cases} \tag{49}$$

$$\Sigma_2 : \quad \begin{cases} \dot{x_1} = x_1 \sin x_2 - x_1^5 \cos x_2 + (x_1^3 x_2 + x_1) u_2 \\ \dot{x_2} = x_2 \end{cases} \tag{50}$$

Choose $u_1 = x_1 x_2$, then the approximate system of the first sub-system of (49) can be expressed as

$$\dot{x_1} = -x_1^3 - x_1 x_2^2 \tag{51}$$

Choose $u_1 = -x_2$, then the approximate system of the first sub-system of (50) can be expressed as

$$\dot{x_1} = -x_1^5 - x_1^3 x_2^2 \tag{52}$$

Choose $V = x_1^2 + x_2^2$

$$\dot{V}|_{(51)} = -2x_1^4 - 2x_1^2 x_2^2 - 2x_2^2 < 0$$

$$\dot{V}|_{(52)} = -2x_1^6 - 2x_1^4 x_2^2 - 2x_2^4 < 0$$

Then V is the common quadratic Lyapunov function of (51)-(52), so the first sub-systems of (50)-(48) are LFHD stabilizable .

Under the switching law

$$\pi = \{(\Sigma_1, 2h), (\Sigma_2, h), (\Sigma_1, 2h), (\Sigma_2, h), \cdots\}$$

where $h > 0$, the second sub-systems of (49)-(50) are exponentially stabilizable.

It is easy to prove that $\beta(x_1)$ and $\frac{\partial V}{\partial x}$ are locally bounded. So the switched nonlinear systems (49)-(50) are asymptotically stabilizable under the switching law π. □

5 Stabilization via Normal Form Approach

In this session we start from a special form of switched nonlinear system, called comparable normal form.

Definition 5.1 *System (1) is said to have a comparable normal form if there exists a coordinate transformation $x = x(z)$, and a state feedback control $u = \alpha(x) + \beta(z)v$, such that (1) can be expressed as:*

$$\begin{cases} \dot{x}^1 = A^{\sigma(t)}x^1 + B^{\sigma(t)}u \\ \dot{x}^2 = f_2^{\sigma(t)}(x) \\ \dot{x}^3 = f_3^{\sigma(t)}(x) \\ \dot{x}^4 = f_4^{\sigma(t)}(x) \end{cases} \tag{53}$$

Moreover, let

$$A_i^\lambda \stackrel{\text{def}}{=} \frac{\partial f_i^\lambda}{\partial x^i}|_{x=0}, \quad i = 2,3,4, \ \lambda \in \Lambda$$

Then A_2^λ, $\lambda \in \Lambda$ have zero real part eigenvalues; A_3^λ, $\lambda \in \Lambda$ have negative real part eigenvalues; A_4^λ, $\lambda \in \Lambda$ have positive real part eigenvalues.

The geometric meaning of (53) is very clear: The uncontrollable states can be decomposed into three parts: x^2 is the linearly central part; x^3 is the linearly stable part; x^4 is the linearly unstable part. Without switching, it is a general form for nonlinear control systems under non-singularity assumption. But for switched system we have to ask when this is true?

Let $G_\lambda = \text{Span}\{g_1^\lambda, \cdots, g_m^\lambda\}$, $\lambda \in \Lambda$. First we give an assumption:

A1. There exists a nonsingular and involutive G, such that $G_\lambda = G$, $\lambda \in \Lambda$.

We have the following

Lamma 5.1 *Assume A1 and there is an auxiliary output $y = (h_1(x), \cdots, h_m(x))^{\mathrm{T}} \in \mathbb{R}^m$, such that*

(a) each switching modes (with respect to this output) have same relative degree vector $(\rho_1, \cdots, \rho_m)$.

(b) The decoupling matrices

$$D_\lambda(x) = \begin{bmatrix} L_{g^\lambda} L_{f^\lambda}^{\rho_1 - 1} h_1(x) \\ \vdots \\ L_{g^\lambda} L_{f^\lambda}^{\rho_m - 1} h_m(x) \end{bmatrix}, \quad \lambda \in \Lambda \tag{54}$$

are nonsingular.

(c) Denote by

$$x_\lambda^1 = (h_1, L_{f^\lambda} h_1, \cdots, L_{f^\lambda}^{\rho_1 - 1} h_1, \cdots, L_{f^\lambda}^{\rho_m - 1} h_m)^{\mathrm{T}}, \quad \lambda \in \Lambda$$

then there exist $T_\lambda \in GL(n_1, \mathbb{R})$, such that

$$T_\lambda x_\lambda^1 = x^1, \quad \lambda \in \Lambda \tag{55}$$

Then system (1), with suitable state feedback, can be expressed as

$$\begin{cases} \dot{x}^1 = A^{\sigma(t)}x^1 + B^{\sigma(t)}u \\ \dot{x}_c^1 = f_c^{\sigma(t)}(x) \end{cases} \tag{56}$$

Proof: (sketch) Choosing x_λ^1 as part of coordinates. Because of (c), we can choose a common complement x_c^1, such that (x_λ^1, x_c^1) is a local coordinate frame. Moreover, because of A1, x_c^1 can be chosen in such a way that, $G \subset (\text{Span}\{dx_c^1\})^\perp$. Now under this coordinate frame, λ-th mode can be expressed into the nonlinear canonical form [15]. An obvious feedback can convert x_λ^1 subsystem into completely controllable form. Finally, using condition (c) again, we can convert the linear subsystems of x_λ^1 , $\lambda \in \Lambda$ into same coordinate x^1 with linear (part) coordinate transformations. □

Consider system (53). Assume

A2. The subsystem of (53) is autonomous. That is:

$$\begin{cases} \dot{x}^3 = f_3^{\sigma(t)}(x) \\ \dot{x}^4 = f_4^{\sigma(t)}(x) \end{cases} \tag{57}$$

can be written as

$$\dot{z} = f(z)$$

Under assumption A2, system (53) can be rewritten as

$$\begin{cases} \dot{x}^1 = A^{\sigma(t)}x^1 + B^{\sigma(t)}u \\ \dot{x}^2 = f_2^{\sigma(t)}(x) \\ \dot{x}^3 = f_3^{\sigma(t)}(x^3) \end{cases} \tag{58}$$

Then we consider only system (58). We have the following result:

Theorem 5.1 *Consider system (58). Assume*

(a) the subsystem

$$\dot{x}^1 = A^{\sigma(t)}x^1 + B^{\sigma(t)}u \tag{59}$$

is quadratically stabilizable;

(b) for the second subsystem

$$\dot{x}^2 = f_2^{\sigma(t)}(x^1, x^2, x^3) \tag{60}$$

the modified form

$$\dot{x}^2 = f_2^i(0, x^2, 0), \quad i = 1, 2, \cdots, N \tag{61}$$

share a common LFHD;

(c) the third subsystem

$$\dot{x}^3 = f_3^{\sigma(t)}(x^3) \tag{62}$$

is exponentially stabilizable by switches.

Then the overall system is stabilizable by both switches and control.

Proof: Assume there V is the LFHD of subsystem (61) such that

$$\dot{V}|_{(61)} \leqslant P_{2m}(x^2) + R(x^2),$$

where $P_{2m}(x^2)$ is a negative definite homogeneous polynomial of degree $2m$, $R(x^2) = O(\|x^2\|^{2m+1})$.

Since for a finite dimensional normed space all the norms are topologically equivalent, in hereafter proof we use $\|\cdot\| \stackrel{\text{def}}{=} \|\cdot\|_{2m}$ for distance. Now we have to prove that there exists a region neighborhood Ω of the origan, which is asymptotically stable under suitable control and switch.

By continuity, we can find $\delta_1 > 0$, such that

$$|R(x^2)| < -\frac{1}{3}P_{2m}(x^2), \quad \|x^2\| < \delta_1$$

Choosing $\delta_2 = \frac{1}{2}\delta_1$, such that

$$\epsilon_1 = \min\{-P_{2m}(x^2) | \delta_2 \leqslant \|x^2\| \leqslant \delta_1\} > 0$$

By continuity, we can find $\delta_3 > 0$, such that $\|x^1\| \leqslant \delta_3$, $\|x^3\| \leqslant \delta_3$

$$\left|\dot{V}|_{(60)} - \dot{V}|_{(61)}\right| < \epsilon_1, \quad \|x^1\| < \delta_3;\ \|x^3\| < \delta_3;\ \delta_2 \leqslant \|x^2\| \leqslant \delta_1$$

Set

$$R = \left\{x \,\middle|\, \|x^1\| < \delta_3;\ \|x^3\| < \delta_3;\ \|x^2\| \leqslant \delta_1 \right\}$$

Now choosing switch to exponentially stabilize subsystem (62), and control to quadratically stabilized subsystem (59). Then we can choose δ_4, such that as $\|x^1(0)\| < \delta_4$ and $\|x^3(0)\| < \delta_4$, we have $\|x^1(t)\| < \delta_3$ and $\|x^3(t)\| < \delta_3$ for $t \geqslant 0$.

Set

$$\Omega = \left\{x \,\middle|\, \|x^1\| < \delta_4;\ \|x^3\| < \delta_4;\ \|x^2\| \leqslant \delta_1 \right\}.$$

Then we can see the following facts:

- As $x_0 \in \Omega$ the trajectory $x(t, x_0)$ will remain in R and after finite time we will have $\|x^2\| < \delta_2$.
- Since both subsystems (59) and (62) are asymptotically stable, we can assume $\|x^1\|$ and $\|x^3\|$ are as small as required.
- Replacing δ_2 by $\frac{1}{2}\delta_2$ and repeat the above argument we also have the conclusion that after finite time $\|x^2\| < \frac{1}{2}\delta_2$.

Based on the above argument we conclude that $x(t, x_0) \to 0$ as $t \to \infty$, $x_0 \in \Omega$. □

Example 5.1 Consider the following system

$$\begin{cases} \dot{x}^1 = A_{\sigma(t)}x + b_{\sigma(t)}u \\ \dot{x}^2 = f_{\sigma(t)}(x) \\ \dot{x}^3 = g_{\sigma(t)}(x) \end{cases} \tag{63}$$

where $\sigma(t) \in \{1, 2\}$, and

$$A_1 = \begin{bmatrix} 0 & 1 \\ 0 & 0 \end{bmatrix}; \quad A_2 = \begin{bmatrix} 1 & 5 \\ -5 & -5 \end{bmatrix}$$

$$b_1 = b_2 = (0, 1)^{\mathrm{T}}$$

$$f_1 = \begin{bmatrix} x_1 - 2x_3^5 + 2(1-\cos x_3)x_4^3 \\ -2x_4^3 + x_3^2 \sin(x_4) \end{bmatrix}, \quad f_2 = \begin{bmatrix} x_2x_5 - x_3^5 + x_4^5 \\ -x_4^2 \sin(x_4) \end{bmatrix}$$

$$g_1 = \begin{bmatrix} -2 & 0 \\ 0 & 1 \end{bmatrix} \begin{bmatrix} x_5 \\ x_6 \end{bmatrix}, \quad g_2 = \begin{bmatrix} 1 & 0 \\ 0 & -2 \end{bmatrix} \begin{bmatrix} x_5 \\ x_6 \end{bmatrix}$$

Denote by $x^1 = (x_1, x_2)^{\mathrm{T}}$, $x^2 = (x_3, x_4)^{\mathrm{T}}$, $x^5 = (x_5, x_6)^{\mathrm{T}}$. Then it is easy to see that the subsystem of x^1 is quadratically stabilizable by

$$u_1^* = (-1,-1) \begin{bmatrix} x_1 \\ x_2 \end{bmatrix}, \quad u_2^* = (0,1) \begin{bmatrix} x_1 \\ x_2 \end{bmatrix}$$

The common quadratic Lyapunov function is

$$V = [x_1, x_2] \begin{bmatrix} 4 & 1 \\ 1 & 4 \end{bmatrix} \begin{bmatrix} x_1 \\ x_2 \end{bmatrix}$$

It is obvious that the subsystem of x^3 is exponentially stablizable by switches. The switching law can be periodic by any $T > 0$ as

$$\sigma^*(t) = \begin{cases} 1, & kT < t \leqslant (k+1/2)T \\ 2, & (k+1/2)T < t \leqslant (k+1)T \end{cases}$$

Finally, consider x^2, we have

$$f_1(0, x^2, 0) = \begin{bmatrix} -2x_3^5 + 2(1-\cos x_3)x_4^3 \\ -2x_4^3 + x_3^2 \sin(x_4) \end{bmatrix}, \quad f_2(0, x^2, 0) = \begin{bmatrix} -x_3^5 + x_4^5 \\ -x_4^2 \sin(x_4) \end{bmatrix}$$

Its approximation is

$$q_1(x^2) = \begin{bmatrix} -2x_3^5 + x_3^2 x_4^3 \\ -2x_4^3 + x_3^2 \sin(x_4) \end{bmatrix}, \quad f_2(0, x^2, 0) = \begin{bmatrix} -x_3^5 + x_4^5 \\ -x_4^2 \sin(x_4) \end{bmatrix}$$

It is easy to check that for this approximation a common QLHD is $V(x_3, x_4) = x_3^2 + \frac{1}{2}x_4^4$.

Bence by Theorem 5.2, the system (63) is stabilizable by the switching law $\sigma^*(t)$ and controls u_1^*, u_2^*. □

6 Conclusions

Firstly, the stabilization of a class of switched linear systems has been considered. The systems considered is in a canonical form, which consists of two subsystems: controllable sub-system and uncontrollable sub-system. Every mode of the uncontrollable sub-system is assumed to be unstable. A design technique was proposed, which consists of two steps: first, a switching law is designed to stabilize the uncontrollable sub-system, and the stabilizing control is designed, using common quadratic Lyapunov function as an auxiliary tool. A sufficient condition was proposed to assure the stabilizability. Secondly, the the local asymptotical stabilization of switched nonlinear systems was considered. We start from two normal forms, controllability normal form and Byrnes-Isidori normal form. Using common quadratic Lyapunov function, LFHD and design switches to stabilize subsystems and then show that the combination can stabilize the overall system. The stabilizers were designed and some examples were provided to demonstrate the methods.

Appendix (For LFHD)

Consider a nonlinear dynamic system

$$\dot{x} = f(x), \quad x \in \mathbb{R}^n \tag{64}$$

Using Taylor series expansion on each component of $f(x)$ and assume the lowest degree of non-vanishing terms of $f_i(x)$ is k_i, then we can express f_i as

$$f_i = g_i(x) = O(\|x\|^{k_i+1}), \quad i = 1, \cdots, n$$

where $g_i(x)$ is a homogeneous polynomial of degree k_i. We call

$$\dot{x} = g(x), \quad x \in \mathbb{R}^n \tag{65}$$

the approximate system of (64).

Definition A.1 *A positive definite polynomial $V(x) > 0$ is c'alled a LFHD of system (65) if its derivative along (65) is a homogeneous polynomial.*

Definition A.2 *System (64) is approximately stable with degrees $(k_1, \cdots, k_n)$, if*

$$\dot{x} = f(x) + r(x)$$

is asymptotically stable as long as $r_i(x) = O(\|x\|^{k_i+1})$.

Theorem A.1 [4] *System (64) is approximately stable with degrees $(k_1, \cdots, k_n)$, if there exists a LFHD, $V(x)$, for system (65) such that*

$$\dot{V}|_{(65)} < 0, \quad x \in U\backslash\{0\},$$

where U is a neighborhood of 0.

References

1. Agrachev, A.A. and D. Liberzon, Lie-algebraic stability criteria for switched systems, *SIAM J. Contr. Opt.*, Vol. 40, No. 1, pp. 253-269, 2001.
2. Branicky, M.S., Multiple Lyapunov functions and other analysis tools for switched hybrid systems, *IEEE Trans. Aut. Contr.*, Vol. 43, No. 4, pp. 475-482, 1998.
3. Chen, W., D.J. Balance, On a switching control scheme for nnlinear systems with ill-defined relative degree, *Sys. Contr. Lett.*, Vol. 47, pp. 159-166, 2002.
4. Cheng, D., C. Martin, Stabilization of nonlinear systmes via designed center manifold, *IEEE Trans. Aut. Contr.*, Vol. 46, No. 9, 1372-1383, 2001.

5. Cheng, D., L. Guo, and J. Huang, On quadratic Lyapunov functions, *IEEE Trans. Aut. Contr.*, Vol. 48, No. 5, pp. 885-890, 2003.
6. Cheng, D., Stabilization via polynomial Lyapunov function, in *New Trends in Nonlinear Dynamics and Control, and their Applications*, W. Kang, M. Xiao, C. Borges (eds), 161-173, Springer, 2003.
7. Cheng, D., Stabilization of planar linear systems, *Sys. Contr. Lett*, Vol. 51, No. 2, 79-88, 2004.
8. Cheng, D., Controllability of switched billinear systems, *IEEE Trans. Aut. Contr.*, Vol. 50, No. 4, 511-515, 2005.
9. Cheng, D., L. Guo, Y. Lin, and Y. Wang, Stabilization of switched linear systems, *IEEE Trans. Aut. Contr.*, Vol. 50, No. 5, 661-666, 2005.
10. Cheng, D., Y. Lin, and Y. Wang, Accessibility of Switched Linear Systems,*IEEE Trans. Aut. Contr.*, Vol. 51 No. 9 1486-1491 2006.
11. Cheng, D., Y. Guo, Stabilization of nonliear systems via center manifold approach, *Sys. Contr. Lett.*, 2006, (to appear)
12. Dayawansa, W.P. and C.F. Martin, A converse Lyapunov theorem for a class of dynamical systems which undergo switching, *IEEE Trans. Aut. Contr.*, Vol. 44, No. 4, pp. 751-760, 1999.
13. Escobar, G, A.J. van der Schaft, R. Ortega, A Hamiltonian viewpoint in the modeling of switching power converters, *Automatica*, Vol.35, No.3, 445-452, 1999.
14. Hu. Q., D. Cheng, Stabilization of switched linear systems via designed switching law, preprint, submitted for publication.
15. Isidori, A., *Non-linear Control Systems*, 3nd ed., Springer-Verlag, 1995.
16. Liberzon, D. and A.S. Morse, Basic problems on stability and design of switched systems, *IEEE Control Systems Magazine*, Vol.19, No. 5, pp. 59-70, 1999.
17. Mancilla-Aguilar, J.L., R.A. Garcua, A convese Lyapunov theorem for nonlinear switched systems, *Sys. Contr. Lett.* Vol. 44, pp. 67-71, 2000.
18. Mancilla-Aguilar, A condition for the stability of switched nonlinear systems, *IEEE Trans. Aut. Contr.*, Vol. 45, No. 11, pp. 2077-2079, 2000.
19. Shorten, R.N. and K.S. Narendra, A sufficient condition for the existence of a common Lyapunov function for two second-order linear systems, *Proc. 36th Conf. on Decision and Control*, pp. 3521-3522, 1997.
20. Shorten, R., K.S. Narendra, In the exitence os a common quadratic Lyapunov functions for linear stable switching system, *Proc. of 10th Yale Workshop on Adaptive and Learning Systems*, 1998.
21. Shorten, R.N. and K.S. Narendra, Necessary and sufficient condition for the existence of a common quadratic Lyapunov function for M-stable linear second order systems, *Proc. 2000ACC*, pp. 359-363, 2000.
22. Sun, Z., S.S. Ge, T.H. Lee, Controllability and reachability criteria for switched linear systems, *Automatica*, Vol. 38, pp. 775-786, 2002.
23. Sun, Z., S. S. Ge, Analysis and synthesis of switched linear controlsystems, *Automatica*, Vol. 41, N0. 2, pp. 181-356. 2005.
24. Sun, Z., S. S. Ge, Switched stabilization of Higher-order switched linear systems, *Proc. 44th CDC and ECC 2005*, Seville, 4873-4878, 2005.
25. Xie, G., L. Wang, Controllability and stabilization of switched linear-systems, *Sys. Contr. Lett.*, Vol. 48, pp. 135-155, 2003.
26. Zhao, J., M.W. Spong, Hubrid control for global stabilization of cart-penduluum system, *Automatica*, Vol.37, 1941-1951, 2001.

Finite-Time Control and Input-to-State Stability

Yiguang Hong[1] and Zhongping Jiang[2]

[1] Institute of Systems Science, Chinese Academy of Sciences, Beijing 100080, China
yghong@iss.ac.cn
[2] Department of Electrical and Computer Engineering, Polytechnic University, Brooklyn, New York 11201, U. S. A.
zjiang@control.poly.edu

1 Introduction

The control synthesis to deal with the stabilization of nonlinear systems becomes more and more important following various practical demands. Many fundamentally nonlinear control approaches, including feedback linearization, sliding mode, backstepping, forwarding, control Lyapunov functions, input-to-state stability, passivity-based control, internal-model principles and nonlinear small-gain techniques were proposed in the last few decades [2,8,14,21,24,25,27,32,33,11~12,17~19] to deal with stabilization or robust and adaptive control. Most of these nonlinear feedback tools focus on the design of smooth controllers for various classes of nonlinear systems.

On the other hand, non-smooth (including discontinuous and contiunous but not Lipschitz continuous) control approaches have drawn increasing attention in nonlinear control system design. One of the main benefits of the non-smooth finite-time control strategy is that it can force a control system to reach a desirable target in finite time. This approach was first studied in the literature of optimal control. In recent years, finite-time control design via non-smooth time-invariant state feedback has become the focal point of several recent studies. Different finite-time stabilizing feedback laws have been constructed for some classes of nonlinear systems [1,4,23]. In addition, finite-time control for nonlinear systems with parametric uncertainties or dynamic uncertainties has gained increasing attention and some control designs have been proposed for specific classes of uncertain nonlinear systems using a backstepping-like procedure [6,7]. Moreover, non-holonomic systems can also be stabilized in finite time using a switching non-smooth controller [5]. These finite-time controllers can also yield, in some sense, fast response and high tracking precision as well as disturbance-rejection properties because of their non-smoothness. Despite its potential application to practical problems, the study of finite-time stabilization is quite under-developed, partially because of the lack of effective and constructive tools in non-smooth analysis and synthesis.

The purpose of this paper is to contribute to the development of novel design tools for nonlinear control systems via the cross-fertilization of two fields.

More specifically, our research is motivated by the fact that Sontag's input-to-state stability (now widely known as ISS) has found its powerful applications in various control problems, and particularly has inspired the development of nonlinear, ISS, small-gain theorems proposed in [12 $\sim$ 14, 31]. We intend to develop a framework for the design of nonsmooth vs. smooth controllers with finite-time stability based on the finite-time variant of ISS, which we term as *finite-time ISS*. Characterizations and further applications of finite-time ISS are under current investigation and will be reported elsewhere. Due to space limitation, we only present preliminary results to show that a combination of Sontag's ISS and nonsmooth feedback yields a new design tool for finite-time stabilization of nonlinear systems. As we will see later, the systematic application of finite-time ISS alleviates the mathematical technicality and complexity associated with the use of nonsmooth feedback approaches. It is our firm belief that finite-time ISS will play a role in finite-time control, as important as what the conventional ISS of Sontag has played in asymptotic stability analysis and smooth feedback stabilization.

The organization of this paper is as follows. Firstly, the problem formulation and preliminaries are given in Section 2. Then, in Section 3, some results on finite-time input-to-state stability are proved, while more discussions on finite time control design or related topics are reported in Section 4. Finally, several concluding remarks are given in Section 5.

2 Preliminaries

The investigation of finite time stability of nonlinear systems is relatively hard because of non-smoothness in the system vector fields. Hence, some generalizations such as Dini derivative have been given to encompass the cases related to less smooth functions [3].

Let a and b ($> a$) be two real numbers and consider a function $h : (a, b) \to \mathbb{R}$ and a point $t^* \in (a, b)$. The upper Dini derivative of h at t^* is defined as

$$D^+h(t^*) = \limsup_{s \to 0+} \frac{h(t^* + s) - h(t^*)}{s}$$

It is known that, when h is continuous on (a, b), h is non-increasing on (a, b) if and only if $D^+h(t^*) \leqslant 0$ for any $t \in (a, b)$.

In stability analysis, we are interested in the Dini derivative of a function along the solutions of a differential equation. Consider a system in the following form

$$\dot{x} = f(t, x) \tag{1}$$

and let $x(t)$ be a generic solution. Further, let $V(t, x) : \mathbb{R} \times \mathbb{R}^n \to \mathbb{R}$ be a continuous functions, satisfying a local Lipschitz condition for x, uniformly with respect to t. Thus, the upper Dini derivative of $V(x, x(t))$ with respect to t is given by

$$D^+V(t, x(t)) = \limsup_{s \to 0+} \frac{V(t + s, x(t + s)) - V(t, x(t))}{s}$$

On the other hand, define

$$D^+V(t,x) = \limsup_{s\to 0^+} \frac{V(t+s, x+sf(t,x)) - V(t,x)}{s}$$

which is called the upper Dini derivative of V along the trajectory of (1). It is shown that

$$D^+V(t^*, x(t^*)) = D^+V(t^*, x^*)$$

when putting $x^* = x(t^*)$. The detailed introduction of Dini derivative can be found in [26].

The following is a basic concept about finite time control [1,4].

Definition 2.1 *The equilibrium $x = 0$ of system (1) is (globally) finite-time stable if it is Laypunov stable and globally finite-time convergent. By "finite time convergence", we mean that, for any initial conditions $x(t_0) = x_0$, there is a settling-time function $T \geqslant 0$, which is a continuous function of x_0, such that every solution $x(t; t_0, x_0)$ satisfies*

$$\lim_{t\to t_0+T} x(t; t_0, x_0, \theta_0) = 0, \quad x(t; t_0, x_0) = 0, \ \forall t > t_0 + T$$

In what follows, we will focus on the finite time stability analysis for autonomous systems. In this case, the considered systems with finite time convergence have to be non-smooth (more precisely, non-Liptchitz).

A function $h : \mathbb{R}_+ \to \mathbb{R}_+$ is K-function if it is continuous, strictly increasing and $h(0) = 0$; it is K_∞-function if it is a K-function and also $h(s) \to \infty$ as $s \to \infty$; and it is a positive definite function if $h(s) > 0$ for all $s > 0$ and $h(0) = 0$. A function $\beta : \mathbb{R}_+ \times \mathbb{R}_+ \to \mathbb{R}_+$ is a KL-function if, for each fixed $t \geqslant 0$, the function $\beta(\cdot, t)$ is a K-function, and for each fixed $s \geqslant 0$ it decreases to zero as $t \to \infty$.

Then, we introduce new concepts to combine finite-time control with ISS ideas. Consider system

$$\dot{z} = f(z, v), \quad f(0,0) = 0, \quad z \in \mathbb{R}^n, \ v \in \mathbb{R}^m \tag{2}$$

Definition 2.2 *System (2) is finite-time input-to-state stable (ISS) (with v as the input), if, for any initial time $t_0 \geqslant 0$, initial state $z(t_0) = z_0$ and bounded input v, we have*

$$||z(t)|| \leqslant \beta(||z_0||, t - t_0) + \gamma\Big(\sup_{t_0 \leqslant \tau \leqslant t} ||v(\tau)||\Big) \tag{3}$$

where γ is a K-function and β is a KL-function with $\beta(||z_0||, t - t_0) \equiv 0$ when $t \geqslant t_0 + T$ for some function T continuous with respect to z_0.

Obviously, finite-time ISS implies ISS. Note that the main difference between ISS and finite time ISS is the finite time convergence of β; that is, "$\beta(||z_0||, t - t_0) \equiv 0$ when $t \geqslant t_0 + T$ for some function T continuous with respect to z_0".

A function V is called an ISS-Lyapunov function for system (2) if there exist K_∞-functions ϕ_1, ϕ_2, and K-functions ϕ_4, ϕ_3, such that

(A1)

$$\phi_1(||z||) \leqslant V(z) \leqslant \phi_2(||z||), \quad \forall z \in \mathbb{R}^n \tag{4}$$

(A2)

$$D^+V(z)f(z,v) \leqslant -\phi_3(||z||), \quad \forall z, v \text{ with } ||z|| \geqslant \phi_4(||v||) \tag{5}$$

which is equivalent to asking that there are K_∞-functions ϕ_3, $\bar{\phi}_4$ such that

$$D^+V(z)f(z,v) \leqslant -\phi_3(||z||) + \bar{\phi}_4(||v||), \quad \forall z \in R^n, \ v \in \mathbb{R}^m \tag{6}$$

Definition 2.3 *A function V is called a finite-time ISS-Lyapunov for system (2) if it is an ISS-Lyapunov function with conditions (A1) and (A2), and $\phi_3(||z||)$ is $O(V(z)^a)$ (as $z \to 0$) for some constant a with $0 < a < 1$.*

Definition 2.4 *System (2) is finite-time input-to-state practically stable (ISPS) with v as the input, if, for any initial state $z(t_0) = z_0$ and bounded input v, we have*

$$||z(t)|| \leqslant \beta(||z_0||, t - t_0) + \gamma(\sup_{t_0 \leqslant \tau \leqslant t} ||v(\tau)||) + D \tag{7}$$

where D is a nonnegative constant, γ is a K-function and β is a KL-function with $\beta(||z_0||, t - t_0) \equiv 0$ when $t \geqslant t_0 + T$ for some function T continuous with respect to z_0. When $D = 0$, finite-time ISPS becomes finite-time ISS.

Remark 2.1 *It is easy to obtain that finite-time ISPS implies input-to-state practical stability (ISPS) [12]. Conversely, if system (2) is ISPS, then according to [12], we have*

$$||z(t)|| \leqslant \hat{\beta}(||z_0||, t - t_0) + \gamma(\sup_{t_0 \leqslant \tau \leqslant t} ||v(\tau)||) + \hat{D}$$

where $\hat{D}$ is a nonnegative constant, γ is a K-function and $\hat{\beta}$ is a KL-function. Note that $\hat{\beta}$ is continuous. Therefore, for any constant $\epsilon > 0$, there is $T \geqslant 0$, which depends only on z_0 and ϵ, such that $\hat{\beta}(||z_0||, t - t_0) \leqslant \epsilon$ when $t \geqslant t_0 + T$. Therefore, there is another KL-function β with $\hat{\beta}(||z_0||, t-t_0) \leqslant \beta(||z_0||, t-t_0)+\epsilon$ and $\beta(||z_0||, t - t_0) = 0$ when $t \geqslant T$, such that (7) holds with $D = \hat{D} + \epsilon$. Thus, finite-time ISPS is equivalent to (asymptotic) ISPS, and an input-to-state stable system is always finite-time ISPS. For wan't of space, we will not discuss finite-time ISPS in this paper.

In fact, the above discussion can be extended to the systems with measured variables. In other words, we can also consider finite time input-to-output properties for nonlinear systems with output variables:

$$\begin{cases} \dot{x} = f(x, u), & x \in \mathbb{R}^n, \ x(t_0) = x_0, \ u \in \mathbb{R}^m \\ y = h(x, u), & y \in \mathbb{R}^l, \ h(0,0) = 0, \ f(0,0) = 0 \end{cases} \tag{8}$$

Definition 2.5 *System (8) is finite-time input-to-output stable (IOS) if there exist a KL-function β and a K-function γ such that, for each initial condition $x(t_0) = x_0$, each measurable essentially bounded control u on $[t_0, \infty)$, and each t in the right maximal interval of the definition of the corresponding solution of system (8), we have*

$$||y(t)|| \leqslant \beta(||x_0||, t - t_0) + \gamma(\sup_{t_0 \leqslant \tau \leqslant t} ||u(\tau)||) \tag{9}$$

with $\beta(||x_0||, t - t_0) \equiv 0$ when $t \geqslant T$ for some function T continuous with respect to x_0.

Here are some useful lemmas for the following analysis.

Lamma 2.1 [12] *For any K-function γ, any K_∞-function ρ such that $\rho - Id$ is a K_∞ function, and any nonnegative real numbers a and b, we have*

$$\gamma(a + b) \leqslant \gamma(\rho(a)) + \gamma(\rho \circ (\rho - Id)^{-1}(b)) \tag{10}$$

Lamma 2.2 *For any continuous function $g(x, z)$, there are C^1 nonnegative functions $g_1(x)$, $g_2(z)$, and $\bar{g}(x, z)$ such that*

$$|g(x, z)| \leqslant \bar{g}(x, z) \leqslant g_1(x) g_2(z)$$

Note that the proof of the above lemma is quite easy and that the inequality has been used in the research work of others, too many to cite.

Lamma 2.3 *(Young's inequality):*

$$ab \leqslant \frac{a^{1+c}}{1+c} + \frac{c\, b^{1+\frac{1}{c}}}{1+c}, \quad a \geqslant 0,\ b \geqslant 0,\ c > 0. \tag{11}$$

Lamma 2.4 [1] *$\dot{x} = f(x)$ is finite time stable if and only if there are a continuous Lyapunov function V and constants $0 < c$, $0 < a < 1$ such that*

$$\dot{V} \leqslant -cV^a \tag{12}$$

Remark 2.2 *Borrowing the proof techniques from [20] and [1], it is possible to prove a stronger result than Lemma 2.4. That is, a dynamic system $\dot{x} = f(x(t), d(t))$ with disturbance taking values in a compact set of $\mathbb{R}^m$ is robustly stable at the origin if and only if there exists a continuous Lyapunov function V satisfying (12). The detailed analysis on finite time robust stability will be given in our future work.*

Remark 2.3 *Obviously, finite time ISS implies that the z-subsystem is globally finite time stable when $v = 0$. However, the converse may not be true. Here is such an example: $\dot{z} = -z^{\frac{1}{3}} + (1 + z^2)v$, $z \in \mathbb{R}$. Note that taking $v = 1$ makes the system unstable. As shown in Theorem 3.1 of Section 3, finite-time ISS also implies existence of an ISS-Lyapunov function guaranteeing finite-time ISS.*

In the following two sections, the above definitions and lemmas will be employed to explore finite time stability analysis and finite-time stabilization for nonlinear systems.

3 Finite Time ISS

In this section, we will prove some basic results for finite time ISS and related concepts.

At first we show the equivalent relationship between ISS and the existence of ISS-Lyapunov function.

Theorem 3.1 *System (2) is finite time ISS with v as input if and only if there is an ISS-Lyapunov function $V_0(z)$, which is a positive-definite and proper function such that*

$$\dot{V}_0 \overset{\text{def}}{=} D^+ V_0 \dot{z} \leqslant -\gamma_3(V_0) + \gamma_4(||v||), \tag{13}$$

where $\gamma_3(V_0) = O(V_0^{\alpha_0})$ as $V_0 \to 0$ for some positive constant $\alpha_0 < 1$, and γ_i $(i = 3, 4)$ are K_∞-functions.

Proof: (Sufficiency) Without loss of generality, we take $t_0 = 0$. It is easy to see that, if

$$\dot{V}_0 \leqslant -\frac{1}{2}\gamma_3(V_0), \tag{14}$$

which implies

$$||z(t)|| \leqslant \beta(||z_0||, t) \tag{15}$$

with a KL-function β with $\beta(||z_0||, t) \equiv 0$, $\forall t \geqslant T$ for a finite constant T depending on z_0.

Let us go back to (13). When $\gamma_3(V_0) \geqslant 2\gamma_4(||v||)$, (14) holds. Therefore, we have

$$||z(t)|| \leqslant \begin{cases} \beta(||z_0||, t), & \gamma_3(V_0) \geqslant 2\gamma_4(||v||) \\ \gamma(\sup_{0 \leqslant \tau \leqslant t} ||v(\tau)||), & \gamma_3(V_0) < 2\gamma_4(||v||) \end{cases} \tag{16}$$

for some K-function γ.

Then rewriting (25) gives that

$$||z(t)|| \leqslant \beta(||z_0||, t) + \gamma(\sup_{0 \leqslant \tau \leqslant t} ||v(\tau)||) \tag{17}$$

Thus, finite time ISS holds since β is a KL-function with $\beta(||z_0||, t) \equiv 0$ when $t \geqslant T$ for some function T continuous with respect to z_0.

(Necessity) We will prove the existence of finite time ISS-Lyapunov function from finite time ISS. In fact, finite time ISS holds if and only if there exist a KL function β and a K function γ such that

$$||z(t, z_0, v)|| \leqslant \max\{\beta(||z_0||, t - t_0), \ \gamma(\sup_{t_0 \leqslant \tau \leqslant t} ||v(\tau)||)\} \tag{18}$$

with $\beta(||z_0||, t - t_0) \equiv 0$ when $t - t_0 \geqslant T$ for some function T continuous with respect to z_0.

According to the analysis for conventional ISS given in Lemma 2.12 of [29], γ in (18) can be assumed to be a K_∞-function, and there is a K_∞-function σ satisfying $\sigma(r) < \gamma^{-1}(\frac{\beta_0^{-1}(r)}{4})$ with $\beta_0(r) = \beta(r, 0)$. Moreover, we have a continuous (or smooth everywhere except possibly at the origin) function φ and a K_∞-function ψ such that

$$\psi(||z||) \leqslant \varphi(z) \leqslant \sigma(||z||), \quad \forall z \in \mathbb{R}^n.$$

Now we consider a system

$$\dot{z}(t) = f(z(t), d(t)\varphi(z(t))) = g(z(t), d(t)) \tag{19}$$

where $d(t)$ is viewed as the disturbance input. Then we will consider the finite time stability of (19).

Let $\zeta(t, z_0, d)$ denote the solution of (19) with initial state z_0 and "disturbance" d. Still invoking the proof of Lemma 2.12 of [29], we can obtain

$$\gamma(||d(t)\varphi(\zeta(t, z_0, d))||) \leqslant \frac{||z_0||}{2}, \quad a.e.\ t \geqslant 0 \tag{20}$$

for any $z_0 \in \mathbb{R}^n$ and any $d \in M$ with

$$M = \{\text{all measurable functions from } R \text{ to } [-1,\ 1]^m\}$$

Moreover, we have that, for each $r > 0$ there is some $T_r \geqslant 0$ so that

$$t \geqslant T_r,\ ||z_0|| \leqslant r \quad \Rightarrow \quad \beta(r, t) \leqslant \frac{r}{2}$$

which implies $||\zeta(t, z_0, d)|| \leqslant \frac{r}{2} \overset{\text{def}}{=} r_1$ due to (18) and (20). Note that there is a finite constant T_* such that $\beta(r, t) = 0$ when $t \geqslant T_*$ (since function T continuous with respect to z_0). Let $r_1 = r/2$ and $r_i = r_{i-1}/2$ $(i = 2, 3, \cdots)$. Then we can pick up a sequence of time instants $\{T_{r_i},\ i = 1, 2, \cdots, \infty\}$ such that $\lim_{i\to\infty} T_{r_i} = T_*$ and that

$$||\zeta(t, z_0, d)|| \leqslant \frac{r}{2^i} \overset{\text{def}}{=} r_i, \quad \forall ||z_0|| \leqslant r,\ d \in M, \quad t \geqslant T_{r_i}$$

This shows that the origin is finite time convergent for system (19). In addition, (18) and (20) imply that $||\zeta(t, z_0, d)|| \leqslant \beta(||z_0||, 0)$ for all $t \geqslant 0$, all $z_0 \in \mathbb{R}^n$, and all $d \in M$. We conclude that system (19) is finite time stable.

Then by Lemma 2.4 and Remark 2.2, there is a Lyapunov function V with (12) for system (19); namely $\dot{V}|_{(19)} \leqslant -cV^a$. Recalling the Definition of ISS-Lyapunov function with $\phi_1(z) = cV(z)^a$ in (5), the existence of finite time ISS-Lyapunov function can be guaranteed. □

The next result is about finite-time ISS properties of cascade-interconnected systems in the following form:

$$\begin{cases} \dot{z} = g(z, v), & g(0, 0) = 0 \\ \dot{x} = f(x, z, v), & f(0, 0, 0) = 0 \end{cases} \tag{21}$$

Theorem 3.2 *If the x-subsystem of system (21) is finite time ISS with (z, v) as the input and the z-subsystem of system (21) is finite time ISS with u as the input, then system (21) is finite time ISS with u as the input.*

Proof: According to the conditions, we have two KL-functions β and β^0 and two K-functions γ and γ^0 such that, for $t \geqslant t_0 \geqslant 0$,

$$||z(t)|| \leqslant \beta(||z(t_0)||, t - t_0) + \gamma(\sup_{t_0 \leqslant \tau \leqslant t} ||v(\tau)||) \tag{22}$$

$$||x(t)|| \leqslant \beta^0(||x(t_0)||, t - t_0) + \gamma^0(\sup_{t_0 \leqslant \tau \leqslant t} ||(u(\tau), z(\tau))||) \tag{23}$$

where $\beta(||z(t_0)||, t - t_0) = 0$ for $t \geqslant t_0 + T$ and $\beta^0(||x(t_0)||, t - t_0) = 0$ for $t \geqslant t_0 + T_0$, with T and T_0 continuous with respect to $z(t_0)$ and $x(t_0)$, respectively.

Firstly, let us notice that, using a triangle inequality as in [12], it holds, for any $t \geqslant t_0 \geqslant 0$,

$$\begin{aligned} ||x(t)|| \leqslant\ & \beta^0(||z(t_0)||, 0) + \gamma^0 \circ (Id + \rho) \circ \beta(||z(t_0)||, 0) \\ & + \gamma^0 \circ (Id + \rho^{-1})(\sup_{t_0 \leqslant \tau \leqslant t} ||u(\tau)|| + \gamma(||v(\tau)||) \end{aligned} \tag{24}$$

where ρ is any K_∞-function and Id stands for the identity function.

Then, by taking $t_0 = t/2$ in (23) and plugging (22) with $t_0 = 0$, we have

$$||x(t)|| \leqslant \beta^0(||x(\frac{t}{2})||, \frac{t}{2}) + \gamma^0(\sup_{t/2 \leqslant \tau \leqslant t} ||(u(\tau)|| + \beta(||z(0)||, \frac{t}{2}) + \gamma(\sup_{0 \leqslant \tau \leqslant t} ||v(\tau)||)$$

Using again the triangle inequality as in [12, Proof of Proposition 3.1], with the help of inequality (24), it follows that there exist a class-KL function $\hat{\beta}$ and a class-K function $\hat{\gamma}$ satisfying

$$||x(t)|| \leqslant \hat{\beta}(||(x(0), z(0))||, t) + \hat{\gamma}(\sup_{0 \leqslant \tau \leqslant t} ||(u(\tau, v(\tau))||) \tag{25}$$

In addition, by hypotheses, it is directly checked that $\hat{\beta}(||(x(0), z(0))||, t) = 0$ for all $t \geqslant \hat{T}$ and some $\hat{T}$ being a nonnegative continuous function with respect to $(x(0), z(0))$. Finally, the proof of Theorem 3.2 is completed. □

4 Control Design

Finite time input-to-state stability and related properties have been discussed in the last section. In this section, we will see how these ISS concepts can be used in the finite-time control. Consider

$$\begin{cases} \dot{z} = g(x, z), & g(0,0) = 0,\ f(0,0) = 0, \\ \dot{x} = f(x, z) + v, & (v, x, z) \in \mathbb{R} \times \mathbb{R} \times \mathbb{R}^l \end{cases} \tag{26}$$

where f and g are analytic functions.

For practical Lyapunov-based design, we usually construct a Lipschitz continuous (or even smooth) Lyapunov function such that (12) holds for finite time stable system $\dot{\xi} = f(\xi)$. Note that, for a finite-time stable system, we are not sure if it admits a smooth Lyapunov function (in fact, it may not be so in general, referring to [1]). However, the assumption of the existence of a Lipschitz continuous (or even smooth) Lyapunov function is not very strict in the finite-time control design [1] because we can try to obtain such Lyapunov function using control input during the feedback design. In fact, most of the existing results on finite time stabilization exhibit the existence of smooth Lyapunov function. Following this idea, when we study how to apply finite time ISS in control design, we can consider a Lipschitz continuous (or even smooth) Lyapunov function.

For addressing the stabilization problem, we give a modified version of finite-time ISS:

Definition 4.1 *System (2) is said to be finite-time ISS with a continuous function $h(z,v)$ as the input, if, for any initial state $z(t_0) = z_0$ and bounded input v, we have*

$$||z(t)|| \leqslant \beta(||z_0||, t-t_0) + \gamma(\sup_{t_0 \leqslant \tau \leqslant t} ||h(\tau)||) \tag{27}$$

where $h(\tau) = h(z(\tau), v(\tau))$, γ is a K-function and β is a KL-function with $\beta(||z_0||, t-t_0) \equiv 0$ when $t \geqslant T$ for some function T continuous with respect to z_0.

In what follows, we will design controllers consisting of the fractional power terms. For convenience, we denote x^p as a shorthand of $|x|^p\, sgn(x)$ (where $sgn(\cdot)$ is the sign function) if there is no big confusion (though the notation is little abused).

Remark 4.1 *It is not hard to show that $|x-\mu| \leqslant 2|x^\iota - \mu^\iota|^{\frac{1}{\iota}}$ if $\iota \geqslant 1$. In fact, if a system is finite time ISS with h, then it is finite time ISS with h^p for a positive constant p (since we can reset function γ as $\gamma^{1/p}$).*

Theorem 4.1 *Suppose $g(x,z)$ is Lipschitzian with respect to x and the z-subsystem of (26) is finite time ISS with C^1 smooth function $h(x,\mu) = [x^{\bar{\iota}} - \mu(z)^{\bar{\iota}}]$ (for some $\bar{\iota} \geqslant 1$) as input. If the z-subsystem of (26) admits a Lipschitz continuous Lyapunov function V_1 such that*

$$\dot{V}_1(z) \leqslant -\gamma_1(V_1(z)) + \gamma_2(h) \tag{28}$$

with K-functions γ_i $(i = 1, 2)$ satisfying

i). there is a constant $\iota \geqslant \bar{\iota} > 1$ such that

$$\gamma_2 = o(|h|^{1+\frac{1}{\iota}}) \tag{29}$$

ii).

$$\left|\frac{\partial \mu^{\bar{\iota}}}{\partial z} g(x,z)\right| \leqslant g_1(h) g_2(z)$$

with some nonnegative function $g_2 = o(\gamma_1(V_1(z))^{1-\frac{1}{\bar{\iota}}})$;

then we can find a non-smooth state feedback $\nu(h,z)$ with $\nu(0,0) = 0$ and ν^ι C^1 smooth for some $\iota > 0$ such that system (26) is finite time ISS with w as input by taking

$$v = \nu(h,z) + w$$

where there is a constant $\iota > 1$ to make $\nu(h,z)^\iota$ C^1 smooth.

Proof: From (28), $\dot{z} = g(\mu(z), z)$ is finite time stable (since $h = 0$).

According to condition i) and Lemma 2.2, there is a C^1 function $\bar{g}_0(h, z)$ such that

$$\gamma_2 \leqslant |h|^{1+\frac{1}{\iota}} \bar{g}_0(h, z) \tag{30}$$

Then, we construct a positive definite function $V = V_1 + \int_\mu^x h(s, z)ds$, and then

$$\dot{V} \leqslant -\gamma_1(V_1(z) + \gamma_2(h) + \frac{\mathrm{d}}{\mathrm{d}t}\int_\mu^x h\,\mathrm{d}s$$

where

$$\frac{\mathrm{d}}{\mathrm{d}t}\int_\mu^x h\,\mathrm{d}s = h[f(x, z) + u] - (x - \mu)\frac{\partial \mu^{\bar{\iota}}}{\partial z} g(x, z).$$

Note that $hf(x, z) = h\{[f(x, z) - f(\mu(z), z)] + f(\mu(z), z)\}$. By Remark 4.1 and Lemma 2.2, $|hf(x, z)| = |h||x - \mu|\tilde{f}_1(h, z) + |hf(\mu, z)|$. It is easy to see that

$$|h|\,|x - \mu|\tilde{f}_1(h, z) \leqslant 2|h|^{1+\frac{1}{\bar{\iota}}} \bar{f}_1(h, z) \leqslant |h|^{1+\frac{1}{\iota}} \bar{f}_1(h, z) \tag{31}$$

for some C^1 nonnegative function $\bar{f}_1(h, z)$ since $\bar{\iota} \leqslant \iota$. Then, the analyticity of f implies that there are positive constants $\alpha_1 < 1$ and $\bar{\alpha}_1 < 1$ such that $f(\mu(z), z) = o(z^{\alpha_1}) = o(\gamma_1(V_1)^{\bar{\alpha}_1})$. Then $|hf(\mu, z)| \leqslant |h|\tilde{f}_1(h, z)\gamma_1(V_1)^{\bar{\alpha}_1}$. Note that we can always take $\iota > (1 - \bar{\alpha}_1)/\bar{\alpha}_1$. Then, by Lemma 2.3 and Lemma 2.2, we have

$$\begin{aligned} |hf(\mu, z)| &\leqslant \frac{\gamma_1(V_1)}{4} + |h|^{1+\frac{1}{\iota}} \cdot 4^{\frac{1}{\bar{\alpha}_1(1-\bar{\alpha}_1)}} |h|^{\frac{1-\bar{\alpha}_1}{\bar{\alpha}_1} - \frac{1}{\iota}} \tilde{f}_1^{1+\frac{\bar{\alpha}_1}{1-\bar{\alpha}_1}} \\ &\leqslant \frac{\gamma_1(V_1)}{4} + |h|^{1+\frac{1}{\iota}} \bar{f}_2(h, z) \end{aligned} \tag{32}$$

with some C^1 function $\bar{f}_2$.

Then, by Remark 4.1, we have

$$(x - \mu)\frac{\partial \mu^{\bar{\iota}}}{\partial z} g(x, z) \leqslant 2h^{\frac{1}{\bar{\iota}}} \left|\frac{\partial \mu^{\bar{\iota}}}{\partial z}\right| |g(x, z)|$$

Recalling condition ii) and Lemma 2.2 and Lemma 2.3, we have

$$\begin{aligned} (x - \mu)\frac{\partial \mu^{\bar{\iota}}}{\partial z} g(x, z) &\leqslant \gamma_1(V_1)^{1-\frac{1}{\bar{\iota}}} \cdot \frac{2|h|^{\frac{1}{\bar{\iota}}} g_1(h)g_2(z)}{\gamma_1(V_1)^{1-\frac{1}{\bar{\iota}}}} \\ &\leqslant \frac{\gamma_1(V_1)}{4} + |h|^{1+\frac{1}{\iota}} \bar{g}_1(h, z) \end{aligned}$$

where there is a suitable nonnegative C^1 function $\bar{g}_1(h, z)$.

Then we can take $\nu = -h^{1/\iota}\Phi(h, z)$, where some function Φ is C^1 and positive and some constant $\iota > 1$ such that Φ dominates $2 + \sum_{i=0}^{1} \bar{g}_i(h, z) + \sum_{i=1}^{2} \bar{f}_i(h, z)$, or equivalently,

$$h\nu + \gamma_2(h) + |h|^{1+\frac{1}{\iota}}[\sum_{i=1}^{2} \bar{f}_i(h, z) + \sum_{i=0}^{1} \bar{g}_i(h, z)] \leqslant -2|h|^{1+\frac{1}{\iota}}$$

Therefore, according to Young's inequality, we have:

$$\dot{V} \leqslant -\frac{1}{2}\gamma_1(\bar{V}_1(z)) - |h^{1+1/\iota}| + |w|^{1+\iota}$$

and it is easy to see that ν^ι is C^1. Thus, the conclusion follows. □

In fact, Theorem 4.1 is consistent with the design procedure given in our recent papers [6,7]. In what follows, we give an illustrate example to show the design of finite-time stabilizing controllers.

Example 4.1 Consider an under-actuated system

$$\begin{cases} \dot{x}_1 = x_1 + x_2^3 \\ \dot{x}_2 = u \end{cases} \tag{33}$$

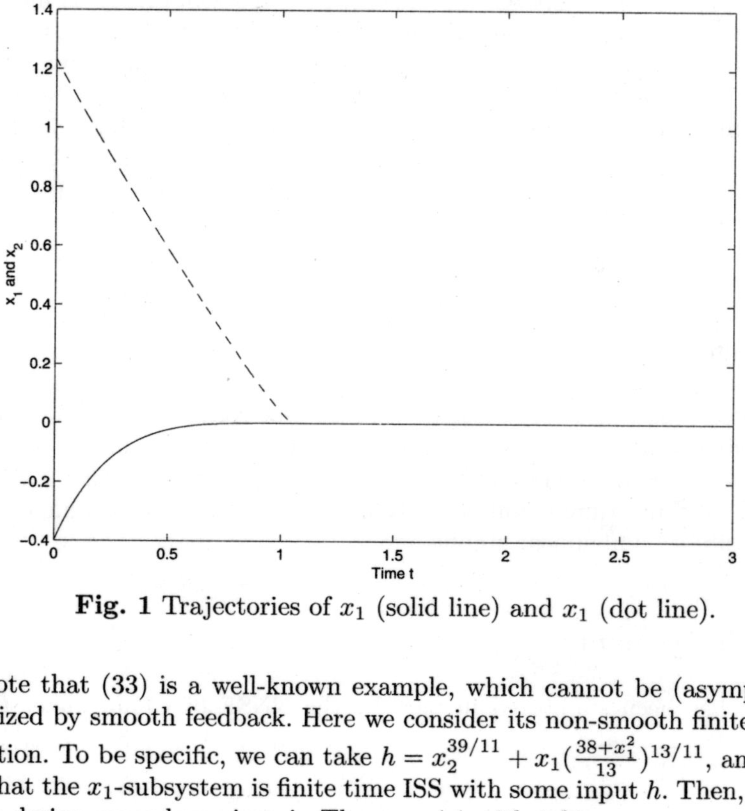

Fig. 1 Trajectories of x_1 (solid line) and x_1 (dot line).

Note that (33) is a well-known example, which cannot be (asymptotically) stabilized by smooth feedback. Here we consider its non-smooth finite time stabilization. To be specific, we can take $h = x_2^{39/11} + x_1(\frac{38+x_1^2}{13})^{13/11}$, and then we find that the x_1-subsystem is finite time ISS with some input h. Then, according to the design procedure given in Theorem 4.1 with taking

$$V = \frac{11}{20}x_1^{20/11} + \int_{(\frac{(38+x_1^2)x_1^{11/13}}{13})^{1/3}}^{x_2} h(s, x_1)\,\mathrm{d}s$$

we can construct its controller as follows:

$$u = -h^{\frac{5}{39}}(2 + \frac{\rho_1^4[15 + |13x_1^{\frac{2}{13}} - 38 - x_1^2)|]^4}{100}) \tag{34}$$

where $\rho_1 = \frac{(x_1^2+15)(38+x_1^2)^{\frac{2}{11}}}{4}$. Fig. 1 shows a numerical result of the finite time control design.

It should be pointed out that finite time ISS provides a general design idea, but the method directly based on finite time ISS is very conservative in the construction of those gain functions in the design procedure (that is, the gain may be relatively high). In other words, the construction of finite time controllers with this method may not be practical because of the high gain. However, this method provides a general design procedure to handle stability problems for (non-smooth) controlled dynamics.

5 Conclusions

In this paper, we have proposed a variant of Sontag's ISS, coined as finite-time ISS, and showed its applications in finite-time stability analysis and finite-time stabilization for nonlinear systems. A relationship between finite-time ISS and finite-time ISS-Lyapunov function is provided. It is also shown that the cascade system composed of two finite-time ISS systems is also finite-time ISS. Preliminary results about finite-time control design based on finite-time ISS were obtained, with two illustrative examples showing the effectiveness of the proposed novel design tool. We believe that finite-time ISS will play a key role for finite-time control, mirroring the power of Sontag's ISS in asymptotic stabilization among many other control applications. Finite-time ISS and its characterizations are a research topic we are currently studying.

Other interesting research problems include but are not limited to: extending the obtained results to generalized finite-time small-gain theorems for interconnected systems, as well as applications to finite time control by partial-state and output feedback of nonlinear systems with parametric and dynamic uncertainties. This design idea based on finite-time ISS should provide a general theoretic framework for finite time stability analysis, leading to the development of new tools for finite-time nonlinear stabilization.

Acknowledgement

This work has been supported in part by the NNSF of China under Grants 60425307, 10472129 and 60221301, and in part by the U.S. NSF under Grants ECS-0093176, OISE-0408925 and DMS-0504462.

References

1. Bhat, S., Bernstein, D., Finite-time stability of continuous autonomous systems, *SIAM J. Control and Optimization*, Vol. 38, No. 2, 751-766, 2000.
2. Desoer C. Vidyasagar, M. , *Feedback Systems: Input-output Properties*, Academic Press, New York, 1975.

3. Filippov, A., *Differential Equations with Discontinuous Right Hand Side*, Kluwer, Dordrecht, 1988.
4. Hong, Y., Huang, J., Xu, Y., On an output feedback finite-time stabilization problem, *IEEE Trans. Automatic Control*, Vol. 46, No. 2, 305-309, 2001.
5. Hong, Y. Wang, J., Xi, Z., Stabilization of uncertain chained form systems within finite settling time, *IEEE Trans. Automatic Control*, Vol. 48, No. 9, 1379-1384, 2005.
6. Hong, Y. Wang, J., Cheng, D., Adaptive finite time control of nonlinear systems with parametric uncertainty, *IEEE Trans. Automatic Control*, Vol. 49, No. 5, 858-862, 2006.
7. Hong Y., Jiang, Z. P., Finite time stabilization of nonlinear systems with parametric and dynamic uncertainties, *IEEE Trans. Automatic Control*, Vol. 49, No. 12, 2006.
8. Huang J., *Nonlinear Output Regulation: Theory and Applications.* SIAM, Phildelphia, 2004.
9. Huang J., Chen, Z., A general framework for tackling the output regulation problems, *IEEE Trans. Automatic Control*, Vol. 49, No. 12, 2203-2218, 2004.
10. Isidori, A., *Nonlinear Control Systems.* 3rd ed. Springer-Verlag, Berlin, 1995.
11. Isidori, A., *Nonlinear Control Systems.* Vol. II. Springer-Verlag, London, 1999.
12. Jiang, Z. P., Teel, A. Praly, L., Small-gain theorem for ISS systems and applications *Mathematics of Control, Signals, and Systems*, Vol. 7, No. 1, 95-120, 1994.
13. Jiang, Z. P., Mareels, I., Wang, Y., A Lyapunov formulation of the nonlinear small-gain theorem for interconnected ISS systems, *Automatica*, Vol. 32, pp. 1211-1215, 1996.
14. Jiang, Z. P., Mareels, I., A small-gain control method for nonlinear cascaded systems with dynamic uncertainties, *IEEE Trans. Automatic Control*, Vol. 42, pp. 292-308, 1997.
15. Jiang, Z. P., Wang, Y., Input-to-state stability for discrete-time nonlinear systems, *Automatica*, Vol 37, No. 6, 857-869, 2001.
16. Jiang, Z. P., Praly, L., Design of robust adaptive controllers for nonlinear systems with dynamic uncertainties, *Automatica*, Vol. 34, No. 6, 825-840, 1998.
17. Khalil, H., *Nonlinear Systems*, 3rd ed., Prentice Hall, Upper Saddle River, 2002.
18. Kokotovic, P. V., Arcak, M. , Constructive nonlinear control: a historical perspective, *Auotmatica*, Vol. 37, pp. 637-662, 2001.
19. Krstic, M., Kanellakopoulos, I., Kokotovic, P., *Nonlinear and Adaptive Control Design*, John Wiley, New York, 1995.
20. Lin, Y., Sontag, E., Wang, Y., A smooth converse Lyapunov theorem for robust stability, *SIAM J. Control and Optimization*, Vol. 34, pp. 124-160, 1996.
21. Marino R., Tomei, P., *Nonlinear Control Design: Geometric, Adaptive, Robust*, Prentice Hall, New York, 1995.
22. Nesic, D., Teel, A., Input to state stability of networked control systems, *Automatica*, Vol. 40, No. 12, 2121-2128, 2004.
23. Orlov, Y., Finite time stability and robust control synthesis of uncertain switched systems, *SIAM J. Control Optim.*, Vol. 43, No. 2, 1253-1271, 2005.
24. Ortega, R., Loria, A., Nicklasson, P.J., Sira-Ramirez, H., *Passivity-based Control of Euler-Lagrange Systems*, Springer-Verlag, London.
25. Priscoli, F. D., Marconi, L., Isidori, A., Adaptive observers as nonlinear internal models, *Systems & Control Letters*, Special Issue "New Trends in Nonlinear Control" (Eds. Z.P. Jiang and I. Mareels), Vol. 55, No. 8, pp. 640-649, 2006.
26. Rouche, N., Habets, P., Laloy, M., *Stability Theory by Liapunov's Direct Method*, Springer-Verlag, New York, 1977.

27. Sontag, E., The ISS philosophy as a unifying framework for stability-like behavior, in: *Nonlinear Control in the Year 2000*, Lecture Notes in Control and Information Sciences, A. Isidori, F. Lamnabhi-Lagarrigue, and W. Respondek (Eds.), pp. 443-468, Springer-Verlag, 2000.
28. Sontag, E., On the input-to-state stability property, *European J. Control*, Vol. 1, No. 1, 24-36, 1995.
29. Sontag, E., Wang, Y., On characterizations of the input to state stability property, *Systems & Control Letters*, Vol. 24, No. 2, 351-359, 1995.
30. Sontag, E., Teel, A., Changing supply functions in input/state stable systems, *IEEE Trans. Automatic Control*, Vol. 40, No. 12, 1476-1478, 1995.
31. Teel, A. R., A nonlinear small-gain theorem for the analysis of control systems with saturation, *IEEE Trans. Automatic Control*, Vol. 41, pp. 1256-1270, 1996.
32. Utkin, V., *Sliding Modes in Control Optimization*, Springer-Verlag, Berlin, 1992.
33. van der Schaft, A. J., *$\mathcal{L}_2$-Gain and Passivity Techniques in Nonlinear Control*, Springer-Verlag, Heidberg, 1996.

Non-synchronized Output Feedback Controller Design of Discrete Time Piecewise Linear Systems

Gang Feng and Tiejun Zhang

Department of Manufacturing Engineering and Engineering Management, City University of Hong Kong, 83 Tat Chee Avenue, Kowloon, Hong Kong, China
{megfeng,tzhang}@cityu.edu.hk

1 Introduction

Piecewise linear systems have been a subject of research in circuits, systems, and control community for some time, see for example $[1 \sim 18]$ and references therein. In fact, piecewise linear systems constitute a special class of hybrid systems and arise often in practical circuits or control systems when piecewise linear components are encountered. These components include diodes, dead-zone, saturation, relays, and hysteresis. It is also known that many chaotic circuits can be constructed by piecewise linear circuits [3,4]. In addition, many general nonlinear systems can also be approximated by piecewise linear systems. Thus piecewise linear systems provide a powerful means of analysis and design for nonlinear circuits including chaotic circuits and nonlinear control systems.

Numerous results have been obtained on analysis and controller design of continuous time or discrete time piecewise linear systems during the last few years. For example, the authors in [6, 7] presented results on stability and optimal performance analysis for piecewise linear systems based on a piecewise continuous Lyapunov function. It has been shown that lower bounds, as well as upper bounds, on the optimal control cost can be obtained by semi-definite programming, and the framework of piecewise linear systems can be used to analyze smooth nonlinear systems with arbitrary accuracy. The authors in [8] discussed stability analysis and controller design of piecewise linear systems which may involve multiple equilibrium points based on a common quadratic Lyapunov function and also a piecewise quadratic Lyapunov function. It has been shown that stability and performance analysis can be cast as convex optimization problems. A controller design method based on a common quadratic Lyapunov function and linear matrix inequalities has been proposed. Similar work to those in $[6 \sim 8]$ has also been reported in [9, 10] where the piecewise Lyapunov function might be discontinuous across the region boundaries. The authors in [13] presented an approach to stabilization of piecewise linear systems based on a common quadratic Lyapunov function. It was shown that the piecewise state feedback control law could be obtained by solving a set of Linear Matrix Inequalities (LMI) and a single non-convex bilinear matrix inequality. The authors in [14, 15] presented a number of results on stability analysis, controller design, H_∞ analysis, and H_∞ controller design for the piecewise linear systems based on a piecewise Lyapunov function. The authors in [16] presented a number of algorithms to test the controllability and observability of the piecewise linear systems. Sontag [18] studied the nonlinear regulation via piecewise linear approach. Issues of state feedback, output feedback and observers were addressed. In a recent paper [19], we proposed a method for stability analysis of the discrete time piecewise linear systems with *affine terms* by constructing a novel piecewise Lyapunov function. It is shown that the piecewise Lyapunov function can be constructed by solving a set of linear matrix inequalities.

More recently, there have appeared some results [20~22] on observer design and output feedback for continuous-time and discrete-time piecewise linear systems. The authors in [20] presented a moving horizon estimation algorithm for discrete time piecewise linear systems. A number of sufficient conditions had been developed to guarantee asymptotic convergence of the moving horizon estimation algorithm, and some practical implementation issues had also been addressed. The authors in [21, 22] presented a number of approaches for observer based output feedback controller design, where the case that both the plant and the controller started in the same region and always switched regions at the same time was dealt with in [21], while the case that the plant and the controller may start in the different region or may switch at the different time was discussed in [22]. However, only a very preliminary result was reported which involves a two-step procedure and bilinear matrix inequalities. We recently studied the observer based output feedback control discrete time of piecewise linear systems using a piecewise Lyapunov function [23]. We have shown that the controller and observer design of the piecewise linear systems based on the piecewise Lyapunov functions can be carried out separately in the sense that the global stability of the combined system can be guaranteed if both the controller and observer design lead to the stability of the corresponding system in the piecewise Lyapunov function sense. The result can be recognized as the separation principle in the context of the piecewise linear systems with piecewise Lyapunov functions. It was assumed that the regions were defined by the output space partition so that the plant and observer always switch to the same regions at the same time. However, many piecewise linear systems are more likely partitioned based on the state space, and in such a case, there is no guarantee that the plant and the observer always switch to the same region at the same time. Then one may wonder what will happen to the observer design.

In this paper, we will consider the observer based output feedback controller design under such asynchronous conditions. We will present a number of approaches to synthesize controllers and observers based on common and piecewise Lyapunov functions respectively for the discrete time piecewise linear systems. It will be shown that the resulting closed loop control system is globally stable and the observer gains can be obtained by solving a set of bilinear matrix inequalities.

The rest of the paper is organized as follows. Section 2 introduces the piecewise linear system model, state feedback controller and observer design for such systems. Section 3 presents a number of results on observer based output feedback controller design based on common and piecewise Lyapunov functions respectively. A number of simulation examples are used to illustrate the performance of the proposed approaches in Section 4, which is followed by conclusions in Section 5.

2 Piecewise Linear System Model, State Feedback Controller, and Observer

Consider autonomous discrete time piecewise linear systems of the form

$$\begin{cases} x(t+1) = A_l x(t) + B_l u(t) \\ y(t) = C_l x(t), \quad x(t) \in S_l, \ l = 1, 2, \cdots, m \end{cases} \tag{1}$$

where $\{S_l\}_{l \in L} \subseteq \mathbb{R}^n$ denotes a partition of the output space into a number of closed polyhedral subspaces, L is the index set of subspaces, $x(t) \in \mathbb{R}^n$ the system state variables, and (A_l, B_l) the l-th local model of the system. For the definition of state trajectory and solution to the piecewise linear system (1) please refer to [$1 \sim 3$], [$7 \sim 9$] for details. Here we assume that given any initial condition $x(0) = x_0$, the difference equation (1) has a unique solution for all $t > 0$. We also assume that when the state of the system transits from the region S_l to S_j at the time t, the dynamics of the system is governed by the dynamics of the local model of S_l at that time. For future use, we also define a set Ω that represents all possible transitions from one region to another, that is,

$$\Omega \overset{\text{def}}{=} \{l, j | x(t) \in X_l, x(t+1) \in X_j, \ j \neq l\}$$

At first, we make the following assumption.

Assumption 2.1 *The system (1) is both locally controllable and observable, that is, $(A_l, B_l), l \in L$ is controllable, and $(A_l, C_l), l \in L$ is observable.*

The following stability results, one based on a common Lyapunov function and the other on a piecewise Lyapunov function, are straightforward [14,15,19].

Lamma 2.1 *Consider the piecewise linear system (1). If there exists a symmetric positive definite matrix P such that the following LMIs are satisfied,*

$$A_l^T P A_l - P < 0, \quad l \in L \tag{2}$$

then the piecewise linear system is globally exponentially stable, that is, $x(t)$ tends to the origin exponentially for every trajectory in the state space.

Lamma 2.2 *Consider the piecewise linear system (1). If there exist symmetric positive definite matrices $P_l, l \in L$ such that the following LMIs are satisfied,*

$$A_l^T P_l A_l - P_l < 0, \quad l \in L \tag{3}$$
$$A_l^T P_j A_l - P_l < 0, \quad l, j \in \Omega \tag{4}$$

then the piecewise linear system is globally exponentially stable, that is, $x(t)$ tends to the origin exponentially for every trajectory in the state space.

Remark 2.1 *The conditions (3) and (4) are linear matrix inequalities in the variable P_l. A solution to those inequalities ensures $V(x) = x^T P_l x$, $x(t) \in S_l$ to be a Lyapunov function for the system. The LMI (3) guarantees that the function is decreasing along all system trajectories in each region. The LMI (4) guarantees that the function is decreasing when the state transits from one region to another.*

Remark 2.2 *The set Ω can be determined by the reachability analysis* [16]. *If it is possible for the transitions happen between all regions, then $\Omega = L \times L$, which is defined as a set of $\{l, j | l, j \in L, \ j \neq l\}$.*

2.1 State Feedback Controller

Consider the following piecewise continuous controller as

$$u(t) = K(x) = K_l x(t), \quad x(t) \in S_l, \ l \in L \tag{5}$$

With the control law (5), the global closed loop system is obtained by combining the system (1) and the controller (5), and can be described by the following equation,

$$x(t+1) = A_{cl} x(t), \quad x(t) \in S_l \tag{6}$$

where

$$A_{cl} = A_l + B_l K_l \tag{7}$$

Then the following results, one based on a common Lyapunov function and the other based on a piecewise Lyapunov function, are straightforward [14,15,19].

Theorem 2.1 *The system (6) is globally stable, if there exist a positive definite matrix X and a set of matrices $Q_l, l \in L$ such that the following LMIs are satisfied,*

$$\begin{bmatrix} -X & X_l^T A_l^T + Q_l^T B_l^T \\ A_l X_l + B_l Q_l & -X \end{bmatrix} < 0, \quad l \in L \tag{8}$$

Moreover, the controller gain for each local subsystem is given by

$$K_l = Q_l X^{-1}, \ l \in L \tag{9}$$

Theorem 2.2 *The system (6) is globally stable, if there exist a set of positive definite matrices $X_l, l \in L$ and two sets of matrices $Q_l, R_l, l \in L$ such that the following LMIs are satisfied,*

$$\begin{bmatrix} X_l - R_l^T - R_l & R_l^T A_l^T + Q_l^T B_l^T \\ A_l R_l + B_l Q_l & -X_l \end{bmatrix} < 0, l \in L \tag{10}$$

$$\begin{bmatrix} X_l - R_l^T - R_l & R_l^T A_l^T + Q_l^T B_l^T \\ A_l R_l + B_l Q_l & -X_j \end{bmatrix} < 0, l, j \in \Omega \tag{11}$$

Moreover, the controller gain for each local subsystem is given by

$$K_l = Q_l R_l^{-1}, \ l \in L \tag{12}$$

Remark 2.3 The conditions (10) and (11) are linear matrix inequalities in the variables $X_l, l \in L$. A solution to those inequalities ensures $x^T X_l^{-1} x, x \in S_l$ to be a Lyapunov function for the system.

Remark 2.4 The results obtained in the theorem are made possible by following the technique of introducing extra slack variables R_l's as in [25]. It should also be noted that the matrices R_l's are not required to be symmetric. Furthermore, it is expected that the results will be less conservative under such circumstances due to the more freedom of those slack variables.

2.2 Observer

Consider the following piecewise continuous observer as

$$\begin{cases} \widehat{x}(t+1) = A_l \widehat{x}(t) + B_l u(t) + G_l(\widehat{y}(t) - y(t)) \\ \widehat{y}(t) = C_l \widehat{x}(t), \quad \widehat{x}(t) \in S_l \end{cases} \tag{13}$$

Define the observer error $\widetilde{x}(t) = \widehat{x}(t) - x(t)$. It should be noted that since the state variable $x(t)$ is not measurable only the estimated $\widehat{x}(t)$ will be used for determining the subspace the observer is working in, in other words, only the estimated $\widehat{x}(t)$ will be used for determining the parameters of the piecewise observer. If the state variable $x(t)$ and its estimate $\widehat{x}(t)$ are always close to each other so that the system dynamics and the observer dynamics synchronize in transition from one region to another, then the results developed in [23] can be applied. However, in practice, the state variable $x(t)$ and its estimate $\widehat{x}(t)$ may not be close to each other, especially in the initial period of the system dynamics, and thus the system dynamics and the observer dynamics may not synchronize in transition from one region to another, in other words, when the state variable $x(t)$ belongs to the region S_l, the estimated $\widehat{x}(t)$ may belong to another region $S_j, j \neq l$. In this case, the results in [23] cannot be used. Instead, we will employ the results from [24] for asynchronized estimation.

Considering the system dynamics for $x(t) \in S_l$ and the observer dynamics for $\widehat{x}(t) \in S_j$, then the observer error dynamic system is obtained by combining the observer (13) and the system (1), and can be described by the following equation,

$$\overline{x}(t+1) = \overline{A}_{lj}\overline{x}(t) + \overline{B}_{lj}u(t), \quad x(t) \in S_l, \ \widehat{x}(t) \in S_j \tag{14}$$

where

$$\overline{x} = \begin{bmatrix} x \\ \widehat{x} - x \end{bmatrix}, \ \overline{A}_{lj} = \begin{bmatrix} A_l & O \\ A_j - A_l + G_j(C_j - C_l) & A_l + G_jC_j \end{bmatrix}, \ \overline{B}_{lj} = \begin{bmatrix} B_l \\ B_j - B_l \end{bmatrix}$$

Then we have the following result.

Theorem 2.3 *Consider the piecewise linear observer error system (14) with $u \equiv 0$. If there exist symmetric positive definite matrices P and Q, and matrices $H_l, l = 1, 2, \cdots, m$ such that the following LMIs are satisfied,*

$$\begin{bmatrix} -P & O & PA_l & O \\ \star & -Q & Q(A_j - A_l) + H_j(C_j - C_l) & QA_j + H_jC_j \\ \star & \star & -P & O \\ \star & \star & \star & -Q \end{bmatrix} < 0, \ l, j \in L \tag{15}$$

where the symbol $\star$ stands for the symmetric terms in the matrix, then the piecewise linear observer error system is globally exponentially stable, that is, both $x(t)$ and $\widetilde{x}(t)$ tend to the origin exponentially for every trajectory in the state space. Moreover, the observer parameters are given by

$$G_l = Q^{-1}H_l, \ l \in L \tag{16}$$

Theorem 2.4 *The observer error system (14) with $u \equiv 0$ is globally stable if there exist two sets of positive definite matrices $P_l, Q_l, l \in L$ and three sets of matrices $R_l, W_l, H_l, l \in L$, such that the following LMIs are satisfied,*

$$\begin{bmatrix} P_i - R_l - R_l^T & O & R_lA_l & O \\ O & Q_k - W_j - W_j^T & W_j(A_j - A_l) + H_j(C_j - C_l) & W_jA_j + H_jC_j \\ A_l^TR_l^T & (A_j^T - A_l^T)W_j^T + (C_j^T - C_l^T)H_j^T & -P_l & O \\ O & A_j^TW_j^T + C_j^TH_j^T & O & -Q_j \end{bmatrix} < 0, \ l, i, j, k \in L \tag{17}$$

Moreover, the observer gain for each local subsystem is given by

$$G_l = W_l^{-1}H_l, \ l \in L \tag{18}$$

3 Output Feedback Controller Design

If the estimated states are used for controller implementation, that is, if the following controller is used,

$$u(t) = K(\widehat{x}) = K_j\widehat{x}(t), \quad \widehat{x}(t) \in S_j, \ j \in L \tag{19}$$

the closed loop system can be expressed as

$$\overline{x}(t+1) = \overline{A}_{lj}\overline{x}(t), \quad x(t) \in S_l,\ \widehat{x}(t) \in S_j \tag{20}$$

where $\overline{x} = \left[x^T\ (\widehat{x}-x)^T\right]^T$ and

$$\overline{A}_{lj} = \begin{bmatrix} A_l + B_l K_j & B_l K_j \\ A_j - A_l + (B_j - B_l)K_j + G_j(C_j - C_l) & A_l + (B_j - B_l)K_j + G_jC_j \end{bmatrix}$$

Then we have the following results based on a common Lypunov function.
Theorem 3.1 *The closed loop control system (20) is globally stable if there exist two positive definite matrices P, Q, and two sets of matrices $K_l, G_l, l \in L$ such that the following matrix inequalities are satisfied,*

$$\Phi_{lj} \overset{\text{def}}{=} \begin{bmatrix} -P & O & P(A_l + B_lK_j) & PB_lK_j \\ \star & -Q & Q\Delta_{lj} & Q[A_j + (B_j - B_l)K_j + G_jC_j] \\ \star & \star & -P & O \\ \star & \star & \star & -Q \end{bmatrix} < 0, \quad l, j \in L \tag{21}$$

where the symbol $\star$ stands for the symmetric terms in the matrix, and

$$\Delta_{lj} = A_j - A_l + (B_j - B_l)K_j + G_j(C_j - C_l)$$

Proof: Consider the Lyapunov function candidate

$$V(\overline{x}) = x^TPx + \widetilde{x}^TQ\widetilde{x} = \overline{x}^T \begin{bmatrix} P & O \\ O & Q \end{bmatrix} \overline{x} \tag{22}$$

Then its difference along the solution of the system (20) can be described by,

$$\begin{aligned} \Delta V(t) &\overset{\text{def}}{=} V(t+1) - V(t) \\ &= \overline{x}(t+1) \begin{bmatrix} P & O \\ O & Q \end{bmatrix} \overline{x}(t+1) - \overline{x}(t) \begin{bmatrix} P & O \\ O & Q \end{bmatrix} \overline{x}(t) \\ &= \overline{x}(t) \left(\overline{A}_{lj}^T \begin{bmatrix} P & O \\ O & Q \end{bmatrix} \overline{A}_{lj} - \begin{bmatrix} P & O \\ O & Q \end{bmatrix} \right) \overline{x}(t) \end{aligned} \tag{23}$$

It follows from (23) that if the following inequality can be shown,

$$\overline{A}_{lj}^T \begin{bmatrix} P & O \\ O & Q \end{bmatrix} \overline{A}_{lj} - \begin{bmatrix} P & O \\ O & Q \end{bmatrix} < 0 \tag{24}$$

then the claims of the theorem can be established by invoking the standard Lyapunov stability theory. Using Schur complement, it is easy to see that (24) is equivalent to

$$\begin{pmatrix} \begin{bmatrix} -P & O \\ O & -Q \end{bmatrix} & \begin{bmatrix} P & O \\ O & Q \end{bmatrix} \overline{A}_{lj} \\ \overline{A}_{lj}^T \begin{bmatrix} P & O \\ O & Q \end{bmatrix} & \begin{bmatrix} -P & O \\ O & -Q \end{bmatrix} \end{pmatrix} < 0 \tag{25}$$

By substituting $\overline{A}_{lj}$ defined in (20) into (25), one obtains (21) directly. Therefore the proof is completed. □

Unfortunately it appears that it is difficult to transform (21) into LMIs, if not impossible. The following V-K algorithm can be used to solve the bilinear matrix inequalities [25].

Algorithm 1

V-Step. Given the fixed controller and observer gains $K_l, G_l, l \in L$, solve the following optimization problem

$$\min_{P,Q} \lambda_{lj}$$
$$s.t.\ \Phi_{lj} - \lambda_{lj} I < 0$$

for positive definite matrices P and Q.

K-Step. Using the matrices P and Q obtained in V-Step, solve the following optimization problem

$$\min_{K_l, G_l} \lambda_{lj}$$
$$s.t.\ \Phi_{lj} - \lambda_{lj} I < 0$$

for two sets of matrices K_l and G_l, $l \in L$.

The above iteration stops when $\lambda_{lj} < 0,\ l, j \in L$. ▽

Before presenting a result based on piecewise Lyapunov function, we introduce the following lemmas.

Lamma 3.1 *The following conditions are equivalent,*

A1 There exist positive definite matrices P_j and P_l such that

$$A_l^T P_j A_l - P_l < 0 \tag{26}$$

A2 There exist positive matrices P_j, P_l, and a matrix R_l such that

$$\begin{bmatrix} P_j - R_l - R_l^T & R_l A_l \\ A_l^T R_l^T & -P_l \end{bmatrix} < 0 \tag{27}$$

Proof: The proof follows from the similar arguments as in the proof of Theorem 1 of [25] and thus omitted. □

Similarly, we have the following results based on a piecewise Lyapunov function.

Theorem 3.1 *The closed loop control system (20) is globally stable if there exist two sets of positive definite matrices $P_l, Q_l, l \in L$, and four sets of matrices $K_l, G_l, R_l, W_l, l \in L$ such that the following matrix inequalities are satisfied,*

$$\Phi_{lijk} \stackrel{\text{def}}{=} \begin{bmatrix} P_i - R_l - R_l^T & O & R_l(A_l + B_l K_j) & R_l B_l K_j \\ \star & Q_k - W_j - W_j^T & W_j \Delta_{lj} & W_j[A_j + (B_j - B_l)K_j + G_j C_j] \\ \star & \star & -P_l & O \\ \star & \star & \star & -Q_j \end{bmatrix} < 0,\ l, i, j, k \in L \tag{28}$$

where the symbol $\star$ stands for the symmetric terms in the matrix, and

$$\Delta_{lj} = A_j - A_l + (B_j - B_l)K_j + G_j(C_j - C_l)$$

Proof: Consider a piecewise Lyapunov function candidate

$$V(\overline{x}) = x^T P_l x + \widetilde{x}^T Q_j \widetilde{x} = \overline{x}^T \begin{bmatrix} P_l & O \\ O & Q_j \end{bmatrix} \overline{x}, \quad x(t) \in S_l,\ \widehat{x}(t) \in S_j \tag{29}$$

Then its difference along the solution of the system (20) can be described by then

$$\begin{aligned} \Delta V(t) &\overset{\text{def}}{=} V(t+1) - V(t) \\ &= \overline{x}(t+1) \begin{bmatrix} P_i & O \\ O & Q_k \end{bmatrix} \overline{x}(t+1) - \overline{x}(t) \begin{bmatrix} P_l & O \\ O & Q_j \end{bmatrix} \overline{x}(t) \\ &= \overline{x}(t) \left(\overline{A}_{lj}^T \begin{bmatrix} P_i & O \\ O & Q_k \end{bmatrix} \overline{A}_{lj} - \begin{bmatrix} P_l & O \\ O & Q_j \end{bmatrix} \right) \overline{x}(t) \end{aligned} \tag{30}$$

where $l = i$ or $(j = k)$ stands for that the state (or its estimate) stays at the same region. It follows from (28) that $\Delta V(t) < 0,\ \forall \overline{x} \neq 0$ if the following inequality can be shown,

$$\overline{A}_{lj}^T \begin{bmatrix} P_i & O \\ O & Q_k \end{bmatrix} \overline{A}_{lj} - \begin{bmatrix} P_l & O \\ O & Q_j \end{bmatrix} < 0,\ \forall l, i, j, k \in L \tag{31}$$

Using Lemma 3.1 and substituting $\overline{A}_{lj}$ defined in (20), one obtains (28) directly. Then the claim of the theorem can be established by invoking the standard Lyapunov stability theory, and thus the proof is completed. □

Similarly, the following V-K algorithm can be used to solve the bilinear matrix inequalities [26].

Algorithm 2

V-Step. Given the fixed controller and observer gains $K_l, G_l, l \in L$, solve the following optimization problem

$$\min_{P_l, Q_l, R_l, W_l} \lambda_{lijk}$$
$$\text{s.t. } \Phi_{lijk} - \lambda_{lijk} I < 0$$

for positive definite matrices $P_l, Q_l, R_l, W_l, l \in L$.

K-Step. Using the matrices $P_l, Q_l, R_l, W_l, l \in L$ obtained in V-Step, solve the following optimization problem

$$\min_{K_l, G_l} \lambda_{lijk}$$
$$\text{s.t. } \Phi_{lijk} - \lambda_{lijk} I < 0$$

for two sets of matrices K_l and G_l, $l \in L$.

The above iteration stops when $\lambda_{lijk} < 0,\ l, i, j, k \in L$. ▽

Remark 3.1 *It appears unfortunate that the separation principle, in the sense that the controller and observer design of the piecewise linear systems can be carried out separately while the global stability of the combined system can be guaranteed, does not hold in this case.*

4 Simulation Examples

In this section, we will use a few examples to illustrate the design approaches for observer based output feedback controllers proposed in this paper. We suppose the state variables are not measurable and the estimated state variables are used to determine the region where the observer gains and controller gains should be used.

Example 4.1 Consider a discrete time piecewise linear system

$$\begin{cases} x(t+1) = A_l x(t) + B_l u(t) \\ y(t) = C_l x(t), \quad l = 1, 2 \end{cases} \tag{32}$$

and the corresponding two sets are defined by $\{l = 1 \ if \ |x_1(t)| < 5\}$ and $\{l = 2 \ if \ |x_1(t)| \geqslant 5\}$ respectively. The system matrices are given by

$$A_1 = \begin{bmatrix} 1 & -0.5 \\ -0.4 & 1 \end{bmatrix}, A_2 = \begin{bmatrix} 1 & -0.4 \\ -0.5 & 1 \end{bmatrix}, B_1 = B_2 = \begin{bmatrix} 0 \\ 1 \end{bmatrix}, C_1 = C_2 = \begin{bmatrix} 1 \; 0 \end{bmatrix}$$

It is noted that the open loop system is unstable. By solving (21) via Algorithm 1 and (28) via Algorithm 2 respectively, one obtains the following solutions,

$$P = \begin{bmatrix} 0.6690 & -0.2558 \\ -0.2558 & 0.4118 \end{bmatrix}, \; Q = \begin{bmatrix} 4.9060 \; 2.3017 \\ 2.3017 \; 2.8130 \end{bmatrix},$$

$$K_1 = \begin{bmatrix} 0.9753 \; -1.1254 \end{bmatrix}, \; K_2 = \begin{bmatrix} 0.9040 \; -1.1120 \end{bmatrix},$$

$$G_1 = \begin{bmatrix} -1.6498 \\ 1.7290 \end{bmatrix}, \; G_2 = \begin{bmatrix} -1.5449 \\ 1.8115 \end{bmatrix}$$

after two iterations for the common Lyapunov function based approach; and

$$P_1 = \begin{bmatrix} 0.4236 & -0.1921 \\ -0.1921 & 0.3021 \end{bmatrix}, \; P_2 = \begin{bmatrix} 0.4132 & -0.1723 \\ -0.1723 & 0.3119 \end{bmatrix},$$

$$Q_1 = \begin{bmatrix} 4.6040 \; 2.0131 \\ 2.0131 \; 1.9956 \end{bmatrix}, \; Q_2 = \begin{bmatrix} 4.6455 \; 1.9739 \\ 1.9739 \; 1.9383 \end{bmatrix},$$

$$K_1 = \begin{bmatrix} 0.8505 \; -0.9816 \end{bmatrix}, \; K_2 = \begin{bmatrix} 0.8582 \; -1.0970 \end{bmatrix},$$

$$G_1 = \begin{bmatrix} -1.7979 \\ 1.9908 \end{bmatrix}, \; G_2 = \begin{bmatrix} -1.7561 \\ 2.1924 \end{bmatrix}$$

after three iterations for the piecewise Lyapunov function based approach. It then follows from Theorem 3.1 and Theorem 3.2 that the resulting closed loop control system (20) in both the cases is globally stable.

Simulation results with the initial conditions $x(0) = [10\ 5]^T$ and $\hat{x}(0) = [0\ 0]^T$ are shown in Fig. 1 for the common Lyapunov function based approach and Fig. 2 for the piecewise Lyapunov function based approach respectively, where (a) and (b) represent the observer errors $\tilde{x}_1$ and $\tilde{x}_2$ respectively; (c) represents the phase-plane response of the system state variables x_1 and x_2; and (d) represents the matching sequence of whether the plant states and the estimated states stay at the same regions for the first few sampling periods. It is noted that the number "1" in the sequence of (d) indicates that the plant state and the estimated state stay at the different regions while the number "0" the same region, and also that the sequence remains to be "0" after the initial period shown in (d).

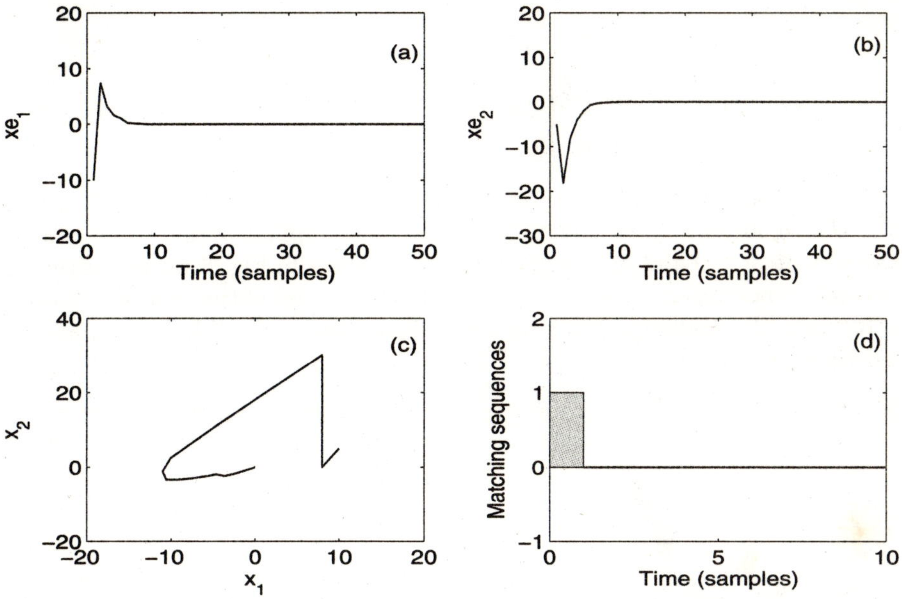

Fig. 1 Closed-loop responses of Example 4.1 based on common Lyapunov function

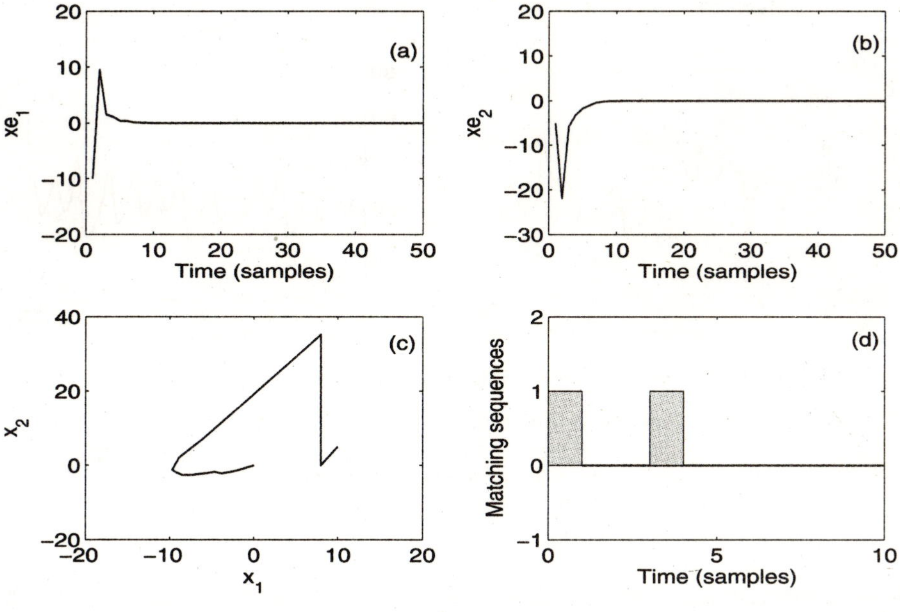

Fig. 2 Closed-loop responses of Example 4.1 based on piecewise Lyapunov function

Next, we will consider controlling the following chaos system from [27], where a discrete time model of chaotic Lorenz system is described.

Example 4.2 Consider the following discrete time chaotic Lorenz system,

$$x(t+1) = \left(\frac{-x_1(t) + M_2}{M_2 - M_1} A_1 + \frac{x_1(t) - M_1}{M_2 - M_1} A_2\right) x(t) + Bu(t) \tag{33}$$

where

$$A_1 = \begin{bmatrix} 1-\sigma T_s & \sigma T_s & 0 \\ rT_s & 1-T_s & -M_1 T_s \\ 0 & M_1 T_s & 1-bT_s \end{bmatrix}, A_2 = \begin{bmatrix} 1-\sigma T_s & \sigma T_s & 0 \\ rT_s & 1-T_s & -M_2 T_s \\ 0 & M_2 T_s & 1-bT_s \end{bmatrix}, B = \begin{bmatrix} 1 \\ 0 \\ 0 \end{bmatrix},$$

$C = \begin{bmatrix} 1 \; 0 \; 0 \end{bmatrix}$ and the parameters are given by $\sigma = 10$, $r = 28$, $b = 8/3$, $M_1 = -20$, $M_2 = 30$ and $T_s = 0.0002$ which is the sampling period. The chaotic response with $u \equiv 0$ and $x(0) = [10\ 10\ 10]^T$ is shown in Fig. 3 for the period of 10 seconds, where (a) represents the three dimension plot of the chaotic response, (b), (c) and (d) represents the responses of each state variable x_1, x_2, and x_3 respectively.

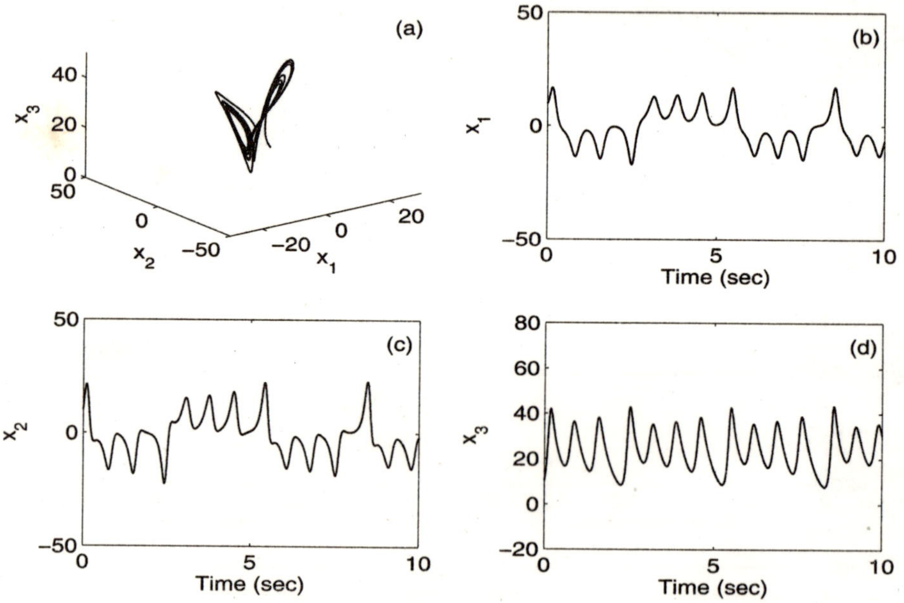

Fig. 3 Chaotic responses of open loop system of Example 4.2

Now we consider the piecewise linear model of this system as follows,

$$\begin{cases} x(t+1) = A_l x(t) + B_l u(t) \\ y(t) = C_l x(t), \quad l = 1, 2 \end{cases} \tag{34}$$

and the corresponding boundary is defined by the middle point, that is, $x_1 = 5$ of $x_1 \in [-20\ 30]$. It should be noted that in this case, $B_1 = B_2 = B$ and

$C_1 = C_2 = C$. It has been found that for this model there is no solution to the Algorithm 1, which is the common Lyapunov function based, but there is a solution to the Algorithm 2, which is the piecewise Lyapunov function based, as follows after 12 iterations.

$$P_1 = \begin{bmatrix} 0.128463 & 0.000328 & -0.000073 \\ 0.000328 & 0.882433 & 0.000106 \\ -0.000073 & 0.000106 & 0.883897 \end{bmatrix},$$

$$P_2 = \begin{bmatrix} 0.135305 & 0.000866 & -0.000084 \\ 0.000866 & 0.882433 & 0.000097 \\ -0.000084 & 0.000097 & 0.883889 \end{bmatrix},$$

$$Q_1 = \begin{bmatrix} 9.107652 & -0.021756 & -0.000911 \\ -0.021756 & 0.000080 & -0.000005 \\ -0.000911 & -0.000005 & 0.000316 \end{bmatrix},$$

$$Q_2 = \begin{bmatrix} 9.287525 & -0.021801 & -0.001000 \\ -0.021801 & 0.000079 & -0.000007 \\ -0.001000 & -0.000007 & 0.000316 \end{bmatrix},$$

$$K_1 = \begin{bmatrix} -0.9890 & 0.01168 & 0.0005423 \end{bmatrix}, \; K_2 = \begin{bmatrix} -0.9896 & 0.01106 & 0.0006216 \end{bmatrix},$$

$$G_1 = \begin{bmatrix} -1.9471 \\ -474.5548 \\ -11.9148 \end{bmatrix}, \; G_2 = \begin{bmatrix} -1.9474 \\ -474.4876 \\ -16.6691 \end{bmatrix}$$

Then we applied the designed observer based output feedback controller to the chaotic Lorenz model (33) and found that the closed loop control system is stable. One simulation result with the initial conditions $x(0) = [10\ 10\ 10]^T$ and $\widehat{x}(0) = [0\ 0\ 0]^T$ is shown in Fig. 4, where the control and observer is activated at $t = 4$ seconds, and (a) represents the three dimension plot of the chaotic response, (b), (c) and (d) represents the responses of each observer error variable $\widetilde{x}_1$, $\widetilde{x}_2$, and $\widetilde{x}_3$ respectively. This example demonstrates that the chaos behavior can be controlled very quickly by the proposed observer based output feedback controller.

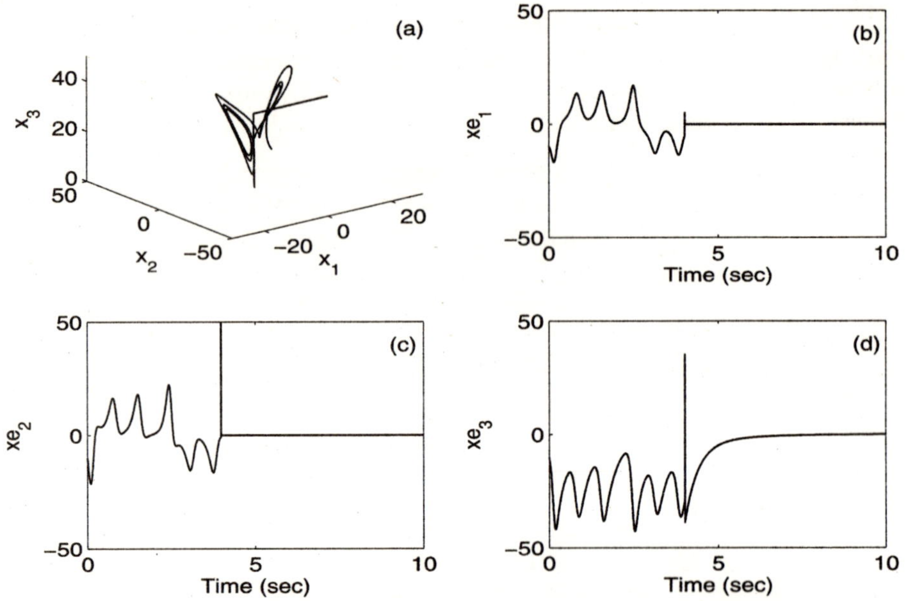

Fig. 4 Responses of the controlled system of Example 4.2

It has also clearly been demonstrated through these examples that the proposed piecewise Lyapunov function based approaches are superior to the common Lyapunov function based approaches.

5 Conclusions

In this paper, novel approaches have been developed to synthesize the observer based output feedback controllers for discrete time piecewise linear systems based on a common and a piecewise Lyapunov function respectively. It is shown that the controller and observer gains can be determined by solving a set of bilinear matrix inequalities. Two examples are also presented to demonstrate the performance of the proposed approaches, and the advantages of the piecewise Lyapunov function based approaches over the common Lyapunov function based approaches.

Acknowledgment

The work described in this paper was partially supported by a grant from the Research Grants Council of the Hong Kong Special Administrative Region, China [Project No.: CityU 1201/04E].

References

1. Chua, L. Deng, A., Canonical piecewise-linear modelling, *IEEE Trans. Circuits and Systems*, Vol.33, 511-525, 1986.
2. Chua, L. Ying, R., Canonical piecewise-linear analysis, *IEEE Trans. Circuits and Systems*, Vol.30, 125-140, 1983.
3. Saito, T., Mitsubori, K., Control of chaos from a piecewise linear hysteresis circuit, *IEEE Trans. Circuits and Systems-I*, Vol.41, 168-172, 1995.
4. Tsubone, T., Saito, T., Stabilizing and destablizing control for a piecewise-linear circuit, *IEEE Trans. Circuits and Systems-I*, Vol.45, 172-177, 1998.
5. Imura, J.I., van der Schaft, A. , Characterization of well-posedness of piecewise-linear systems, *IEEE Trans. Automat. Contr.*, Vol.45, 1600-1619, 2000.
6. Johansson, M., Rantzer, A. , Computation of piecewise quadratic Lyapunov functions for hybrid systems, *IEEE Trans. Automat. Contr.*, Vol.43, 555-559, 1998.
7. Rantzer, A., Johansson, M. , Piecewise linear quadratic optimal control, *IEEE Trans. Automat. Contr.*, Vol.45, 629-637, 2000.
8. Hassibi, A., Boyd, S., Qradratic stabilization and control of piecewise-linear systems, *Proc. American Control Conf.*, Philadelphia, 3659-3664, 1998.
9. Pettersson, S., Lennartson, B., LMI approach for stability and robusness of hybrid systems, *Proc. American Control Conf.*, Albuquerque, 1714-1718, 1997.
10. Pettersson, S., Lennartson, B., Exponential stability analysis of nonlinear systems using LMIs, *Proc. the 36th IEEE Conf. Decision and Control*, San Diego, 199-204, 1997.
11. Pettit, N.B.O.L., Wellstead, P.E., Analyzing piecewise linear dynamical systems, *IEEE Control Systems Magazine*, Vol.15, 43-50, 1995.
12. Goncalves, J. M., *Constructive global analysis of hybrid systems*, Ph.D. Thesis, Massachusetts Institute of Technology, Cambridge, MA, 2000.
13. Slupphaug, O., Foss, B.A., Constrained quadratic stabilization of discrete time uncertain nonlinear multi-model systems using piecewise affine state feedback, *Int. J. Control*, Vol.72, No.7, 686-701, 1999.
14. Cuzzola, F.A., Morari, M., A generalized approach for analysis and control of discrete time piecewise affine and hybrid systems, *Hybrid Systems: Computation and Control - Lecture Notes in Computer Sciences 2034*, Springer Verlag, 189-203, 2001.
15. Mignone, D., Ferrari-Trecate, G., Morari, M., Stability and stabilization of piecewise affine and hybrid systems: An LMI approach, *Proc. the 39th IEEE Conf. Decision and Control*, Sydney, Australia, 504-509, 2000.
16. Bempard, A., Ferrari-Trecate, G., Maorari, M., Observability and controllability of piecewise affine and hybrid systems, *IEEE Trans. Automat. Contr.*, Vol.45, No.10, 1864-1876, 2000.
17. Kantner, M., Robust stability of piecewise linear discrete time systems, *Proc. American Control Conf.*, Albuquerque, 1241-1245, 1997.
18. Sontag, E.D., Nonlinear regulation: the piecewise linear approach, *IEEE Trans. Automat. Contr.*, Vol.26, 346-357, 1981.
19. Feng, G., Stability analysis of piecewise discrete time linear systems, *IEEE Trans. Automat. Contr.*, Vol. 47, No.7, 1108-1112, 2002.
20. Ferrari-Trecate, G., Mignone, D., Morari, M., Moving horizon estimation for hybrid systems, *IEEE Trans. Automat. Contr.*, Vol.47, No.10, 1663-1676, 2002.
21. Rodrigues, L., Hassibi, A., How, J., Output feedback controller synthesis for piecewise affine systems with multiple equilibia, *Proc. 2000 American Contr. Conf.*, Chicago, 1784-1789, 2000.

22. Rodrigues, L., How, J., Observer based control of piecewise affine systems, *Proc. 40th Conf. on Decision and Contr.*, Orlando, 1366-11371, 2001.
23. Feng, G., Observer based output feedback controller design of piecewise discrete time linear systems, *IEEE Trans. Circuits and Systems-I*, Vol.50, No.3, 448-451, 2003.
24. Feng, G., Non-synchronized state estimation of discrete time piecewise linear systems, *IEEE Trans. Signal Processing*, Vol.54, No.1, 295-303, 2006.
25. De Oliveira, M.C., Bernussou, J., Geromel, J.C., A new discrete time robust stability condition, *Systems and Control Letters*, Vol.36, No.2, 135-141, 1999.
26. Goh, K.C., Turan, L., Safonov, M.G., Papavassilopoulos, G.P., Ly, J.H., Biaffine matrix inequality properties and computational methods, *Proc. Ameri. Contr. Conf.*, Baltimore, MD, 850-855, 1994.
27. Lee, J. H., Park, J. B., Chen, G., Robust fuzzy control of nonlinear system with parametric uncertainties, *IEEE Trans. Fuzzy Systems*, Vol.9, No.2, 369-379, 2001.

Coordination Stability of Multi-Agent Systems with Switching Topology

Yiguang Hong[1], Jiangping Hu[1] and Lixin Gao[2]

[1] Institute of Systems Science, Chinese Academy of Sciences, Beijing 100080, China
yghong@iss.ac.cn
[2] Institute of Systems Science, Wenzhou University, Wenzhou 325035, China

1 Introduction

For the past two decades, cooperative behaviors of large numbers of autonomous agents have drawn a broad interest from various research communities. Researchers from different disciplines including physics, ecology, and engineering have worked on the distributed coordination problems with differences regarding the types of agent dynamics, the properties of the interconnection nature, and the varieties of the control schemes[1~5,12]. However, the basic ideas in the coordination of multi-agent systems are to achieve a cooperative goal with decentralized control laws. In many applications, the interconnection topology between individual agents may change dynamically. Some works have explored the topology conditions to achieve the coordination for a group of mobile agents in recent years. In [10], Jadbabaie et al. proved that all the jointly-connected agents can move in the same direction, where the nearest neighbor rules were used. Moreover, Lin et al. showed the agreement of multi-agent systems with switching interconnection structure and nonlinear agent dynamics[11]. In addition, the consensus stability can be achieved for a multi-agent network with an active leaders[7] or with delayed communication interconnection[9]. The Laplacian of a formation graph was used to determine a Nyquist-type criterion for stability analysis of multi-vehicle formations in closed-loop with linear controllers [5].

In the study of variable topologies, "joint connection" is an important condition because it does not require the connection of switching interconnection graphs at any moment. For multi-agent systems with simple neighbor-based average rules under joint-connection-like conditions, many research works focused on each agent in the single-integrator form.

Our aim in this paper is to solve the formation problem of multi-agent systems with jointly-connected interconnection and agents in the form of a double integrator. However, the analysis idea (mainly based on graph theory and related stochastic matrix) that served single-integrator agent system effectively cannot be extended straightforward to study double-integrator systems with jointly-connected interconnection structures since their state matrix along with the nearest-neighbor average rule does not satisfy some properties directly associated with stochastic matrices. Although the existence and the construction of common Lyapunov functions are usually difficult to solve for switching multi-agent networks, a Lyapunov-based approach is proposed to deal with switching jointly-connected topologies and solve the corresponding coordination problem with a space decomposition technique.

The paper is organized as follows. In Section 2, the preliminary knowledge and problem formulation are presented. Then in Section 3, convergence analysis based on common Lyapunov functions is given. Following that, based on the joint-connection assumption, sufficient conditions are given for the formation problem of the considered multi-agent system with the help of matrix analysis and space decomposition in Section 4. Finally, concluding remarks are made in Section 5.

2 Preliminaries and Problem Formulation

In this paper, we consider a dynamical system consisting of n agents. The interconnection topology of n agents (as n vertices) can be conveniently described by a simple graph $\mathcal{G} = \{V, \varepsilon, A\}$, where $V = \{v_i, i \in \mathcal{I}\}$ (with $\mathcal{I}$ an index set) is the set of vertices, $\varepsilon \subset V \times V$ is the set of edges of the graph. A graph is called undirected if $\forall\,(v_i, v_j) \in \varepsilon$ implies $(v_j, v_i) \in \varepsilon$. If $(v_i, v_j) \in \varepsilon$, then v_i is said to be a neighbor of v_j and the set of all neighbor vertices of vertex v_j is denoted by $\mathcal{N}_j = \{i|(v_i, v_j) \in \varepsilon\}$. A path from vertex v_i to vertex v_j is a sequence of distinct vertices starting with v_i and ending with v_j through some edges of the graph.If there is a path between any two vertices of a graph $\mathcal{G}$, then $\mathcal{G}$ is connected. The adjacency matrix associated with $\mathcal{G}$ is denoted by $A = [a_{ij}] \in \mathbb{R}^{n \times n}$ with $a_{ii} = 0$ and $a_{ij} = a_{ji} \geqslant 0$ ($a_{ij} > 0$ if there is an edge between agent i and agent j). Its degree matrix D is a diagonal matrix with diagonal elements $D_i = \sum_{j=1}^{n} a_{ij}$ for $i = 1, \cdots, n$. The Laplacian of $\mathcal{G}$ is defined as $L = D - A$[6] .

The next lemma is well-known in graph theory (e.g. [6]) and establishes a relationship between the graph connectivity and its Laplacian.

Lamma 2.1 *Let $\mathcal{G}$ be an undirected graph on n vertices with weighted Laplacian L. Denote the eigenvalues of L by $\lambda_1, \cdots, \lambda_n$ satisfying $\lambda_1 \leqslant \cdots \leqslant \lambda_n$. Then $\lambda_1 = 0$ and $\mathbf{1} = [1, 1, \cdots, 1]^T \in R^n$ is its eigenvector. Furthermore, L has exactly one zero eigenvalue if and only if the graph $\mathcal{G}$ is connected.*

Joint connection is an important concept in the following analysis:

Definition 2.1 *A union graph of a collection of simple graphs $\mathcal{G}_1, \cdots, \mathcal{G}_m$, each with vertex set $\mathcal{V}$ for some $m \geqslant 1$ is defined as a simple graph, denoted by $\mathcal{G}_1, \cdots, \mathcal{G}_m$ with vertex set $\mathcal{V}$ and edge set as the union of the edge sets of all the graphs in the collections, and connection weight between edge i and edge j is the sum of nonzero a_{ij}'s of $\mathcal{G}_1, \cdots, \mathcal{G}_m$. Moreover, a collection of simple graphs $\mathcal{G}_1, \cdots, \mathcal{G}_m$ is jointly connected if the union graph $\mathcal{G}_1, \cdots, \mathcal{G}_m$ of this collection is connected.*

A subspace $S \subset \mathbb{R}^n$ is trivial if it is either $\{0\}$ or the whole space $\mathbb{R}^n$. Let S and S' be two nontrivial subspaces. If $\langle s,\ s'\rangle = 0$ for any $s \in S$ and $s' \in S'$, then we say the two subspaces orthogonal, denoted by $S \perp S'$. Then a new subspace $S^* = S + S'$ with $S \perp S'$ will be denoted by $S^* = S \oplus_\perp S'$. If $\mathbb{R}^n = S \oplus_\perp S'$, then S' is called the orthogonal complement of S, denoted by $S_\perp$. Moreover, the angle between a vector $z \in \mathbb{R}^n$ and a subspace $S \subset \mathbb{R}^n$ is defined as

$$\theta_{z,S} = \min_{s\in S} \theta_{s,z} = \min_{s\in S} \arccos \frac{|\langle s,\ z\rangle|}{||s||\ ||z||}$$

with $0 \leqslant \theta_{z,S} \leqslant \frac{\pi}{2}$. The angle between two subspaces S and S' is defined as

$$\theta_{S,S'} = \min_{s\in S,\ s'\in S'} \theta_{s,s'} = \min_{s\in S,\ s'\in S'} \arccos \frac{|\langle s,\ s'\rangle|}{||s||\ ||s'||}$$

Thus, we can obtain that, for two nontrivial subspaces S and S', $S' \cap S = \{0\}$ if and only if $\theta_{S,S'} > 0$. Moreover, for any $z \in \mathbb{R}^n$, $\theta_{S,S'} \leqslant \theta_{z,S} + \theta_{z,S'}$.

Consider two positive semi-definite matrices G_1 and G_2. Clearly,

$$rank(G_1 + G_2) \geqslant \max\{rank(G_1),\ rank(G_2)\} \tag{1}$$

Denote $rank(G_1) = \tilde{r}_1$ and $rank(G_1 + G_2) = \tilde{r}_{1,2}$. It is not hard to get the following lemma.

Lamma 2.2 *For any positive semi-definite matrices G_1 and G_2, there is an orthogonal matrix U, such that*

$$U^T(G_1 + G_2)U = \begin{bmatrix} \tilde{G}_{1,2} & 0 \\ 0 & 0 \end{bmatrix} \tag{2}$$

with

$$U^T G_1 U = \begin{bmatrix} \Lambda & 0 \\ 0 & 0 \end{bmatrix}, \quad U^T G_2 U = \begin{bmatrix} \tilde{G}_2 & 0 \\ 0 & 0 \end{bmatrix}$$

where $\Lambda \in \mathbb{R}^{\tilde{r}_1 \times \tilde{r}_1}$ is a diagonal matrix with positive diagonal elements, $\tilde{G}_{1,2} \in \mathbb{R}^{\tilde{r}_{1,2} \times \tilde{r}_{1,2}}$ is a positive definite matrix, and $\tilde{G}_2 \in \mathbb{R}^{\tilde{r}_{1,2} \times \tilde{r}_{1,2}}$ is positive semi-definite matrix.

In this paper, the dynamics of each agent in the considered multi-agent system is described by

$$\begin{cases} \dot{\phi}_i = w_i, \\ \dot{w}_i = u_i, \end{cases} \quad \phi_i,\ w_i,\ u_i \in \mathbb{R}, \quad i = 1, \cdots, n \tag{3}$$

where ϕ_i and u_i are the position (or angle) and control input, respectively, and w_i its velocity (or angular velocity) of agent i for $i = 1, \cdots, n$.

For the multi-agent system under consideration, the relationship among neighbors can change over time and the interconnection topology may be varying dynamically. In this case, the weights for the connections (i.e. edges) between the vertices are time-varying in the following ways:

$$a_{ij}(t) = \begin{cases} \alpha_{ij}, & \text{if agent } i \text{ is connected to agent } j \text{ at time } t \\ 0, & \text{otherwise} \end{cases}$$

where $\alpha_{ij} > 0$ is a fixed constant $(i, j = 1, \cdots, n)$. Denote

$$\alpha = 2 \max_{i=1,\cdots,n} \sum_{j=1}^{n} \alpha_{ij} + 1 \tag{4}$$

and $\mathcal{S} = \{\mathcal{G}_1, \mathcal{G}_2, \cdots, \mathcal{G}_{N_0}\}$ as a set of the graphs of all possible topologies. Let $\mathcal{P}_0 = \{1, 2, \cdots, N_0\}$ be the index set.

We consider a perfect formation problem for system (1), by which we mean that all the relative inter-agent position vectors are fixed over time (with the same desired velocity). In other words, given a vector set d_{ij} for all $(v_i, v_j) \in \varepsilon$, such that, for any given initial values $\phi_i(0)$ and $w_i(0)$ $(i = 1, 2, \cdots, n)$, and some desired velocity w_0, we have

$$\lim_{t\to\infty} (\phi_i(t) - \phi_j(t)) = d_{ij}, \quad \lim_{t\to\infty} w_i(t) = w_0, \quad i, j = 1, 2, \cdots, n$$

Obviously, $d_{ji} = -d_{ij}$ and d_{ij} may be not independent of each other. In fact, we can select a set of constants d_i, $i = 1, \cdots, n$ such that $d_{ij} = d_i - d_j$, though the selection is not unique. For any edge $(v_i, v_j) \in \varepsilon$, we make a formation constraint $\varphi_{ij} = 0$, $\forall i, j = 1, \cdots, n$, where $\varphi_{i,j} = \phi_i - \phi_j - d_{ij}$.

To achieve the formation, we take the neighbor-based control law as

$$u_i = - \sum_{j\in\mathcal{N}_i(\sigma(t))} a_{ij}\varphi_{i,j} - \kappa(w_i - w_0), \quad i = 1, \cdots, n \tag{5}$$

where

$$\kappa > \frac{1}{4}\alpha + 1 \tag{6}$$

and $\sigma : [0, \infty) \to \mathcal{P}_0$ is is a piecewise constant switching signal with successive switching times.

Suppose that there is an infinite sequence of contiguous, nonempty, and bounded time interval $[t_k, t_{k+1})$, $k \geqslant 0$ (with upper bound T), starting at $t_0 = 0$. Also suppose that in interval $[t_k, t_{k+1})$ there is a sequence of non-overlapping subintervals $[t_{k_{i-1}}, t_{k_i})$ (determined by σ) for $i = 1, \cdots, m_k$ with lower bound τ.

Remark 2.1 *As done in many works on switching control, we assume that there is a positive dwell time τ (as the lower bound of each interval length). Then there will be no infinite switchings between the connected graphs and unconnected graphs during any finite time interval. In this case, strict discussion about derivative of a Lyapunov function in the Filippov's sense for a switched system can be omitted without loss of clarity.*

For simplicity, set

$$s = \begin{bmatrix} \phi_1 - d_1 - w_0 t \\ \phi_2 - d_2 - w_0 t \\ \vdots \\ \phi_n - d_n - w_0 t \end{bmatrix} \in \mathbb{R}^n, \quad q = \begin{bmatrix} w_1 - w_0 \\ w_2 - w_0 \\ \vdots \\ w_n - w_0 \end{bmatrix} \in \mathbb{R}^n$$

then, after simple manipulation, we have a simper expression for our problem:

$$\begin{cases} \dot{s} = q \\ \dot{q} = u_\sigma = -L_\sigma s - \kappa q \end{cases} \tag{7}$$

Let

$$x = \begin{bmatrix} x_1 \\ \vdots \\ x_n \end{bmatrix} \in \mathbb{R}^{2n}, \quad x_i = \begin{bmatrix} s_i \\ q_i \end{bmatrix} \in \mathbb{R}^2 \tag{8}$$

The closed-loop system (4) can be expressed in a compact form as follows:

$$\dot{x} = F_\sigma x \tag{9}$$

with

$$F_\sigma = I_n \otimes \begin{bmatrix} 0 & 1 \\ 0 & -\kappa \end{bmatrix} + L_\sigma \otimes \begin{bmatrix} 0 & 0 \\ -1 & 0 \end{bmatrix}$$

3 Analysis

In this section, we analyzed the consensus stability of system (9). At first, we simplify the expression of (9). By Lemma 2.1, it easily follows that there exists an orthogonal matrix

$$\bar{U} = \begin{bmatrix} * & * & \cdots & \frac{1}{\sqrt{n}} \\ * & * & \cdots & \frac{1}{\sqrt{n}} \\ \vdots & \vdots & \vdots & \vdots \\ * & * & \cdots & \frac{1}{\sqrt{n}} \end{bmatrix} \in \mathbb{R}^{n \times n} \tag{10}$$

where $*$ denotes other entries, such that

$$\bar{U}^T L_\sigma \bar{U} = \begin{bmatrix} H_\sigma & 0 \\ 0 & 0 \end{bmatrix}, \quad H_\sigma \in \mathbb{R}^{(n-1)\times(n-1)} \tag{11}$$

where H_σ is positive semi-definite matrix by Lemma 2.1. It is easy to see that $\bar{U}$ can be fixed for to obtain (11) for any switching graphs. From Lemma 2.1, a graph is connected if and only if H_σ associated with the grapn is of full rank.

With coordinates transformation $\bar{s} = \bar{U}^{\mathrm{T}} s$ and $\bar{q} = \bar{U}^{\mathrm{T}} q$, system (4) is rewritten as

$$\begin{cases} \dot{\bar{s}} = \bar{q} \\ \dot{\bar{q}} = \begin{bmatrix} H_\sigma & 0 \\ 0 & 0 \end{bmatrix} \bar{s} - \kappa \bar{q} \end{cases} \tag{12}$$

Take

$$\bar{x} = \begin{bmatrix} \bar{x}_1 \\ \vdots \\ \bar{x}_{n-1} \end{bmatrix} \in \mathbb{R}^{2(n-1)}, \quad \bar{x}_i = \begin{bmatrix} \bar{s}_i \\ \bar{q}_i \end{bmatrix} \in \mathbb{R}^2, \ i = 1, \cdots, n-1$$

Then system (4) can be decoupled into two subsystems as follows: a $2(n-1)$-dimensional subsystem

$$\dot{\bar{x}} = \bar{F}_\sigma \bar{x} \tag{13}$$

with

$$\bar{F}_\sigma = I_n \otimes \begin{bmatrix} 0 & 1 \\ 0 & -\kappa \end{bmatrix} + H_\sigma \otimes \begin{bmatrix} 0 & 0 \\ -1 & 0 \end{bmatrix}$$

and a 2-dimensional subsystem:

$$\begin{cases} \dot{\bar{s}}_n = \bar{q}_n \\ \dot{\bar{q}}_n = -\kappa \bar{q}_n \end{cases} \tag{14}$$

In fact, we can view $\bar{x}_i$ as the state of virtual agent i, and then we focus on system (13) related to space $\{\mathbf{1}\}^\perp$.

Lamma 3.1 *Suppose that $L_{i_1}, \cdots, L_{i_m}$ are Laplacians associated with graphs $\mathcal{G}_{i_1}, \cdots, \mathcal{G}_{i_m}$, respectively. For $H_{i_j}, j = 1, 2, \cdots, m$, obtained with transformation (11), if $\mathcal{G}_{i_1}, \cdots, \mathcal{G}_{i_m}$ is connected jointly, $\sum_{j=1}^m H_{i_j}$ is positive definite.*

Proof: From Definition 2.1, it is obvious that the Laplacian L of the union graph $\mathcal{G}_{1_1,\cdots,i_m}$ satisfies

$$L = \sum_{j=1}^{m} L_{i_j}$$

Thus, we can get the matrix $\bar{U}$ of form (10) such that

$$\bar{U}^T L \bar{U} = \begin{bmatrix} H & 0 \\ 0 & 0 \end{bmatrix} = \begin{bmatrix} \sum_{j=1}^m H_{i_j} & 0 \\ 0 & 0 \end{bmatrix}$$

Then the conclusion follows directly from Lemma 2.1 by considering the eigenvalues of $L = \sum_{j=1}^m L_{i_j}$. □

Remark 3.1 *According to (4), the matrix $L - \alpha I$ is negative definite due to its negative dominant diagonal elements. Then we have that all the eigenvalues of H_p, $p \in \mathcal{P}$ are less than α.*

Therefore, in what follows, we only need to consider the stability of system (13) in order to make $\lim_{t\to\infty} \bar{x}(t) = 0$ in $2(n-1)$-dimensional space, instead of the formation of system (9). To this end, we propose a Lyapunov-based approach for system (13) and construct a common Lyapunov function

$$V(\bar{x}) = \bar{x}^{\mathrm{T}} P \bar{x}, \quad P = I_{n-1} \otimes P_0 \in \mathbb{R}^{2(n-1)\times 2(n-1)}, \quad P_0 = \begin{bmatrix} \kappa & 1 \\ 1 & 1 \end{bmatrix}. \tag{15}$$

For any given orthogonal matrix $U \in \mathbb{R}^{(n-1)\times(n-1)}$, the vector $\bar{x}$ can be transformed to:

$$\bar{x}^0 = \begin{bmatrix} x_1^0 \\ \vdots \\ x_{n-1}^0 \end{bmatrix} = (U \otimes I_2)^{\mathrm{T}} \bar{x}, \quad x_i^0 = \begin{bmatrix} s_i^0 \\ q_i^0 \end{bmatrix} \in \mathbb{R}^2, \quad i = 1, \cdots, n-1, \tag{16}$$

with $\bar{s}^0 = (s_1^0, \cdots, s_{n-1}^0)^{\mathrm{T}}$ and $\bar{q}^0 = (q_1^0, \cdots, q_{n-1}^0)^{\mathrm{T}}$. Denote $\tilde{V}(\xi) = \xi^{\mathrm{T}} P_0 \xi$, $\xi \in \mathbb{R}^2$, and then the form of Lyapunov function $V(\bar{x}) = \sum_{i=1}^{n} \tilde{V}(\bar{x}_i)$ keeps unchanged through any orthogonal transformations $U \otimes I_2$.

Take an interval $[t_k, t_{k+1})$ with m_k subintervals, and, without loss of generality, we denote the matrix associated with the (time-invariant) interconnection graph on subinterval $[t_{k_{i-1}}, t_{k_i})$ by H_i ($i = 1, \cdots, m_k$). Note that interval $[t_k, t_{k_{j-1}})$ consists of $j-1$ subintervals: $[t_k, t_{k_1})$, $[t_{k_1}, t_{k_2})$, and $[t_{k_{j-2}}, t_{k_{j-1}})$. It is easy to see that $H_{\widehat{j-1}} = \sum_{i=1}^{j-1} H_i$ is a matrix associated with the union graph of interval $[t_k, t_{k_{j-1}})$ (for $2 \leqslant j \leqslant m_k$). For convenience, we denote the rank of H_i as r_i and the rank of $H_{\widehat{i}}$ as $r_{\widehat{i}}$ ($i = 1, \cdots, m_k$).

Then we study the considered system during $[t_k, t_{k_j})$ based on the results in $[t_k, t_{k_{j-1}})$ and $[t_{k_{j-1}}, t_{k_j})$ (for $j \leqslant m_k$). As we discussed, we have two matrices $H_{\widehat{j-1}}$ and H_j for $[t_k, t_{k_{j-1}})$ and $[t_{k_{j-1}}, t_{k_j})$, respectively. Then $H_{\widehat{j}} = H_{\widehat{j-1}} + H_j$ is associated with the union graph on $[t_k, t_{k_j})$.

In fact, according to Lemma 2.2 (by taking $G_1 = H_{\widehat{j-1}}$ and $G_2 = H_j$, along with an orthogonal matrix $U = U^1$), there is a normalized orthogonal basis $\{\mathbf{e}_1, \cdots, \mathbf{e}_n\}$ of $\mathbb{R}^n$ (that is, $\mathbf{e}_i \perp \mathbf{e}_l$ when $i \neq l$ and $||\mathbf{e}_i|| = 1$, $i = 1, \cdots, n$) such that we can obtain the following three subspaces:

- $S_{\widehat{j},0}$ is the kernel of $H_{\widehat{j}}$ with $\{\mathbf{e}^1_{r_{\widehat{j}}+1}, \cdots, \mathbf{e}^1_{n-1}\}$ as its orthogonal basis.
- $S_{\widehat{j-1},\perp}$ with $\{\mathbf{e}^1_1, \cdots, \mathbf{e}^1_{r_{\widehat{j-1}}}\}$ as its basis of the subspace spanned by eigenvectors corresponding to nonzero eigenvalues of $H_{\widehat{j-1}}$.
- $S_{\widehat{j-1},-}$ with $\{\mathbf{e}^i_{r_{\widehat{j-1}}+1}, \cdots, \mathbf{e}^i_{r_{\widehat{j}}}\}$ as its orthogonal basis. Clearly, $H_{\widehat{j-1}} s = 0$ for any $s \in S_{\widehat{j-1},-}$.

Denote $S_{\widehat{j},\perp} = S_{\widehat{j-1},\perp} \oplus_{\perp} S_{\widehat{j-1},-}$, which is the orthogonal complement of $S_{\widehat{j},0}$. Moreover, we have a new expression of a vector, denoted by $\bar{x}^1$ (recalling (16))

$$\bar{x}^1 = (U^1 \otimes I_2)^{\mathrm{T}} \bar{x} = \begin{bmatrix} \bar{x}^1_1 \\ \vdots \\ \bar{x}^1_{n-1} \end{bmatrix} \in \mathbb{R}^{2(n-1)} \tag{17}$$

As we did before, we define Lyapunov functions and related energy vectors in following subspaces:

$$V_{\widehat{j},0}(\bar{x}) = \sum_{l=r_{\widehat{j}}+1}^{n} \tilde{V}(\bar{x}^1_l), \quad \nu_{\widehat{j},0} = \sum_{l=r_{\widehat{j}}+1}^{n} \sqrt{\tilde{V}(\bar{x}^1_l)}\mathbf{e}^1_l \in \mathbb{R}^n$$

$$V_{\widehat{j-1},\perp}(\bar{x}) = \sum_{l=1}^{r_{\widehat{j-1}}} \tilde{V}(\bar{x}^1_l), \quad \nu_{\widehat{j-1},\perp} = \sum_{l=1}^{r_{\widehat{j-1}}} \sqrt{\tilde{V}(\bar{x}^1_l)}\mathbf{e}^1_l \in \mathbb{R}^n$$

$$V_{\widehat{j-1},-}(\bar{x}) = \sum_{l=r_{\widehat{j-1}}+1}^{r_{\widehat{j}}} \tilde{V}(\bar{x}^1_l), \quad \nu_{\widehat{j-1},-} = \sum_{l=r_{\widehat{j-1}}+1}^{r_{\widehat{j}}} \sqrt{\tilde{V}(\bar{x}^1_l)}\mathbf{e}^1_l$$

Furthermore, we have the kernel of $H_{\widehat{j-1}}$, denoted by $S_{\widehat{j-1},0} (= S_{\widehat{j},0} \oplus_\perp S_{\widehat{j-1},-})$, which is the orthogonal complement of $S_{\widehat{j-1},\perp}$. Correspondingly, we have

$$V_{\widehat{j-1},0}(\bar{x}) = \sum_{l=r_{\widehat{j-1}}+1}^{n} \tilde{V}(\bar{x}_l^1)$$

On the other hand, recalling Lemma 2.2 (with taking $G_1 = H_j$ and $G_2 = H_{\widehat{j}}$ with an orthogonal matrix $U = U^2$), there are a normalized orthogonal basis denoted by $\{\mathbf{e}_1^2, \cdots, \mathbf{e}_{n-1}^2\}$, and a new expression of a vector in the new coordinates: $\bar{x}^2 = (U^2 \otimes I_2)^{\mathrm{T}} \bar{x} \in \mathbb{R}^{2(n-1)}$. Also, we have three subspaces, still with the first subspace $S_{\widehat{j},0}$, the kernel of $H_{\widehat{j}}$. Thus, we can take $\mathbf{e}_{r_l}^1 = \mathbf{e}_{r_l}^2$ for $l = \widehat{j} + 1, \cdots, n-1$. The other two subspaces are:

- $S_{j,\perp}$, with its orthogonal basis $\{\mathbf{e}_1^2, \cdots, \mathbf{e}_{r_j}^2\}$, is spanned by the eigenvectors corresponding to nonzero eigenvalues of H_j. Set

$$V_{j,\perp}(\bar{x}) = \sum_{l=1}^{r_j} \tilde{V}(\bar{x}_l^2), \quad \nu_{j,\perp} = \sum_{l=1}^{r_j} \sqrt{\tilde{V}(\bar{x}_l^2)} \mathbf{e}_l^2$$

- $S_{j,-}$ is a subspace with $\{\mathbf{e}_{r_j+1}^2, \cdots, \mathbf{e}_{r_{\widehat{j}}}^2\}$ as its orthogonal basis. Set

$$V_{j,-}(\bar{x}) = \sum_{l=r_j+1}^{r_{\widehat{j}}} \tilde{V}(\bar{x}_l^2), \quad \nu_{j,-} = \sum_{l=r_j+1}^{r_{\widehat{j}}} \sqrt{\tilde{V}(\bar{x}_l^2)} \mathbf{e}_i^2$$

Obviously,

$$S_{\widehat{j},\perp} = S_{\widehat{j-1},\perp} \oplus_\perp S_{\widehat{j-1},-} = S_{j,\perp} \oplus_\perp S_{j,-} \tag{18}$$

For convenience, we denote

$$V_{\widehat{j},\perp}(\bar{x}) = V_{\widehat{j-1},\perp} + V_{\widehat{j-1},-} = V_{j,\perp} + V_{j,-} \tag{19}$$

and, correspondingly, a vector $\nu_{\widehat{j},\perp} = \nu_{\widehat{j-1},\perp} + \nu_{\widehat{j-1},-} = \nu_{j,\perp} + \nu_{j,-} \in \mathbb{R}^n$. Then, it is not hard to obtain

$$S_{\widehat{j-1},-} \cap S_{j,-} = \{0\} \tag{20}$$

Remark 3.2 *Set* $0 < \delta < 1$. *For a constant* $0 < \gamma_0 < 1$, *define a sequence of constants*

$$\gamma_{l+1} = (1 - \delta^2)(1 - \gamma_l) + \gamma_l, \quad l = 0, 1, \cdots \tag{21}$$

Then we have $\gamma_{l+1} > \gamma_l$ *and* $0 < \gamma_l < 1$, $l = 0, 1, \cdots$.

4 Main Results

In this section, we will present our main results. At first, a lemma is given for the recursive convergence analysis.

Lamma 4.1 *Suppose that there is a positive constant* $\gamma_{j-2} < 1$ $(j \geqslant 2)$ *such that*

$$V_{\widehat{j-1},0}(\bar{x}(t_{k_{j-1}})) \leqslant V_{\widehat{j-1},0}(\bar{x}(t_k)) \tag{22}$$

and

$$V_{\widehat{j-1},\perp}(\bar{x}(t_{k_{j-1}})) \leqslant \gamma_{j-2} V_{\widehat{j-1},\perp}(\bar{x}(t_k)) \tag{23}$$

Then there is a constant $0 < \gamma_{j-1} < 1$ *defined in (21) such that*

$$V_{\hat{j},0}(\bar{x}(t_{k_j})) \leqslant V_{\hat{j},0}(\bar{x}(t_k)) \tag{24}$$

and

$$V_{\hat{j},\perp}(\bar{x}(t_{k_j})) \leqslant \gamma_{j-1} V_{\hat{j},\perp}(\bar{x}(t_k)) \tag{25}$$

Proof: Let us first discuss a given subinterval, where the interconnection graph is associated with H_p $(p \in \mathcal{P})$ of rank $r_p > 0$. Then there is a special orthogonal matrix U_p such that

$$U_p^T H_p U_p = \begin{bmatrix} \Lambda_p & 0 \\ 0 & 0 \end{bmatrix}, \quad \Lambda_p \in \mathbb{R}^{r_p \times r_p} \tag{26}$$

where diagonal matrix $\Lambda_p = diag\{\lambda_1(H_p) \ \cdots \ \lambda_{r_p}(H_p)\}$ is positive definite with $\lambda_i(H_p)$ $(i = 1, \cdots, r_p)$ denoting the nonzero eigenvalue of H_p. Correspondingly, we have $\bar{x}^p = (U_p \otimes I_2)^{\mathrm{T}} \bar{x}$, and $V(\bar{x}) = V(\bar{x}^p) = \sum_{i=1}^{n-1} \tilde{V}(\bar{x}_i^p)$. Since $\bar{F}_p$ is a constant matrix during any subinterval, we have

$$\dot{V}(\bar{x})|_{(9)} = \bar{x}^T(\bar{F}_p^T P + P\bar{F}_p)\bar{x} = -\bar{x}^T Q_p \bar{x}, \quad t \in [t_{k_l}, t_{k_{l+1}})$$

Then, based on (26),

$$(U_p \otimes I_2)^{\mathrm{T}} Q_p (U_p \otimes I_2) = I_{n-1} \otimes \begin{bmatrix} 0 & 0 \\ 0 & -2(\kappa - 1) \end{bmatrix} + \begin{bmatrix} \Lambda_p & 0 \\ 0 & 0 \end{bmatrix} \otimes \begin{bmatrix} 2 & 1 \\ 1 & 0 \end{bmatrix} \tag{27}$$

where $\Lambda_p = diag\{\lambda_1(H_p) \ \cdots \ \lambda_{r_p}(H_p)\}$ is positive definite (defined in (26)). By Remark 3.1, (6) yields that

$$Q_p^i = \begin{bmatrix} 2\lambda_i(H_p) & \lambda_i(H_p) \\ \lambda_i(H_p) & 2(\kappa - 1) \end{bmatrix}, \qquad i = 1, \cdots, r_p$$

is positive definite. Therefore, Q_p is positive semi-definite, which implies

$$\dot{V}(\bar{x}(t)) \leqslant 0, \quad \forall t \in [t_{k_l}, t_{k_{l+1}}) \tag{28}$$

Moreover, from (27), $\dot{\tilde{V}}(\bar{x}_i^p) \leqslant 0$, $(i = 1, \cdots, n-1)$. Note that $\dot{\tilde{V}}(\bar{x}_i^p) = -(\bar{x}_i^p)^{\mathrm{T}} Q_p^i \bar{x}_i^p$ $(i = 1, \cdots, r_p)$. Again, based on (6), it is not hard to obtain a positive constant β such that $\dot{\tilde{V}}(\bar{x}_i^p) \leqslant -\beta \tilde{V}(\bar{x}_i^p)$, $\quad i = 1, \cdots, r_p$. Thus,

$$V_{p,0}(\bar{x}(t_{k_{l+1}})) \leqslant V_{p,0}(\bar{x}(t_{k_l})), \quad V_{p,\perp}(\bar{x}(t_{k_{l+1}})) \leqslant \gamma_0 V_{p,\perp}(\bar{x}(t_{k_l})) \tag{29}$$

where $\gamma_0 = \mathrm{e}^{-\beta\tau} < 1$ because $t_{k_{l+1}} - t_{k_l} \geqslant \tau$.

Therefore, (24) is obvious. Meanwhile, due to (19), it is easy to obtain:

$$\dot{V}_{\widehat{j},\perp} \leqslant 0, \quad t \in [t_k, t_{k_j}) \tag{30}$$

In what follows, we only need to prove (25).

By (1), we have the following two cases; $r_{\widehat{j}} = \max\{r_{\widehat{j-1}}, r_j\}$ and

$$r_{\widehat{j}} > \max\{r_{\widehat{j-1}}, r_j\} \tag{31}$$

Let us first consider the case of $r_{\widehat{j}} = \max\{r_{\widehat{j-1}}, r_j\}$. If $r_{\widehat{j}} = r_{\widehat{j-1}}$, then $S_{\widehat{j},\perp} = S_{\widehat{j-1},\perp}$ and $S_{\widehat{j},0} = S_{\widehat{j-1},0}$. Based on the conditions and $\gamma_{j-1} > \gamma_{j-2}$ (from Remark 3.2), we have the conclusion. If $r_{\widehat{j}} = r_j$, then we have (29) with $p = j$. Clearly, $S_{\widehat{j},\perp} = S_{j,\perp}$, $S_{\widehat{j},0} = S_{j,0}$, and $\gamma_{j-1} \geqslant \gamma_0$, which implies the conclusion.

Next, we study the case of $r_{\widehat{j}} > \max\{r_{\widehat{j-1}}, r_j\}$. According to (20), $S_{\widehat{j-1},-} \neq \{0\}$ and $S_{j,-} \neq \{0\}$, and the angle θ_j between these two subspaces is positive. Since there are at most $[\frac{T}{\tau}] + 1$ subintervals in each interval, define

$$\hat{\mathcal{H}} = \{\sum_{i=1}^{\hat{m}} H_{l_i} \in \mathbb{R}^{(n-1)\times(n-1)} \mid H_{l_i} \neq H_{l_{i+1}}, \ l_i \in \mathcal{P}_0, \ i \leqslant \hat{m} \leqslant [\frac{T}{\tau}] + 1\}$$

which is a finite set because $\mathcal{P}_0$ is finite. Therefore, there is a positive constant $\theta_* \leqslant \frac{\pi}{2}$ such that

$$\min_{H_{\widehat{j-1}}, H_j \in \hat{\mathcal{H}} \text{ with satisfying (31)}} \theta_j > \theta_*$$

Define

$$S_l^\delta = \{z \in S_{\widehat{j},\perp} : \ z \neq 0 \ \& \ \frac{||z_{l,\perp}||}{||z||} \leqslant \delta\} \subset S_{\widehat{j},\perp}, \quad l = \widehat{j-1} \text{ or } j \tag{32}$$

where δ is a fixed constant with $0 < \delta < \sin\frac{\theta_*}{2}$. It is not hard to prove that $S_{\widehat{j-1}}^\delta \cap S_j^\delta = \phi$.

For any $\nu_{\widehat{j},\perp} \in S_{\widehat{j},\perp}$, we have

$$\nu_{\widehat{j},\perp} \notin S_l^\delta \quad \text{if and only if} \quad \frac{V_{l,-}}{V_{\widehat{j},\perp}} \leqslant 1 - \delta^2 \tag{33}$$

with l representing either $\widehat{j-1}$ or j. Then we discuss the problem in the following cases:

If $V_{\widehat{j},\perp}(t_{k_{j-1}}) \leqslant \gamma_{j-2} V_{\widehat{j},\perp}(t_k)$, then we have (25) because $V_{\widehat{j},\perp}(t_{k_j}) \leqslant V_{\widehat{j},\perp}(t_{k_{j-1}})$ by (30) and $\gamma_{j-2} \leqslant \gamma_{j-1}$.

If $V_{\widehat{j},\perp}(t_{k_{j-1}}) > \gamma_{j-2} V_{\widehat{j},\perp}(t_k)$, then, with (23), we have

$$\frac{V_{\widehat{j-1},\perp}(t_{k_{j-1}})}{V_{\widehat{j},\perp}(t_{k_{j-1}})} \leqslant \frac{V_{\widehat{j-1},\perp}(t_k)}{V_{\widehat{j},\perp}(t_k)} \tag{34}$$

Thus, we have the following two situations:

When $\nu_{\widehat{j},\perp}(t_k) \notin S^{\delta}_{\widehat{j-1}}$: From (33), we have $\frac{V_{\widehat{j-1},-}(t_k)}{V_{\widehat{j},\perp}(t_k)} \leqslant 1 - \delta^2$. Note that, from (21) and $V_{\widehat{j},\perp} = V_{\widehat{j-1},\perp} + V_{\widehat{j-1},-}$, we have

$$\frac{V_{\widehat{j},\perp}(t_{k_{j-1}})}{V_{\widehat{j},\perp}(t_k)} \leqslant \max_{\nu_{\widehat{j},\perp}(t_k)\notin S^{\delta}_{\widehat{j-1}}} \frac{V_{\widehat{j-1},-}(t_k) + \gamma_{j-2} V_{\widehat{j-1},\perp}(t_k)}{V_{\widehat{j},\perp}(t_k)} \leqslant \gamma_{j-1} \tag{35}$$

Then, according to (30), $V_{\widehat{j},\perp}(t_{k_j}) \leqslant V_{\widehat{j},\perp}(t_{k_{j-1}})$ in $[t_{k_{j-1}}, t_{k_j})$, which implies (25) in light of (35).

When $\nu_{\widehat{j},\perp}(t_k) \in S^{\delta}_{\widehat{j-1}}$: According to (34), $\nu_{\widehat{j},\perp}(t_{k_{j-1}}) \in S^{\delta}_{\widehat{j-1}}$ if $\nu_{\widehat{j},\perp}(t_k) \in S^{\delta}_{\widehat{j-1}}$. Similar analysis leads to $V_{\widehat{j},\perp}(t_{k_j}) \leqslant \gamma_1 V_{\widehat{j},\perp}(t_k)$, which implies (25) since $\gamma_{j-1} \geqslant \gamma_1$.

In a sum of all the above cases, the conclusion follows directly. □

Here the main result is given as follows:

Theorem 4.1 *Consider any given initial conditions* $\phi(0)$ *and* $w(0)$ *of system (1) and a switching signal* $\sigma : [0,\infty) \to \mathcal{P}_0$. *If, in each interval* $[t_k, t_{k+1})$, *the collection of simple graphs (each graph is associated with the interconnection topology of system (1) during each subinterval) is jointly connected, then*

$$\begin{cases} \lim\limits_{t\to\infty} (\phi_i(t) - \phi_j(t)) = d_{ij} \\ \lim\limits_{t\to\infty} w_i(t) = w_0 \end{cases} \quad i,j = 1,2,\cdots,n \tag{36}$$

Proof: Consider interval $[t_k, t_{k+1})$ consisting of a series of subintervals $[t_{k_l}, t_{k_{l+1}})$ ($k_0 = k$, $k_{m_k} = k+1$) without topological switching in-between (corresponding to a switching signal σ). Without loss of generality, a sequence of matrices, corresponding to m_k graphs $\mathcal{G}_{k_1}, \cdots, \mathcal{G}_{k_{m_k}}$ in these m_k subintervals, are denoted by $H_1, H_2, \cdots, H_{m_k}$, respectively. Set

$$\gamma = \gamma_{[\frac{T}{\tau}]+1} \tag{37}$$

according to (21) with $\gamma_0 = \mathrm{e}^{-\beta\tau}$ given in Lemma 4.1 and δ given in Lemma 4.1.

Repeatedly using Lemma 4.1, we can start with subinterval $[t_k,\ t_{k_1})$ and then extend it to the whole interval $[t_k, t_{k+1})$ step by step. Since a collection of m_k graphs, $H_1, H_2, \cdots, H_{m_k}$, are jointly connected in $[t_k, t_{k+1})$, $\sum_{p=1}^{m_k} H_p$ is positive definite and its rank is $r_{\widehat{m_k}} = n$ by Lemma 3.1. Therefore, $V = V_{\widehat{m_k},\perp}$. Note that $\gamma = \gamma_{[\frac{T}{\tau}]+1} \geqslant \gamma_{m_k-1}$ according to Remark 3.2 and (37). By Lemma 4.1, we have $V(\bar{x}(t_{k+1})) \leqslant V(\bar{x}(t_{k_{m_k}})) = V_{\widehat{m_k},\perp}(x(t_{k+1})) \leqslant \gamma_{m_k-1} V_{\widehat{m_k},\perp}(x(t_k)) = \gamma V(\bar{x}(t_k))$. Therefore, for any given switching signal σ and any initial value $x_0 = x(0)$,

$$V(\bar{x}(t_{k+1})) \leqslant \gamma V(\bar{x}(t_k)) \tag{38}$$

Thus, for any $t > 0$, let j_t be the largest nonnegative integer such that $t_{j_t} \leqslant t$. According to (38) and (28), $V(\bar{x}(t)) \leqslant V(\bar{x}(t_{j_t}))$ and $V(\bar{x}(t_{j_t})) \leqslant \gamma^{j_t} V(\bar{x}(0))$, which yields $V(\bar{x}(t)) \leqslant \gamma^{j_t} V(\bar{x}(0))$. Since $j_t \to \infty$ as $t \to \infty$, we have $\lim_{t\to\infty} V(\bar{x}(t) = 0$.

Moreover, to study the consensus of the whole multi-agent system (9), we need to check the dynamics of system (14). In fact, based on the above discussion, there exists a constant a such that

$$\lim_{t\to\infty} \bar{s}_n = a, \quad \text{or} \quad \lim_{t\to\infty} s_i = \lim_{t\to\infty} \phi_i - d_i - w_0 t = \frac{a}{\sqrt{n}}; \quad i = 1, \cdots, n$$

and

$$\lim_{t\to\infty} \bar{q}_n = 0, \quad \text{or} \quad \lim_{t\to\infty} q = 0$$

which implies the conclusion. □

Therefore, the following result can be obtained straightforwardly.

Corollary 4.1 *For any given initial condition $\phi(0)$ and $w(0)$ of system (1) and a switching signal $\sigma : [0, \infty) \to \mathcal{P}_0$. If, in each interval $[t_k, t_{k+1})$, there is at least one subinterval when the interconnection graph is connected and the length of each subinterval is no less than τ, then (36) holds.*

In fact, this common Lyapunov function approach is naturally applicable to the case when the dynamics of each agent is single integrator, which has been widely studied:

$$\dot{\phi}_i = u_i, \quad \phi_i,\ u_i \in R, \quad i = 1, \cdots, n, \tag{39}$$

where ϕ_i is the state (e.g., position or angle) of agent i and u_i its local control input for $i = 1, \cdots, n$. Suppose each agent is equipped with a neighbor-based rule as follows:

$$\dot{\phi}_i = u_i = -\sum_{j\in\mathcal{N}_i,} a_{ij}(\phi_i - \phi_j - d_{ij})$$

Then we have

$$\dot{s} = -L_\sigma s, \quad s = \begin{bmatrix} \phi_1 - d_1 \\ \vdots \\ \phi_n - d_n \end{bmatrix} \in \mathbb{R}^n \tag{40}$$

Take the common Lyapunov function $V(s) = s^{\mathrm{T}} s$. Following the proposed recursive procedure, we have:

Theorem 4.2 *For any given initial condition $\phi(0)$ of system (40), if the collection of simple graphs in the subintervals of this interval is jointly connected, then we have*

$$\lim_{t\to\infty} (\phi_i(t) - \phi_j(t)) = d_{ij}, \quad i, j = 1, \cdots, n$$

The proof is similar to that of Theorem 4.1. Actually, this result is consistent with those obtained using stochastic matrix approach (see [10]).

5 Conclusions

In this paper, we discussed leaderless formation problems of multi-agent systems with jointly-connected interconnection topologies by a proposed Lyapunov-based approach. Although the interconnection graph need not be connected at each moment, sufficient conditions were obtained for the formation of these multiple agents in the double-integrator form to converge to a specific configuration.

6 Acknowledgement

This work was supported by the NNSF of China under Grants 60425307, 50595411, 10472129, and 60221301.

References

1. Buhl, J., Stumpter, D., Couzin, I., Hale, J., Despland, E., Miller, E., Simpson, S., From disorder to order in marching locusts, *Science*, Vol. 312, 1402-1406, 2006.
2. Chu, T., Wang, L., Chen, T., Mu, S., Complex emergent dynamics of anisotropic swarms: covergence vs. oscillation, *Chaos, Solitons, and Fractals*, Vol. 30, No. 7, 875-885, 2006.
3. Couzin, I., Krause, J., Franks, R., Levin, S., Effective leadership and decisionmaking in animal groups on the move, *Nature*, Vol. 433, 513-516, 2005.
4. Egerstedt, M., Hu. X., Formation constrained multi-agent control, *IEEE Trans. on Robotics and Automation*, Vol. 17, No. 6, 947-951, 2001.
5. Fax, A., Murray, R., Information flow and cooperative control of vehicle formations, *IEEE Trans. on Automatic Control*, Vol. 49, No. 9, 1453- 1464, 2004.
6. Godsil, C., Royle, G., *Algebraic Graph Theory,* Springer-Verlag, New York, 2001.
7. Hong, Y., Hu, J., Gao, L., Tracking control for multi-agent consensus with an active leader and variable topology, *Automatica*, Vol. 42, No. 7, 1177-1182, 2006.
8. Horn, R., Johnson, C., *Matrix Analysis,* Cambridge Univ. Press, Cambridge, 1985.
9. Hu, J., Hong, Y., Leader-following coordination of multi-agent systems with coupling time delays, *Physica A*, (to appear), 2006.
10. Jadbabaie, A., Lin, J., Morse, S., Coordination of groups of mobile agents using nearest neighbor rules, *IEEE Trans. on Automatic Control*, Vol. 48, No. 6, 988-1001, 2003.
11. Lin, Z., Francis, B., Maggiore, M., State agreement for coupled nonlinear systems with time-varying interaction, *SIAM J. Control and Opt.*, (to appear), 2006.
12. Olfati-Saber, R., Flocking for multi-agent dynamic systems: algorithms and theory, *IEEE Trans. on Automatic Control*, Vol. 51, No. 3, 410-420, 2006.

Position Servo System Design for a Flight Simulation Table with Discontinuous Uncertainties

Kai Zheng[1], Tielong Shen[2] and Yu Yao[1]

[1] Dept. of Control Science and Engineering, Harbin Institute of Technology, Harbin 150080, China
hitkzh@gmail.com, yaoyu@hit.edu.cn

[2] Dept. of Mechanical Engineering Sophia University, Tokyo, Japan
tetu-sin@hoffman.cc.shophia.ac.jp

1 Introduction

Multi-axis rotational table is a typical simulator for the ground-based test of the attitudes of a spacecraft. From the view of control, there are two main issues in the motion control of the simulation table, position servo control, or say set-point control, and the trajectory tracking control. In the past, many researchers contributed to the control issues for the simulation table[1~3]. However, improving the control accuracy under the existence of unknown friction is still a challenging problem, since the mechanism of static-friction is not yet a fairly well-understood nature[4]. Particularly, in the set-point control, the static friction is main reason that causes steady state errors, limit cycles, and poor performance.

In the past two decades, modeling of the friction for improving the control performance has been investigated by a number of studies. The survey paper [5] summarizes the common friction models and compensation methods used in control theory. Furthermore, many control approaches with the models for compensation of the effort of the friction have been proposed. For example, the feedforward compensation methods are proposed by [6] and [7], and the state feedback regulation approach is provided by [8]. In [9], a state observer-based control scheme is reported to cope with the unknown frictions. As is well known, control with switching action is an effective method to reduce the effort of static friction. Several approaches have been investigated along this research line such as [10]. However, the systems with the static friction are essentially a discontinuous system since most effective modeling of the friction is based on the discontinuous function. The behavior of the systems with discontinuity should be investigated with the theory of differential equation with discontinuous right-hand side [11]. Hence, more effective synthesis tool for the motion control of the systems with static friction is expected by employing the Filippov-framework that is developed for dealing with the differential equation with the discontinuity.

In this paper, we focus our attention on the set-point control problem for the flight simulation table. The friction model is described by discontinuous static maps from the velocity of the plant output which is motivated by the friction model in Southward et al. [3]. We will propose a smooth control law that can render the position error to be any given small bounded set. The control law is derived by a Lyapunov function which is well-known in the control community of mechanical systems. The physics of Lagrange system is used to construct the Lyapunov function, and the behavior of the closed loop system on the discontinuous surface will be precisely analyzed with the Filippov-framework. It will be shown that with the smooth controller we can avoid undesired chattering that usually appears in the systems with switching control. Finally, some simulation results will be demonstrated.

2 Problem Formulation

A typical three-axis flight simulation table is shown in Fig. 1. There are three degrees of freedom for the motion of pitching, yawing and rolling respect to y-axis, z-axis and x-axis in inertial frame. The motion of each freedom generates a user defined 3-dimensional motion profile by using three PMSM direct drive motors fixed along the center of each axis.

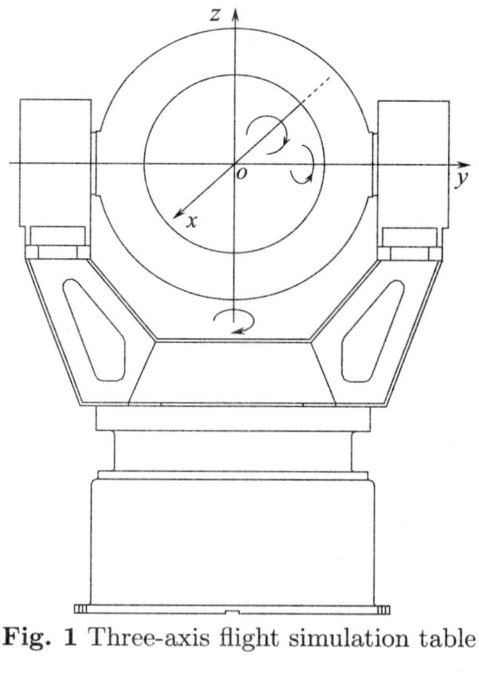

Fig. 1 Three-axis flight simulation table

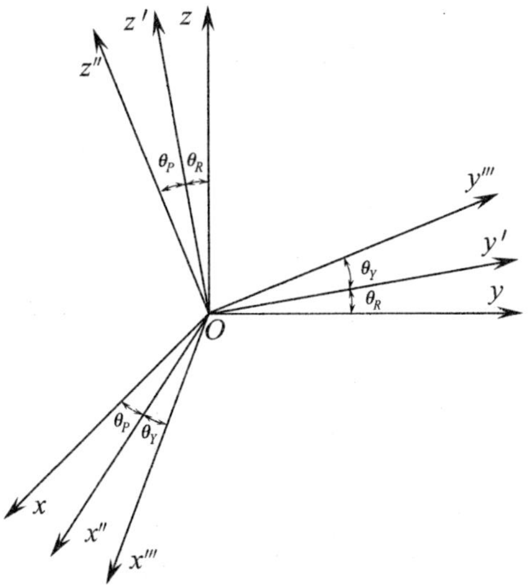

Fig. 2 Axial representation based on classical *Euler* angles.

The table is designed and modeled based on classical *Euler* angle system. Suppose that each axis is axisymmetric and normal to others and they meet at a single point in the space. The *Euler* angles θ_R, θ_P, θ_Y shown in Fig.2 are defined as classical. From [1] and [2], the elementary equation for each freedom can be derived by the generalized dynamics of rigid bodies

$$\begin{cases} J_{R_z}(\ddot{\theta}_R+\ddot{\theta}_Y\cos\theta_P)-J_{R_z}\dot{\theta}_Y\dot{\theta}_P\sin\theta_P+\Delta f_R(\theta_R,\dot{\theta}_R,t)=\tau_R \\ (J_{P_y}+J_{R_x})\ddot{\theta}_P+(J_{R_z}+J_{P_z}-J_{R_x}-J_{P_x})\dot{\theta}_Y^2\sin 2\theta_P/2 \\ \qquad +J_{R_z}\dot{\theta}_R\dot{\theta}_Y\sin\theta_P+\Delta f_P(\theta_P,\dot{\theta}_P,t)=\tau_P \\ [J_{Y_x}+J_{P_x}+J_{R_x}+(J_{P_z}+J_{R_z}-J_{R_x}-J_{P_x})\cos^2\theta_P]\ddot{\theta}_Y-J_{R_z}\dot{\theta}_R\dot{\theta}_P\sin\theta_P \\ -(J_{R_z}+J_{P_z}-J_{R_x}-J_{P_x})\dot{\theta}_Y\dot{\theta}_P\sin 2\theta_P+J_{R_z}\cos\theta_P\ddot{\theta}_R+\Delta f_Y(\theta_Y,\dot{\theta}_Y,t)=\tau_Y \end{cases} \tag{1}$$

where $J_{R_{x,y,z}}$, $J_{P_{x,y,z}}$, $J_{Y_{x,y,z}}$ represent the moment of inertia of rolling, pitching and yawing part about the x, y, z axis, respectively. $\Delta f_{R,P,Y}$ note the static friction acting on the rolling, pitching and yawing parts of the table, respectively and is modeled by

$$\Delta f_i(\theta_i,\dot{\theta}_i,t)=d_i\,\mathrm{sgn}(\dot{\theta}_i),\quad i=R,P,Y \tag{2}$$

where d_i $(i = R, P, Y)$ states the bound of the static friction acting on each freedom. τ_i $(i = R, P, Y)$ is the driving torque produce by the PMSM of each freedom and its dynamic is modeled by [12]

$$L_i\dot{I}_i+R_iI+K_{i_e}\dot{\theta}_i=\nu_i,\quad \tau_R=K_{i_t}I_i,\quad i=R,P,Y \tag{3}$$

where I_i and ν_i $(i = R, P, Y)$ are the armature currents and voltages of PMSM in each freedom, R_i and L_i $(i = R, P, Y)$ are the PMSM resistance and inductance in each freedom. And K_{i_t} $(i = R, P, Y)$ are the coefficients of the conversion from electrical current and mechanical torque in each freedom, K_{i_e} $(i = R, P, Y)$ are the voltage constants of motor back-electromotive forces.

For convenience of description, the dynamic mechanical model of the three-axis simulation table can be written in the typical form of Lagrange system with the dynamic of the actuator as follows

$$\begin{cases} J(\theta)\ddot{\theta} + C(\theta,\dot{\theta})\dot{\theta} + D\,\mathcal{S}gn(\dot{\theta}) = K_t I \\ L\dot{I} + RI + K_e\dot{\theta} = \nu \end{cases} \tag{4}$$

where θ, I and ν are vectors defined by $\theta = [\theta_R \ \ \theta_P \ \ \theta_Y]^{\mathrm{T}}$, $I = [I_R \ \ I_P \ \ I_Y]^{\mathrm{T}}$, $\nu = [\nu_R \ \ \nu_P \ \ \nu_Y]^{\mathrm{T}}$. D, K_t, L, R and K_e are diagonal matrixes defined by $D = \mathrm{diag}\{d_R, d_P, d_Y\}$, $L = \mathrm{diag}\{L_R,\ L_P,\ L_Y\}$, $K_t = \mathrm{diag}\{K_{t_R},\ K_{t_P},\ K_{t_Y}\}$, $R = \mathrm{diag}\{R_R,\ R_P,\ R_Y\}$ and $K_e = \mathrm{diag}\{K_{e_R},\ K_{e_P},\ K_{e_Y}\}$. If define $J_1 = J_{R_z}$, $J_2 = J_{P_y} + J_{R_x}$, $J_3 = J_{P_z} + J_{R_z} - J_{R_x} - J_{P_x}$ and $J_4 = J_{Y_x} + J_{R_x} + J_{P_x}$, the inertia matrix $J(\theta)$ and the coefficients matrix of centripetal and Coriolis forces $C(\theta,\dot{\theta})$ are expressed by

$$J(\theta) = \begin{bmatrix} J_1 & 0 & J_1\cos\theta_P \\ 0 & J_2 & 0 \\ J_1\cos\theta_P & 0 & J_4 + J_3\cos^2\theta_P \end{bmatrix} \tag{5}$$

$$C(\theta,\dot{\theta}) = \begin{bmatrix} 0 & -J_1\dot{\theta}_Y\sin\theta_P & 0 \\ J_1\dot{\theta}_Y\sin\theta_P & 0 & J_3\dot{\theta}_Y\sin 2\theta_P/2 \\ -J_1\dot{\theta}_P\sin\theta_P & -J_3\dot{\theta}_Y\sin 2\theta_P/2 & -J_3\dot{\theta}_P\sin 2\theta_P/2 \end{bmatrix} \tag{6}$$

The sign function $\mathcal{S}gn(\dot{\theta})$ is defined as a vector of discontinuous terms in (2), that is

$$\mathcal{S}gn(\dot{\theta}) = [\mathrm{sgn}(\dot{\theta}_R) \ \ \mathrm{sgn}(\dot{\theta}_P) \ \ \mathrm{sgn}(\dot{\theta}_Y)]^{\mathrm{T}} \tag{7}$$

In what follows, we will consider the set-point control problem which should find a continuous control input $\nu(\theta,\dot{\theta},I)$, with $\nu(\theta,\dot{\theta},I)$ the closed loop is stable and the trajectories of the system will enter the area whose bound is determined by the parameters of $\nu(\theta,\dot{\theta},I)$ in finite time, i.e., find a admissible controller $\nu(\theta,\dot{\theta},I)$ such that

A1) the closed loop is table
A2) $|\theta_i| < \varepsilon_i$, $i = R, P, Y$, ε is a small positive constant determined by $\nu(\theta,\dot{\theta},I)$, for $t < \infty$.

3 Controller Design Based on Fillippov-Framework

Assume that all the states of above system are measurable, use x_1 and x_2 to note θ, $\dot{\theta}$. Use $K_t I$ to catch the feedback law $-P_1 x_1$ where the positive definite diagonal matrix $P_1 = \mathrm{diag}\{p_R, p_P, p_Y\}$ is the feedback gain matrix determined by user. Define a new state noted by $x_3 = [x_{3_R} \ \ x_{3_P} \ \ x_{3_Y}]^{\mathrm{T}}$ to describe the error between K_tI and $-P_1x_1$, that is $x_3 = K_tI + P_1x_1$. The equation of the system is changed into

$$\begin{cases} \dot{x}_1 = x_2 \\ \dot{x}_2 = -J^{-1}(x_1)(P_1x_1 - x_3) - J^{-1}(x_1)C(x_1,x_2)x_2 - J^{-1}(x_1)D\,\mathcal{S}gn(x_2) \\ \dot{x}_3 = -K_tL^{-1}RI - K_tL^{-1}K_ex_2 + P_1x_2 + K_tL^{-1}\nu \end{cases} \tag{8}$$

Obviously, the equation (8) has a discontinuous right-hand side due to the sign function $\mathcal{S}gn(x_2)$. The stability of system at the discontinuous point, i.e., when $x_2 = 0$ can not be derived by classical Lyapunov stability theory directly. The discontinuous property of system motivates us to utilize the Filippov's theory about nonsmooth differential equations [11,13].

Choose the control input ν as follows so as to make the dynamic of x_3 stable

$$\nu = RI + K_ex_2 - LK_t^{-1}(P_1x_2 + Gx_3 + \nu') \tag{9}$$

where the diagonal matrix $G = \mathrm{diag}\{g_R, g_P, g_Y\}$ is positive definite whose parameters are determined by user. And ν' is an auxiliary control input which is determined later. The closed loop equation is

$$\begin{cases} \dot{x}_1 = x_2 \\ \dot{x}_2 = -J^{-1}(x_1)(P_1x_1 - x_3) - J^{-1}(x_1)C(x_1,x_2)x_2 - J^{-1}(x_1)D\,\mathcal{S}gn(x_2) \\ \dot{x}_3 = -Gx_3 + \nu' \end{cases} \tag{10}$$

Define a Lyapunov candidate function given by

$$V = \frac{1}{2}x_1^{\mathrm{T}}x_1 + \frac{1}{2}x_2^{\mathrm{T}}P_1^{-1}J(x_1)x_2 + \frac{1}{2}x_3^{\mathrm{T}}x_3 \tag{11}$$

the generalized time derivative of V is defined by [14]

$$\dot{\tilde{V}} = \bigcap_{\xi\in\partial V} \xi^{\mathrm{T}} \cdot K[f](x,t) \tag{12}$$

where ∂V is the Clarke's generalized gradient [15] and $K[f](x,t)$ is the differential inclusion in Filippov sense.

When $x_2 \neq 0$, $\dot{\tilde{V}}$ is the same as the normal time derivative of V

$$\begin{aligned} \dot{\tilde{V}} =& x_1^{\mathrm{T}}x_2 + x_2^{\mathrm{T}}P_1^{-1}J(x_1)\dot{x}_2 + x_2^{\mathrm{T}}P_1^{-1}\dot{J}(x_1)x_2/2 + x_3^{\mathrm{T}}\dot{x}_3 \\ =& \frac{1}{2}x_2^{\mathrm{T}}P_1^{-1}[\dot{J}(x_1) - 2C(x_1,x_2)]x_2 - x_3^{\mathrm{T}}Gx_3 - x_3^{\mathrm{T}}(P_1^{-1}x_2 + \nu') \\ & - x_2^{\mathrm{T}}P_1^{-1}D\,\mathcal{S}gn(x_2) \end{aligned} \tag{13}$$

By applying the skew-symmetric property of Lagrange systems to the first term of the right-hand side of (13) and choosing the control input $\nu' = -P_1^{-1}x_2$, we have

$$\begin{aligned}\dot{\tilde{V}} &= -x_2^{\mathrm{T}} P_1^{-1} D\, Sgn(x_2) - x_3^{\mathrm{T}} G x_3 \\ &= -p_R^{-1} d_R |\dot{\theta}_R| - p_P^{-1} d_P |\dot{\theta}_P| - p_Y^{-1} d_Y |\dot{\theta}_Y| - x_3^{\mathrm{T}} G x_3 \leqslant 0\end{aligned} \tag{14}$$

This implies that if and only if $x_2 = 0$ and $x_3 = 0$, the value of the generalized time derivative of V is zero and if some element of $x_2 \neq 0$ or $x_3 \neq 0$ the value of $\dot{\tilde{V}}$ is less than zero and the trajectory is convergent. Then we turn our focus on the point set when $x_2 = 0$ and $x_3 = 0$. Define the set $\Omega \in \mathbb{R}^9$ as the whole state space. From the derivation of (14), $\forall x = [x_1 \ \ x_2 \ \ x_3]^{\mathrm{T}} \in \Omega, \ \ \dot{\tilde{V}} \leqslant 0$. Using set S to express the point set when $\dot{\tilde{V}} = 0$, that is

$$S = \{x \in \Omega \mid 0 \in \dot{\tilde{V}}\} \tag{15}$$

From the above discussion, S satisfies

$$S = \{x \in \Omega \mid 0 \in \dot{\tilde{V}}\} = \{x \in \Omega \mid x_2 = 0, x_3 = 0\} \tag{16}$$

When the trajectories enter S, the dynamic of closed loop should be expressed by the following differential inclusion

$$\dot{x} \in K \begin{bmatrix} \mathbf{0} \\ -J^{-1}(x_1) P_1 x_1 - J^{-1}(x_1) D\, Sgn(x_2) \\ \mathbf{0} \end{bmatrix} \tag{17}$$

$J^{-1}(x_1)$ is a continuous function respect ot x_1, noted by $j_{m \times n}(x_1), m, n = 1, 2, 3,$ we can get

$$K \begin{bmatrix} \mathbf{0} \\ -J^{-1}(x_1) P_1 x_1 - J^{-1}(x_1) D\, Sgn(x_2) \\ \mathbf{0} \end{bmatrix} =$$

$$K \begin{bmatrix} \mathbf{0} \\ -j_{11}(x_1)(p_R\theta_R + d_R\eta_R) - j_{12}(x_1)(p_P\theta_P + d_P\eta_P) - j_{13}(x_1)(p_Y\theta_Y + d_Y\eta_Y) \\ -j_{21}(x_1)(p_R\theta_R + d_R\eta_R) - j_{22}(x_1)(p_P\theta_P + d_P\eta_P - j_{23}(x_1)(p_Y\theta_Y + d_Y\eta_Y) \\ -j_{31}(x_1)(p_R\theta_R + d_R\eta_R) - j_{32}(x_1)(p_P\theta_P + d_P\eta_P) - j_{33}(x_1)(p_Y\theta_Y + d_Y\eta_Y) \\ \mathbf{0} \end{bmatrix},$$
$$\eta_i \in [-1, 1], i = R, P, Y \tag{18}$$

Without loss of generality, we discuss the state θ_R separately at first and the result can be extended to all the states easily. Note $\Pi_R = \{x \in \mathbb{R}^9 \mid S_R(x) = \dot{\theta}_R = 0\}$ as the switching surface which divides the state space into two region S_R^+ and S_R^-, that is

$$S_R^+ = \{x \in \mathbb{R}^9 \mid \dot{\theta}_R > 0\}, \qquad S_R^- = \{x \in \mathbb{R}^9 \mid \dot{\theta}_R < 0\} \tag{19}$$

when the trajectories approach the switching surface Π_R from S_R^+ and S_R^-, the limit dynamic of the trajectories noted by $f_R^+(x,t)$ $f_R^-(x,t)$ are given by

$$f_{R}^{+}(\theta_R, t) = \left\{ \begin{array}{c} \mathbf{0} \\ -j_{11}(x_1)(p_R\theta_R + d_R) - j_{12}(x_1)(p_P\theta_P + d_P\eta_P) - j_{13}(x_1)(p_Y\theta_Y + d_Y\eta_Y) \\ -j_{21}(x_1)(p_R\theta_R + d_R) - j_{22}(x_1)(p_P\theta_P + d_P\eta_P) - j_{23}(x_1)(p_Y\theta_Y + d_Y\eta_Y) \\ -j_{31}(x_1)(p_R\theta_R + d_R) - j_{32}(x_1)(p_P\theta_P + d_P\eta_P) - j_{33}(x_1)(p_Y\theta_Y + d_Y\eta_Y) \\ \mathbf{0} \end{array} \right. \tag{20a}$$

$$f_{R}^{-}(\theta_R, t) = \left\{ \begin{array}{c} \mathbf{0} \\ -j_{11}(x_1)(p_R\theta_R - d_R) - j_{12}(x_1)(p_P\theta_P + d_P\eta_P) - j_{13}(x_1)(p_Y\theta_Y + d_Y\eta_Y) \\ -j_{21}(x_1)(p_R\theta_R - d_R) - j_{22}(x_1)(p_P\theta_P + d_P\eta_P) - j_{23}(x_1)(p_Y\theta_Y + d_Y\eta_Y) \\ -j_{31}(x_1)(p_R\theta_R - d_R) - j_{32}(x_1)(p_P\theta_P + d_P\eta_P) - j_{33}(x_1)(p_Y\theta_Y + d_Y\eta_Y) \\ \mathbf{0} \end{array} \right. \tag{20b}$$

Since the normal vector N_R of Π_R is $N_R = [0\ 0\ 0\ 1\ 0\ 0\ 0\ 0\ 0]^{\mathrm{T}}$, $f_{N_R}^{+}(\theta_R, t)$ and $f_{N_R}^{-}(\theta_R, t)$ are calculated as follows

$$f_{N_R}^{+}(\theta_R, t) = -j_{11}(x_1)(p_R\theta_R + d_R) - j_{12}(x_1)(p_P\theta_P + d_P\eta_P) - j_{13}(x_1)(p_Y\theta_Y + d_Y\eta_Y) \tag{21a}$$

$$f_{N_R}^{-}(\theta_R, t) = -j_{11}(x_1)(p_R\theta_R - d_R) - j_{12}(x_1)(p_P\theta_P + d_P\eta_P) - j_{13}(x_1)(p_Y\theta_Y + d_Y\eta_Y) \tag{21b}$$

From Filippov's differential theory, we define the set S_{eR} with

$$S_{eR} = \{x \in \Pi_R \mid f_{N_R}^{+} \leqslant 0, f_{N_R}^{-} \geqslant 0, f_{N_R}^{-} - f_{N_R}^{+} > 0\} \tag{22}$$

From Lemma 3 in the reference [11], we can get the existence conditions of solution at the switching surface Π_R

$$S_{eR} = \{[x_1\ \mathbf{0}\ \mathbf{0}]^{\mathrm{T}} \Big| \forall \theta_R \in [-\frac{j_{12}(x_1)}{p_R j_{11}(x_1)}(p_P\theta_P + d_P\eta_P) - \frac{j_{13}(x_1)}{p_R j_{11}(x_1)}(p_Y\theta_Y + d_Y\eta_Y) - \frac{d_R}{p_R}, -\frac{j_{12}(x_1)}{p_R j_{11}(x_1)}(p_P\theta_P + d_P\eta_P) - \frac{j_{13}(x_1)}{p_R j_{11}(x_1)}(p_Y\theta_Y + d_Y\eta_Y) + \frac{d_R}{p_R}]\} \tag{23}$$

The solution is given by

$$f_{R}^{\circ}(\alpha, t) = m f_{R}^{+}(\alpha, t) + (1 - m) f_{R}^{+}(\alpha, t) = \left\{ \begin{array}{c} \mathbf{0} \\ 0 \\ -j_{21}(x_1)(p_R\theta_R + d_R) - j_{22}(x_1)(p_P\theta_P + d_P\eta_P) - j_{23}(x_1)(p_Y\theta_Y + d_Y\eta_Y) \\ -j_{31}(x_1)(p_R\theta_R + d_R) - j_{32}(x_1)(p_P\theta_P + d_P\eta_P) - j_{33}(x_1)(p_Y\theta_Y + d_Y\eta_Y) \\ \mathbf{0} \end{array} \right. \tag{24}$$

where

$$m = \frac{f_{N_R}^-}{f_{N_R}^- - f_{N_R}^+} = \frac{f_{N_R}^-}{2d_R} \tag{25}$$

Equation (24) implies the solution of state θ_R is non-trivial at the switching surface, and by LaSalle invariance principle the state θ_R will stay in the largest invariance set given by (23). And the bound of the invariance set is d_R/p_R which is determined by p_R. In the same way, we can get the similar results for the other two freedom. The largest invariance sets of θ_P and θ_Y are

$$S_{e_P} = \\ \{[x_1\ \mathbf{0}\ \mathbf{0}]^{\mathrm{T}} \Big| \forall\theta_P \in [-\frac{j_{21}(x_1)}{p_P j_{22}(x_1)}(p_R\theta_R + d_R\eta_R) - \frac{j_{23}(x_1)}{p_P j_{22}(x_1)}(p_Y\theta_Y + d_Y\eta_Y) - \frac{d_P}{p_P}, \\ -\frac{j_{21}(x_1)}{p_P j_{22}(x_1)}(p_R\theta_R + d_R\eta_R) - \frac{j_{23}(x_1)}{p_P j_{22}(x_1)}(p_Y\theta_Y + d_Y\eta_Y) + \frac{d_P}{p_P}]\} \tag{26}$$

$$S_{e_Y} = \\ \{[x_1\ \mathbf{0}\ \mathbf{0}]^{\mathrm{T}} \Big| \forall\theta_Y \in [-\frac{j_{31}(x_1)}{p_Y j_{33}(x_1)}(p_R\theta_R + d_R\eta_R) - \frac{j_{32}(x_1)}{p_Y j_{33}(x_1)}(p_P\theta_P + d_P\eta_P) - \frac{d_Y}{p_Y}, \\ -\frac{j_{31}(x_1)}{p_Y j_{33}(x_1)}(p_R\theta_R + d_R\eta_R) - \frac{j_{32}(x_1)}{p_Y j_{33}(x_1)}(p_P\theta_P + d_P\eta_P) + \frac{d_Y}{p_Y}]\} \tag{27}$$

And the bounds of these two invariant set are d_P/p_P and d_Y/p_Y, respectively.

From the above discussion, we can obtain the following proposition.

Proposition 3.1 *The system given by (4) with the feedback controller*

$$\nu = -LK_t^{-1}GP_1x_1 + [K_e - LK_t^{-1}(P_1 + P_1^{-1})]x_2 + (R - LG)I \tag{28}$$

is stable. And the trajectories of system will approach the invariant set given by (23), (26) and (27) whose bounds are determined by the feedback gain P_1.

Form the above proposition, the invariant set of each freedom is bounded and can be regulated by the feedback gain matrix P_1. In other words, we can design the gain matrix P_1 to make the servo error in an arbitrary small bound. The following simulation examples verify the conclusion.

4 Simulation Examples

In order to inspect and verify the performance of the derived controller at the nonsmooth points in state space, a simulation is set up. The parameters used in the simulation is shown in Table 1.

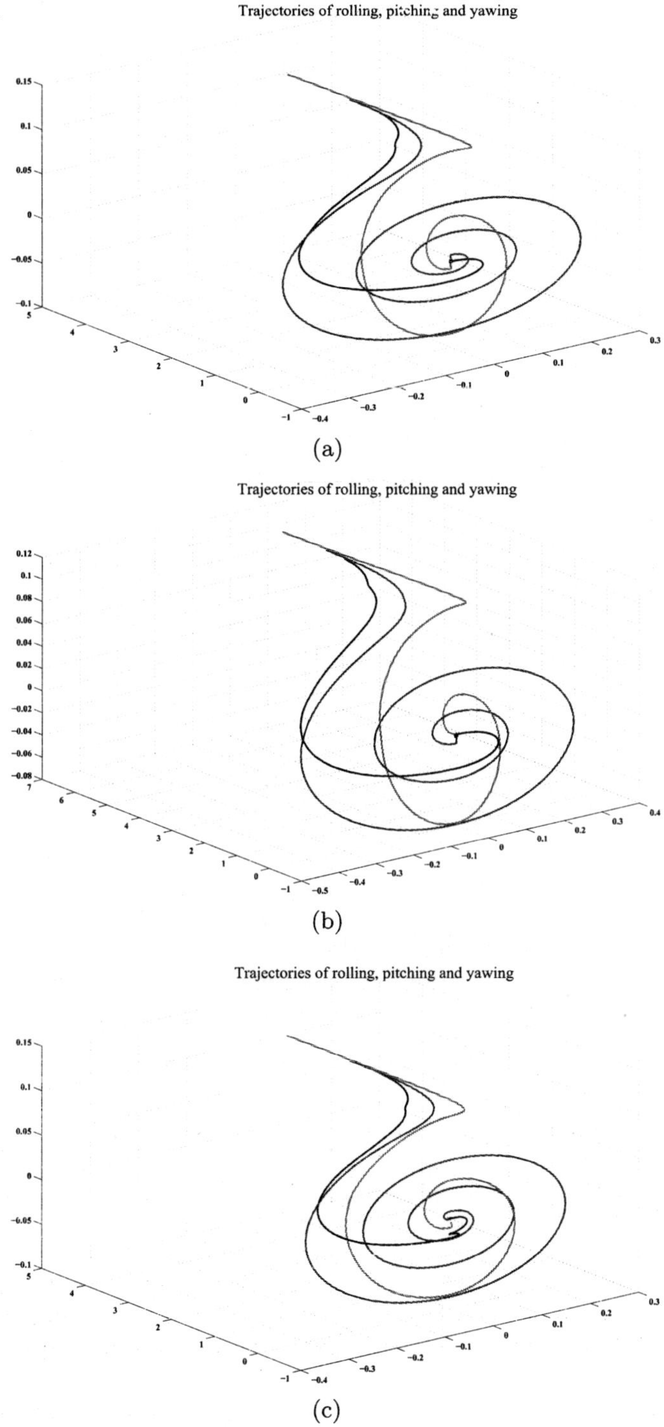

Fig. 3 Simulation results with the initial condition $x_1 = \{0.1 \;\; 0.1 \;\; 0.1\}$, $x_2 = \{0.1 \;\; 0.1 \;\; 0.1\}$.

Table 1 Parameter sets for simulation

Parameters	In Fig. 3 (a)	In Fig. 3 (b)	In Fig. 3 (c)
$[J_1\ J_2\ J_3\ J_4]$	$[1.2\ \ 2.9\ \ -0.3\ \ 19.9]$	$[1.2\ \ 2.9\ \ -0.3\ \ 19.9]$	$[1.5\ \ 4.2\ \ 0.3\ \ 14.0]$
L	diag$\{0.1\ \ 0.05\ \ 0.2\}$	diag$\{0.1\ \ 0.05\ \ 0.2\}$	diag$\{0.1\ \ 0.05\ \ 0.2\}$
R	diag$\{1\ \ 0.05\ \ 0.1\}$	diag$\{1\ \ 0.05\ \ 0.1\}$	diag$\{1\ \ 0.05\ \ 0.1\}$
K_e	diag$\{40\ \ 40\ \ 80\}$	diag$\{40\ \ 40\ \ 80\}$	diag$\{40\ \ 40\ \ 80\}$
K_t	diag$\{40\ \ 40\ \ 80\}$	diag$\{40\ \ 40\ \ 80\}$	diag$\{40\ \ 40\ \ 80\}$
D	diag$\{0.5\ \ 0.2\ \ 1\}$	diag$\{0.8\ \ 0.4\ \ 1.5\}$	diag$\{0.5\ \ 0.2\ \ 1\}$
P_1	diag$\{30\ \ 40\ \ 60\}$	diag$\{50\ \ 60\ \ 80\}$	diag$\{30\ \ 40\ \ 60\}$
G	diag$\{10\ \ 15\ \ 20\}$	diag$\{10\ \ 15\ \ 20\}$	diag$\{10\ \ 15\ \ 20\}$

In Fig. 3, subfigure (a) shows the trajectories with the standard parameters, subfigure (b) shows the trajectories with the variation of the bound of friction, subfigure (c) shows the trajectories with changed mechanical parameters. Comparison with the trajectories shown in Fig. 3(a) and 3(b) implies the fact that it just needs to change the gain matrix P_1 to achieve the enough precision when the bound of friction is changed. And from Fig. 3(a) and 3(b), we can find that the servo error is independent of the mechanical parameters. The robust property can be obviously found in the process of controller design, because the mechanical parameters is not used in the designed of control law.

5 Conclusions

In this research, a simple and effectual controller is designed to compensating the nonsmooth friction in multi-axis spacecraft simulation table based on Filippov framework. And backstepping method is used to get the control voltage of actuator. By means of regulating the gain of the controller, the positioning accuracy can be set in a arbitrary small bound. And the robust property is represented by its insensibility for the variation of the mechanical parameters. Simulations are set up to evaluate the performance of the proposed controller. The results give evidence for our conclusion.

References

1. Liu Yan-bin, Jin Guang, and He Huiyang. Model ing of three axis simulator and decoupl ing control. *Journal of Harbin Institute of Technology*, 35:323–328, 2003.
2. Xie Yue, Mahinda Vilathgamuwa, K. J. Tseng, and N. Nagarajan. Modeling and robust adaptive control of a 3-axis motion simulator. In *Power Electronics Specialists Conference, IEEE 33rd Annual*, 2002.
3. Xie Yue, D. Mahinda Vilathgamuwa, and King-Jet Tseng. Robust adaptive control of a three-axis motion simulator with state observers. *IEEE/ASME Transaction on Mechatronics*, 10:437–448, 2005.
4. C. Canudas de Wit, H. Olsson, K.J. Astrom, and P. Lischinsky. A new model for control of systems with friction. *IEEE Transactions on Automatic Control*, 40(3):419–425, 1995.

5. B. Armstrong-Helouvry, P. Dupont, and C. Canudas de Wit. A survey of models, analysis tools and compensation methods for the control of machines with friction. *Automatica*, 30:1083–1138, 1994. A survey of models, analysis tools and compensation methods for the control of machines with friction.
6. E. D. Tung, G. Anwar, and M. Tomizuka. Low velocity friction compensation and feedforward solution based on repetitive control. *ASME Journal of Dynamic Systems, Measurement, and Control*, 115:279–284, 1993.
7. N. Koreta, H. Okitomo, K. Tsumura, K. Takeuchi, and T. Egawa. Study of high accuracy of machine tool with bang-bang control. *Journal of Japan Society for Precision Engineering*, 60(3):427–431, 1994.
8. C. T. Johnson and R. D. Lorenz. Experimental identification of friction and its compensation in precise, position controlled mechanisms. *IEEE Transactions on Industry Applications*, 28:1392–1398, 1992.
9. C. Canudas de Wit and P. Lischinsky. Adaptive friction compensation with partially known dynamic friction model. *International Journal of Adaptive Control and Signal Processing*, 11:65–80, 1997.
10. Tielong Shen, Katsutoshi Tamura, Hiroshi Kaminaga, Noriaki Henmi, and Toru Nakazawa. Robust nonlinear control of parametric uncertain systems with unknown friction and its application to a pneumatic control valve. *Journal of Dynamic Systems, Measurement, and Control*, 122:257–262, 2000.
11. A. Filippov. Differential equations with discontinous right-hand side. *American Mathematical Society Translations*, 42:354–362, 1964.
12. Chiharu Ishii, Tielong Shen, and Zhihua Qu. Lyapunov resursive design of robust adaptive tracking control with l_2-gain performance for electrically-driven robot manipulators. *International Journal of Control*, 74:811–828, 2001.
13. A.Filippov. *Differential Equations with Discontinuous Righthand Sides.* Kluwer Academic Publishers, Netherlands, 1988.
14. Brad E. Paden and Shankar S. Sastry. A calculus for computing filippov's differential inclusion with application to the variable structure control of robot manipulatore. *IEEE Transactions on Circuits and Systems*, 34:73–82, 1987.
15. F. Clarke. *Optimization and Nonsmooth Analysis.* SIAM, New York, 1990.

Robust Exponential Stabilization for a Class of Nonlinear Singular Delay Systems

Renquan Lu and Anke Xue

Institute of Information and Control, Hangzhou Dianzi University, Hangzhou 310018, China
rqlu@hdu.edu.cn

1 Introduction

The model of singular system is built based on the concept of singular perturbation, and commonly encountered in various engineering systems, such as power system, machine system, flight control system, robotic system, chemical engineering system, and so on. Singular system is also referred to as descriptor system, generalized state-space system or semistate system. Due to the fact that singular system better describe physical system than regular one, the study of singular system has been a topic of recurring interest over the past decades, and is of theoretical and practical importance.

In recent years, a great number of results based on the theory of regular systems have been extended to the area of singular systems, increasing attention has been devoted to the problem of robust stability analysis for uncertain singular systems. It should be pointed out that when the robust stability problem for singular systems is investigated, the regularity and absence of impulses (for continuous systems) and causality (for discrete systems) are required to be considered simultaneously[1,3]. Hence, the robust stability problem for singular time-delay systems is much more complicated than that for state-space ones. In the continuous context, the robust stability and robust stabilization problems were solved based on the concepts of generalized quadratic stability and generalized quadratic stabilization[4,2], where the obtained results were presented in terms of strict linear matrix inequalities (LMIs). The same conclusion was reached by using an alternative approach[5]. Some delay-dependent stability criteria for singular time-delay systems were also presented in[6, 7], where it was required to assume that the considered system is regular and impulse free. In the discrete setting, Wang *et al.* [8] studied the robust stability problem by using the spectral radius inequality of modulus matrix, where the considered uncertainty is highly structured. The same approach was applied to investigate the problem of robust D-stability analysis[9]. To the best of our knowledge, when a class of nonlinear perturbation appears, there are no results on the problems of robust exponential stability and stabilization for uncertain singular delay systems in the literature.

In this paper, the delay-dependent robust exponential stability and stabilization conditions are presented for uncertain Lur'e singular system with time-varying delay and nonlinear perturbation. The time delay considered here is assumed to be size-bounded but otherwise arbitrarily fast time-varying, and nonlinear perturbation is constrained on the set of Hurwctiz. It worth pointing out that the analysis of robust exponential stability and robust stabilization for nonlinear singular systems is not the same as that for singular linear systems, therefore the new concept of generalized robust exponentially stability and generalized robust stabilization is presented based on the Barbalat's lemma by considering the initial state in this note. The sufficient conditions for generalized robust exponentially stability and generalized robust stabilization is obtained in term of the strict LMIs, moreover, a state-feedback control law is also given such that the resultant closed-loop system is regular, impulse free and exponentially stable for admissible uncertainties.

2 Problem Formulation

Consider an uncertain Lur'e singular time-delay system described by

$$\begin{aligned} E\dot{x}(t) &= (A_0 + \Delta A_0(\bullet))x(t) + (A_1 + \Delta A_1(\bullet))x(t-h(t)) \\ &\quad + E_0\varphi(\sigma(t)) + (B_0 + \Delta B_0(\bullet))u(t) \\ \sigma(t) &= Cx(t), x(t) = \phi(t), t \in [-max(h(t)), 0] \end{aligned} \tag{1}$$

where $x(t) \in \mathbb{R}^n$ is the state vector, $u(t) \in \mathbb{R}^m$ is the input vector. E, A_0, A_1,E_0,B_0 and C are constant matrices with appropriate dimensions, and E may be singular, we shall assume that rank $E = r \leqslant n$. $\Delta A_0(\bullet)$, $\Delta A_1(\bullet)$ and $\Delta B_0(\bullet)$ are time-variant matrices representing the admissible parameter uncertainties, which can be described as

$$\left[\Delta A_0(\bullet)\ \Delta A_1(\bullet)\ \Delta B_0(\bullet)\right] = G_1 F(x,t)\left[H_1\ H_2\ H_3\right] \tag{2}$$

where G_1,H_1,H_2 and H_3 are known constant matrices with appropriate dimensions and $F(x,t)$ is an unknown time-variant matrix bounded by

$$F^{\mathrm{T}}(x,t)F(x,t) \leqslant I, \forall t \tag{3}$$

$h(t)$ is time-varying delay with known bound in system (1) such that

$$0 \leqslant h(t) \leqslant h, \dot{h}(t) \leqslant d \leqslant 1 \tag{4}$$

$\phi(t)$ is continuous vector valued initial function. Setting

$$\begin{aligned} \sigma(t) &= \left[\sigma_1(t)\ \sigma_2(t) \cdots \sigma_n(t)\right]^{\mathrm{T}} \\ \varphi(t) &= \left[\varphi(\sigma_1(t))\ \varphi(\sigma_2(t)) \cdots \varphi(\sigma_n(t))\right]^{\mathrm{T}} \end{aligned}$$

Every nonlinear term is uniform continuous function and constrained in the set of Hurwctiz, that is, for any $\alpha > 0$ there exists scalars $k_j (j = 1, 2, \cdots, n)$ such that

$$\varphi_j(\bullet) \in K_j[0,k_j] = \{\varphi(\sigma_j)|\varphi_j(0)=0, \|\dot{\varphi}_j(\sigma_j)\| \leqslant \alpha, \\ 0 < \sigma_j\varphi_j(\sigma_j) \leqslant k_j\sigma_j^2(\sigma_j \neq 0)\} \tag{5}$$

To facilitate the following discussion, we introduce the following definitions and lemmas.

Definition 2.1 [1]
A1) *The pair* (E, A) *is said to be regular, if* $\det(sE - A)$ *is not identically zero.*
A2) *The pair* (E, A) *is said to be impulse free, if* $\deg(\det(sE - A)) = \text{rank } E$.

Definition 2.2 [9,12]
A1) *The singular system* (1) *is said to regular and impulse free if the pair* (E, A) *is regular and impulse free.*
A2) *The singular* (1) *is said to exponentially stable if for any* $\varepsilon < 0$ *there exists a scalar* $\delta(\varepsilon) > 0$ *such that, for any compatible initial conditions* $\phi(t)$ *satisfying* $\sup\limits_{-h(t)\leqslant t\leqslant 0} \|\phi(t)\| \leqslant \delta(\varepsilon)$, *the solution* $x(t)$ *of system*(1) *satisfies*

$$\lim_{t\to\infty} \sup(\log\|x(t)\|^2) \leqslant -\beta < 0$$

for a positive scalar β.

Definition 2.3 *The uncertain Lur'e singular delay system* (1) *is said to be generalized robustly exponentially stable if the system* (1) *with* $u(t) \equiv 0$ *is regular, impulse free and asymptotically stable for all admissible uncertainties.*

Definition 2.4 *The uncertain Lur'e singular delay system* (1) *is said to be generalized robustly exponentially stabilizable if there exists a linear state feedback control law* $u(t) = \Lambda x(t), \Lambda \in \mathbb{R}^n$ *such that the resultant closed-loop system is regular, impulse free and exponentially stable for all admissible uncertainties.*

Lamma 2.1 [10] *Given matrices* U, V *and* W *of appropriate dimensions, then for any scalar* $\alpha > 0$, *the following matrix inequality holds,*

$$U^{\mathrm{T}}V + V^{\mathrm{T}}U \leqslant \alpha U^{\mathrm{T}} + \alpha^{-1}V^{\mathrm{T}}V$$

Lamma 2.2 [10] *Given a symmetric matrix* Ω *and matrices* Γ, Ξ *with appropriate dimensions, then*

$$\Omega + \Gamma F \Xi + \Xi^{\mathrm{T}}F^{\mathrm{T}}\Gamma^{\mathrm{T}} < 0$$

for any matrix F *satisfying* $F^{\mathrm{T}}F \leqslant I$, *if and only if there exists a scalar* $\varepsilon > 0$ *such that*

$$\Omega + \varepsilon^{-1}\Gamma\Gamma^{\mathrm{T}} + \varepsilon\Xi^{\mathrm{T}}\Xi < 0.$$

Lamma 2.3 [1] *The singular system*

$$E\dot{x}(t) = Ax(t)$$

is regular, impulse free and asymptotically stable if and only if there exists a matrix P *such that*

$$EP^{\mathrm{T}} = PE^{\mathrm{T}} \geqslant 0$$

$$AP^{\mathrm{T}} + PA^{\mathrm{T}} < 0$$

Lamma 2.4 *(Barbalat's Lemma)* [12] *Consider the function* $\phi : \mathbb{R}^+ \to \mathbb{R}$. *If* ϕ *is uniformly continuous and* $\int_0^\infty \phi(s)\mathrm{d}s < \infty$, *then*

$$\lim_{t\to\infty} \phi(t) = 0$$

3 Main Results

In this section, the problems of robust stability and robust stabilization based on LMI approach for the system (1) are discussed. First, we present Theorem 3.1, which gives the the sufficient condition of robust stability for system (1) with $u(t) = 0$, and will paly a key role in solving the aforementioned problems.

Theorem 3.1 *For the initial condition* $x(t) = \phi(t)$, *the uncertain Lur'e singular delay system* (1) *with* $u(t) = 0$ *is said to be generalized robustly exponentially stable, if there exists a matrix* P, *a positive definite matrix* Q, *and scalars* $\varepsilon > 0$ *and* $\theta > 0$ *such that the matrix inequalities* (6) *and the equation* (7) *hold,*

$$EP^{\mathrm{T}} = PE^{\mathrm{T}} \geqslant 0 \tag{6a}$$

$$M = \begin{bmatrix} M_{11} & A_1P^{\mathrm{T}} & E_0 & PC^{\mathrm{T}}K^{\mathrm{T}} & PH_1^{\mathrm{T}} & G_1 \\ * & M_{22} & 0 & 0 & PH_2^{\mathrm{T}} & 0 \\ * & * & -\varepsilon^{-1}I & 0 & 0 & 0 \\ * & * & * & -\varepsilon I & 0 & 0 \\ * & * & * & * & -\theta I & 0 \\ * & * & * & * & * & -\theta^{-1}I \end{bmatrix} < 0 \tag{6b}$$

where $M_{11} = A_0P^{\mathrm{T}} + PA_0^{\mathrm{T}} + Q$, $M_{22} = -(1-d)Q$, $K = \mathrm{diag}\{k_1, \cdots, k_n\}$, *and* $\beta > 0$ *is the unique root to the following equation* (7),

$$\beta(\lambda_1 + \lambda_2 he^{\beta h}) = \lambda_M \tag{7}$$

where $\lambda_1 = \lambda_{max}(P^{-1}E)$, $\lambda_2 = \lambda_{max}(P^{-1}QP^{-\mathrm{T}})$, $\lambda_M = \lambda_{max}(P^{-1}MP^{-\mathrm{T}})$.

Proof: when $u(t) = 0$, the uncertain Lur'e singular delay system (1) can be described as

$$E\dot{x}(t) = A_{0\Delta}x(t) + A_{1\Delta}x(t-h(t)) + E_0\varphi(\sigma(t)) \tag{8}$$

where $A_{0\Delta} = A_0 + \Delta A_0(\bullet)$, $A_{1\Delta} = A_1 + \Delta A_1(\bullet)$.

By using Schur complement argument, it easy to see from(6b) that $A_0P^{\mathrm{T}} + PA_0^{\mathrm{T}} < 0$, it follows from (6a) and Lemma 2.3 that the pair (E, A) is regular and impulse free, therefore, if we can deduce that the system (8) is exponentially stable, then, it completes the proof of Theorem 3.1 by Definition 2.3. To this end, we note that the regularity and the absence of impulse of the pair (E, A) implies that there exists two orthogonal matrices L_1 and $L_2 \in \mathbb{R}^{n\times n}$ such that

$$\bar{E} = L_1 E L_2 = \begin{bmatrix} I_r & 0 \\ 0 & 0 \end{bmatrix}, \qquad \bar{A}_0 = L_1 A L_2 = \begin{bmatrix} A_r & 0 \\ 0 & I_{n-r} \end{bmatrix} \tag{9}$$

where $I_r \in \mathbb{R}^{r\times r}$ and $I_{n-r} \in \mathbb{R}^{(n-r)\times(n-r)}$ are identity matrices. According to (9), let

$$\bar{A}_1 = L_1 A_1 L_2 = \begin{bmatrix} \bar{A}_{11} & \bar{A}_{12} \\ \bar{A}_{21} & \bar{A}_{22} \end{bmatrix} \qquad \bar{B}_0 = L_1 B_0 L_2 \tag{10a}$$

$$\bar{E}_0 = L_1 E_0 = \begin{bmatrix} \bar{E}_{01} \\ \bar{E}_{02} \end{bmatrix} \qquad \bar{C}_0 = L_2^{-1} C L_2 \tag{10b}$$

$$\bar{K} = K L_2 \qquad \bar{H}_1 = H_1 L_2 \qquad \bar{H}_2 = H_2 L_2 \tag{10c}$$

$$\bar{H}_3 = H_1 L_3 \qquad \bar{G}_1 = L_1 G_1 \tag{10d}$$

$$\bar{P} = L_1 P L_2^{-\mathrm{T}} = \begin{bmatrix} \bar{P}_{11} & \bar{P}_{12} \\ \bar{P}_{21} & \bar{P}_{22} \end{bmatrix} \tag{10e}$$

$$\bar{Q} = L_1 Q L_2^T = \begin{bmatrix} \bar{Q}_{11} & \bar{Q}_{12} \\ \bar{Q}_{21} & \bar{Q}_{22} \end{bmatrix} \tag{10f}$$

Pre-multiplying diag$\{L_1, L_1, L_1, I, I, I\}$ and post-multiplying diag$\{L_1^{\mathrm{T}}, L_1^{\mathrm{T}}, L_1^{\mathrm{T}}, I, I, I\}$ to the left and right side of (6b), yield

$$\bar{E}\bar{P}^{\mathrm{T}} = \bar{P}\bar{E}^{\mathrm{T}} \geqslant 0 \tag{11a}$$

$$\bar{M} = \begin{bmatrix} \bar{M}_{11} & \bar{A}_1\bar{P}^{\mathrm{T}} & \bar{E}_0 & \bar{P}\bar{C}^{\mathrm{T}}\bar{K}^{\mathrm{T}} & \bar{P}\bar{H}_1^{\mathrm{T}} & \bar{G}_1 \\ * & \bar{M}_{22} & 0 & 0 & \bar{P}\bar{H}_2^{\mathrm{T}} & 0 \\ * & * & -\varepsilon^{-1}I & 0 & 0 & 0 \\ * & * & * & -\varepsilon I & 0 & 0 \\ * & * & * & * & -\theta I & 0 \\ * & * & * & * & * & -\theta^{-1}I \end{bmatrix} < 0 \tag{11b}$$

Noting that the expression of $\bar{E}$ in (9) and using (11a) and similar techniques as in the work by Xu [4], we can easily deduce that

$$\bar{P} = \begin{bmatrix} \bar{P}_{11} & \bar{P}_{12} \\ 0 & \bar{P}_{22} \end{bmatrix} \tag{12a}$$

$$\bar{P}_{11} = \bar{P}_{11}^{\mathrm{T}} > 0 \tag{12b}$$

$$\rho(\bar{A}_{22}) < 1 \tag{12c}$$

Now, Let

$$\xi(t) = L_2^{-1}x(t) = \begin{bmatrix} \xi_1(t) \\ \xi_2(t) \end{bmatrix}$$

where $\xi_1(t) \in \mathbb{R}^r$, $\xi_2(t) \in \mathbb{R}^{n-r}$. Substituting (9) and (10) into the singular system (8), we get

$$\bar{E}\dot{\xi}(t) = \bar{A}_{0\Delta}\xi(t) + \bar{A}_{1\Delta}\xi(t - h(t)) + \bar{E}_0\varphi(\eta(t)) \tag{13}$$

where $\eta(t) = \bar{C}\xi(t)$. It is easy to see that the exponential stability of the uncertain Lur'e singular delay system (13) is equivalent to the system (8). The singular delay system (13) can also be decomposed as

$$\begin{aligned}\dot{\xi}_1(t) = \bar{A}_{r\Delta}\xi_1(t) + \bar{A}_{11\Delta}\xi_1(t-h(t)) + \bar{A}_{12\Delta}\xi_2(t-h(t))\\ + \bar{E}_{01}\varphi(\eta(t))\end{aligned} \tag{14}$$

$$\begin{aligned}0 = \xi_2(t) + \bar{A}_{21\Delta}\xi_1(t-h(t)) + \bar{A}_{22\Delta}\xi_2(t-h(t))\\ + \bar{E}_{02}\varphi(\eta(t)).\end{aligned} \tag{15}$$

Define

$$\begin{aligned}V(\xi(t)) &= \xi_1^{\mathrm{T}}(t)\bar{P}_{11}^{-1}\xi_1(t) + \int_{t-h(t)}^{t} \xi^{\mathrm{T}}(s)\bar{P}^{-1}\bar{Q} \times \bar{P}^{-\mathrm{T}}\xi(s)\mathrm{d}s\\ &= \xi^{\mathrm{T}}(t)\bar{P}^{-1}\bar{E}\xi(t) + \int_{t-h(t)}^{t} \xi^{\mathrm{T}}(s)\bar{P}^{-1}\bar{Q}\bar{P}^{-\mathrm{T}}\xi(s)\mathrm{d}s\end{aligned} \tag{16}$$

Then, the time-derivative of $V(\xi(t))$ along the solution of (13) is given by

$$\begin{aligned}\dot{V}(\xi(t)) &= \xi^{\mathrm{T}}(t)\bar{P}^{-1}\bar{E}\dot{\xi}(t) + \dot{\xi}^{\mathrm{T}}(t)\bar{P}^{-1}\bar{E}\xi(t)\\ &\quad + \xi^{\mathrm{T}}(t)\bar{P}^{-1}\bar{Q}\bar{P}^{-\mathrm{T}}\xi(t) - (1-\dot{h}(t))\\ &\quad \times \xi^{\mathrm{T}}(t-h(t))\bar{P}^{-1}\bar{Q}\bar{P}^{-\mathrm{T}}\xi(t-h(t))\\ &\leqslant 2\xi^{\mathrm{T}}(t)\bar{P}^{-1}[\bar{A}_{0\Delta}\xi(t) + \bar{A}_{1\Delta}\xi(t-h(t))\\ &\quad + \bar{E}_0\varphi(\eta(t))] + \xi^{\mathrm{T}}(t)\bar{P}^{-1}\bar{Q}\bar{P}^{-\mathrm{T}}\xi(t)\\ &\quad - (1-d)\xi^{\mathrm{T}}(t-h(t))\bar{P}^{-1}\bar{Q}\bar{P}^{-\mathrm{T}}\xi(t-h(t))\end{aligned} \tag{17}$$

Note that the nonlinear terms described in (5), which are equivalent to the following expression,

$$\varphi_j(\sigma)(\varphi_j(\sigma) - k_jCx(t)) \leqslant 0.$$

It implies that

$$\|\varphi_j(\sigma)\|^2 \leqslant \|k_jCx(t)\|$$

Therefore

$$\varphi^{\mathrm{T}}\varphi \leqslant \xi^{\mathrm{T}}(t)\bar{C}^{\mathrm{T}}\bar{K}^{\mathrm{T}}\bar{K}\bar{C}\xi(t) \tag{18}$$

According to Lemma 2.1 and (18), we can deduce that there exists a postive scalar ε such that

$$\begin{aligned}2\xi^{\mathrm{T}}(t)\bar{P}^{-1}\bar{E}_0\varphi(\eta(t)) \leqslant \varepsilon\xi^{\mathrm{T}}(t)\bar{P}^{-1}\bar{E}_0\bar{E}_0^{\mathrm{T}}\bar{P}^{-\mathrm{T}}\xi(t)\\ + \varepsilon^{-1}\xi^{\mathrm{T}}(t)\bar{C}^{\mathrm{T}}\bar{K}^{\mathrm{T}}\bar{K}\bar{C}\xi(t)\end{aligned}$$

Therefore, considering (17), it follows in terms of the above analysis

$$\dot{V}(\xi(t)) \leqslant \tilde{\xi}^{\mathrm{T}}(t)\bar{P}^{-1}\bar{M}_{1\Delta}\bar{P}^{-\mathrm{T}}\tilde{\xi}(t) \tag{19}$$

where $\tilde{\xi}(t) = [\xi^{\mathrm{T}}(t)\ \xi^{\mathrm{T}}(t-h(t))]$, and

$$\bar{M}_{1\Delta} = \begin{bmatrix} \bar{A}_{0\Delta}\bar{P}^{\mathrm{T}} + \bar{P}\bar{A}_{0\Delta}^{\mathrm{T}} + \bar{Q} + \varepsilon\bar{E}_0\bar{E}_0^{\mathrm{T}} \\ + \varepsilon^{-1}\bar{P}\bar{C}^{\mathrm{T}}\bar{K}^{\mathrm{T}}\bar{K}\bar{C}\bar{P}^{\mathrm{T}} & \bar{A}_{1\Delta}\bar{P}^{\mathrm{T}} \\ * & -(1-d)\bar{Q} \end{bmatrix}$$

Considering the uncertain expressions (2) and (3), the matrix $\bar{M}_{1\Delta}$ can be rewritten as

$$\bar{M}_{1\Delta} = \bar{M}_1 + \Omega_1 F(x,t)\Omega_2 + (\Omega_1 F(x,t)\Omega_2)^{\mathrm{T}} \tag{20}$$

where the matrix $\bar{M}_1$ is the matrix $\bar{M}_{1\Delta}$ which not contain uncertain matrices $\Delta\bar{A}_0(\bullet)$ and $\Delta\bar{A}_0(\bullet)$, and

$$\Omega_1^{\mathrm{T}} = \begin{bmatrix}\bar{G}_1^{\mathrm{T}} & 0\end{bmatrix}, \qquad \Omega_2 = \begin{bmatrix}\bar{H}_1\bar{P}^{\mathrm{T}} & \bar{H}_2\bar{P}^{\mathrm{T}}\end{bmatrix}$$

On the other hand, by using Schur complement argument, it follows from (11b) that

$$\bar{M}_1 + \theta\Omega_1\Omega_1^{\mathrm{T}} + \theta^{-1}\Omega_2^{\mathrm{T}}\Omega_1 < 0 \tag{21}$$

According to Lemma 2.2, (20) and (21), it can be deduced that

$$\bar{M}_{1\Delta} = \bar{M}_1 + \theta\Omega_1\Omega_1^{\mathrm{T}} + \theta^{-1}\Omega_2^{\mathrm{T}}\Omega_1 < 0 \tag{22}$$

Substituting (22) into (19), for all $\xi(t) \neq 0$, one eventually gets (23) shown as follows,

$$\dot{V}(\xi(t)) \leqslant -\lambda_{\bar{M}}\|\tilde{\xi}(t)\|^2 \leqslant -\lambda_{\bar{M}}\|\xi(t)\|^2 \tag{23}$$

where $\lambda_{\bar{M}} = -\lambda_{max}[\bar{P}^{-1}(\bar{M}_1 + \theta\Omega_1\Omega_1^{\mathrm{T}} + \theta^{-1}\Omega_2^{\mathrm{T}}\Omega_1)\bar{P}^{-\mathrm{T}}]$.

Then we obtain for a scalar $\beta > 0$,

$$\begin{aligned}\frac{\mathrm{d}e^{\beta t}V(\xi(t))}{\mathrm{d}t} &= e^{\beta t}[\beta V(\xi(t)) + \dot{V}(\xi(T))] \\ &\leqslant e^{\beta t}(\bar{\lambda}_1\beta - \lambda_{\bar{M}})\|\xi(t)\|^2 \\ &\quad + \bar{\lambda}_2\beta e^{\beta t}\int_{t-h(t)}^{t}\|\xi(s)\|^2\mathrm{d}s\end{aligned} \tag{24}$$

where $\bar{\lambda}_1 = \lambda_{max}(\bar{P}^{-1}\bar{E})$, $\bar{\lambda}_2 = \lambda_{max}(\bar{P}^{-1}\bar{Q}\bar{P}^{-\mathrm{T}})$.

Since L_1 and L_2 are orthogonal matrix, it implies from (7) that $\beta > 0$ is the unique root to the equation

$$\beta(\bar{\lambda}_1 + \bar{\lambda}_2 h e^{\beta h}) = \lambda_{\bar{M}}$$

Integrating both sides of (24) from 0 to t and then taking into account the following inequality [12]

$$\int_0^t e^{\beta t}\left(\int_{t-h(t)}^{t}\|\xi(s)\|^2\mathrm{d}s\right)\mathrm{d}t \leqslant h e^{\beta h}\int_0^t e^{\beta s}\|\xi(s)\|^2\mathrm{d}s$$

yield

$$V(\xi(t)) \leqslant e^{-\beta t}V(\bar{\phi}(t)) \tag{25}$$

where $\bar{\phi}(t) = L_2^{-1}\phi(t)$. Furthermore, it is straightforward to see from (16) that

$$V(\xi(t)) \geqslant \lambda_{min}(\bar{P}_{11}^{-1})\|\xi_1(t)\|^2 \tag{26}$$

Therefore, from (25) and (26) we have

$$\|\xi_1(t)\|^2 \leqslant \frac{e^{-\beta t}}{\lambda_{min}(\bar{P}_{11})} V(\bar{\phi}(t)) \tag{27}$$

which implies that

$$\lim_{t\to\infty} \sup(\log \|\xi_1(t)\|^2) \leqslant -\beta < 0 \tag{28}$$

Now, together with (16) and (23), implies that

$$\lambda_{min}(\bar{P}_{11}^{-1})\|\xi_1(t)\|^2 - V(\bar{\phi}(t)) \leqslant \int_0^t \dot{V}(\xi(s))\mathrm{d}s \leqslant -\lambda_{\bar{M}} \int_0^t \|\xi(s)\|^2 \mathrm{d}s \tag{29}$$

It follows this inequality that

$$\int_0^t \|\xi_1(s)\|^2 \mathrm{d}s \quad \text{or} \quad \int_0^t \|\xi_2(s)\|^2 \mathrm{d}s \leqslant \frac{1}{\lambda_{\bar{M}}} V(\bar{\phi}(t)) \tag{30}$$

According to (18), we have

$$\int_0^t \|\bar{E}_{02}\varphi(\eta(t))\|\mathrm{d}t \leqslant \int_0^t \sqrt{\lambda_3}(\|\xi_1(t)\| + \|\xi_2(t)\|)\mathrm{d}t \tag{31}$$

where $\lambda_3 = \lambda_{max}[\bar{C}^{\mathrm{T}}\bar{K}^{\mathrm{T}}\bar{E}_{02}^{\mathrm{T}}\bar{E}_{02}\bar{K}\bar{C}]$.

Noting (5) and using the Barbalat's Lemma, we obtain by (30) and (31)

$$\lim_{t\to\infty} \bar{E}_{02}\varphi(\eta(t)) = 0 \tag{32}$$

This, together with (12), (15), (28) and (32), implies that

$$\lim_{t\to\infty} \sup(\log \|\xi_2(t)\|^2 \leqslant -\beta < 0 \tag{33}$$

Thus, the system (8) is exponentially stable. This completes the proof. □

Remark 3.1 *Theorem 3.1 provides a sufficient condition for the uncertain Lur'e singular delay system* (1) *to be regular, impulse free and exponentially stable. when* $E = I$, *the uncertain Lur'e singular delay system* (1) *reduces to a state-space uncertain Lur'e delay system and it is easy to show that Theorem 3.1 coincides with Theorem 1 (see [13]). Therefore, Theorem 3.1 can be viewed as extension of existing results on state-space uncertain Lur'e delay system to uncertain Lur'e singular delay system.*

Now, we are in a position to present the solution to the robust stabilization problem for uncertain Lur'e singular delay system (1).

Theorem 3.1 gives the condition of generalized robust quadratical stability for the uncertain Lur'e singular delay system (1) with $u(t) = 0$, when there exists a linear state feedback law $u(t) = \Lambda x(t), \Lambda \in \mathbb{R}^{m\times n}$, the resultant closed-loop system can be described as follows,

$$\begin{aligned} E\dot{x}(t) &= (A_{0K} + \Delta A_{0K}(\bullet))x(t) + (A_1 + \Delta A_1(\bullet)) \\ &\quad \times x(t-h(t)) + E_0\varphi(\sigma(t)) \\ \sigma(t) &= Cx(t), x(t) = \phi(t), t \in [-max(h(t)), 0] \end{aligned} \tag{34}$$

where $A_{0K} = A_0 + B_0\Lambda$, $\Delta A_{0K} = \Delta A_0 + \Delta B_0\Lambda$. According to Theorem 3.1 and Definition 2.4, the generalized robust exponential stabilizability result can be easily derived shown as follows,

Corollary 3.1 *For the initial condition $x(t) = \phi(t)$, the uncertain Lur'e singular delay system (1) with $u(t) = \Lambda x(t)$ is said to be generalized robustly exponentially stabilizable, if there exists a matrix P, a positive definite matrix Q, and scalars $\varepsilon > 0, \theta > 0$ such that the matrix inequalities (6) and the equation (7) hold, where $M_{11} = A_{0K}P^{\mathrm{T}} + PA_{0K}^{\mathrm{T}} + Q$, and $H_1 + H_3\Lambda$ instead of H_1.*

Remark 3.2 *Though Corollary 3.1 provides the sufficient conditions of generalized robust exponential stabilizability based on matrix inequality and exponential equation, the linear state feedback control law can not be solved based on linear matrix inequality technology due to the fact that some terms of the matrix inequality (6b) is nonlinear, such as $(A_0 + B_0\Lambda)P^{\mathrm{T}}$ and $(H_1 + H_3\Lambda)P^{\mathrm{T}}$ with two unknown variables.*

In view of this, next problem consists in how to eliminate nonlinear terms in the matrix inequality (6b) such that the linear state feedback control law can be solved based on Matlab/LMI Toolbox.

From the proof of Theorem 3.1, there exists two orthogonal matrices L_1 and $L_2 \in \mathbb{R}^{n\times n}$ such that

$$\bar{P} = L_1 P L_2^{-\mathrm{T}} = \begin{bmatrix} \bar{P}_{11} & \bar{P}_{12} \\ 0 & \bar{P}_{22} \end{bmatrix} \tag{35}$$

where $\bar{P}_{11} = \bar{P}_{11}^{\mathrm{T}} > 0$, $\bar{P}_{12} \in \mathbb{R}^{r\times(n-r)}$ and $\bar{P}_{22} \in \mathbb{R}^{(n-r)\times(n-r)}$.

On the other hand, from rank $E = r \leqslant n$, it can be shown that there exists a matrix $\Phi \in \mathbb{R}^{n\times n-r}$ such that $E\Phi = 0$, and rank $\Phi = n - r$, then, we can derive that there exists an invertible matrix $\Gamma \in \mathbb{R}^{(n-r)\times(n-r)}$ such that

$$\Phi = L_2^{-1} \begin{bmatrix} 0 \\ I_{n-r} \end{bmatrix} \Gamma \tag{36}$$

Hence

$$\begin{aligned} P &= L_1 \begin{bmatrix} \bar{P}_{11} & \bar{P}_{12} \\ 0 & \bar{P}_{22} \end{bmatrix} L_2^{-\mathrm{T}} \\ &= (L_1 \begin{bmatrix} I_r & 0 \\ 0 & 0 \end{bmatrix} L_2^{-\mathrm{T}})(L_2^{\mathrm{T}} \begin{bmatrix} \bar{P}_{11} & 0 \\ 0 & I_{n-r} \end{bmatrix} L_2^{-\mathrm{T}}) \\ &\quad + (L_1 \begin{bmatrix} \bar{P}_{12} \\ \bar{P}_{22} \end{bmatrix} \Gamma^{-\mathrm{T}})(\Gamma^{\mathrm{T}} \begin{bmatrix} 0 & I_{n-r} \end{bmatrix} L_2^{-\mathrm{T}}) \\ &= EX + Y\Phi^{\mathrm{T}} \end{aligned} \tag{37}$$

where $X = L_2^{\mathrm{T}} \begin{bmatrix} \bar{P}_{11} & 0 \\ 0 & I_{n-r} \end{bmatrix} L_2^{-\mathrm{T}} > 0$, $Y = L_1 \begin{bmatrix} \bar{P}_{12} \\ \bar{P}_{22} \end{bmatrix} \Gamma^{-\mathrm{T}}$.

Furthermore, we can obtain from (37)

$$\begin{aligned} EP^{\mathrm{T}} &= E(EX + Y\Phi^{\mathrm{T}})^{\mathrm{T}} = EXE^{\mathrm{T}} \\ &= (EX + Y\Phi^{\mathrm{T}})E^{\mathrm{T}} = PE^{\mathrm{T}} \geqslant 0 \end{aligned} \tag{38}$$

Define

$$\Theta = \Lambda(EX + Y\Phi^{\mathrm{T}})^{\mathrm{T}} \overset{\mathrm{def}}{=} \Lambda\Xi^{\mathrm{T}}$$

Without loss of generality, we can assume that $\Xi = EX + Y\Phi^{\mathrm{T}}$ is invertible, otherwise we can choose a sufficiently small scalar $\varepsilon > 0$ such that $\hat{\Xi} = EX + Y\Phi^{\mathrm{T}} + \varepsilon I$ is invertible.

Finally, by replacing Ξ instead of P into Corollary 3.1, and replacing Θ instead of ΛP^{T} into Corollary 3.1, the desired result follows immediately. The generalized exponential stabilizability result is presented in the following Theorem 3.2.

Theorem 3.2 *For the initial condition $x(t) = \phi(t)$, the uncertain Lur'e singular delay system (1) with $u(t) = \Lambda x(t)$ is said to be generalized robustly exponentially stabilizable, if there exists matrices Y and Θ, a positive definite matrices X and Q, and scalars $\varepsilon > 0$ and $\theta > 0$ such that the following conditions hold,*

$$M_K = \begin{bmatrix} M_{11K} & A_1\Xi^{\mathrm{T}} & E_0 & \Xi C^{\mathrm{T}}K^{\mathrm{T}} & M_{15K} & G_1 \\ * & M_{22K} & 0 & 0 & \Xi H_2^{\mathrm{T}} & 0 \\ * & * & -\varepsilon^{-1}I & 0 & 0 & 0 \\ * & * & * & -\varepsilon I & 0 & 0 \\ * & * & * & * & -\theta I & 0 \\ * & * & * & * & * & -\theta^{-1}I \end{bmatrix} < 0 \tag{39}$$

where $M_{11K} = A_0\Xi^{\mathrm{T}} + \Xi A_0^{\mathrm{T}} + B_0\Theta + \Theta^{\mathrm{T}}B_0^{\mathrm{T}} + Q$, $M_{15K} = \Xi H_1^{\mathrm{T}} + \Theta^{\mathrm{T}}H_3^{\mathrm{T}}$, $M_{22K} = -(1-d)Q$ and $\beta > 0$ is the unique root to the following equation (40),

$$\beta(\lambda_{1K} + \lambda_{2K}he^{\beta h}) = \lambda_{M_K} \tag{40}$$

where $\lambda_{1K} = \lambda_{max}(\Xi^{-1}E)$, $\lambda_{2K} = \lambda_{max}(\Xi^{-1}Q\Xi^{-\mathrm{T}})$, $\lambda_{M_K} = \lambda_{max}(\Xi^{-1}M_K\Xi^{-\mathrm{T}})$. In this case, a robustly stabilizing state feedback control law is given by

$$u(t) = \Theta\Xi^{-\mathrm{T}}x(t) \tag{41}$$

4 Numerical Example

In this section, we give an example to demonstrate the effectiveness of the proposed method.

Consider the uncertain Lur'e singular delay system (1) with parameters as follows,

$$E = \begin{bmatrix} 1 & 1 & 0 \\ 1 & -1 & 1 \\ 2 & 0 & 1 \end{bmatrix} \quad A_0 = \begin{bmatrix} 1.5 & 0.5 & 1 \\ -1 & 0 & 1 \\ 0.5 & 0 & 1 \end{bmatrix} \quad A_1 = \begin{bmatrix} -9 & 0 & 1 \\ 5 & -1 & 0.5 \\ 0.3 & 0.5 & -1 \end{bmatrix} \quad B_0 = \begin{bmatrix} 0.4 & 0.2 \\ 0.5 & 0.2 \\ 0.3 & 0.1 \end{bmatrix}$$

$$E_0 = \begin{bmatrix} 0.4 & 0.1 & 0.1 \\ 0.3 & 0 & 0.2 \\ 0.4 & 0.3 & 0.5 \end{bmatrix} \quad C = \begin{bmatrix} 1 & 0 & 1.2 \\ 0 & 1.5 & 1.3 \\ 1.2 & -0.9 & -0.7 \end{bmatrix} \quad K = \begin{bmatrix} 0.5 & 0 & 0 \\ 0 & 0.7 & 0 \\ 0 & 0 & 0.8 \end{bmatrix} \quad G_1 = \begin{bmatrix} 0.2 \\ -0.2 \\ 0.1 \end{bmatrix}$$

$$H_1 = \begin{bmatrix} 0 & -0.1 & 0.2 \end{bmatrix} \quad H_2 = \begin{bmatrix} 0.1 & 0 & 0.4 \end{bmatrix} \quad H_3 = \begin{bmatrix} 0.1 & 0.2 \end{bmatrix} \quad F(x,t) = \cos\sin t^2$$

The purpose is the design of a state feedback control law such that the resultant closed-loop system is regular, impulse free and exponential stable for all admissible uncertainties. To this end, we choose

$$\Phi = \begin{bmatrix} -1 & 1 & 2 \end{bmatrix}^{\mathrm{T}}$$

According to Remark 3, using Matlab LMI Toolbox to solve the LMI (39) and exponential equation (40), it can be shown that the feasible solution of the LMI (39) and exponential equation (40) is simultaneously existent if the upper bound of delays h and d satisfies $0 \leqslant h \leqslant 0.4976$ and $0 \leqslant d \leqslant 0.8696$, respectively, when $h = 0.1$ and $d = 0.2$, we obtain the corresponding solution shown as follows,

$$X = \begin{bmatrix} 0.7856 & -0.6694 & -1.3387 \\ -0.6694 & 0.5726 & 1.1452 \\ -1.3387 & 1.1452 & 2.2940 \end{bmatrix} \quad Q = \begin{bmatrix} 2.1899 & 2.1306 & 1.0409 \\ 2.1306 & 3.0888 & 2.0216 \\ 1.0409 & 2.0216 & 1.4977 \end{bmatrix}$$

$$\Theta = \begin{bmatrix} 0.4910 & -0.9097 & -1.1580 \\ -2.1749 & 0.7922 & 1.8834 \end{bmatrix} \quad Y = \begin{bmatrix} 0.0770 \\ 1.1585 \\ 2.3169 \end{bmatrix}$$

$$\Xi = \begin{bmatrix} 1.0855 & -0.8905 & -1.7810 \\ 0.0041 & 0.1909 & 0.3818 \\ 0.0082 & 0.3818 & 0.7637 \end{bmatrix} \quad \lambda_{1K} = 4.3631$$

$$\lambda_{2K} = 2.1955 \qquad \lambda_{M_K} = 2.1817$$

From above solutions, we can also illustrate that exponential equation (40) is satisfied when $\beta = 0.2856$, and LMI (39) is also simultaneously stasfied. Therefore, by Theorem 3.2, a robustly stabilizing state feedback control law can be obtained as

$$\Lambda = \begin{bmatrix} -0.0001 & 1.1543 & -0.5772 \\ -0.0012 & 0.5218 & -0.2609 \end{bmatrix}$$

5 Conclusions

The problems of generalized robust exponential stability and generalized robust stabilizability for uncertain Lur'e singular delay systems have been studied. A LMI approach has been developed to design a robustly stabilizing state feedback control law which guarantees the resultant closed-loop system is regular, impulse free and exponentially stable for all admissible uncertainties. An illustrative examples has been provided to show the effectiveness of the proposed approach.

Acknowledgments

This work is supported by the the National Nature Science Foundation of China (NNSFC: 60604003 and 60434020).

References

1. L. Dai, *Singular Control Systems.* Berlin, Germany: Springer-Verlag, 1989.
2. T.-L. Shen, *Basis of robot robust control.* Beijing, China: Tsinghua University Press, 2000.
3. F. L. Lewis, A survey of linear singular systems, *Circuits. Syst. Signal Processing,* vol. 5, pp. 3-36, 1986.
4. S. Xu, P. V. Dooren, R. Stefan and J. Lam, Robust stability and stabilization for singular systems with state delay and parameter uncertainty, *IEEE Trans. Automat. Contr.*, vol. 47, pp. 1122-1128, 2002.
5. J. Feng, S. Zhu and Z. Chen,Guaranteed cost control of linear uncertain singular time-delay systems, *Proc. Conf. Decision and Control,* pp. 1820-1807, 2002.
6. E. K. Boukas and Z. K. Liu, Delay-dependent stability analysis of singular linear continuous-time system, *IEE Proc. Control Theory Appl.*, vol. 150, pp. 325-330. 2003.
7. E. Fridman, A Lyapunov-based approach to stability of descriptor systems with delay, *Proc. Decision and Control,* pp. 2850-2855, 2001.
8. R. Wang and Y. Liu, Asymptotic stability and robustness for discrete-time singular systems with multiple delays, *Proc. World Congress in Intel. Contr. and Auto.*, pp. 1227-1232, 2000.
9. S. Xu, J. Lam, L. Zhang, Robust *D*-stability analysis for uncertain discrete singular systems with state delay, *IEEE Trans. Automat. Contr.*, vol. 49, pp. 551-555, 2004.
10. S. Boyd, L. Ei Ghaoui, E. feron and V. Balakrishnan, *Linear Matrix Inequalities in Systems and Control Theory* . Philadelphia, PA:SIAM, 1994.
11. M. Krstic and H. Deng, *Stabilization of Nonlinear Uncertain System.* London, U. K.: Springer-Verlag,1998.
12. X. Mao, Exponential stability of stochastic delay interval systems with Markovian switching, *IEEE Trans. Automat. Contr.*, vol. 47, pp. 1604-1612, 2002.
13. R.-Q. Lu, H.-Y. Su and J. Chu, Robust stabilization for a class of uncertain singular systems with time-delays and saturating controls, *American Control Conference, Boston, Massachusetts USA*, pp.4986-4991, 2004.

Part II

Control of Mechanical and Electrical Systems

Blended Lateral Jet and Aerodynamic Control

Kemao Ma and Yu Yao

Control and Simulation Center, Harbin Institute of Technology, Harbin 150080, China
makemao@hit.edu.cn, yaoyu@hit.edu.cn

1 Introduction

In modern interception engagement, targets of point defense are characterized by a higher speed and increased escape maneuverability. For such targets, higher guidance and control precision is needed for a successful interception with structural destruction, up to hit-to-kill. High guidance and control precision can only be obtained by a missile with enough maneuverability and agility, i.e., the missile can provide lateral overload (roughly speaking, the overload is the ratio of acceleration and gravitation acceleration) large enough in time. In the endgame phase of terminal guidance, the time-to-go is short (about 1.0 sec to 1.5 sec), and the missile needs to establish swift and large lateral overload to compensate the expected miss distance caused by target escape maneuver, which is realizable only with a very short guidance time constant. The response of conventional aerodynamic overload is dissatisfactory compared with the required short guidance time constant. A possible mechanism to improve overload response is the lateral (or side) jet control, which can shorten the overload response by about one order of magnitude.

The conventional aerodynamic overload is generated as follows. The aerodynamic operating surfaces are driven by motors to change certain angles, which makes the attitude of the missile to change. Since the attitude change is faster than the change of the direction of missile velocity, the angle of attack or the sideslip angle of the missile changes. The change of angle of attack or the sideslip angle results in the change of the lateral aerodynamic overload of the missile, which changes the direction of the missile velocity. Thus, the trajectory control of missile is realized. While missiles equipped with lateral jet mechanism can provide blended control consisting of lateral jet control and aerodynamic control. The aerodynamic control is conventionally realized by movable aerodynamic fins. Lateral pulse jet mechanism consists of a ring of thrusters mounted near the centroid, or away from the centroid of a missile, for trajectory change or attitude change, respectively. For example, there are 180 thrusters in Erint of U.S. PAC-III. Each thruster on the ring can impart a single, short duration, large lateral force, or a lateral torque, usually both constant, to the missile, thus to provide lateral overload directly, or to speed up the establishment of lateral aerodynamic overload. By overload response mechanism, the blended control can be classified into two types, trajectory control and attitude control. In the former control type, the lateral jet thrusters are installed near the centroid, and can impart a large lateral force to the missile to provide lateral overload directly, as shown in Fig. 1.

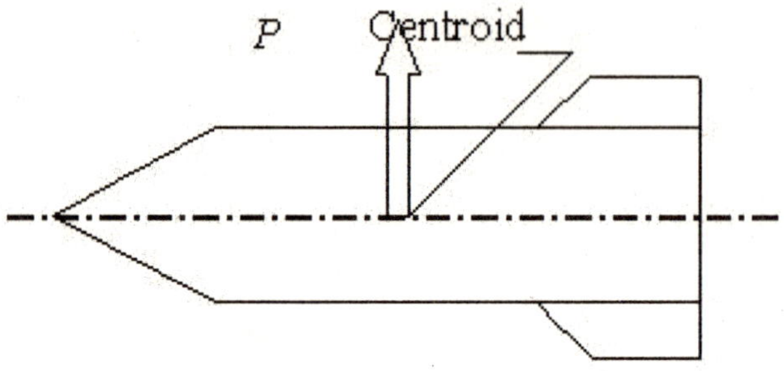

Fig. 1 Trajectory control mode

In the latter type, the lateral jet thrusters are installed away from the centroid, see Fig. 2, and can impart lateral torque to the missile, thus the missile can establish certain attitude through lateral jet mechanism more quickly than through conventional aerodynamic fin control. The quickly established attitude leads to the change of attack angle (or sideslip angle) of the missile, and thus the change of the aerodynamic overload of the missile.

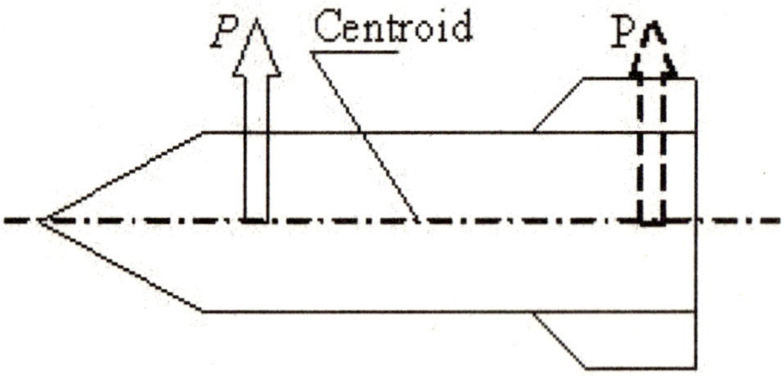

Fig. 2 Attitude control mode

2 Modeling

The modeling of missiles equipped with blended control mechanism is more difficult than that of conventional aerodynamic controlled missiles. The difficulties arise mainly from the so-called lateral jet interaction effects.

The side jet thruster provides lateral force by discharging jet stream, usually supersonic. For a missile with high speed, also supersonic, the supersonic side jet interacts strongly with the coming supersonic stream, thus exerts significant interaction effects on the flow field around the missile, and results in a very complicated flow field. Such effects are called lateral jet interaction effects[1,2]. An illustrative chart of the jet interaction effects is shown in Fig. 3.

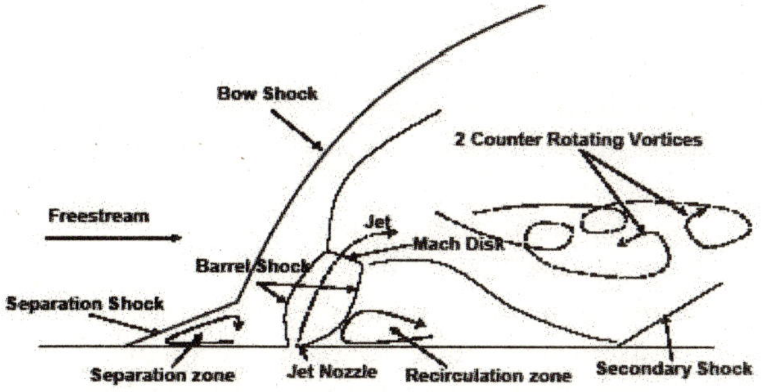

Fig. 3 Side jet interaction flow field

From Fig. 3, we can see that before the jet stream, there is a separation zone, while behind the jet stream, there is a recirculation zone. In the interaction flow field, there are many shocks, including separation shock before the separation zone, barrel shocks around the jet stream, bow shocks before the jet stream, and secondary shock behind the recirculation zone. Besides, there are also Mach disks and rotating vortices. The interaction flow field results in a high pressure zone, and a low pressure zone, before and behind the net nozzle, respectively. For trajectory controlled lateral jet thrusters, the two zones provide an additional rotating torque with respect to the centroid of the missile, since the thrusters are equipped near the centroid of the missile. The lateral jet provides lateral control force or control torque to the missile. In the construction of a mathematical model for control synthesis, the interaction effects are usually described with jet magnification factors of control force and control torque. Generally, the magnification factors are formulated as follows

$$K = 1 + \frac{F_i}{F_j} \tag{1}$$

$$F_i = F_{jeton} - F_{jetoff} \tag{2}$$

$$F_i + F_j = KF_j = F_j + \Delta F_j \tag{3}$$

where F_i is the jet-caused interfering force, F_j is jet force without coming free stream, F_{jeton} and F_{jetoff} are aerodynamic forces in jet direction with the jet thruster on, and off, respectively. A magnification factor changes with such parameters as Mach number of coming free stream (M_∞), Mach number of jet stream (M_j), angle of attack of the missile(α),or sideslip angle(β). Other conditions, such as location and configuration of jet nozzles, also have certain effects on the magnification factor.

The thrust magnification factor in trajectory control mode, and the torque magnification factor in attitude control mode, can give the lateral control force and control torque in the respective control mode, as shown in equations (2)(3).The characteristic of side jet changes along with the change of aerodynamic conditions. It is also worth noting that the magnification factors are estimated through theoretical analysis and experimental data, thus significant differences exist between the approximation and the real effects. Furthermore, in trajectory control mode, the additional torque caused by side jet interaction effects exerts turning effects on attitude of the missile. And in attitude control mode, the lateral force away from the centroid of the missile exerts motion effects on the centroid of the missile. Thus the constructed model contains many uncertainties. The model simplification for control law design also introduces uncertainties in the final constructed model.

Generally, the model of a missile can be divided into two parts, the translational motion and rotation motion, which, roughly speaking, are used to design guidance law and attitude control law, respectively. For blended control system, in attitude control mode, the general kinetic equations of translational motion are as follows

$$\begin{aligned} m\dot{V} =& P\cos\alpha\cos\beta - X - mg\sin\theta - (F_{jy} + \Delta F_{jy})\sin\alpha\cos\beta \\ &+ (F_{jz} + \Delta F_{jz})\sin\beta \end{aligned} \tag{4}$$

$$\begin{aligned} mV\dot{\theta} =& P(\sin\alpha\cos\gamma_V + \cos\alpha\sin\beta\sin\gamma_V) + Y\cos\gamma_V - Z\sin\gamma_V \\ &- mg\cos\theta + (F_{jy} + \Delta F_{jy})(\cos\alpha\cos\gamma_V - \sin\alpha\sin\beta\sin\gamma_V) \\ &- (F_{jz} + \delta F_{jz})\cos\beta\sin\gamma_V \end{aligned} \tag{5}$$

$$\begin{aligned} -mV\cos\theta\dot{\psi}_c =& P(\sin\alpha\sin\gamma_V - \cos\alpha\sin\beta\cos\gamma_V) + Y\sin\gamma_V + Z\cos\gamma_V \\ &+ (F_{jy} + \Delta F_{jy})(\cos\alpha\sin\gamma_V + \sin\alpha\sin\beta\cos\gamma_V) \\ &+ (F_{jz} + \Delta F_{jz})\cos\beta\cos\gamma_V \end{aligned} \tag{6}$$

where, and throughout this section, the notations are common used in aeronautics, and about their meaning, readers are refered to [3]. The equations of rotational motion, i.e. attitude motion, are as follows

$$\begin{aligned} J_x\dot{\omega}_x =& M_{x0} + M_x^{\beta}\beta + M_x^{\delta_x}\delta_x + M_x^{\delta_y}\delta_y \\ &+ M_x^{\omega_x}\omega_x + M_x^{\omega_y}\omega_y \end{aligned} \tag{7}$$

$$\begin{aligned} J_y\dot{\omega}_y + (J_x - J_z)\omega_x\omega_z =& M_y^{\beta}\beta + M_y^{\delta_y}\delta_y + M_y^{\omega_y}\omega_y + M_x^{\dot{\beta}}\dot{\beta} \\ &+ M_y^{\dot{\delta}_y}\dot{\delta}_y + (F_{jz}l_m + \Delta M_{jy}) \end{aligned} \tag{8}$$

$$\begin{aligned} J_z\dot{\omega}_z + (J_y - J_x)\omega_x\omega_y =& M_{z0} + M_z^{\alpha}\alpha + M_z^{\delta_z}\delta_z + M_z^{\omega_z}\omega_z + M_z^{\dot{\alpha}}\dot{\alpha} \\ &+ M_z^{\dot{\delta}_z}\dot{\delta}_z + (F_{jy}l_m + \Delta M_{jz}) \end{aligned} \tag{9}$$

$$\dot{\gamma} = \omega_{1x} - (\omega_{1y}\cos\gamma - \omega_{1z}\sin\gamma)\tan\vartheta \tag{10}$$

$$\dot{\varphi} = \frac{1}{\cos\vartheta}(\omega_{1y}\cos\gamma - \omega_{1z}\sin\gamma) \tag{11}$$

$$\dot{\vartheta} = \omega_{1y}\sin\gamma + \omega_{1z}\cos\gamma \tag{12}$$

For simplicity and without loss of generality, the models are simplified in short period mode in longitudinal plane as follows

$$\begin{bmatrix} \dot{\omega_z} \\ \dot{\alpha} \\ \dot{\vartheta} \end{bmatrix} = \begin{bmatrix} \frac{M_z^{\alpha}\alpha}{J_z} + \frac{M_z^{\omega_z}\omega_z}{J_z} + \frac{M_z^{\dot{\alpha}}\dot{\alpha}}{J_z} \\ \omega_z - \frac{P\sin\alpha}{mV} \\ \omega_z \end{bmatrix} + \begin{bmatrix} \frac{M_z^{\delta_z}}{J_z} & \frac{l_m}{J_z} \\ 0 & -\frac{\cos\alpha}{mV} \\ 0 & 0 \end{bmatrix} \begin{bmatrix} \delta_z \\ F_{jy} \end{bmatrix}$$

$$+ \begin{bmatrix} \frac{M_{z0}}{J_z} + \frac{\Delta M_{jz}}{J_z} + \frac{M_z^{\delta_z} \dot{delta}_z}{J_z} \\ -\frac{Y + \Delta J_{jy}\cos\alpha}{mV} \\ 0 \end{bmatrix} \tag{13}$$

$$y = \frac{V}{g}\dot{\theta} + \cos\theta \tag{14}$$

where y, the output of the system, is the lateral overload.

Similarly, the short period mode dynamic equations in longitudinal plane of a missile in trajectory mode are as follows

$$\begin{bmatrix} \dot{\vartheta} \\ \dot{\omega_z} \\ \dot{\alpha} \end{bmatrix} = \begin{bmatrix} \omega_z \\ \frac{M_z^{\alpha}\alpha}{J_z}\alpha + \frac{M_z^{\omega_z}}{J_z}\omega_z \\ \omega_z - \frac{P\sin\alpha}{mV} + \frac{c_y^{\alpha}\alpha q s}{mV} - \frac{g\cos(\vartheta-\alpha)}{V} \end{bmatrix} + \begin{bmatrix} 0 & 0 \\ 0 & \frac{M_z^{\delta_z}}{J_z} \\ \frac{\cos\alpha}{mV} & \frac{c_y^{\delta}qs}{mV} \end{bmatrix} \begin{bmatrix} u_1 \\ u_2 \end{bmatrix}$$

$$+ \begin{bmatrix} 0 \\ \frac{M_{z0}}{J_z} + \frac{\Delta u_1\cos\alpha}{mV} + \frac{\Delta u_1 L_T}{J_z} + \frac{M_{gz}}{J_z} \\ \frac{F_{gy}}{mV} + \frac{\Delta u_1\cos\alpha}{mV} \end{bmatrix} \tag{15}$$

$$y = \frac{V}{g}\left(\frac{u_1\cos\alpha}{mV} + \frac{c_y^{\delta}u_2\alpha q s}{mV}\right) + \frac{P\sin\alpha}{mV} \tag{16}$$

$$+ \frac{c_y^{\alpha}\alpha q s}{mV} - \frac{g\cos(\vartheta-\alpha)}{V} + \frac{F_{gy}}{mV} \tag{17}$$

The relative motion model in longitudinal plane between a missile and its target is as follows

$$\ddot{\rho} = \rho\dot{\lambda}^2 - a_{M1} \tag{18}$$

$$\ddot{\lambda} = -\frac{2\dot{\rho}\dot{\lambda}}{\rho} - \frac{a_{MZ}}{\rho} + \frac{a_{TZ}}{\rho} \tag{19}$$

where ρ is the relative range between the missile and the target, λ is the line-of-sight(LOS) angle in longitudinal plane, a_{TZ} is the lateral acceleration of the target, and a_{MZ} and a_{M1} are the lateral and axial accelerations of the missile, respectively.

3 Essential Control Problems and Main Control Methods

For a blended control system, a key research is the study of side jet interaction effects, which is essential to system modeling and is briefly discussed in the above section. Another key factor involved in modeling is the lateral jet mechanism and its description. When the model of the blended control system is constructed, the design tasks are followed to design suitable control methods to realize rapid response, and endgame guidance law with high precision. Even from the simplified models (13)∼(17)of the blended control system, it is not difficult to find that the blended control problem can be characterized by three aspects: 1) coupling, 2) uncertainties, and 3) nonlinearity, which make the design tasks, together with corresponding simulation validations, highly complicated.

To accomplish the researches, some essential control problems are to be tackled. The first is to design control strategy scheduling multi-control actuators.The actuators in a blended control system are classified into two parts, lateral jet mechanism and aerodynamic control surfaces. They have different characteristics and are to be scheduled to effect in different time durations or under different flying conditions.

The second problem is multi-variable nonlinear control with strong coupling. The coupling mainly arises from two aspects, the coupling between different kinds of actuators, and the strong coupling between control channels when the missile flies with a large angle of attack (or sideslip angle). And the latter coupling also results in the increase of nonlinearity.

The third problem is high precision guidance and control law design. This is the step leading to the purpose of the adoption of blended control mechanism.

It is worth noting that there exist the following discrete events in a blended control system: the switching on and off of lateral jet thrusters; switching from conventional aerodynamic control to blended control; significant differences between flow fields with and without side jet streams. So the description of a blended control system can be formulated in a hybrid system architecture. Different to traditional two-layer hybrid system architecture, here we adopt hierarchical model architecture with two layers to describe a blended control system. The first layer, the decision layer, is used to accommodate control strategy of multiple actuators and the guidance law, while the control layer is used for nonlinear robust control to cope with uncertainties and strong coupling. Based on the hybrid model, performance optimization of guidance and control system can be considered.

In a hybrid control system architecture, blended control strategy can be described by a single-state discrete event input-output automation

$$H = < U, E, D, T >$$

where U is the discrete state set of decision-maker used to describe the state of lateral jet thrusters; E is the discrete event sets, which consist of output event set used to describe on and off of lateral jet thrusters, switching between lateral jet control and aerodynamic control, and input event set used to describe time-to-go, relative range, pulse duration of lateral jet thrust; D is decision algorithm including guidance law, control switch; T is decision-maker state transition function used to describe pulse duration limitation of lateral jet thrusters.

4 Remarks on Future Research

It is easy to understand that an effective way to improve the research is to improve the depiction of side jet interaction effects. But it is very difficult, since the study of side jet interaction effects involve not only theoretical analysis and computation, but, more importantly, also real wind tunnel experiments and tests, which is difficult both in technology and in finance.

In control design, due to the nonlinearity and uncertainties in blended control system, nonlinear robust control law must be employed. Also, coupling must be considered.

Most importantly, for guidance and control design, traditional decoupled principle cannot provide effective design, an integrated guidance and control design can be employed to give an optimized performance. Traditional guidance and control design are usually conducted in a decoupled architecture, as shown in Fig. 4[4], where the guidance loop consists of such parts as target sensing, guidance filter, guidance law, autopilot and airframe/propulsion. Each part can be designed, separately, using different theory, as Kalman filter theory in guidance filter part, optimal control theory in guidance law part, and servomechanism theory in autopilot part.

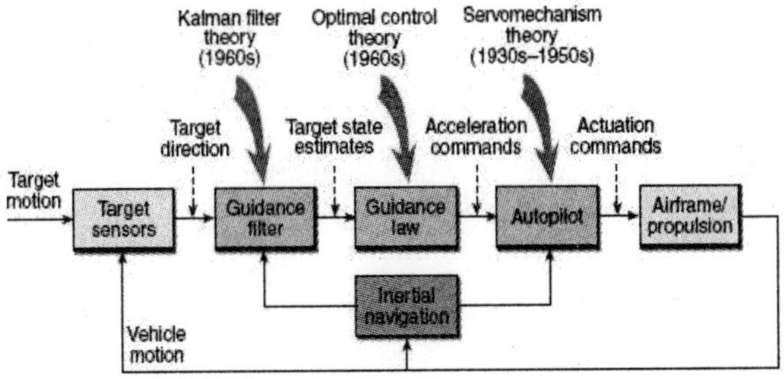

Fig. 4 Traditional architecture of guidance and control design

If the designed guidance loop cannot meet the required performance parameters, some parts must be redesigned with stricter performance requirement, which will inevitably introduce certain conservativeness. But in reality, each part in the loop interacts with others to different degrees. But with the increase of precision requirement, the interactions among different parts take more serious impacts to final precision. It is more reasonable to design in an integrated guidance and control design architecture, as shown in Fig. 5[4], where different parts are considered and designed as a whole.

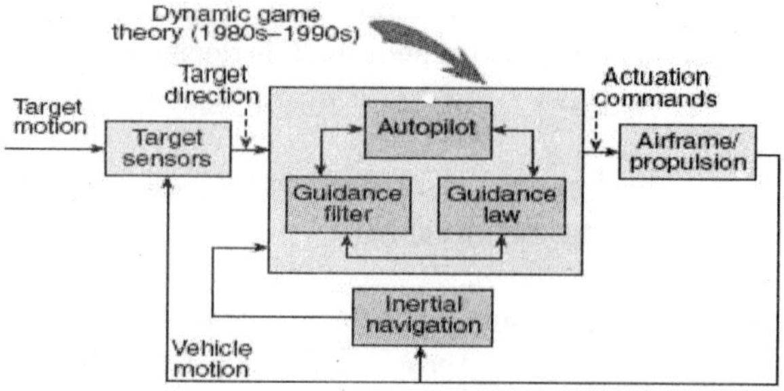

Fig. 5 Integrated architecture of guidance and control design

For a blended control system, the interactions among different parts can be viewed in the following ways. First, the time delay in the guidance information filter becomes crucial to the final miss distance, since the rapid response. Second, rapid response of lateral jet control seriously affects the filtering accuracy. As a result, an integrated guidance and control design should be employed to optimize the final precision.

References

1. Jitpraphal, T.,B. Burchett, and M. Costello. A comparison of different guidance schemes for a direct fire rocket with pulse jet control mechanism. AIAA Atmospheric Flight Mechanics Conference and Exhibit. Montreal, 6-9 August, 2001, Quebec
2. Jeffrey L. P., Christopher J. Roy, and Steven J. Beresh A comparison of turbulence models for a supersonic jet in transonic crossflow. 39th AIAA Aerospace Sciences Meeting and Exhibit. 8-11 January, Reno, 2001, NV Neil
3. Lou Shouchun.Missile guidance technology, Beijing Aerospace Press,1989.
4. Palumbo,N. F., Reardon,B. E. and Blauwkamp.R. A. Integrated guidance and control for homing missiles.JOHNS HOPKINS APL TECHNICAL DIGEST, Vol. 25, No. 2, 2004

Passivity-based Robust Control of Electrically-Driven Bilateral Teleoperation Systems

Chiharu Ishii[1] and Hiroshi Hashimoto[2]

[1] School of Global Engineering, Kogakuin University, 139, Inume-cho, Hachioji-shi, Tokyo 193-0802, Japan
c-ishii@cc.kogakuin.ac.jp
[2] School of Bionics, Tokyo University of Technology, 1404-1, Katakura-cho, Hachioji-shi, Tokyo 192-0982, Japan
hasimoto@cc.teu.ac.jp

1 Introduction

Bilateral teleoperation systems such as master-slave manipulators have been studied for long years (e.g. [1, 2]). They are used for the remote operations, in which the position of the slave manipulator follows the position signal from the master manipulator manipulated by operator, and the back driving force of actuator of the master manipulator tracks the force of the slave manipulator, i.e. the operator can feel as if he manipulates the object by himself. In control design for teleoperation systems, an important issue is to design a controller with high maneuverability. In [3] and [4], bilateral control scheme which achieves the ideal kinesthetic coupling with the operator is proposed, and stability of the control system is proved by the concept of passivity. While, in [5] a robust H_∞ control approach is proposed for the master-slave systems with uncertain objects to obtain robust performance of maneuverability.

In recent years, teleoperation systems are put in practical use in the areas such as a nuclear power plants, space stations, undersea, and robotic surgery. Especially in surgical operation, enhanced trackability and maneuverability are required. In such a background, it is expected that the more excellent maneuverability can be achieved if an electrical property of actuators is taken into consideration in controller design.

Therefore, in this work we focus on the dynamics of electrical motors. In practice, we have proposed a design method of tracking control for electrically-driven robot manipulators taking the dynamics of motors into consideration, and demonstrated that proposed control system has enhanced trackability compared with the conventional control systems through experimental works[6]. To the best of our knowledge, such a control scheme that considers dynamics of the motors in bilateral control design for teleoperation systems has not been proposed. In this work, using a backstepping technique the control law proposed in [4] is extended so as to ensure passivity of the whole system including dynamics of motors under certain assumption. Besides, control law is derived so as to guarantee robust performance of maneuverability in the presence of uncertainty for the objects and the operators. The effectiveness of the proposed control scheme was verified through experimental works.

2 System Description

The dynamics of master-slave manipulator system considered in this work are given by
Master:

$$\begin{cases} K_{Nm}I_m + f_m = m_m\ddot{x}_m + b_m\dot{x}_m + c_m x_m \\ L_m\dot{I}_m + R_m I_m + K_{em}\dot{x}_m = v_m \end{cases} \tag{1}$$

Slave:

$$\begin{cases} K_{Ns}I_s - f_s = m_s\ddot{x}_s + b_s\dot{x}_s + c_s x_s \\ L_s\dot{I}_s + R_s I_s + K_{es}\dot{x}_s = v_s \end{cases} \tag{2}$$

where subscripts m and s denote master and slave respectively, x_m and x_s represent the displacements, m_m and m_s the masses, b_m and b_s the viscous coefficients, and c_m and c_s the spring coefficients of the master and slave arms. f_m stands for the force applied to the master arm by human operator, f_s the force of the slave arm due to the mechanical interaction between slave arm and handling object, I_m and I_s the armature currents, v_m and v_s the armature voltages in each joint actuator, L_m and L_s the actuator inductances, R_m and R_s the actuator resistances, K_{em} and K_{es} the voltage constants of motor back-electromotive forces, and K_{Nm} and K_{Ns} the coefficients that characterizes the electromechanical conversion from electrical current and mechanical torque.

Note that, in general, the lower equations of (1) and (2) are not considered in control design, and in the upper equations of (1) and (2), actuator driving torques τ_m and τ_s are appeared instead of $K_{Nm}I_m$ and $K_{Ns}I_s$.

The dynamics of objects and operators are modeled by the following spring - damper systems with uncertain perturbation.

$$f_s = (b_w + \Delta b_w)\dot{x}_s + (c_w + \Delta c_w)x_s \tag{3}$$

$$\tau_{op} - f_m = (b_{op} + \Delta b_{op})\dot{x}_m + (c_{op} + \Delta c_{op})x_m \tag{4}$$

where τ_{op} is combined force of muscular power of the operator, b_w, c_w, b_{op} and c_{op} denote nominal values of viscous coefficient and stiffness of objects and operators, respectively. Δb_w, Δc_w, Δb_{op} and Δc_{op} denote uncertain perturbation satisfying the following gain bounded conditions

$$\begin{array}{c} |\Delta b_w| \leqslant \sigma_{bw},\ |\Delta c_w| \leqslant \sigma_{cw} \\ |\Delta b_{op}| \leqslant \sigma_{bop},\ |\Delta c_{op}| \leqslant \sigma_{cop} \end{array} \tag{5}$$

where σ_{bw}, σ_{cw}, σ_{bop} and σ_{cop} are known positive constants.

The dynamic models (1) and (2) consist of two cascade loops, respectively. Unlike dynamic model of manipulators assuming the joint torque can be commanded directly, the torque terms $K_{Ni}I_i$ $(i = m, s)$ in the upper equations of (1) and (2) can not be synthesized directly. Instead, they are outputs of the actuator dynamics. In accordance with the backstepping control strategy described in [7], the design procedure is organized as following two steps. First, the armature currents I_i $(i = m, s)$ are regarded as control variables for subsystems, i.e. the upper equations of (1) and (2), and using a bilateral torque control input derived by conventional method, an embedded control inputs $I_{di} = \frac{\tau_i}{K_{Ni}}$ $(i = m, s)$ are set up so that the bilateral control objective may be achieved. Then, voltage level control inputs v_i $(i = m, s)$ are designed such that I_i tracks I_{di}. To this end, we rewrite torque terms $K_{Ni}I_i$ $(i = m, s)$ as follows.

$$K_{Ni}I_i = K_{Ni}I_{di} + K_{Ni}\eta_i \quad (i = m, s) \tag{6}$$

where $\eta_i \stackrel{\text{def}}{=} I_i - I_{di}$ $(i = m, s)$ represent current level perturbation to the manipulator dynamics. The subsystems, the upper equations (1) and (2), can be viewed as rigid model systems with input disturbances $K_{Ni}\eta_i$ $(i = m, s)$, controlled by torque level inputs $K_{Ni}I_{di}$ $(i = m, s)$ (See Fig. 1). Hereafter, the upper equations of (1) and (2) are called manipulator loop and the lower equations of (1) and (2) are called actuator loop.

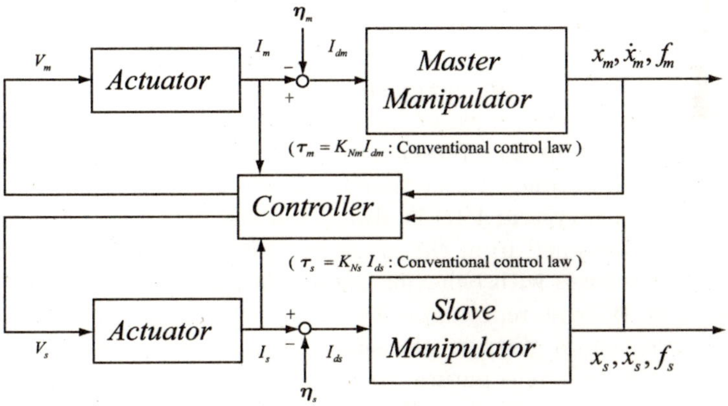

Fig. 1 Block Diagram.

In this work, bilateral control law proposed in [3] in the case of without using an acceleration signal developed for the achievement of ideal kinesthetic coupling with the operator is adopted as conventional torque control inputs τ_i $(i = m, s)$, which are given by

$$\tau_m = \begin{bmatrix} K_{mpm} + K'_{mpm}\frac{\mathrm{d}}{\mathrm{d}t} & K_{mfm} \end{bmatrix} \begin{bmatrix} x_m \\ f_m \end{bmatrix} + \begin{bmatrix} K_{mps} + K'_{mps}\frac{\mathrm{d}}{\mathrm{d}t} & K_{mfs} \end{bmatrix} \begin{bmatrix} x_s \\ f_s \end{bmatrix} \quad (7)$$

$$\tau_s = \begin{bmatrix} K_{spm} + K'_{spm}\frac{\mathrm{d}}{\mathrm{d}t} & K_{sfm} \end{bmatrix} \begin{bmatrix} x_m \\ f_m \end{bmatrix} + \begin{bmatrix} K_{sps} + K'_{sps}\frac{\mathrm{d}}{\mathrm{d}t} & K_{sfs} \end{bmatrix} \begin{bmatrix} x_s \\ f_s \end{bmatrix} \quad (8)$$

where K_{mpm}, K'_{mpm}, K_{mfm}, K_{mps}, K'_{mps} and K_{mfs} are feedback gains of position, velocity and force of the master and slave arms to determine τ_m, respectively. Similarly, K_{spm}, K'_{spm}, K_{sfm}, K_{sps}, K'_{sps} and K_{sfs} are feedback gains of position, velocity and force of the master and slave arms to determine τ_s.

In [3], under the assumption that environments and operators are passive, the stability of the control system is shown from the view point of passivity of the electrical circuit. In this case, velocities $\dot{x}_m$ and $\dot{x}_s$ are regarded as currents and forces f_m and f_s are regarded as voltages.

From the definition of passivity[8], this is interpreted as follows.

"There exists a positive semi-definite function V depending on the state variables such that the following inequality is satisfied,

$$V(t) \leqslant V(0) + \int_0^t \dot{\boldsymbol{x}}^{\mathrm{T}}(\tau)\boldsymbol{f}(\tau)d\tau, \quad \forall t \geqslant 0 \quad (9)$$

where $\boldsymbol{x} = [\ x_m\ x_s\ ]^{\mathrm{T}}$ and $\boldsymbol{f} = [\ f_m\ f_s\ ]^{\mathrm{T}}$. In other words, if $V \in C^1$ then

$$\dot{V} \leqslant \dot{\boldsymbol{x}}^{\mathrm{T}}\boldsymbol{f}, \quad \forall t \geqslant 0 \quad (10)$$

holds. "

In (9), $V(t)$ is called as an energy storage function. If $\dot{\boldsymbol{x}}^{\mathrm{T}}\boldsymbol{f}$ is interpreted as a supply rate of the energy injected into a system from the exterior with input signal, the second term in (9) represents total of the energy which is injected into the system from initial time 0 to the time t. Therefore, this inequality shows that present energy of the system $V(t)$ is always less than the sum of initial energy $V(0)$ and energy obtained from the exterior. This means that consumption of the energy always arises with behavior of the system.

For Lagrange systems represented by the robot manipulators, normally energy storage function is given as the sum of kinetic energy and potential energy. Based on this fact, it is natural to consider that V includes kinetic energy $\frac{1}{2}\dot{\boldsymbol{x}}^{\mathrm{T}}\mathrm{diag}\{m_m\ m_s\}\dot{\boldsymbol{x}}$. Besides, along the research line of backstepping synthesis in [6], assume the following condition for the derivative of energy storage function of manipulator loop.

Assumption 2.1 *For the manipulator closed-loop subsystem imposed by control inputs* $I_{di} = \tau_i/K_{Ni}$ $(i = m, s)$ *based on (8) and (8), there exists a positive semi-definite function* $V_1 \in C^1$ *depending on the state variables such that the following inequality is satisfied.*

$$\dot{V}_1 \leqslant \dot{\boldsymbol{x}}^{\mathrm{T}}\boldsymbol{f} + \dot{\boldsymbol{x}}^{\mathrm{T}}K_N\boldsymbol{\eta}, \quad \forall t \geqslant 0 \quad (11)$$

where $K_N = \mathrm{diag}\{K_{Nm}\ K_{ms}\}$ *and* $\boldsymbol{\eta} = [\ \eta_m\ \eta_s\ ]^{\mathrm{T}}$.

Note that the second term of right hand-side in (11) is supposed to be generated by time derivative of $\frac{1}{2}\dot{\boldsymbol{x}}^{\mathrm{T}}\mathrm{diag}\{m_m\ m_s\}\dot{\boldsymbol{x}}$ along the trajectory of the manipulator closed-loop subsystem.

On the other hand, operators are not said to be passive in a strict sense because they generate power themselves. Therefore, [3] assumes that operators do not generate such a power τ_{op} that makes the control system unstable. This assumption is important for stability analysis of the closed-loop system. In this work, along this meaning the following condition is assumed for its derivative $\dot{\tau}_{op}$.

Assumption 2.2 $\dot{\tau}_{op} \approx 0$ *holds.*

From the above arguments, the design objective of voltage control inputs v_i $(i = m, s)$ are described as follows.

Design Problem Under the Assumptions 2.1 and Assumption 2.2, find a voltage level state feedback control law such that the closed-loop system of the whole system satisfies the following design specification. There exists a positive semi-definite function $V_2 \in C^1$ depending on the state variables such that the following inequality is satisfied,

$$V_2(t) \leqslant V_2(0) + \int_0^t \dot{\boldsymbol{x}}^{\mathrm{T}}(\tau)\boldsymbol{f}(\tau)d\tau + \varepsilon_0, \quad \forall t \geqslant 0 \tag{12}$$

where ε_0 is a sufficiently small positive constant.

3 Derivation of the Control Law

Along the same line in [6], in order to design voltage control inputs v_i $(i = m, s)$ to regulate current errors η_i $(i = m, s)$ to 0 using backstepping technique, it is required to calculate the derivative of I_{di} $(i = m, s)$. From $I_{di} = \tau_i / K_{Ni}$ $(i = m, s)$, (8) and (8), calculation of $\dot{I}_{di}$ requires the measurement of the acceleration $\ddot{x}_i$ and derivative of the force $\dot{f}_i$. In order to avoid the intensive computation of $\dot{I}_{di}$, consider to use bounds of $\dot{I}_{di}$, rather than $\dot{I}_{di}$ itself. Bounding functions $\rho_{Idi}(\cdot)$ such that

$$|\dot{I}_{di}| \leqslant \rho_{Idi}(\cdot) \quad i = m, s \tag{13}$$

holds are determined as follows.

The acceleration term $\ddot{x}_i$ in $\dot{I}_{di}$ is evaluated from the dynamics of master-slave manipulators appeared in the upper equations of (1) and (2), and the force derivative term $\dot{f}_i$ is evaluated from the time derivative of (3) and (4) representing the dynamics of objects and operators, respectively. Substituting these computations to $\dot{I}_{di}$, the following equation is obtained,

$$
\begin{aligned}
\dot{I}_{di} &= \frac{1}{K_{Ni}}\left\{K_{ipm}\dot{x}_m + K'_{ipm}\ddot{x}_m + K_{ifm}\dot{f}_m + K_{ips}\dot{x}_s + K'_{ips}\ddot{x}_s + K_{ifs}\dot{f}_s\right\}\\
&= \frac{1}{K_{Ni}}\left[\left\{K_{ipm} - \frac{K'_{ipm}}{m_m}b_m - K_{ifm}(c_{op}+\Delta c_{op}) + \frac{K_{ifm}}{m_m}(b_{op}+\Delta b_{op})b_m\right\}\dot{x}_m\right.\\
&\quad + \left\{-\frac{K'_{ipm}}{m_m}c_m + \frac{K_{ifm}}{m_m}(b_{op}+\Delta b_{op})c_m\right\}x_m\\
&\quad + \left\{\frac{K'_{ipm}}{m_m} - \frac{K_{ifm}}{m_m}(b_{op}+\Delta b_{op})\right\}f_m\\
&\quad + \left\{\frac{K'_{ipm}}{m_m}K_{Nm} - \frac{K_{ifm}}{m_m}(b_{op}+\Delta b_{op})K_{Nm}\right\}I_m\\
&\quad + \left\{K_{ips} - \frac{K'_{ips}}{m_s}b_s + K_{ifs}(c_w+\Delta c_w) - \frac{K_{ifs}}{m_s}(b_w+\Delta b_w)b_s\right\}\dot{x}_s\\
&\quad + \left\{-\frac{K'_{ips}}{m_s}c_s - \frac{K_{ifs}}{m_s}(b_w+\Delta b_w)c_s\right\}x_s\\
&\quad + \left\{-\frac{K'_{ips}}{m_s} - \frac{K_{ifs}}{m_s}(b_w+\Delta b_w)\right\}f_s\\
&\quad \left. + \left\{\frac{K'_{ips}}{m_s}K_{Ns} + \frac{K_{ifs}}{m_s}(b_w+\Delta b_w)K_{Ns}\right\}I_s + K_{ifm}\dot{\tau}_{op}\right] \qquad i = m, s \qquad (14)
\end{aligned}
$$

Observing the above equations, determine bounding functions by

$$
\begin{aligned}
&\rho_{Idi}(\dot{x}_m, x_m, f_m, I_m, \dot{x}_s, x_s, f_s, I_s)\\
&= K_{1i}|\dot{x}_m| + K_{2i}|x_m| + K_{3i}|f_m| + K_{4i}|I_m|\\
&\quad + K_{5i}|\dot{x}_s| + K_{6i}|x_s| + K_{7i}|f_s| + K_{8i}|I_s| \qquad i = m, s \qquad (15)
\end{aligned}
$$

From Assumption 2.2, $\dot{\tau}_{op}$ is regarded as 0. Thus, considering the absolute value of (14) with (5), the coefficients $K_{1i} \sim K_{8i}$ $(i = m, s)$ in (15) are estimated as follows.

$$
\begin{cases}
K_{1i} \geqslant \dfrac{1}{K_{Ni}} \left\{ \left| K_{ipm} - \dfrac{K'_{ipm}}{m_m} b_m - K_{ifm} c_{op} \dfrac{K_{ifm}}{m_m} b_{op} b_m \right| \right. \\
\qquad \left. + \left| K_{ifm} \sigma_{cop} \right| + \left| \dfrac{K_{ifm}}{m_m} \sigma_{bop} b_m \right| \right\} \\
K_{2i} \geqslant \dfrac{1}{K_{Ni}} \left\{ \left| -\dfrac{K'_{ipm}}{m_m} c_m + \dfrac{K_{ifm}}{m_m} b_{op} c_m \right| + \left| \dfrac{K_{ifm}}{m_m} \sigma_{bop}) c_m \right| \right\} \\
K_{3i} \geqslant \dfrac{1}{K_{Ni}} \left\{ \left| \dfrac{K'_{ipm}}{m_m} - \dfrac{K_{ifm}}{m_m} b_{op} \right| + \left| \dfrac{K_{ifm}}{m_m} \sigma_{bop} \right| \right\} \\
K_{4i} \geqslant \dfrac{1}{K_{Ni}} \left\{ \left| \dfrac{K'_{ipm}}{m_m} K_{Nm} - \dfrac{K_{ifm}}{m_m} b_{op} K_{Nm} \right| + \left| \dfrac{K_{ifm}}{m_m} \sigma_{bop} K_{Nm} \right| \right\} \\
K_{5i} \geqslant \dfrac{1}{K_{Ni}} \left\{ \left| K_{ips} - \dfrac{K'_{ips}}{m_s} b_s + K_{ifs} c_w - \dfrac{K_{ifs}}{m_s} b_w b_s \right| \right. \\
\qquad \left. + \left| K_{ifs} \sigma_{cw} \right| + \left| \dfrac{K_{ifs}}{m_s} \sigma_{bw} b_s \right| \right\} \\
K_{6i} \geqslant \dfrac{1}{K_{Ni}} \left\{ \left| -\dfrac{K'_{ips}}{m_s} c_s - \dfrac{K_{ifs}}{m_s} b_w c_s \right| + \left| \dfrac{K_{ifs}}{m_s} \sigma_{bw} c_s \right| \right\} \\
K_{7i} \geqslant \dfrac{1}{K_{Ni}} \left\{ \left| -\dfrac{K'_{ips}}{m_s} - \dfrac{K_{ifs}}{m_s} b_w \right| + \left| \dfrac{K_{ifs}}{m_s} \sigma_{bw} \right| \right\} \\
K_{8i} \geqslant \dfrac{1}{K_{Ni}} \left\{ \left| \dfrac{K'_{ips}}{m_s} K_{Ns} + \dfrac{K_{ifs}}{m_s} b_w K_{Ns} \right| + \left| \dfrac{K_{ifs}}{m_s} \sigma_{bw} K_{Ns} \right| \right\} \qquad i = m, s
\end{cases}
\tag{16}
$$

For a simplification of derivation of a control law, let the dynamics of actuator loop subsystems appeared in the lower equations in (1) and (2) describe as a vector representation

$$
L\dot{\boldsymbol{I}} + R\boldsymbol{I} + K_e \dot{\boldsymbol{x}} = \boldsymbol{v} \tag{17}
$$

where

$$
L = \begin{bmatrix} L_m & 0 \\ 0 & L_s \end{bmatrix}, \quad R = \begin{bmatrix} R_m & 0 \\ 0 & R_s \end{bmatrix}, \quad K_e = \begin{bmatrix} K_{em} & 0 \\ 0 & K_{es} \end{bmatrix},
$$

$$
\boldsymbol{I} = \begin{bmatrix} I_m \\ I_s \end{bmatrix}, \quad \boldsymbol{x} = \begin{bmatrix} x_m \\ x_s \end{bmatrix}, \quad \boldsymbol{v} = \begin{bmatrix} v_m \\ v_s \end{bmatrix}
$$

We simply apply the following voltage control input $\boldsymbol{v}$ given by

$$
\boldsymbol{v} = R\boldsymbol{I_d} + K_e \dot{\boldsymbol{x}} + \boldsymbol{u} \tag{18}
$$

where $\boldsymbol{I_d} = [\ I_{dm}\ I_{ds}\ ]^{\mathrm{T}}$, and $\boldsymbol{u} = [\ u_m\ u_s\ ]^{\mathrm{T}}$ is an auxiliary control input, which is determined later. Then, the error dynamics of the actuator loop is given by

$$
L\dot{\boldsymbol{I}} + R\boldsymbol{\eta} = \boldsymbol{u} \tag{19}
$$

Subtracting a 'fictitious' term $L\dot{\boldsymbol{I}}_{\boldsymbol{d}}$ from the both side of (19), the error dynamics (19) is rewritten as follows

$$
L\dot{\boldsymbol{\eta}} = -R\boldsymbol{\eta} - L\dot{\boldsymbol{I}}_{\boldsymbol{d}} + \boldsymbol{u} \tag{20}
$$

Let a positive semi-definite function V_2 be

$$V_2(\boldsymbol{x}, \dot{\boldsymbol{y}}, \boldsymbol{f}, \boldsymbol{\eta}) = V_1(\boldsymbol{x}, \dot{\boldsymbol{x}}, \boldsymbol{f}) + \frac{1}{2}\boldsymbol{\eta}^{\mathrm{T}} L \boldsymbol{\eta} \tag{21}$$

Using Assumption 2.1, the time derivative of $V_2(\boldsymbol{x}, \dot{\boldsymbol{y}}, \boldsymbol{f}, \boldsymbol{\eta})$ along the trajectory of (20) is given by

$$\begin{aligned}
\dot{V}_2(\boldsymbol{x}, \dot{\boldsymbol{x}}, \boldsymbol{f}, \boldsymbol{\eta}) &= \dot{V}_1(\boldsymbol{x}, \dot{\boldsymbol{x}}, \boldsymbol{f}) + \boldsymbol{\eta}^{\mathrm{T}} L \dot{\boldsymbol{\eta}} \\
&\leqslant \dot{\boldsymbol{x}}^{\mathrm{T}} \boldsymbol{f} + \dot{\boldsymbol{x}}^{\mathrm{T}} K_N \boldsymbol{\eta} + \boldsymbol{\eta}^{\mathrm{T}} L \dot{\boldsymbol{\eta}} \\
&= \dot{\boldsymbol{x}}^{\mathrm{T}} \boldsymbol{f} + \dot{\boldsymbol{x}}^{\mathrm{T}} K_N \boldsymbol{\eta} + \boldsymbol{\eta}^{\mathrm{T}} (-R\boldsymbol{\eta} - L\dot{\boldsymbol{I}}_{\boldsymbol{d}} + \boldsymbol{u}) \\
&= \dot{\boldsymbol{x}}^{\mathrm{T}} \boldsymbol{f} - \boldsymbol{\eta}^{\mathrm{T}} R \boldsymbol{\eta} - \sum_{i=m,s} \eta_i L_i \dot{I}_{di} + \boldsymbol{\eta}^{\mathrm{T}} (K_N^{\mathrm{T}} \dot{\boldsymbol{x}} + \boldsymbol{u}) \\
&\leqslant \dot{\boldsymbol{x}}^{\mathrm{T}} \boldsymbol{f} - \boldsymbol{\eta}^{\mathrm{T}} R \boldsymbol{\eta} + \sum_{i=m,s} |\eta_i L_i| \cdot |\dot{I}_{di}| + \boldsymbol{\eta}^{\mathrm{T}} (K_N^{\mathrm{T}} \dot{\boldsymbol{x}} + \boldsymbol{u}) \\
&\leqslant \dot{\boldsymbol{x}}^{\mathrm{T}} \boldsymbol{f} + \sum_{i=m,s} |\eta_i L_i| \cdot \rho_{Idi} + \boldsymbol{\eta}^{\mathrm{T}} (K_N^{\mathrm{T}} \dot{\boldsymbol{x}} + \boldsymbol{u})
\end{aligned} \tag{22}$$

Determine $\boldsymbol{u}$ as follows so as to cancel the second and the third terms in (22)

$$\boldsymbol{u} = -K_N^{\mathrm{T}} \dot{\boldsymbol{x}} - \gamma(\boldsymbol{\eta}, \boldsymbol{\rho_{Id}}) - \alpha L \boldsymbol{\eta} \tag{23}$$

where

$$\gamma(\boldsymbol{\eta}, \boldsymbol{\rho_{Id}}) = \begin{bmatrix} \dfrac{L_m^2 \eta_m \rho_{Idm}^2}{|\eta_m L_m| \rho_{Idm} + \varepsilon \mathrm{e}^{-\beta t}} \\[2ex] \dfrac{L_s^2 \eta_s \rho_{Ids}^2}{|\eta_s L_s| \rho_{Ids} + \varepsilon \mathrm{e}^{-\beta t}} \end{bmatrix},$$

ε is a sufficiently small positive scalar control gain, β is an adequate positive constant, and α is an arbitrary positive constant chosen by the designer which plays important role in stability analysis. Substituting (23) into (22), finally we have the following inequality.

$$\begin{aligned}
&\dot{V}_2\ (\boldsymbol{x}, \dot{\boldsymbol{x}}, \boldsymbol{f}, \boldsymbol{\eta}) \\
&\leqslant \dot{\boldsymbol{x}}^{\mathrm{T}} \boldsymbol{f} + \sum_{i=m,s} |\eta_i L_i| \cdot \rho_{Idi} - \sum_{i=m,s} \frac{|\eta_i L_i|^2 \cdot \rho_{Idi}^2}{|\eta_i L_i| \cdot \rho_{Idi} + \varepsilon \mathrm{e}^{-\beta t}} - \alpha \boldsymbol{\eta}^{\mathrm{T}} L \boldsymbol{\eta} \\
&\leqslant \dot{\boldsymbol{x}}^{\mathrm{T}} \boldsymbol{f} + \sum_{i=m,s} \frac{|\eta_i L_i|^2 \cdot \rho_{Idi}^2 + |\eta_i L_i| \cdot \rho_{Idi} \cdot \varepsilon \mathrm{e}^{-\beta t}}{|\eta_i L_i| \cdot \rho_{Idi} + \varepsilon \mathrm{e}^{-\beta t}} - \sum_{i=m,s} \frac{|\eta_i L_i|^2 \cdot \rho_{Idi}^2}{|\eta_i L_i| \cdot \rho_{Idi} + \varepsilon \mathrm{e}^{-\beta t}} \\
&\leqslant \dot{\boldsymbol{x}}^{\mathrm{T}} \boldsymbol{f} + \sum_{i=m,s} \frac{|\eta_i L_i| \cdot \rho_{Idi} \cdot \varepsilon \mathrm{e}^{-\beta t}}{|\eta_i L_i| \cdot \rho_{Idi}} \\
&= \dot{\boldsymbol{x}}^{\mathrm{T}} \boldsymbol{f} + 2\varepsilon \mathrm{e}^{-\beta t}
\end{aligned} \tag{24}$$

Thus, integrating (24) from 0 to t, (12) is obtained.

4 Experimental Example

In order to verify the effectiveness of the proposed scheme, experimental works were executed for a master-slave arm of one degree of freedom. Configuration of the master-slave arm is shown in Fig. 2. Left-hand side is a master arm operated by operator and right-hand side is a slave arm that actually works. The motion of the arm part of the slave side tracks opening and closing motions of the arm part of the master side operated by the operator, and restitution of the slave side when the object has been grasped is transmitted to the operator.

Fig. 2 Configuration of master-slave arm

In experimental equipments, direct drive motors produced by KOLLMORGEN Corp. is used for the actuators. Hence, any deceleration mechanism is not utilized. The positions of master and slave arms are detected by rotary encoder, and a standard backwards difference algorithm applied to the position measurements and then passed through a low-pass filter was used to generate the velocity signals. The forces are measured through strain gages, and currents are measured by transducer.

The parameters of the system are shown in Table 1.

Table 1 Parameter Values of System ($i = m, s$)

m_i	0.768	kg	K_{Ni}	0.5017	Nm/A
b_i	420.7	Ns/m	L_i	0.016	H
c_i	0.0	N/m	R_i	7.5	Ω
			K_{ei}	0.4994	Vs/rad

The grasping experiments were executed using a rubber ball as an object. The rubber ball is inserted between the arms of the slave side previously, and operator repeats opening and closing motions of the arms of the master side periodically. The parameters of the object and operator were set as shown in Table 2.

Table 2 Parameter values of object and operator

b_w	30	Ns/m	b_{op}	10	Ns/m
c_w	1000	N/m	c_{op}	500	N/m
σ_{bw}	20	Ns/m	σ_{bop}	10	Ns/m
σ_{cw}	500	N/m	σ_{cop}	500	N/m

Table 3 Parameter values of actual object

b_w(real)	40	Ns/m	c_w(real)	1250	N/m

The real parameters of the rubber ball was obtained as shown in Table 3 through the parameter identification.

From Table 2 and Table 3, it is observed that the real parameter values of the rubber ball exceed the nominal values of the rubber ball, however, in the case where uncertainty is considered the real parameter values of the rubber ball remain in the upper bounds of the uncertainty.

For comparison, the grasping experiments were carried out using the following two control laws.

(A) A conventional torque level control laws (8) and (8) proposed in [3] (hereafter denoted as control law A).

(B) A voltage level control law proposed in this work based on the control law in [3], which guarantees the passivity of the whole closed-loop system including actuator dynamics (hereafter denoted as control law B).

In the experimental equipments, current control type driver is not used, hence in control law A, voltage level control inputs to electrical motors are calculated from the expression of relations of torque and voltage given by

$$\tau_i = \frac{K_{Ni}}{R_i}(v_i - K_{ei}\dot{x}_i) \quad i = m, s \tag{25}$$

From (25), voltage level control inputs are obtained as follows.

$$v_i = \frac{R_i}{K_{Ni}}\tau_i + K_{ei}\dot{x}_i \quad i = m, s \tag{26}$$

In control law B, desired currents $I_{di}, i = m, s$ are obtained through $I_{di} = \frac{\tau_i}{K_{Ni}}$ $(i = m, s)$ with torque level control law A. Then, from (23) and I_{di}, the voltage level control law (18) is determined. Control design parameters were tuned by trial-and-error until the best performance was achieved. They were determined as $\alpha = 10$, $\beta = 1.0$ and $\varepsilon = 0.01$. The sampling time of the experiments were 0.5ms.

Substituting $\tau_i = K_{Ni}I_i, i = m, s$ into (26), the following equations are obtained

$$v_i = R_i I_i + K_{ei}\dot{x}_i \quad i = m, s$$

These are what $L_i\dot{I}_i, i = m, s$ representing the dynamics of motor are omitted in the lower equations of (1) and (2). The meaning for comparison of the two control laws in the experiments is to see the improvement of maneuverability and trackability in positions and forces of master-slave manipulator by taking the dynamics of motor into consideration in controller design.

The experimental results are shown in Fig. 3 and Fig. 4. The upper figures in Fig. 3 and Fig. 4 show the positions of master and slave arms, while the lowers show the forces of master and slave arms, respectively.

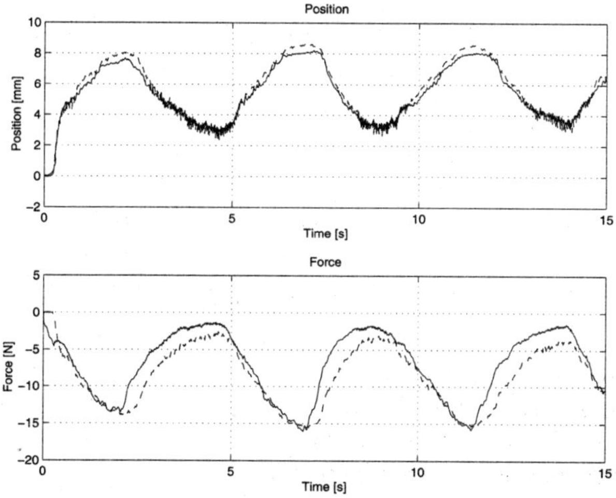

———: Master Manipulator
⋯⋯: Slave Manipulator

Fig. 3 Experimental results of position and force with control law A

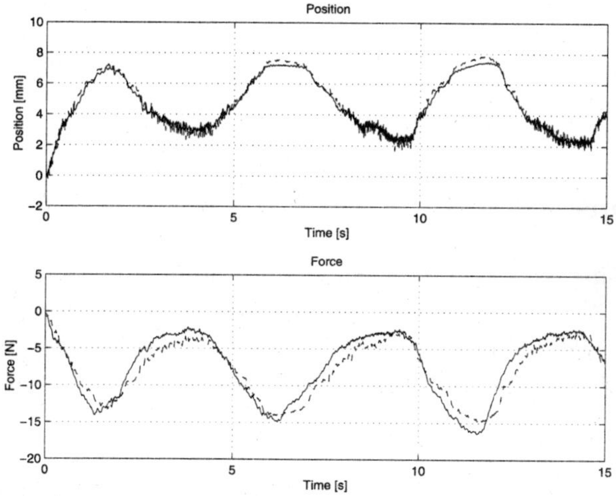

———: Master Manipulator
⋯⋯: Slave Manipulator

Fig. 4 Experimental results of position and force with control law B

From Fig. 3 and Fig. 4, although big difference is not seen in positions between master and slave arms, as for forces between master and slave arms, it can be observed that transmission delay of force in the experimental result using control law B is much smaller than that of using control law A. To see more details, integrated values of absolute value of the position and force errors are shown in Fig. 5.

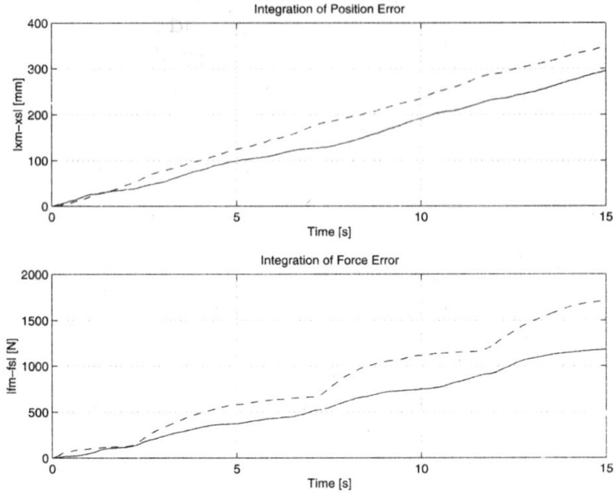

——: Master Manipulator
⋯⋯: Slave Manipulator

Fig. 5 Integration of position error and force error

From Fig. 5, it is clear that the integrated values of both position and force using control law B is smaller than that of using control law A. Although a little difference is observed in the experimental results depending on the characteristics of operator, almost same results were obtained through the repetition of experiments. In terms of these observations, we conclude that the effectiveness of the proposed control scheme for improvement of trackability of master-slave manipulator was verified.

5 Conclusions

In this work, using backstepping technique we proposed such a control law for electrically-driven bilateral teleoperation systems that ensures passivity of the whole systems including actuator dynamics under the certain proper assumption in the physical sense based on the conventional torque control law for master-slave manipulator systems. Besides, the control law is designed so as to possess robustness in the presence of uncertainty for the objects and the operators. The proposed control scheme is regarded as an extension of the conventional control scheme for master-slave manipulators. Experimental results showed an improvement for trackability and maneuverability compared with the conventional control scheme proposed in [4].

References

1. K. Kosuge, Master Slave Manipulator based on Virtual Internal Model Following Control Concept, *IEEE International Conference on Robotics and Automation*, pp.567-572, 1987.
2. R.J. Anderson and M.W. Spong, Bilateral Control of Teleoperators with Time Delay, *IEEE Transactions on Automatic Control*, Vol.34, No.5, pp.494-501, 1989.
3. Y. Yokokohji and T. Yoshikawa, Bilateral Control of Master-Slave Manipulators for Ideal Kinesthetic Coupling, *Transactions on Society of Instrument and Control Engineers*, Vol.27, No.1, pp.56-63, 1991. (in Japanese)
4. Y. Yokokohji and T. Yoshikawa, Bilateral Control of Master-Slave Manipulators for Ideal Kinesthetic Coupling-Formulation and Experiment, *IEEE Transactions on Robotics and Automation*, Vol.10, No.5, pp.605-620, 1994.
5. T. Shen, M. Itoyama and K. Tamura, A New Approach to Robust Control of Master-Slave Manipulators with Uncertain Objects, *Proceeding of the International Conference on Advanced Robotics*, pp.585-590, 1995.
6. C. Ishii, T. Shen and Z. Qu, Robust Adaptive Tracking Control with L2-Gain Disturbance Attenuation for Electrically-Driven Robot Manipulators, *Proceedings of IEEE Conference on Decision and Control*, pp.3388-3393, 1999.
7. C. Ishii and T. Shen, Robust Adaptive Control with Disturbance Attenuation for Nonlinear Systems with Uncertainty, *Proceedings of the American Control Conference*, pp.3504-3505, 2002.
8. P.J. Moylan, Implications of Passivity for a Class of Nonlinear Systems, *IEEE Transactions on Automatic Control*, Vol.19, No.4, pp.373-381, 1974.

Positioning Control of Hydraulic Actuator with Uncertain Input Nonlinearity

Kazuhisa Ito and Tielong Shen

Department of Mechanical Engineering, Sophia University, Kioicho 7-1, Chiyoda-ku, Tokyo 102-8554, Japan
kazu-ito@me.sophia.ac.jp

1 Introduction

In designing a controller for mechanical system, many uncertainties e.g. unmodeled dynamics, parameter uncertainties, disturbances, should be considered to achieve the control specifications. Many design methods to compensate the effects of these uncertainties are proposed, however, the existence of input uncertainty is more serious because designer needs precise information to cancel other uncertainties by designing the control input.

One good example of such mechanical systems is the hydraulic control system. It is usually composed of the power source (pressure source), the flow control valve and the actuator (cylinder and/or motor). The flow control valves, proportional valve or servo valve, usually show nonlinear flow characteristics around its neutral position for the positive lap between sleeve and lands of spool. These can be interpreted as a nonlinear change of flow coefficient physically and this affects much on the precise control performance. In this research, we call it as an uncertain input nonlinearity problem. Such nonlinearity is treated with various methods. [1, 2] discussed broader input nonlinearity problem including saturation and dead zone, the resulting controller demands the solution of a certain Riccati equation. Also [3, 4] solved controller design problem for these uncertainty with LMI approach. The key idea common to these designs is to approximate the uncertainty with a sector condition.

In this paper, the input nonlinearity problem for hydraulic servo system is solved. Motivated by Wu's Lyapunov function[5] and the saturated input control[1,2], the new design for input nonlinearity is proposed. Considering the saturation and the lower boundary sector condition of the input, the approximation of input nonlinearity with optimal gradient is introduced, and then its worst error is estimated as a known bound of input uncertainty. Based on this information, we construct a proper Lyapunov function and state feedback input for set-point regulation. The numerical simulations show the effectiveness of the proposed controller.

2 Modeling and the Control Problem

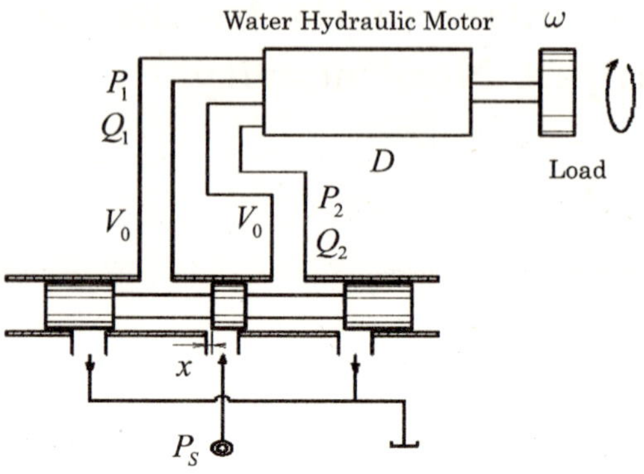

Fig. 1 Diagram of water hydraulic servo motor

The dynamics of hydraulic motor system is given as follows[6] (see Fig.1):

$$\begin{cases} \dot{\theta} = \omega \\ \dot{\omega} = -c_e \dfrac{D\mu}{2\pi I}\omega + (1 - c_f)\dfrac{D}{2\pi I}p \\ \dot{p} = -\dfrac{DK}{\pi V_0}\omega + \dfrac{2K}{V_0}q(u) \end{cases} \tag{1}$$

where state variables $p\,(= p_1 - p_2)(\mathrm{Pa})$ and $q(u) = (\frac{Q_1+Q_2}{2})(\mathrm{m}^3/\mathrm{s})$ are the load pressure and the flow, respectively; $D(\mathrm{m}^3/\mathrm{rev})$ is the displacement of pump or motor, I is the load inertia including actuator, $K(\mathrm{Pa})$ is the bulk modulus of pressure medium; $V_0(\mathrm{m}^3)$ is the piping volume. c_e and c_f are the viscous and Coulomb friction coefficient, respectively, and are obtained by experiments. In (1), the first two equations represent the rotational or translational motion of motor with the displacement θ and the velocity ω, and the last equation describes the equation of continuity with the pressure p. Note that in this formulation the static friction term is neglected.

The flow with load pressure p can be written as

$$q(u) = c_d w k_u u \sqrt{\frac{p_s - \mathrm{sgn}(u)p}{\rho_w}} \tag{2}$$

where c_d is discharge coefficient of servo valve, $\rho_w(\mathrm{kg/m}^3)$ is density of pressure medium, $w(\mathrm{m}^2)$ is width of opening area of servo valve, $p_s(\mathrm{Pa})$ is supply pressure and $k_u(\mathrm{m/V})$ is gain of amplifier, respectively.

From above, the system can be simply described as follows:

$$\begin{cases} \dot{\theta} = \omega \\ \dot{\omega} = -a_1\omega + a_2 p \\ \dot{p} = -b_1\omega - b_2 p + \sigma[u]H\sqrt{p_s - \mathrm{sgn}(u)p} \end{cases} \tag{3}$$

The parameters $a_i, b_i (i = 1, 2)$ and H, p_s that all parameters here are positive constants from the physical consideration.

The nonlinear function $\sigma[u]$ is unknown but satisfies the following sector bound condition

$$\begin{cases} \sigma[u] = 0, & |u| \leqslant \epsilon_0 \\ \{u - \epsilon_0 - \sigma[u]\}\{\sigma[u] - \epsilon_m(u - \epsilon_0)\} \geqslant 0, & \epsilon_0 \leqslant |u| \leqslant 1 \\ \{1 - \sigma[u]\}\{\sigma[u] - \epsilon_m(u - \epsilon_0)\} \geq 0, & u > 1, u < -\epsilon_0 \end{cases} \quad (4)$$

where $\epsilon_0 \geqslant 0$ and $\epsilon_m > 0$ are known constants. Fig.2 shows the region of the unknown $\sigma[\cdot]$. Obviously, this definition targets the unknown input nonlinearities such as saturation and dead zone with minimum value ϵ_0. As is well-known, the effort for known ϵ_0, can be pre-compensated by replacing u by $u - \text{sign}(u)\epsilon_0$. Hence, in this paper, we consider without loss of generality the case $\epsilon_0 = 0$ only.

Consider the positioning control with bounded input which is less than a pre-specified maximum level $1 + \rho$ $(\rho \geqslant 0)$. Motivated by the technique used in the control design for saturated systems[3], the basic idea in this paper is to deal with the unknown nonlinearity to replace the $\sigma[u]$ by a linear function $\rho_1 u$ and to choose an optimal ρ_1 in such a way where the error

$$\delta(u) = \sigma[u] - \rho_1 u \quad (5)$$

is bounded by the smallest sector bound, i.e.

$$|\delta(u)| \leqslant \rho_2 |u| \quad \forall |u| \leqslant \rho + 1 \quad (6)$$

with the smallest $\rho_2 > 0$. As shown in Fig.2, it is easy to determine the optimal $\rho_i (i = 1, 2)$ as follows:

$$\rho_1 = \frac{1 + \epsilon_m}{2}, \quad \rho_2 = \frac{1 - \epsilon_m}{2}, \quad \rho \leqslant \frac{1 - \epsilon_m}{\epsilon_m} \quad (7)$$

$$\rho_1 = \frac{2 + \rho}{2(1 + \rho)}, \quad \rho_2 = \frac{\rho}{2(1 + \rho)}, \quad \rho > \frac{1 - \epsilon_m}{\epsilon_m} \quad (8)$$

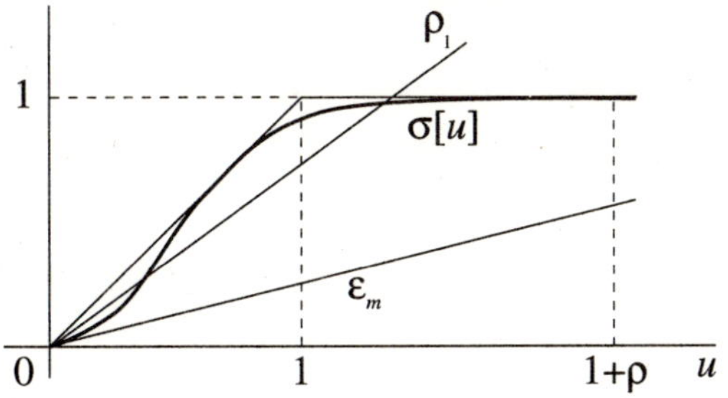

Fig. 2 Uncertain input nonlinearity and the sector condition

For a given set-point θ_d, define error as $e = \theta - \theta_d$. We now give the statement of positioning control problem considered in this paper as follows:

Problem 1 For a given set-point θ_d and a maximum level of input $1+\rho$, find a linear time-invariant feedback control law

$$u = c_1 e + c_2 \omega + c_3 p \tag{9}$$

such that the $e \to 0$ subject to $|u| \leqslant 1+\rho$, and the domain of attraction of the origin $(e,\omega,p)=(0,0,0)$, contained in the region where $|u| \leqslant 1+\rho$, as larger as possible.

3 Controller Design

With the positioning error e, the system can be rewritten as

$$\begin{cases} \dot{e} = \omega \\ \dot{\omega} = -a_1\omega + a_2 p \\ \dot{p} = -b_1\omega - b_2 p + \{\rho_1 u + \delta(u)\}H\sqrt{p_s - \mathrm{sgn}(u)p} \end{cases} \tag{10}$$

We have the following results.

Theorem 3.1

$$u = -\alpha\left\{\kappa_1\kappa_3 e + \kappa_2\kappa_3\omega + (\kappa_3^2 + \varrho_2^2)p\right\} \tag{11}$$

Furthermore, the origin $(e,\omega,p)=(0,0,0)$ *is attractive in the ellipsoid defined by*

$$\Omega_\rho = \left\{(e,\omega,p)\ :\ x^{\mathrm{T}}Mx \leqslant \mu_\rho^2 = \frac{(1+\rho)^2}{2\alpha^2(\kappa_3^2+\varrho_2^2)}\right\} \tag{12}$$

with $x=[e,\omega,p]^{\mathrm{T}}$, $M=T^{\mathrm{T}}T$ *where*

$$T = \begin{bmatrix} \kappa_1 & \kappa_2 & \kappa_3 \\ 0 & \varrho_1 & 0 \\ 0 & 0 & \varrho_2 \end{bmatrix}$$

and $\kappa_1, \varrho_1 > 0$ *are design parameters.*

Proof: Consider the positive definite function V defined as

$$V(e,\omega,p) = \frac{1}{2}(\kappa_1 e + \kappa_2\omega + \kappa_3 p)^2 + \frac{\varrho_1^2}{2}\omega^2 + \frac{\varrho_2^2}{2}p^2 \tag{13}$$

where $\kappa_i > 0, (i=1,2,3)$ and $\varrho_i (i=1,2)$ are design parameters determined later.

Along any trajectories of the system, straightforward calculation of the time derivative of V yields

$$\begin{aligned}\dot{V} = &-a_1\varrho_1^2\omega^2 - b_2\varrho_2^2p^2 + [\Sigma_\kappa(x)\kappa_3 + \varrho_2^2 p]\sigma[u]g(p,u) \\ &+\Sigma_\kappa\{(\kappa_1 - a_1\kappa_2 - b_1\kappa_3)\omega + (a_2\kappa_2 - b_2\kappa_3)p\} \\ &+(a_2\varrho_1^2 - b_1\varrho_2^2)\omega p \end{aligned} \tag{14}$$

where $\Sigma_\kappa(x) = \kappa_1 e + \kappa_2\omega + \kappa_3 p$, and for seeking of simplicity, we take

$$g(p,u) = H\sqrt{p_s - \text{sgn}(u)p} \tag{15}$$

Thus, choose the design parameters such that

$$\begin{cases} a_1\kappa_2 + b_1\kappa_3 = \kappa_1, & \kappa_1 > 0 \\ a_2\kappa_2 - b_2\kappa_3 = 0 \\ a_2\rho_1^2 - b_1\varrho_2^2 = 0, & \varrho_1 > 0 \end{cases} \tag{16}$$

we get

$$\dot{V} = -a_1\varrho_1^2\omega^2 - b_2\varrho_2^2p^2 + [\Sigma_\kappa(x)\kappa_3 + \varrho_2^2p]\{\rho_1 u + \delta\}g(p,u) \tag{17}$$

Furthermore, by utilizing the sector bound, we have the following inequalities

$$\begin{aligned} \dot{V} &\leqslant -a_1\varrho_1^2\omega^2 - b_2\varrho_2^2p^2 + \{\Pi(x)\rho_1 u + \frac{1}{2}(\Pi^2(x) + \delta^2)\}g(p,u) \\ &\leqslant -a_1\varrho_1^2\omega^2 - b_2\varrho_2^2p^2 + \{\Pi(x)\rho_1 u + \frac{1}{2}(\Pi^2(x) + \rho_2^2u^2)\}g(p,u) \end{aligned} \tag{18}$$

where $\Pi(x) = \Sigma_\kappa(x)\kappa_3 + \varrho_2^2p$.

Let the feedback control law be given as (11), *i.e.*

$$u = -\alpha\{\Sigma_\kappa(x)\kappa_3 + \varrho_2^2p\} = -\alpha\Pi(x)$$

Then, we can conclude from (18) that

$$\dot{V} \leqslant -a_1\varrho_1^2\omega^2 - b_2\varrho_2^2p^2 + \frac{1}{2}(\rho_2^2\alpha^2 - 2\rho_1\alpha + 1)\Pi^2(x)g(p,u) \tag{19}$$

Since $\rho_2 \leqslant \rho_1$, we can find $\alpha > 0$ such that $\rho_2^2\alpha^2 - 2\rho_1\alpha + 1 < 0$, *i.e.*

$$\dot{V} < 0, \quad \forall(e,\omega,p) \neq 0 \tag{20}$$

In order to complete the proof, we need to show that $(e,\omega,p) \in \Omega_\rho$ if and only if $V(e,\omega,p) \leqslant \mu_\rho^2$ and V is strictly decreasing inside of Ω_ρ. Furthermore, $|u| \leqslant 1+\rho, \ \ \forall x \in \Omega_\rho$. To see rewrite the function V as

$$V(e,\omega,p) = \frac{1}{2}x^{\mathrm{T}}T^{\mathrm{T}}Tx \tag{21}$$

where

$$T = \begin{bmatrix} \kappa_1 & \kappa_2 & \kappa_3 \\ 0 & \varrho_1 & 0 \\ 0 & 0 & \varrho_2 \end{bmatrix}$$

and the feedback control law as

$$u = -\alpha FTx$$

with $F = [\kappa_3 \ 0 \ \varrho_2]$.

Since the time derivative of V is negative subject to $|u| \leqslant 1+\rho$, so, all we need to show is that μ_ρ given in Theorem 3.1 is the largest value in sense where $|u| \leqslant 1+\rho, \forall x \in \Omega_\rho$, that is we need to determine the largest μ_ρ such that

$$\max_{x^{\mathrm{T}}T^{\mathrm{T}}Tx \leqslant 2\mu_\rho^2} |\alpha F T x| = 1 + \rho \tag{22}$$

Let $y = Tx/\sqrt{2}$. Then,

$$\max_{x^{\mathrm{T}}T^{\mathrm{T}}Tx \leqslant 2\mu_\rho^2} |\alpha F T x| = \sqrt{2}\alpha \max_{\|y\| \leqslant \mu_\rho} |Fy| \tag{23}$$

Seeking for a solution η_0 of the following maximization problem

$$\max_{\|y\| \leqslant \mu_\rho} |Fy| \tag{24}$$

obtains

$$y_0 = \frac{\mu_\rho}{\|F\|} F^{\mathrm{T}} \tag{25}$$

So that, let

$$\sqrt{2}\alpha |F y_0| = \sqrt{2}\alpha\mu_\rho \|F\| = 1 + \rho \tag{26}$$

We get μ_ρ as follows:

$$\mu_\rho = \frac{1+\rho}{\sqrt{2}\alpha\|F\|} = \frac{1+\rho}{\alpha\sqrt{2(\kappa_3^2 + \varrho_2^2)}} \tag{27}$$

□

Remark 3.1 *There are two free design parameters, $\kappa_1 > 0$ and $\varrho_1 > 0$. A way to choose these two parameters is to make the given initial state belong to the domain of attraction. These parameter effects to the performance of the system.*

4 Illustrative Simulation

To illustrate the proposed controller, consider the following water hydraulic cylinder system:

$$\begin{cases} \dot{x} = v \\ \dot{v} = \frac{A}{m} p \\ \dot{p} = -\dfrac{2KA}{V} v + \sigma[u] \dfrac{2K}{V} c_d w \sqrt{\dfrac{1}{\rho_w}} k_u \sqrt{p_s - \operatorname{sgn}(u) p} \end{cases} \tag{28}$$

where each physical parameter is given in Table 1.

Table 1 Physical parameters and its value

physical parameter	value
mass of cylinder rod and load m(kg)	100
effective cross-section area of cylinder A(m^2)	6.32×10^{-4}
volume of pipe V(m^3)	1.272×10^{-4}
bulk modulus K(GPa)	2.25
flow coefficient c_d	0.62
water density ρ_w(kg/m^3)	1000
width of opening area of servo valve w(m)	3×10^{-3}
gain of servo valve amplifier k_u(m/V)	1×10^4
supply pressure p_s(MPa)	5.0

The control aims to track the cylinder displacement x to a given reference trajectory x_r under the initial condition $(x, v, p)(0) = (0, 0, 0)$.

In order to compensate a large numerical difference between displacement x and pressure p, a variable change

$$\bar{p} = S_p p = 1 \times 10^{-6} p \tag{29}$$

is introduced. Defining the error as $e = x - x_r$, the error system can be transferred into

$$\begin{cases} \dot{e} = v \\ \dot{v} = a_2 \bar{p} \\ \dot{\bar{p}} = -b_1 v + \sigma[u] H \sqrt{S_p p_s - \mathrm{sgn}(u) S_p \bar{p}} \end{cases} \tag{30}$$

where $a_2 = A/S_p m = 6.32, b_1 = 2KAS_p/V = 2.24 \times 10^4, H = \frac{2K}{V} c_d w k_u \sqrt{S_p/\rho_w}$ $= 2.083 \times 10^3$. For this model, we have $a_1 = b_2 = 0$ and these lead to

$$\kappa_2 = 0,\ \kappa_3 = \frac{\kappa_1}{b_1},\ \varrho_2 = \sqrt{\frac{a_2}{b_1}} \varrho_1 \tag{31}$$

and the designed control input

$$u = -\alpha \left\{ \kappa_1 \kappa_3 e + (\kappa_3^2 + \varrho_2^2) \bar{p} \right\} \tag{32}$$

Fig.3 shows the typically uneven input nonlinearity used in the simulation. We set $\epsilon_m = 2/3, \rho = 9$ where the input saturation 10V is considered. In this case $\rho_1 = 0.5455, \rho_2 = 0.4545$ and the gain α satisfying $\rho_2^2 \alpha^2 - 2\rho_1 \alpha + 1 < 0$ is chosen as $\alpha = 1.154$. As a controller parameter, we set $\kappa_1 = 500$, $\varrho_2 = 1$. On the other hand, the ellipsoid Ω_ρ is given as $\mu_\rho = 1.88 \times 10^3$ and this satisfies $V(0) < \mu_\rho^2$.

In Fig. 4 and Fig. 5, the simulation results are shown. It is observed in Fig. 4 that the trajectory tracking is achieved. In these figures, the result for normal position feedback control $u = 3(x - x_r) = 3e$ are also plotted. In this example, however P-control strategy is enough for position control because this servo cylinder system has no friction, the obtained results showed longer settling time. The reason is that the proposed controller maximizes the effect of given input amplitude, on the other hand, normal P-controller makes no care of the information.

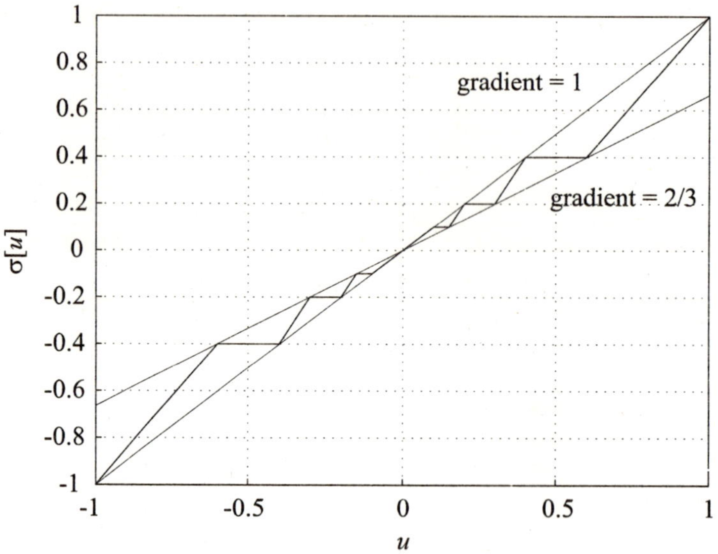

Fig. 3 Input nonlinearity

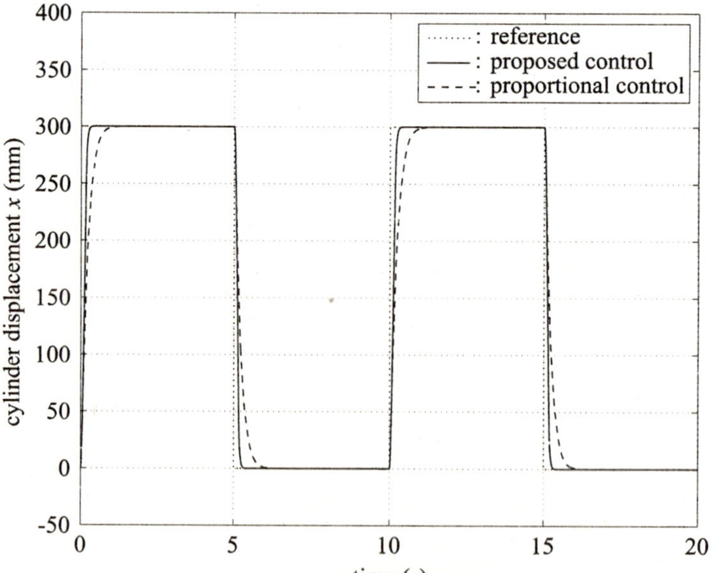

Fig. 4 Simulation result (position x)

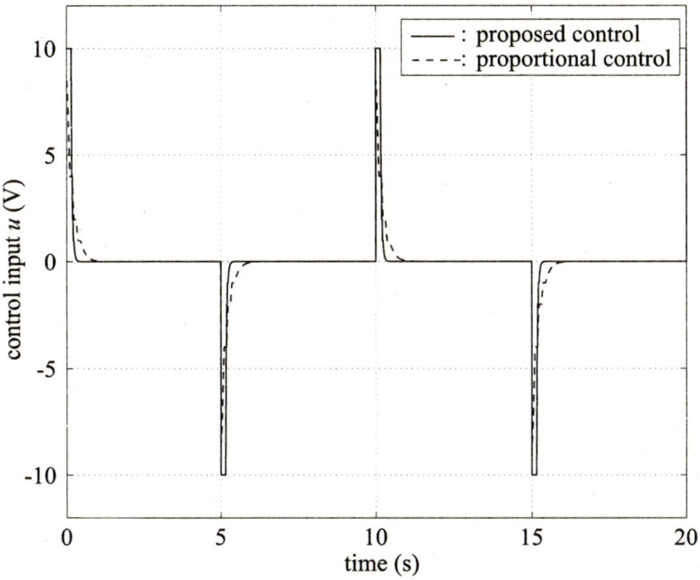

Fig. 5 Simulation result (control input u)

5 Conclusions

Many mechanical systems possess inherently input nonlinearity and the controller for these problems was constructed with dominant design or LMI approach. In this paper, the novel controller which allows input uncertainty was proposed and applied to the water hydraulic cylinder system numerically. The key idea is, first, to introduce a proper input approximation function, then to estimate the error. Moreover the design of the control input was reduced to solve a simple quadratic equation. This is much intuitive than other existing method.

References

1. Z.Lin, *Low gain feedback*, Springer, 1999.
2. A. Saberi, Z. Lin and A. R. Teel, Control of linear systems with saturation actuators, *IEEE Transaction on Automatic Control,* Vol.41, No.3, pp.368-378, 1996.
3. T. Kiyama and T. Iwasaki, On the use of multi-loop circle criterion for saturating control systems, *System & Control Letters,* Vol.41, pp.105-114, 2000.
4. T. Iwasaki and M. Fu, "Regional H_2 performance synthesis", Chapter 6 of Actuator Saturation Control, Editors: V. Kapila and K. M. Grigoriadis, Marcel Dekker, Inc., (To appear), 2006
5. P.Sekhavat, Q.Wu and N.Sepehri: Lyapunov-based Friction Compensation for Accurate Positioning of a Hydraulic Actuator, Proceeding of the 2004 American Control Conference, Boston, U.S.A., 2004.

6. K.Ito, Nonlinear Robust Velocity Control for Water Hydraulic Servomotor System with Uncertainty, in Daizhan Cheng et al. Ed., Advanced Robust and Adaptive Control Theory and Applications, Tsinghua-Springer, pp.257-269, 2005.

Robust Coordinated Control for Tension-Looper of Hot Strip Mill

Liping Shao[1], Xiaohong Jiao[1] and Yan Peng[2]

[1] Institute of Electrical Engineering, Yanshan University, Qinhuangdao 066004, China
jiaoxh@tsinghua.edu.cn
[2] Institute of Mechanical Engineering, Yanshan University, Qinhuangdao 066004, China
pengyan@ysu.edu.cn

1 Introduction

In hot strip rolling mill process, slabs are in general heated in a reheating furnace and then rolled on two reversing roughing mills. After rough rolling, the strip is transported to the finishing mills composed of typically six or seven rolling stands to be further rolled. The rolled strip is cooled down in a run-out table and coiled by a down coiler. The major specifications associated with control problem in hot rolling mills are the dimensional quality and proper mass flow of a strip and stable operation of the process.

Tension control is the key to the stable mill operations and to the proper product qualities such as gage, width and mechanical properties. The strip tension should be kept to a desired value during operation to ensure proper product quality and strip threading. Meanwhile, in the finishing mills, a looper is installed at inter-stand positions to reduce tension variations by changing looper angle and stabilize operation of the process by absorbing an excessive loop of the strip arising from a mass flow unbalance via adjusting the loop length of the strip between the stands. Ideally, the looper angle also should be kept to a desired value to absorb large changes in loop length during an abnormal rolling condition. Thus, the specifications of dimensional quality and mass flow can be satisfied by simultaneous control of the strip tension and looper angle in hot strip mills. Conventionally, each of them is controlled independently.

However, the looper position and the tension have strongly interacted through the mechanics of the inter-stand system. The most difficult challenge in controller design and control performance arises from the interaction between the looper angle and the strip tension in the finishing mill process. To improve the control performance, many control schemes considering the interactions are proposed to solve this control problem. For instance, multivariable control scheme and decoupling controller[1], or optimum regulator and decoupling controller[2,3], or impedance control with decentralization and coordination[4]. These methods are presented on the basis of ignoring the tension-looper system parameter variations and tension or mass flow disturbances from several sources which affect both control performance and stability. Hence, robust and adaptive control scheme as well as neural network and fuzzy technique are adopted to solve the tension-looper control problem under consideration the parameter uncertainties and disturbances[5~9]. However, most of these methods are based on the linearization of system at the operation point and the neglect of nonlinear characteristic of system.

Therefore, in this paper, under the consideration of the essential nonlinearity of system and the presence of the unavoidable parameter variations and external disturbances, the robust coordinated control is investigated for the looper angle and the strip tension of a hot strip finishing mill. Based on the nonlinear recursive technique, a robust coordinated controller is designed not only to regulate simultaneously the looper angle and the strip tension, but also to enhance the robustness for the system parameter variations and external disturbances.

The remaining of the paper is organized as follows. The tension-looper system mathematical model and control problem of the looper angle and tension regulation are presented in Section 2. In Section 3, based on the robust adaptive recursive design technique, a robust coordinated controller achieving the tension and looper angle regulation as well as disturbance attenuation is designed. Simulation results on a model tuned in agreement with the measures obtained from a real hot strip finishing mill will be given in Section 4 to support the theoretical claims. Concluding remarks follow in final Section.

2 System Model And Control Problem Formulation

2.1 System Model

In this paper, a typical finishing rolling process consisted of seven rolling stands and six loopers is considered. And a pair of consecutive rolling stands with the looper is depicted in Fig.1. The strip is approximately to a straight line. The looper is located approximately midway between the adjacent stands of the finishing mill. The looper roll is set at the top of the arm, which pivots on the drive axis driven by an electric motor. And each work roll is driven by a main motor which controls speed from Automatic speed regulator (ASR).

The interstand tension is governed by the length and Young's modulus of the strip. The looper is raised above the pass line so that it changes the length of the strip between the adjacent stands. So the loop length which can be adjusted by manipulating the looper angle can regulate the tension. Since excess fluctuation of the angle may lead to unstable rolling, the looper angle should also be considered as a controlled variable. Therefore, the control problem is to regulate the looper angle and tension simultaneously by manipulating the looper motor torque and the speed of the stand.

In the following subsections, the dynamic models of each part of the system will be developed.

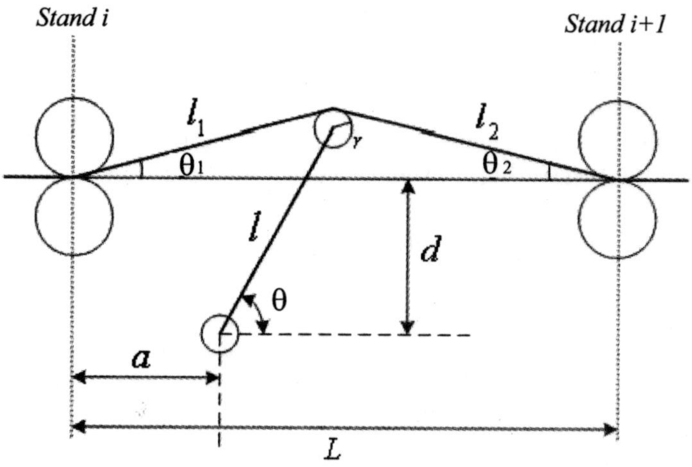

Fig. 1 Looper geometry

2.1.1 Looper Dynamics

The looper model can be derived by applying Newton's second law,

$$J\ddot{\theta} = T_u - T_{load} + T_d \tag{1}$$

where, θ denotes the looper angle, J is the inertia, T_u, T_{load} represent the torque applied to the looper and the total load acting on the looper, respectively. T_d denotes unmodeled phenomena such as the torque necessary for bending of the strip cover the looper roil, and the external disturbance from the several sources.

The torque T_u is provided by the motor, which can be represented as

$$T_u = C_T\phi i_a \tag{2}$$

where $C_T\phi$ is the electromagnetism constant, i_a is the armature current.

The load can be considered to be composed of two main components due to the strip tension T_θ, the weight of the whole system T_s, respectively. These quantities are evaluated as follows:

$$T_\theta = \theta Bhl[\sin(\tau + \tau_1) - \sin(\tau - \tau_2)] \tag{3}$$

$$T_s = Mgl\cos\tau \tag{4}$$

where θ is the strip tension, B is the strip width, h is the strip exit thickness for ith stand, l is the length of the looper, M is the mass of the looper and strip, τ_1, τ_2 are the angle between the strip and the pass line (see Fig.1), r is the radius of the looper roll.

Then, the dynamics of the looper system is described by the following form

$$\ddot{\tau} = \frac{1}{J}\{C_T\phi i_a - \theta Bhl[\sin(\tau + \tau_1) - \sin(\tau - \tau_2)] - Mgl\cos\tau + T_d\} \tag{5}$$

It should be noted that the strip exit thickness h and the strip width B are considered to be constant values regulated by AGC (Automatic Gauge Control) and AWC (Automatic Width Control), respectively. But there exist uncertainties in their values, which arise from the AGC and AWC actions.

2.1.2 Strip Tension

The strip tension is approximately proportional to both the Young's modulus and the strip stretch according to the following equation:

$$\theta(t) = \frac{E}{L+\xi(t)}[l_1(\tau) + l_2(\tau) - L - \xi(t)] \tag{6}$$

where E is the strip Young's modulus, L is the distance between two stands, $l_1(\tau)$ denotes the loop length between the ith stand and the looper roll, and $l_2(\tau)$ denotes the loop length between the looper roll and the $(i+1)$th stand (see Fig.1). These quantities are evaluated as follows:

$$l_1(\tau) = \sqrt{(l\sin\tau + r - d)^2 + (a + l\cos\tau)^2} \tag{7}$$

$$l_2(\tau) = \sqrt{(l\sin\tau + r - d)^2 + (L - a - l\cos\tau)^2} \tag{8}$$

where a is the distance between looper and stand, d is the height from looper motor shaft to stand shaft.

Moreover, $\xi(t)$ denotes the deviation of the interstand strip length with respect to L and its dynamic behavior is described by the following differential equation:

$$\dot{\xi}(t) = v^i(t) - v^{i+1}(t) + w_\xi \tag{9}$$

where $v^i(t)$ is the exit speed from the ith stand, $v^{i+1}(t)$ is the entry speed to the $(i+1)$th stand. w_ξ generically denotes the unmodeled dynamics phenomena like, for instance, the effect of the temperature, the plastic deformation of the steel strip, the uncertainty of the geometric quantities, etc. The relation between $v^i(t)$ and the stand speed v_R^i, $v^{i+1}(t)$ and v_R^{i+1} can be defined by the following equation:

$$v^i(t) = (1+f)v_R^i, \quad v^{i+1}(t) = (1-\varphi)v_R^{i+1} \tag{10}$$

where f is the forward slip, φ is the backward slip.

Furthermore, it is also worth noting that:

(A1) $\xi(t)$ can be assumed to be very small in normal operation as compared with L, and it can be simplified assuming $L + \xi(t) = L$.

(A2) v_R^{i+1} can be assumed to be invariable. But f and φ would be changed by following the strip tension. Hence, their influence on the strip tension is represented as a term with the uncertain parameter.

Then, the strip tension model is described as follow:

$$\dot{\theta} = \frac{E}{L}\left[\left(\frac{dl_1(\tau)}{d\tau} + \frac{dl_2(\tau)}{d\tau}\right)\omega - (1+f)v_R + \epsilon\theta + w_\xi\right] \tag{11}$$

where ϵ denotes the uncertain parameter.

2.1.3 Driving Motor Model

The models of motors driving work roll and looper are considered as the first-order systems with time constants.

$$\dot{i}_a = -\frac{1}{T_i} i_a + \frac{1}{T_i} i_a^{ref} \tag{12}$$

$$\dot{v}_R = -\frac{1}{T_v} v_R + \frac{1}{T_v} v_R^{ref} \tag{13}$$

where T_i, T_R are the time constants of looper motor and of mill motor, respectively.

2.1.4 State space model of the stand-looper system

Let $\tau_d, \omega_d, \theta_d, i_{ad}, v_{Rd}$ denote the desired value of $\tau, \omega, \theta, i_a, v_R$, respectively. And define x_1, x_2, x_3, x_4, x_5 denote the looper angle error, the looper angular velocity error, the interstand tension error, the current error and the roll velocity error, respectively, i.e.

$$x_1 = \tau - \tau_d, \; x_2 = \omega - \omega_d, \; x_3 = \theta - \theta_d, \; x_4 = i_a - i_{ad}, \; x_5 = v_R - v_{Rd}$$

Form (5), (11), (12), (13), the dynamics of the whole system can be described as the following dynamical differential equation:

$$\begin{cases} \dot{x}_1 = x_2 \\ \dot{x}_2 = a_1\delta_1 f_1(x_1)x_3 + a_2\delta_1 f_2(x_1) + a_3 f_3(x_1) + a_4 x_4 + w_1 \\ \dot{x}_3 = b_1 f_4(x_1)x_2 + b_2 f_5(x_1) + b_1\delta_2 x_3 + b_3 x_5 + w_2 \\ \dot{x}_4 = c_1(u_1 - x_4) \\ \dot{x}_5 = c_2(u_2 - x_5) \end{cases} \tag{14}$$

where

$$a_1 = -\frac{1}{J} l, \quad a_2 = a_1\theta_d, \quad a_3 = -\frac{1}{J} Mgl, \quad a_4 = \frac{1}{J} C_T\phi,$$
$$b_1 = \frac{E}{L}, \quad b_2 = b_1\omega_d, \quad b_3 = -\frac{E}{L}(1+f), \quad c_1 = \frac{1}{T_i}, \quad c_2 = \frac{1}{T_v},$$
$$\delta_1 = Bh, \quad \delta_2 = \epsilon, \quad u_1 = i_a^{ref} - i_{ad}, \quad u_2 = v_R^{ref} - v_{Rd}$$
$$w_1 = \frac{1}{J} T_d, \quad w_2 = \frac{E}{L} w_\xi$$

$$f_1(x_1) = \sin(x_1 + \tau_d + \tau_1) - \sin(x_1 + \tau_d - \tau_2),$$
$$f_2(x_1) = f_1(x_1) - [\sin(\tau_d + \tau_1) - \sin(\tau_d - \tau_2)],$$
$$f_3(x_1) = \cos(x_1 + \tau_d) - \cos\tau_d,$$
$$f_4(x_1) = \frac{dl_1(x_1+\tau_d)}{d(x_1+\tau_d)} + \frac{dl_2(x_1+\tau_d)}{d(x_1+\tau_d)},$$
$$f_5(x_1) = f_4(x_1) - \left[\frac{dl_1(\tau_d)}{d\tau_d} + \frac{dl_2(\tau_d)}{d\tau_d}\right]$$

The system parameters δ_1, δ_2 are unknown, w_1, w_2 denote the disturbances and u_1, u_2 are control inputs. Moreover, It can be seen that the equilibrium point of the system (14) is at $x = 0$ and $f_2(0) = f_3(0) = f_5(0) = 0$.

2.2 Control Problem Formulation

For the rolling stands and looper system in the finishing mills, the objective of the looper and tension controller is to maintain the tension and looper angle at their desired values regardless of disturbance, modeling errors and process interactions. The schematic diagram of the tension-looper control system is depicted in Fig. 2.

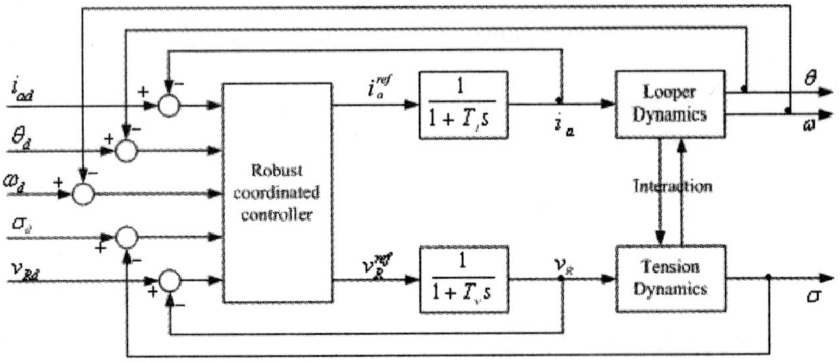

Fig. 2 The tension-looper system with a robust coordinated controller

In general, the design specifications for controller are classified as follows [10]:

(A1) The stability of the closed-loop system is guaranteed under interaction, parameter uncertainties and disturbances.

(A2) Proper closed-loop performance is obtained by quicker control action for reference changes and disturbances, and proper strip quality and stable mill operation is ensured.

(A3) The interaction effects are minimized by having a proper control structure and systematic handling of interactions.

(A4) Tension performance is more important than looper angle performance, because tension has a direct affect on the width, shape and thickness of a strip, and so looper angle performance can be sacrificed for quicker tension recovery.

Therefore, based on the above design specifications, the robust coordinated control problem in this paper is formulated as follows:

For the system (14), to find a smooth robust adaptive coordinated controller

$$\begin{cases} u = \alpha(x, \hat{\delta}) \\ \dot{\hat{\delta}} = \beta(x, \hat{\delta}) \end{cases} \tag{15}$$

with the system states $x = [x_1 \ \ x_2 \ \ x_3 \ \ x_4 \ \ x_5]^{\mathrm{T}}$ and the adaptive parameter estimates $\hat{\delta} = [\hat{\delta}_1 \ \ \hat{\delta}_2]^{\mathrm{T}}$ such that for all admissible parameter uncertainties $\delta = [\delta_1 \ \ \delta_2]^{\mathrm{T}}$ and disturbances $w = [w_1 \ \ w_2]^{\mathrm{T}}$, the following performances are satisfied:

[P1] When $w = 0$, the resulting closed-loop system is globally stable in the sense of Lyapunov, and the system states x can converge to the origin, i.e. $x \to 0$ as $t \to \infty$.

[P2] When $w \neq 0$, the resulting closed-loop system has robust L_2 disturbance attenuation, i.e. the closed-loop system from the disturbance input w to the penalty output y has L_2-gain less than or equal to γ

$$\int_0^T \|y(t)\|^2 \mathrm{d}t \leqslant \gamma^2 \int_0^T \|w(t)\|^2 \mathrm{d}t, \quad \forall w \tag{16}$$

where $T > 0$ is any given scalar, γ is any given positive value.

3 Robust Coordinated Controller Design

In this section, a solution of the robust coordinated control problem for the system (14) will be given by utilizing the nonlinear recursive design technique based Lyapunov function.

Proposition 3.1 *For the system (14) with uncertain parameters δ and disturbance w, a robust adaptive controller designed as the following form is a solution of the robust coordinated control problem.*

$$\begin{aligned} u_1 = \frac{1}{c_1}\Bigg[& \frac{\partial \alpha_2}{\partial x_1} x_2 + \frac{\partial \alpha_2}{\partial x_2}(a_3 f_3(x_1) + a_4 x_4 + (a_1 f_1(x_1)x + a_2 f_2(x_1))\hat{\delta}_1) \\ & + \frac{\partial \alpha_2}{\partial x_3}(b_1 f_4(x_1)x_2 + b_2 f_5(x_1) + b_3 x_5 + b_1 \hat{\delta}_2 x_3) + \frac{\partial \alpha_2}{\partial \hat{\delta}_1}\dot{\hat{\delta}}_1 \\ & - a_4 z_2 + c_1 x_4 - k_4 z_4 - \frac{3}{4\gamma^2} z_4 \left(\frac{\partial \alpha_2}{\partial x_2}\right)^2 - \frac{3}{4\gamma^2} z_4 \left(\frac{\partial \alpha_2}{\partial x_3}\right)^2 \Bigg] \end{aligned} \tag{17}$$

$$\begin{aligned} u_2 = \frac{1}{c_2}\Bigg[& \frac{\partial \alpha_3}{\partial x_1} x_2 + \frac{\partial \alpha_3}{\partial x_2}(a_3 f_3(x_1) + a_4 x_4 + (a_1 f_1(x_1)x + a_2 f_2(x_1))\hat{\delta}_1) \\ & + \frac{\partial \alpha_3}{\partial x_3}(b_1 f_4(x_1)x_2 + b_2 f_5(x_1) + b_3 x_5 + b_1 \hat{\delta}_2 x_3) + \frac{\partial \alpha_3}{\partial \hat{\delta}_2}\dot{\hat{\delta}}_2 \\ & - b_3 x_3 + c_2 x_5 - k_5 z_5 - \frac{3}{4\gamma^2} z_5 \left(\frac{\partial \alpha_3}{\partial x_2}\right)^2 - \frac{3}{4\gamma^2} z_5 \left(\frac{\partial \alpha_3}{\partial x_3}\right)^2 \Bigg] \end{aligned} \tag{18}$$

$$\begin{aligned} \dot{\hat{\delta}} &= \Gamma^{-1}\Psi(x), \\ \Psi(x) &= \begin{bmatrix} \left\{ z_2 - z_4 \dfrac{\partial \alpha_2}{\partial x_2} - z_5 \dfrac{\partial \alpha_3}{\partial x_2} \right\} (a_1 f_1(x_1)x_3 + a_2 f_2(x_1)) \\ \left\{ x_3 - z_4 \dfrac{\partial \alpha_2}{\partial x_3} - z_5 \dfrac{\partial \alpha_3}{\partial x_3} \right\} b_1 x_3 \end{bmatrix} \end{aligned} \tag{19}$$

where k_4, k_5 are chosen positive constants, α_2, α_3 are determined in the design procedure.

Proof: First, the design procedure of a robust adaptive coordinated controller is given as follows:

Step 1: For the subsystem x_1, a positive definite function defined by

$$V_1(x_1) = \frac{1}{2}x_1^2 \tag{20}$$

it's derivative along the trajectories of the closed-loop system is obtained as

$$\dot{V}_1(x_1) = x_1 x_2 \tag{21}$$

Let $z_2 = x_2 - \alpha_1(x_1)$, $\alpha_1(x_1) = -k_1 x_1$ where k_1 is a positive constant. Then, it follows

$$\dot{V}_1(x_1) = -k_1 x_1^2 + x_1 z_2 \tag{22}$$

Step 2: For the subsystem (x_1, x_2, x_3), a positive definite function is constructed as following form:

$$V_2(x_1, z_2, x_3) = V_1(x_1) + \frac{1}{2}z_2^2 + \frac{1}{2}x_3^2 \tag{23}$$

the derivative of V_2 along the trajectories of the closed-loop system is calculated as follows:

$$\begin{aligned} V_2(x_1, z_2, x_3) = & -k_1 x_1^2 + z_2[x_1 + a_1\delta_1 f_1(x_1)x_3 + a_2\delta_1 f_2(x_1) \\ & + a_3 f_3(x_1) + a_4 x_4 + w_1 - \frac{\alpha_1}{x_1}x_2] \\ & + x_3[b_1 f_4(x_1)x_2 + b_2 f_5(x_1) + b_1\delta_2 x_3 + b_3 x_5 + w_2] \end{aligned} \tag{24}$$

Let $z_4 = x_4 - \alpha_2(x_1, x_2, x_3, \hat{\delta}_1)$, $z_5 = x_5 - \alpha_3(x_1, x_2, x_3, \hat{\delta}_2)$, and choose

$$\begin{aligned} \alpha_2(x_1, x_2, x_3, \hat{\delta}_1) = & \frac{1}{a_4}[-x_1 - a_1\hat{\delta}_1 f_1(x_1)x_3 - a_2\hat{\delta}_1 f_2(x_1) \\ & - a_3 f_3(x_1) + \frac{\partial \alpha_1}{\partial x_1}x_2 - k_2 z_2] \end{aligned} \tag{25}$$

$$\alpha_3(x_1, x_2, x_3, \hat{\delta}_2) = \frac{1}{b_3}[-b_1 f_4(x_1)x_2 - b_2 f_5(x_1) - b_1\hat{\delta}_2 x_3 - k_3 x_3] \tag{26}$$

where k_2, k_3 are positive constants, $\hat{\delta}_1, \hat{\delta}_2$ are the estimates of uncertain parameters δ_1, δ_2, respectively. Then, the derivative of V_2 satisfies the following inequality

$$\begin{aligned} \dot{V}_2(x_1, x_2, x_3) = & -k_1 x_1^2 - k_2 z_2^2 - k_3 x_3^2 + a_4 z_2 z_4 + b_3 x_3 z_5 + z_2 w_1 + x_3 w_2 \\ & + [a_1 f_1(x_1)x_3 + a_2 f_2(x_1)]z_2(\delta_1 - \hat{\delta}_1) + b_1 x_3^2(\delta_2 - \hat{\delta}_2) \end{aligned} \tag{27}$$

Step 3: For the system (14), a positive definite function is constructed as the following form

$$V_3(x) = V_2(x_1, x_2, x_3) + \frac{1}{2}z_4^2 + \frac{1}{2}z_5^2 \tag{28}$$

then, the derivative of $V_3(x)$ along the trajectories of the closed-loop system is calculated as

$$
\begin{aligned}
\dot{V}_3(x) &= z_4\left[a_4z_2 + c_1u_1 - c_1x_4 - \frac{\partial\alpha_2}{\partial x_1}x_2 - \frac{\partial\alpha_2}{\partial x_2}\dot{x}_2 - \frac{\partial\alpha_2}{\partial x_3}\dot{x}_3 - \frac{\partial\alpha_2}{\partial\hat{\delta}_1}\dot{\hat{\delta}}_1\right] \\
&\quad + z_5\left[b_3x_3 + c_2u_2 - c_2x_5 - \frac{\partial\alpha_3}{\partial x_1}x_2 - \frac{\partial\alpha_3}{\partial x_2}\dot{x}_2 - \frac{\partial\alpha_3}{\partial x_3}\dot{x}_3 - \frac{\partial\alpha_3}{\partial\hat{\delta}_2}\dot{\hat{\delta}}_2\right] \\
&\quad + [a_1f_1(x_1)x_3 + a_2f_2(x_1)]z_2(\delta_1 - \hat{\delta}_1) + b_1x_3^2(\delta_2 - \hat{\delta}_2) \\
&\quad - k_1x_1^2 - k_2z_2^2 - k_3x_3^2 + z_2w_1 + x_3w_2 \\
&= z_4\left[a_4z_2 + c_1u_1 - c_1x_4 - \frac{\partial\alpha_2}{\partial x_1}x_2\right. \\
&\quad - \frac{\partial\alpha_2}{\partial x_2}(a_3f_3(x_1) + a_4x_4 + w_1 + (a_1f_1(x_1)x_3 + a_2f_2(x_1))\delta_1) \\
&\quad \left. - \frac{\partial\alpha_2}{\partial x_3}(b_1f_4(x_1)x_2 + b_2f_5(x_1) + b_3x_5 + b_1\delta_2x_3 + w_2) - \frac{\partial\alpha_2}{\partial\hat{\delta}_1}\dot{\hat{\delta}}_1\right] \\
&\quad + z_5\left[b_3x_3 + c_2u_2 - c_2x_5 - \frac{\partial\alpha_3}{\partial x_1}x_2\right. \\
&\quad - \frac{\partial\alpha_3}{\partial x_2}(a_3f_3(x_1) + a_4x_4 + w_1 + (a_1f_1(x_1)x_3 + a_2f_2(x_1))\delta_1) \\
&\quad \left. - \frac{\partial\alpha_3}{\partial x_3}(b_1f_4(x_1)x_2 + b_2f_5(x_1) + b_3x_5 + b_1\delta_2x_3 + w_2) - \frac{\partial\alpha_3}{\partial\hat{\delta}_2}\dot{\hat{\delta}}_2\right] \\
&\quad + [a_1f_1(x_1)x_3 + a_2f_2(x_1)]z_2(\delta_1 - \hat{\delta}_1) + b_1x_3^2(\delta_2 - \hat{\delta}_2) \\
&\quad - k_1x_1^2 - k_2z_2^2 - k_3x_3^2 + z_2w_1 + x_3w_2
\end{aligned} \tag{29}
$$

Thus, a robust coordinated controller chosen as the form (17) and (18) can render the derivative of $V_3(x)$ to satisfy the following inequality

$$
\begin{aligned}
\dot{V}_3(x) &= \left\{z_2 - z_4\frac{\partial\alpha_2}{\partial x_2} - z_5\frac{\partial\alpha_3}{\partial x_2}\right\}(a_1f_1(x_1)x_3 + a_2f_2(x_1))(\delta_1 - \hat{\delta}_1) \\
&\quad + \left\{x_3 - z_4\frac{\partial\alpha_2}{\partial x_3} - z_5\frac{\partial\alpha_3}{\partial x_3}\right\}b_1x_3(\delta_2 - \hat{\delta}_2) \\
&\quad + \left\{z_2 - z_4\frac{\partial\alpha_2}{\partial x_2} - z_5\frac{\partial\alpha_3}{\partial x_2}\right\}w_1 + \left\{x_3 - z_4\frac{\partial\alpha_2}{\partial x_3} - z_5\frac{\partial\alpha_3}{\partial x_3}\right\}w_2 \\
&\quad - \frac{3}{4\gamma^2}z_4^2\left[\left(\frac{\partial\alpha_2}{\partial x_2}\right)^2 + \left(\frac{\partial\alpha_2}{\partial x_3}\right)^2\right] - \frac{3}{4\gamma^2}z_5^2\left[\left(\frac{\partial\alpha_3}{\partial x_2}\right)^2 + \left(\frac{\partial\alpha_3}{\partial x_3}\right)^2\right] \\
&\quad - k_1x_1^2 - k_2z_2^2 - k_3x_3^2 - k_4z_4^2 - k_5z_5^2
\end{aligned} \tag{30}
$$

Step 4: For the whole closed-loop system, a positive definite function is defined as

$$
V(x, \hat{\delta}) = V_3(x) + \frac{1}{2}(\delta - \hat{\delta})^{\mathrm{T}}\Gamma(\delta - \hat{\delta}) \tag{31}
$$

then, the derivative of V along the trajectories of the closed-loop system is obtained as follows

$$
\begin{aligned}
\dot{V}(x,\hat{\delta}) = & -k_1x_1^2 - k_2z_2^2 - k_3x_3^2 - k_4z_4^2 - k_5z_5^2 + (\delta-\hat{\delta})^{\mathrm{T}}\left\{\Psi(x) - \Gamma\dot{\hat{\delta}}\right\} \\
& + \left\{z_2 - z_4\frac{\partial\alpha_2}{\partial x_2} - z_5\frac{\partial\alpha_3}{\partial x_2}\right\}w_1 + \left\{x_3 - z_4\frac{\partial\alpha_2}{\partial x_3} - z_5\frac{\partial\alpha_3}{\partial x_3}\right\}w_2 \\
& - \frac{3}{4\gamma^2}z_4^2\left[\left(\frac{\partial\alpha_2}{\partial x_2}\right)^2 + \left(\frac{\partial\alpha_2}{\partial x_3}\right)^2\right] - \frac{3}{4\gamma^2}z_5^2\left[\left(\frac{\partial\alpha_3}{\partial x_2}\right)^2 + \left(\frac{\partial\alpha_3}{\partial x_3}\right)^2\right] \quad (32)
\end{aligned}
$$

If an adaptive law is chosen as the form (1), the following inequality can be obtained

$$
\begin{aligned}
\dot{V}(x,\hat{\delta}) = & \left\{z_2 - z_4\frac{\partial\alpha_2}{\partial x_2} - z_5\frac{\partial\alpha_3}{\partial x_2}\right\}w_1 + \left\{x_3 - z_4\frac{\partial\alpha_2}{\partial x_3} - z_5\frac{\partial\alpha_3}{\partial x_3}\right\}w_2 \\
& - \frac{3}{4\gamma^2}z_4^2\left[\left(\frac{\partial\alpha_2}{\partial x_2}\right)^2 + \left(\frac{\partial\alpha_2}{\partial x_3}\right)^2\right] - \frac{3}{4\gamma^2}z_5^2\left[\left(\frac{\partial\alpha_3}{\partial x_2}\right)^2 + \left(\frac{\partial\alpha_3}{\partial x_3}\right)^2\right] \\
& - k_1x_1^2 - k_2z_2^2 - k_3x_3^2 - k_4z_4^2 - k_5z_5^2 \quad (33)
\end{aligned}
$$

Step 5: A function is constructed as

$$
H = \dot{V}(x,\hat{\delta}) + y^{\mathrm{T}}y - \gamma^2 w^{\mathrm{T}}w \quad (34)
$$

with the penalty output $y = [\rho_1 x_2 \quad \rho_2 x_3]^{\mathrm{T}}$. Then, by using the inequalities $2ab \leqslant a^2 + b^2$ and $(a+b+c)^2 \leqslant 3a^2 + 3b^2 + 3c^2$, H satisfies the following inequality

$$
\begin{aligned}
H = & \left\{z_2 - z_4\frac{\partial\alpha_2}{\partial x_2} - z_5\frac{\partial\alpha_3}{\partial x_2}\right\}w_1 + \left\{x_3 - z_4\frac{\partial\alpha_2}{\partial x_3} - z_5\frac{\partial\alpha_3}{\partial x_3}\right\}w_2 \\
& - \frac{3}{4\gamma^2}z_4^2\left[\left(\frac{\partial\alpha_2}{\partial x_2}\right)^2 + \left(\frac{\partial\alpha_2}{\partial x_3}\right)^2\right] - \frac{3}{4\gamma^2}z_5^2\left[\left(\frac{\partial\alpha_3}{\partial x_2}\right)^2 + \left(\frac{\partial\alpha_3}{\partial x_3}\right)^2\right] \\
& - k_1x_1^2 - k_2z_2^2 - k_3x_3^2 - k_4z_4^2 - k_5z_5^2 + y^T y - \gamma^2 w^T w \\
= & -\left\{\gamma w_1 - \frac{1}{2\gamma}\left[z_2 - z_4\frac{\partial\alpha_2}{\partial x_2} - z_5\frac{\partial\alpha_3}{\partial x_2}\right]\right\}^2 + \frac{1}{4\gamma^2}\left[z_2 - z_4\frac{\partial\alpha_2}{\partial x_2} - z_5\frac{\partial\alpha_3}{\partial x_2}\right]^2 \\
& - \left\{\gamma w_2 - \frac{1}{2\gamma}\left[x_3 - z_4\frac{\partial\alpha_2}{\partial x_3} - z_5\frac{\partial\alpha_3}{\partial x_3}\right]\right\}^2 + \frac{1}{4\gamma^2}\left[x_3 - z_4\frac{\partial\alpha_2}{\partial x_3} - z_5\frac{\partial\alpha_3}{\partial x_3}\right]^2 \\
& - \frac{3}{4\gamma^2}z_4^2\left[\left(\frac{\partial\alpha_2}{\partial x_2}\right)^2 + \left(\frac{\partial\alpha_2}{\partial x_3}\right)^2\right] - \frac{3}{4\gamma^2}z_5^2\left[\left(\frac{\partial\alpha_3}{\partial x_2}\right)^2 + \left(\frac{\partial\alpha_3}{\partial x_3}\right)^2\right] \\
& - k_1x_1^2 - k_2z_2^2 - k_3x_3^2 - k_4z_4^2 - k_5z_5^2 + \rho_1^2x_2^2 + \rho_2^2x_3^2 \\
\leqslant & \frac{3}{4\gamma^2}z_2^2 + \frac{3}{4\gamma^2}x_3^2 + \rho_1^2(z_2 - k_1x_1)^2 + \rho_2^2x_3^2 - k_1x_1^2 - k_2z_2^2 - k_3x_3^2 - k_4z_4^2 - k_5z_5^2 \\
\leqslant & -k_1(1 - 2\rho_1^2k_1)x_1^2 - \left(k_2 - \frac{3}{4\gamma^2} - 2\rho_1^2\right)z_2^2 \\
& - \left(k_3 - \frac{3}{4\gamma^2} - \rho_2^2\right)x_3^2 - k_4z_4^2 - k_5z_5^2 \quad (35)
\end{aligned}
$$

Thus, the control parameters k_1, k_2, k_3 are chosen to satisfy the inequalities

$$0 < k_1 < \frac{1}{2\rho_1^2}, \quad k_2 > \frac{3}{4\gamma^2} + 2\rho_1^2, \quad k_3 > \frac{3}{4\gamma^2} + \rho_2^2 \tag{36}$$

then, H satisfies the inequality

$$H \leqslant -Q(x) \leqslant 0 \tag{37}$$

where

$$Q(x) = k_1(1-2\rho_1^2 k_1)x_1^2 + \left(k_2 - \frac{3}{4\gamma^2} - 2\rho_1^2\right) z_2^2 + \left(k_3 - \frac{3}{4\gamma^2} - \rho_2^2\right) x_3^2 + k_4 z_4^2 + k_5 z_5^2$$

From (34), it follows

$$\dot{V}(x, \hat{\delta}) \leqslant -Q(x) - y^{\mathrm{T}} y + \gamma^2 w^{\mathrm{T}} w \tag{38}$$

In the following, the Lyapunov stability of the closed-loop system and the convergence of the states x_1, x_2, x_3, x_4 and x_5, as well as the L_2 disturbance attenuation performance will be proved.

When $w = 0$, it follows from (38) that

$$\dot{V}(x, \hat{\delta}) \leqslant -Q(x) \leqslant 0 \tag{39}$$

hence, it can be concluded from (31) and (39) that the closed-loop system consisting of (14) and (17-1) is globally stable in the sense of Lyapunov at the point $(x_1 = 0, z_2 = 0, x_3 = 0, z_4 = 0, z_5 = 0, \delta - \hat{\delta} = 0)$.

Furthermore, with the inequality (39), it can be concluded from LaSalle invariance principle that $x_1 \to 0, z_2 \to 0, x_3 \to 0, z_4 \to 0$ and $z_5 \to 0$ as $t \to \infty$. Then, by the definition of z_2, z_4, z_5, $x_2 \to 0, x_4 \to 0, x_5 \to 0$ as $t \to \infty$. Hence, the result is concluded that the system states x can converge to the origin, i.e. $\tau \to \tau_d, \omega \to \omega_d, \theta \to \theta_d, i_a \to i_{ad}$ and $v_r \to v_{Rd}$ as $t \to \infty$.

When $w \neq 0$, it follows from (38) that

$$\dot{V}(x, \hat{\delta}) \leqslant -y^{\mathrm{T}} y + \gamma^2 w^{\mathrm{T}} w \tag{40}$$

hence,

$$\int_0^T \|y(t)\|^2 \mathrm{d}t \leqslant \gamma^2 \int_0^T \|w(t)\|^2 \mathrm{d}t, \quad \forall w \tag{41}$$

holds, i.e the resulting closed-loop system from the disturbance input w to the penalty output y has L_2-gain less than or equal to γ. □

4 Simulation Results

The simulation results on a model of a hot strip finishing mill are provided to show the effectiveness of the proposed control scheme. The physical parameters of the hot strip mill system are chosen as follows[8]:

$J = 7.85kg \cdot m^2, \quad C_T\phi = 4.144WB, \quad E = 150MPa, \quad L = 6m, \quad l = 0.769m,$
$r = 0.11m, \quad d = 0.18m, \quad \tau_1 = 0.0774rad, \quad \tau_2 = 0.0743rad, \quad M = 2000kg,$
$f = 0.082, \quad T_i = 0.18, \quad T_v = 0.09$

The tuning parameters of the designed robust coordinated controller are chosen respectively:

$$k_1 = 5, \quad k_2 = 3.1, \quad k_4 = 10, \quad k_5 = 50, \quad r_1 = 100, \quad r_2 = 20, \quad \gamma = 0.5$$

The desired values of the system states are chosen as:

$$\tau_d = 0.4363 \text{ rad}, \quad \omega_d = 0.2 \text{ rad/s}, \quad \theta_d = 4.8 \text{ MPa}$$

Several disturbances are considered in the simulation: disturbance on the strip tension, departure of the looper angle, external disturbance. The simulation results shown in Fig. 3~6 are the case with disturbances of the looper angle and the strip tension at $t = 0.5s$. And the simulation results shown in Fig. 7 and Fig. 8 are the case with disturbances of looper angle and strip tension, as well as additional external disturbance $w_1 = w_2 = 0.3 \sin 2t$.

From the simulation results it can be illustrated that the proposed robust coordinated controller can not only regulate promptly both the strip tension and the looper angle in the presence of disturbances, but also attenuate the external disturbance to a desired level.

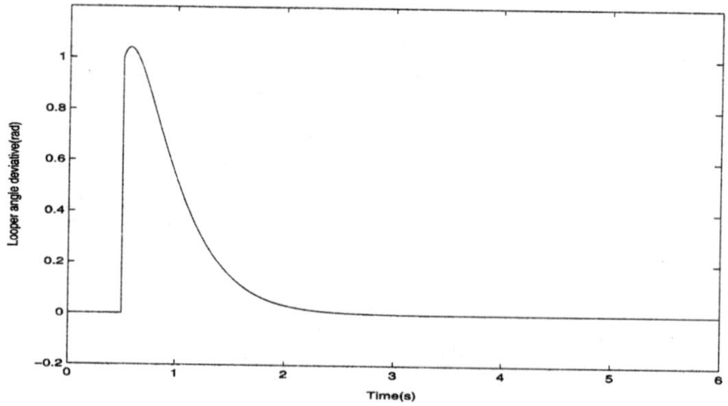

Fig. 3 Looper angle deviation without external disturbance

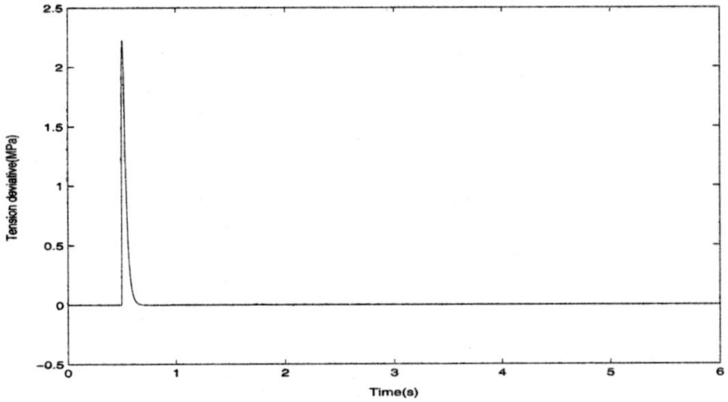

Fig. 4 Tension deviation without external disturbance

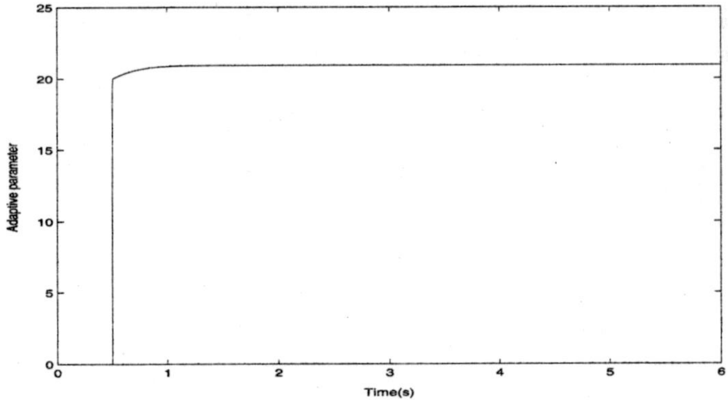

Fig. 5 Adaptive parameter $\hat{\delta}_1$ without external disturbance

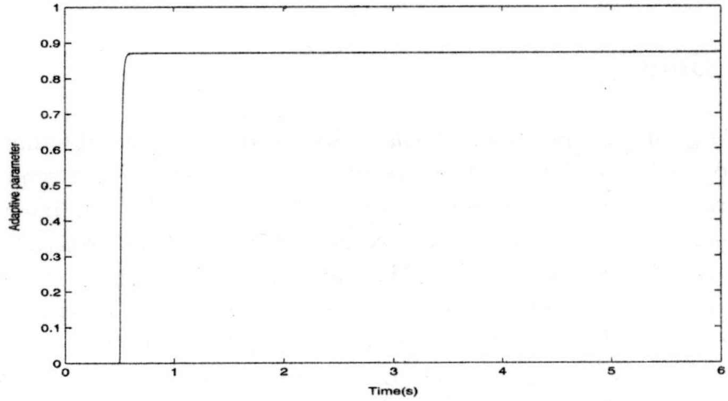

Fig. 6 Adaptive parameter $\hat{\delta}_2$ without external disturbance

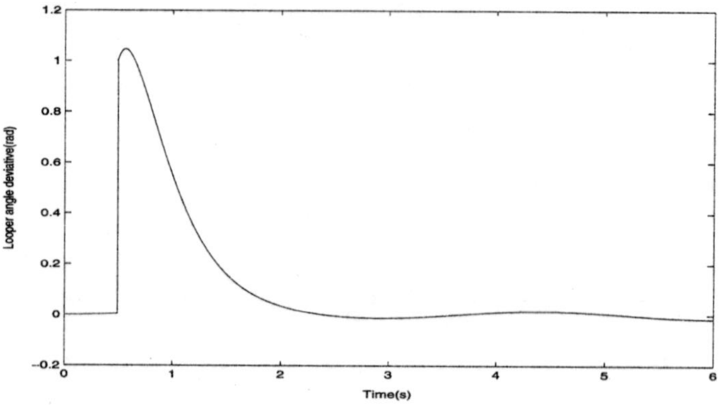

Fig. 7 Looper angle deviation with external disturbance

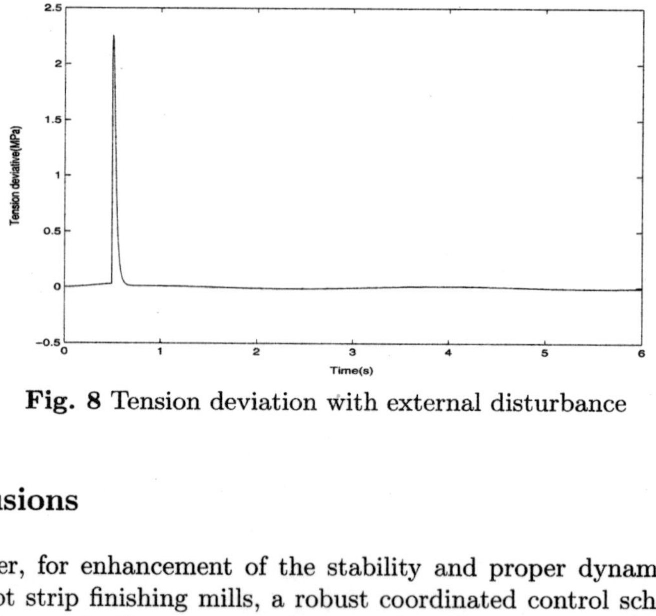

Fig. 8 Tension deviation with external disturbance

5 Conclusions

In this paper, for enhancement of the stability and proper dynamical performance of hot strip finishing mills, a robust coordinated control scheme is proposed for the tension-looper control system based on the nonlinear adaptive recursive design technique. The proposed robust coordinated controller takes an advantage both in regulating promptly the strip tension and the looper angle and in attenuating the external disturbance during rolling operation process. Irrespective of the rolling conditions with disturbances of looper angle and strip tension, as well as additional external disturbance, the resulting closed-loop system can be rendered to converge quickly to the desired operating point.

References

1. Kotera, Y. and Watanabe, F., Multivariable control of hot strip mill looper, *Proc. 8th IFAC World Congr.*, Kyoto, Japan, vol. XVIII, 1-6, 1981.

2. Seki, Y., Sekiguchi, K. and Anbe, Y. et al., Optimal multivariable looper control for hot strip finishing mill, *IEEE Transactions on Industry Applications*, 27, 124-130, 1991.
3. Okada, M., Murayama, K. and Urano, A. et al., Optimal control system for hot strip finishing mill, *Control Engineering Practice*, 6, 1029-1034, 1998.
4. Kazuya, A., Kazuhiro, Y., Takashi, K. and Nobuaki, N., Hot strip mill tension-looper control based on decentralization and coordination, *Control Engineering Practice*, 8, 337-344, 2000.
5. Imanari, H., Morimatsu, Y. and Sekiguchi, K. et al, Looper H-Infinity control for hot-strip mills, *IEEE Transactions on Industry Applications*, 33, 790-796, 1997.
6. Hearns, G. and Grimble, M.J., Robust multivariable control for hot strip mills, *ISIJ International*, 40(10), 995-1002, 2000.
7. Asada, H., Kitamura, A., Nishino, S. and Konishi, M., Adaptive and robust control method with estimation of rolling characteristics for looper angle control at hot strip mill, *ISIJ International*, 43(3), 358-365, 2003.
8. Bo-qun Li, Ke-jun Zhang, Jian Fu and Yi-kang Sun, Diagonal recurrent neural network decoupling control on the loopers' height and tension system, *Proceedings of the 6th World Congress on Intelligent Control and Automation*, June 21 - 23, 2006, Dalian, China, 2787-2791.
9. Janabi-Sharifi, F., A neuro-fuzzy system for looper tension control in rolling mills, *Control Engineering Practice*, 13(1), 1-13, 2005.
10. Choi, I.S., Rossiter, J.A. and Fleming, P.J., Looper and tension control in hot rolling mills: A survey, *Journal of Process Control*, 17, 509-521, 2007.

Hybrid Control Strategy for Attitude Stabilization of an Under-actuated Spacecraft with Two Moving Mass

Yu Jiang, Fenghua He and Yu Yao

Control and Simulation Center, Harbin Institute of Technology, Harbin 150080, China
hefenghua@hit.edu.cn

1 Introduction

We consider the attitude control problem of an under-actuated multi-rigid spacecraft, which has been the subject of numerous research articles in the last decade[1,2]. As we all know, in order to direct the spacecraft to a specified orientation, the attitude control is an important issue for a spacecraft. Meanwhile, the trends on reducing weight and cost and improvement reliability of spacecraft make the architecture of a spacecraft more compact. Underactuated spacecraft is a kind of design to achieve such objects. However, the new obstacle in attitude control stands out due to fewer actuators than degrees of freedom. In this paper, we discuss the control design of an underactuated spacecraft whose actuators are only two moving mass fixed on a given direction of the plant. We try to stabilize the three-axis attitude by means of hybrid control strategies. Actually, the problem is interesting both from a practical and theoretic point of view. Furthermore, as will shown, its dynamics are complicated, which rules out any attempt to design a controller for such a spacecraft with two mass that would rely on its kinematic and dynamics equations only.

The research on attitude control of under-actuated spacecraft is a continuation on the research on nonholonomic systems, as attitude systems of many under-actuated spacecraft are subject to nonholonomic constraints. Nonholonomic constraints can be divided into first-order and second-order nonholonomic constraints. First-order constraints are non-integral constrains on velocities. Second-order constraints are on acceleration of the system. In this paper attitude systems of under-actuated spacecraft with two moving mass belong to first-order nonholonomic systems, as a result of angular momentum conservation in multi-rigid spacecraft between two moving mass and spacecraft body, as satellites with two reaction wheels for attitude stabilization problem.

A common property of nonholonomic systems is that they can not be stabilized with a time-invariant pure state feedback control law because it fails the so-called Brockett's necessary condition. Only non-smooth (discontinuous or time varying or hybrid) control law can be utilized in this case. An excellent introduction to nonholonomic systems can be referred to [3]. Continuous time-varying feedback methods are proposed in [4 $\sim$ 6]. Discontinuous feedback methods are proposed in [7, 8]. Hybrid (switching and time-varying feedback) methods are proposed in [9, 10]. In all of these works, the objective is to achieve either exponential or asymptotic stabilization/tracking, which is, as pointed out in [11], "too restrictive or too constraining". But in practical engineering sense control objective of attitude is set as the convergence to arbitrarily small neighborhood of the origin in finite time instead of asymptotic stability, i.e. practical stability. This objective is meaningful and realistic. However A simple control approach for the first nonholonomic system so-called chain system is proposed in [12], which based on a switching algorithm of two sets of steering laws. Global exponential convergence to any prescribed norm bound is guaranteed and the convergence rate is explicitly given. This approach has a distinctive feature that one of the inputs is free; all control inputs are continuous and piecewise smooth, therefore, physically feasible. For the design of steering laws, a method based on back-stepping is proposed and analyzed in detail.

Hybrid control has been applied extensively in recent years, which has special advantage for control of dynamic system whose smooth control law does not exist, such as feedback stabilization of under-actuated and nonhonomic system. Hybrid controllers in the form of a switching control architecture is introduced in [13]. Using hybrid feedback law the attitude stabilization problem of an under-actuated rigid spacecraft with control torques supplied by gas jet actuators about only two of its principal axes is proposed in [14]. A stabilizing hybrid hybrid scheme to control a class of underactuated mechanical systems is discussed in [15], Lyapunov theory is used to determine the switching boundaries and guarantee the stability of the closed-loop hybrid system.

In this paper, we discuss a hybrid control strategy for attitude stabilization of an under-actuated spacecraft with two moving mass actuator. The spacecraft is modeled based on principle of conservation of momentum as an ideal multi-rigid body and characteristic of model is analyzed in Section 2. Hybrid control architecture for attitude system is described and a continuous and piecewise smooth hybrid feedback law is designed in Section 3. In Section 4, the proposed feedback control method is summarized. The paper concludes with a summary of results and recommendations for further research.

2 Modeling

This section describes the equations of the under-actuated spacecraft with two mass and address the problem of controlling it to a desired orientation.

We consider a spacecraft equipped with two mass actuators for pitch and yaw motion control and roll motion is left uncontrolled, shown in Fig.1.

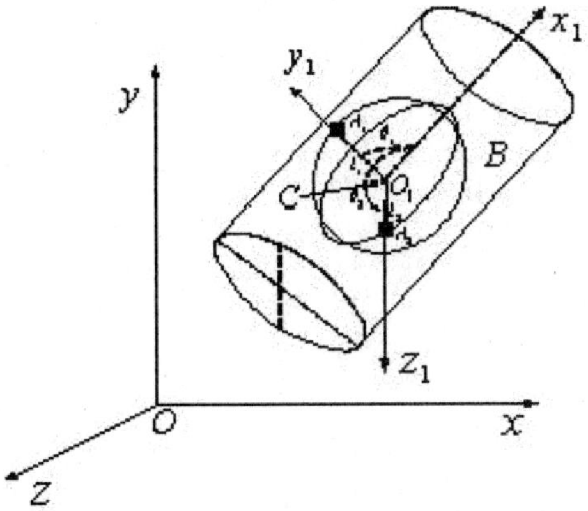

Fig. 1 A spacecraft with two moving mass

The spacecraft composed of three rigid bodies, the main body B, two moving mass A_1 and A_2. Following the standard practice, the kinematic and dynamic equations of motion of the spacecraft can be developed using a frame n fixed in an inertial space and a frame n_1 fixed in body B, as depicted in Fig.1. The origin of n_1 is the total center of mass of the three bodies and can be assumed to be identical with the origin of n. Each axis of a frame n_1 is a same direction with a principal axis of inertia of a main body. The moving masses are set on the positive direction of y_1 and z_1 axis. By pass z_1 axis and y_1 axis rotational angle is θ_1 and θ_2 , rotational radius is l_1 and l_2, respectively.

The following notation is required:

$\left[l_{x1}\; l_{y1}\; 0\right]^{\mathrm{T}}$ is position vector of m_1 in frame n_1, here we have

$$l_{x1} = l_1 \cos\theta_1$$

$$l_{y1} = l_1 \sin\theta_1$$

$\left[l_{x2}\; 0\; l_{z2}\right]^{\mathrm{T}}$ is position vector of m_2 in frame n_1, here we have

$$l_{x2} = l_2 \cos\theta_2$$

$$l_{z2} = l_2 \sin\theta_2$$

J_x, J_z and J_z are inertia of the main body about the origin of n_1 expressed in the frame n_1; ω is angular velocity of n_1 with respect to n expressed in the frame n_1; $\dot{\theta}$ is angular velocity of the two moving mass in frame n_1; H_0 is initial angular momentum of the total system about the origin of n_1 expressed in the frame n.

Assume that there is no external force and moment to a spacecraft, the conservation of angular momentum derives the constraint equation of the attitude maneuver. With this notation, the constraint equation is expressed as follows:

$$J_t\omega + J_m\dot{\theta} = LH_0 \tag{1}$$

$$J_t = \begin{bmatrix} J_x + a_1 l_{y1}^2 + a_2 l_{z2}^2 & (bl_{x2} - a_1 l_{x1})l_{y1} & (a_2 l_{x2} - bl_{x1})l_{z2} \\ (bl_{x2} - a_1 l_{x1})l_{y1} & J_y + a_1 l_{x1}^2 + a_2 l_2^2 & -bl_{y1}l_{z2} \\ (a_2 l_{x2} - bl_{x1})l_{z2} & -bl_{y1}l_{z2} & J_z + a_1 l_1^2 + a_2 l_{x2}^2 \end{bmatrix} \tag{2}$$

$$\omega = \begin{bmatrix} \omega_{x1} \\ \omega_{y1} \\ \omega_{z1} \end{bmatrix} \tag{3}$$

$$J_m = \begin{pmatrix} -bl_{x1}l_{z2} & bl_{y1}l_{x2} \\ -bl_{y1}l_{z2} & a_2l_2^2 - bl_{x1}l_{x2} \\ a_1l_1^2 - bl_{x1}l_{x2} & -bl_{y1}l_{z2} \end{pmatrix} \tag{4}$$

$$\dot{\theta} = \begin{bmatrix} \dot{\theta}_1 \\ \dot{\theta}_2 \end{bmatrix} \tag{5}$$

Where

$$a_1 = \frac{(M + m_2)m_1}{M + m_1 + m_2}$$

$$a_2 = \frac{(M + m_1)m_2}{M + m_1 + m_2}$$

$$b = \frac{m_2 m_1}{M + m_1 + m_2}$$

M, m_1 and m_2 are mass of the main body B and the two mass A_1, A_2, respectively.

Let γ, ψ and φ are Euler Angles in frame n, and L is a coordinate transform matrix from n to n_1, i.e.

$$L^{\mathrm{T}} = \begin{bmatrix} 1 & -\tan\psi\cos\gamma & \tan\psi\sin\gamma \\ 0 & \frac{\cos\gamma}{\cos\psi} & -\frac{\sin\gamma}{\cos\psi} \\ 0 & \sin\gamma & \cos\gamma \end{bmatrix} \tag{6}$$

γ_1, ψ_1 and φ_1 denote Euler Angles in frame n_1, so attitude of the spacecraft is expressed as follows:

$$\begin{bmatrix} \dot{\gamma}_1 \\ \dot{\psi}_1 \\ \dot{\varphi}_1 \end{bmatrix} = \omega \tag{7}$$

$$\begin{bmatrix} \dot{\gamma}_1 \\ \dot{\psi}_1 \\ \dot{\varphi}_1 \end{bmatrix} = -J_t^{-1}J_m\dot{\theta} + J_t^{-1}LH_0 \tag{8}$$

Throughout the paper, angular velocities $\dot{\theta}$ of two moving mass are input variables of the system (8), i.e.

$$u = \begin{bmatrix} u_1 \\ u_2 \end{bmatrix} = \begin{bmatrix} \dot{\theta}_1 \\ \dot{\theta}_2 \end{bmatrix}$$

and $x = \begin{bmatrix} \gamma_1 & \psi_1 & \varphi_1 & \theta_1 & \theta_2 \end{bmatrix}^{\mathrm{T}}$ denotes the state vector of the system described by equation (8).

The control objective is to design a feedback control law for system that make the state $(\gamma_1, \psi_1, \varphi_1)$ converges to an arbitrarily small neighborhood of the state $(\gamma_{1c}, \psi_{1c}, \varphi_{1c})$ the in finite time, i.e.

$$\begin{cases} |\gamma_{1c} - \gamma_1| < \delta \\ |\psi_{1c} - \psi_1| < \delta \\ |\varphi_{1c} - \varphi_1| < \delta \end{cases}$$

Characteristics of the model are summarized to a few way:

A1) Moment matrix J_t of inertia is changed, they involve that initial diagonal form is transfer to off-diagonal form, moreover diagonal and off-diagonal term is variational along with rotational movement of moving mass actuator, so system model represent strong nonlinear and coupling characteristic.

A2) Due to two actuators are only building in body, but there are requirements of control for three attitude angle, system again represent under-actuated characteristic. single control of three attitude angle is not achieved by decoupling method, we can but utilize the coupling relation that control of three attitude angle is achieved by correspond with two actuator.

Therefore we may research attitude control problem of spacecraft with two moving mass on frame of under-actuated control theory. Due to complexity of model, difficulty of attitude control is greatly increased when design is processed.

3 Hybrid Control Strategy

In this section, we present a hybrid discontinuous feedback strategy, which obtained by requiring that the spacecraft undergo a sequence of specified maneuvers.

Control strategy design builds on hybrid system theory. Typically, hybrid controllers combine continuous-time features with either discrete-event features or discrete-time features. The operation of hybrid controllers is based on switching at discrete-time instants between various low-level continuous-time controllers. The time-instants at which switches occur may be either specified a priori or be determined in the process of controller operation. A hybrid strategy is applied to regulate the actions between the two mass and satisfy the desired specifications, such as attitude control precision.Hybrid control architecture is usually conducted in this paper, as shown in Fig. 2, where they consists of such parts as supervisor, many attitude control laws, moving mass actuator, spacecraft dynamic.

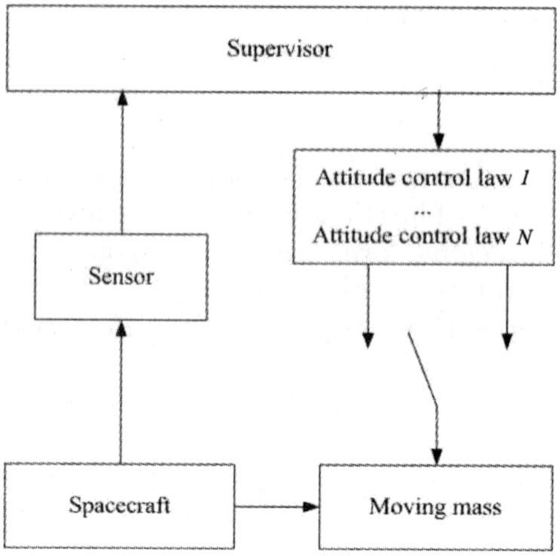

Fig. 2 Hybrid control architecture of attitude stabilization

Using a hybrid control theory, attitude stabilization problem in equations (8) is translated into many phases decision-making problem, the supervisor at a higher level configures the low-level attitude feedback control law according to the current attitude control law and output of the spacecraft dynamic system and accomplishes switching between them in a way that provides stabilization of the system. Each of the low-level attitude feedback control law forces the attitude to trace a specific trajectory, which is selected by the supervisor to produce the desired geometric phase change. The feedback law provides finite time responses with output or state feedback.

In this section, we make the assumption that the initial angular momentum H_0 is zero. And assume that the angular precision is still satisfied when the mass A_1 and A_2 rotate around no more than $\pi/2$.

The hybrid system will evolve in continuous time and the continuous state evolution function may have discontinuities as a result of the switching between controllers. The continuous-time hybrid control spacecraft system can be described by a hybrid I/O automata which is a turple as follows:

$$H = \{M, X, U, Y, f, E, h, I, G, Init\} \tag{9}$$

Where $M = \{M_1, M_2, M_3, M_4, M_5, M_6, M_7\}$ is a set of finite discrete states which describe a sequence of maneuver behavior M_1 to M_7.

X is a set of continuous states and

$$x(t) = \left[\gamma_1 \; \psi_1 \; \varphi_1 \; \theta_1 \; \theta_2\right]^{\mathrm{T}} \in X \subset \mathbb{R}^n$$

U is a set of a continuous input variables and

$$u(t) = \left[u_1 \; u_2\right]^{\mathrm{T}} = \left[\dot{\theta}_1 \; \dot{\theta}_2\right]^{\mathrm{T}} \in U$$

Y is a set of piecewise continuous output variables, $y \in Y \subset \mathbb{R}^p$ denotes a continuous output vector, $f : X \times M \to \mathbb{R}^n$ is vector field which satisfies the local

Lipschitz condition, the continuous state trajectory $x(t)$ evolves in $\mathbb{R}^n$ according to the differential equation:

$$\dot{x}(t) = f(x(t), M_i(t), u(t)), i \in \{1, \cdots, 7\} \tag{10}$$

which can be simplified to

$$\dot{x}(t) = f_{M_i}(x(t), u(t)), M_i \in M, i \in \{1, \cdots, 7\} \tag{11}$$

and are described in detail as follows.

Maneuver 1 M1:

$$\begin{bmatrix} J_x + a_1 l_{y1}^2 + a_2 l_{z2}^2 & (bl_{x2} - a_1 l_{x1}) l_{y1} & (a_2 l_{x2} - bl_{x1}) l_{z2} & 0 & 0 \\ (bl_{x2} - a_1 l_{x1}) l_{y1} & J_y + a_1 l_{x1}^2 + a_2 l_2^2 & -bl_{y1} l_{z2} & 0 & 0 \\ (a_2 l_{x2} - bl_{x1}) l_{z2} & -bl_{y1} l_{z2} & J_z + a_1 l_1^2 + a_2 l_{x2}^2 & 0 & 0 \\ 0 & 0 & 0 & 1 & 0 \\ 0 & 0 & 0 & 0 & 1 \end{bmatrix} \begin{bmatrix} \dot{\gamma}_1 \\ \dot{\psi}_1 \\ \dot{\varphi}_1 \\ \dot{\theta}_1 \\ \dot{\theta}_2 \end{bmatrix} + \begin{bmatrix} -bl_{x1} l_{z2} & bl_{y1} l_{x2} \\ -bl_{y1} l_{z2} & a_2 l_2^2 - bl_{x1} l_{x2} \\ a_1 l_1^2 - bl_{x1} l_{x2} & -bl_{y1} l_{z2} \\ -1 & 0 \\ 0 & -1 \end{bmatrix} \begin{bmatrix} u_1^1 \\ u_2^1 \end{bmatrix} = 0 \tag{12}$$

where

$$\begin{bmatrix} u_1^1 \\ u_2^1 \end{bmatrix} = \begin{bmatrix} 0 \\ K_1(\theta_2) \end{bmatrix}$$

u_2^1 is used to drive the mass A_2 to $\theta_2 = \pi/2$.

Maneuver 2 M2:

$$\begin{bmatrix} J_x + a_1 l_{y1}^2 + a_2 l_2^2 & -a_1 l_{x1} l_{y1} & -bl_{x1} l_2 & 0 & 0 \\ -a_1 l_{x1} l_{y1} & J_y + a_1 l_{x1}^2 + a_2 l_2^2 & -bl_{y1} l_2 & 0 & 0 \\ -bl_{x1} l_2 & -bl_{y1} l_2 & J_z + a_1 l_1^2 & 0 & 0 \\ 0 & 0 & 0 & 1 & 0 \\ 0 & 0 & 0 & 0 & 1 \end{bmatrix} \begin{bmatrix} \dot{\gamma}_1 \\ \dot{\psi}_1 \\ \dot{\varphi}_1 \\ \dot{\theta}_1 \\ \dot{\theta}_2 \end{bmatrix} + \begin{bmatrix} -bl_{x1} l_2 & 0 \\ -bl_{y1} l_2 & a_2 l_2^2 \\ a_1 l_1^2 & -bl_{y1} l_2 \\ -1 & 0 \\ 0 & -1 \end{bmatrix} \begin{bmatrix} u_1^2 \\ u_2^2 \end{bmatrix} = 0 \tag{13}$$

where

$$\begin{bmatrix} u_1^2 \\ u_2^2 \end{bmatrix} = \begin{bmatrix} K_2(\gamma_1) \\ 0 \end{bmatrix}$$

Maneuver 2 is accomplished using the control u_1^2 only. The control u_1^2 is used to drive the mass A_1 to stabilize γ_1 to γ_{1c} in finite time.

Maneuver 3 M3:

$$\begin{bmatrix} J_x + a_1 l_{y1}^2 + a_2 l_2^2 & -a_1 l_{x1} l_{y1} & -b l_{x1} l_2 & 0 & 0 \\ -a_1 l_{x1} l_{y1} & J_y + a_1 l_{x1}^2 + a_2 l_2^2 & -b l_{y1} l_2 & 0 & 0 \\ -b l_{x1} l_2 & -b l_{y1} l_2 & J_z + a_1 l_1^2 & 0 & 0 \\ 0 & 0 & 0 & 1 & 0 \\ 0 & 0 & 0 & 0 & 1 \end{bmatrix} \begin{bmatrix} \dot{\gamma}_1 \\ \dot{\psi}_1 \\ \dot{\varphi}_1 \\ \dot{\theta}_1 \\ \dot{\theta}_2 \end{bmatrix} + \begin{bmatrix} -b l_{x1} l_2 & 0 \\ -b l_{y1} l_2 & a_2 l_2^2 \\ a_1 l_1^2 & -b l_{y1} l_2 \\ -1 & 0 \\ 0 & -1 \end{bmatrix} \begin{bmatrix} u_1^3 \\ u_2^3 \end{bmatrix} = 0 \qquad (14)$$

where

$$\begin{bmatrix} u_1^3 \\ u_2^3 \end{bmatrix} = \begin{bmatrix} K_3(\theta_1) \\ 0 \end{bmatrix}$$

The control u_1^3 is used to drive the mass A_1 to $\theta_1 = 0$.

Maneuver 4 M4:

$$\begin{bmatrix} J_x + a_2 l_{z2}^2 & 0 & (a_2 l_{x2} - b l_1) l_{z2} & 0 & 0 \\ 0 & J_y + a_1 l_1^2 + a_2 l_2^2 & 0 & 0 & 0 \\ (a_2 l_{x2} - b l_1) l_{z2} & 0 & J_z + a_1 l_1^2 + a_2 l_{x2}^2 & 0 & 0 \\ 0 & 0 & 0 & 1 & 0 \\ 0 & 0 & 0 & 0 & 1 \end{bmatrix} \begin{bmatrix} \dot{\gamma}_1 \\ \dot{\psi}_1 \\ \dot{\varphi}_1 \\ \dot{\theta}_1 \\ \dot{\theta}_2 \end{bmatrix} + \begin{bmatrix} -b l_1 l_{z2} & 0 \\ 0 & a_2 l_2^2 - b l_1 l_{x2} \\ a_1 l_1^2 - b l_1 l_{x2} & 0 \\ -1 & 0 \\ 0 & -1 \end{bmatrix} \begin{bmatrix} u_1^4 \\ u_2^4 \end{bmatrix} = 0 \qquad (15)$$

where

$$\begin{bmatrix} u_1^4 \\ u_2^4 \end{bmatrix} = \begin{bmatrix} 0 \\ K_4(\psi_1) \end{bmatrix}$$

Maneuver 4 is accomplished using the control u_2^4 only. The control u_2^4 is used to stabilize ψ_1 to ψ_{1c}.

Maneuver 5 M5:

$$\begin{bmatrix} J_x + a_2 l_{z2}^2 & 0 & (a_2 l_{x2} - b l_1) l_{z2} & 0 & 0 \\ 0 & J_y + a_1 l_1^2 + a_2 l_2^2 & 0 & 0 & 0 \\ (a_2 l_{x2} - b l_1) l_{z2} & 0 & J_z + a_1 l_1^2 + a_2 l_{x2}^2 & 0 & 0 \\ 0 & 0 & 0 & 1 & 0 \\ 0 & 0 & 0 & 0 & 1 \end{bmatrix} \begin{bmatrix} \dot{\gamma}_1 \\ \dot{\psi}_1 \\ \dot{\varphi}_1 \\ \dot{\theta}_1 \\ \dot{\theta}_2 \end{bmatrix} + \begin{bmatrix} -b l_1 l_{z2} & 0 \\ 0 & a_2 l_2^2 - b l_1 l_{x2} \\ a_1 l_1^2 - b l_1 l_{x2} & 0 \\ -1 & 0 \\ 0 & -1 \end{bmatrix} \begin{bmatrix} u_1^5 \\ u_2^5 \end{bmatrix} = 0 \qquad (16)$$

where

$$\begin{bmatrix} u_1^5 \\ u_2^5 \end{bmatrix} = \begin{bmatrix} 0 \\ K_5(\theta_2) \end{bmatrix}$$

u_2^5 is used to drive the mass A_2 to $\theta_2 = 0$.

Maneuver 6 M6:

$$\begin{bmatrix} J_x + a_1 l_{y1}^2 & (bl_2 - a_1 l_{x1}) l_{y1} & 0 & 0 & 0 \\ (bl_2 - a_1 l_{x1}) l_{y1} & J_y + a_1 l_{x1}^2 + a_2 l_2^2 & 0 & 0 & 0 \\ 0 & 0 & J_z + a_1 l_1^2 + a_2 l_2^2 & 0 & 0 \\ 0 & 0 & 0 & 1 & 0 \\ 0 & 0 & 0 & 0 & 1 \end{bmatrix} \begin{bmatrix} \dot{\gamma}_1 \\ \dot{\psi}_1 \\ \dot{\varphi}_1 \\ \dot{\theta}_1 \\ \dot{\theta}_2 \end{bmatrix} + \begin{bmatrix} 0 & bl_{y1} l_2 \\ 0 & a_2 l_2^2 - bl_{x1} l_2 \\ a_1 l_1^2 - bl_{x1} l_2 & 0 \\ -1 & 0 \\ 0 & -1 \end{bmatrix} \begin{bmatrix} u_1^6 \\ u_2^6 \end{bmatrix} = 0 \quad (17)$$

where

$$\begin{bmatrix} u_1^6 \\ u_2^6 \end{bmatrix} = \begin{bmatrix} K_6(\varphi_1) \\ 0 \end{bmatrix}$$

Maneuver 6 is accomplished using the control u_1^6 only. The control u_1^6 is used to stabilize φ_1 to φ_{1c}.

Maneuver 7 M7:

$$\begin{bmatrix} J_x + a_1 l_{y1}^2 & (bl_2 - a_1 l_{x1}) l_{y1} & 0 & 0 & 0 \\ (bl_2 - a_1 l_{x1}) l_{y1} & J_y + a_1 l_{x1}^2 + a_2 l_2^2 & 0 & 0 & 0 \\ 0 & 0 & J_z + a_1 l_1^2 + a_2 l_2^2 & 0 & 0 \\ 0 & 0 & 0 & 1 & 0 \\ 0 & 0 & 0 & 0 & 1 \end{bmatrix} \begin{bmatrix} \dot{\gamma}_1 \\ \dot{\psi}_1 \\ \dot{\varphi}_1 \\ \dot{\theta}_1 \\ \dot{\theta}_2 \end{bmatrix} + \begin{bmatrix} 0 & bl_{y1} l_2 \\ 0 & a_2 l_2^2 - bl_{x1} l_2 \\ a_1 l_1^2 - bl_{x1} l_2 & 0 \\ -1 & 0 \\ 0 & -1 \end{bmatrix} \begin{bmatrix} u_1^7 \\ u_2^7 \end{bmatrix} = 0 \quad (18)$$

where

$$\begin{bmatrix} u_1^7 \\ u_2^7 \end{bmatrix} = \begin{bmatrix} 0 \\ 0 \end{bmatrix}$$

E is a set of discrete events which is used to describe discrete behavior i.e. switching from one maneuver behavior to another. Here we have

$$E = \{e_{12}, e_{23}, e_{34}, e_{45}, e_{56}, e_{67}, e_{71}, e_{73}, e_{75}\}$$

$h : E \times M \to M$ defines switch between between different maneuver.

$$M_j = h(M_i, e_{ij}), e_{ij} \in E$$

$I : M \rightarrow X$ assigns to each discrete state $M_i \in M$ an invariant of the form $I(M_i) \subseteq X$, where continuous variables must assure to satisfy the invariant conditions, otherwise the system dynamic leaves the location and trigger an event.

$G : E \rightarrow X$ assigns to each event $e_{ij} \in E$ a guard set which a union of the surface of $I(M_i)$. Guard sets are described as follows:

$$
\begin{aligned}
G(e_{12}) &= \{x \in X | \theta_2 = \pi/2\} \\
G(e_{23}) &= \{x \in X || \gamma_1 - \gamma_{1c}| \leqslant \delta\} \\
G(e_{34}) &= \{x \in X | \theta_1 = 0\} \\
G(e_{45}) &= \{x \in X || \psi_1 - \psi_{1c}| \leqslant \delta\} \\
G(e_{56}) &= \{x \in X | \theta_2 = 0\} \\
G(e_{67}) &= \{x \in X || \varphi_1 - \varphi_{1c}| \leqslant \delta\} \\
G(e_{71}) &= \{x \in X || \gamma_1 - \gamma_{1c}| > \delta\} \\
G(e_{73}) &= \{x \in X | \psi_1 - \psi_{1c}| > \delta\} \\
G(e_{75}) &= \{x \in X || \varphi_1 - \varphi_{1c}| > \delta\}
\end{aligned}
$$

A discrete switch may generate only when the guard condition is satisfied.

$Init = X_0 \cup M_0$ is a set of initial states, $M_0 \subset M$ is a set of initial discrete states and $X_0 \subset \mathbb{R}^n$ is a set of initial continuous states, where we let

$$M_0 = M1$$

$$X_0 = (\gamma_{10}, \psi_{10}, \varphi_{10}, \theta_1^0, \theta_2^0)$$

The feedback law for each maneuver mode are designed following simple rules: if $i = 1$, the moving mass actuator A_1 must be driven away from zero to $\pi/2$; when $i = 2$, the roll angle $\gamma_1(t)$ must move and reach a given bound of γ_{1c} in finite time; when $i = 3$, the moving mass actuator must be driven to $\theta_1 = 0$; when $i = 4$, the pitch angle ψ_1 must move and reach a given bound of ψ_{1c} in finite time; when $i = 5$, the moving mass actuator must be driven to $\theta_2 = 0$; when $i = 6$, the yaw angle $\varphi_1(t)$ must move and reach a given bound of $varphi_{1c}$ in finite time; finally when $i = 7$, $(\gamma_1, \psi_1, \varphi_1)$ must remain in a given bound of $(\gamma_{1c}, \psi_{1c}, \varphi_{1c})$ and the two moving mass actuator A_1 and A_2 stay in rest. The hybrid controller consists of a collection of state feedback controllers designed above and a discrete event supervisor. When the continuous state hits the switching boundary define by the guard sets, a new controller is applied to the spacecraft.

The dynamics of the system H can now be described as follows: starting at (x_0, M_i) with $x_0 \in X_0$ and $M_i \in M$, the continuous state trajectory $x(t)$ evolves according to $\dot{x} = f_{M_i}(x(t), u_{M_i}(t))$. When $h(x(t), e_{ij})$ becomes equal to $j \neq i$ and this could happen when $x(\cdot)$ hits the boundary of the set $G(e_{ij})$. The continuous dynamics switches to $\dot{x} = f_{M_j}(x(t), u_{M_j}(t))$ from which the process continues. Evolution of the hybrid control laws proposed is shown in Fig.3.

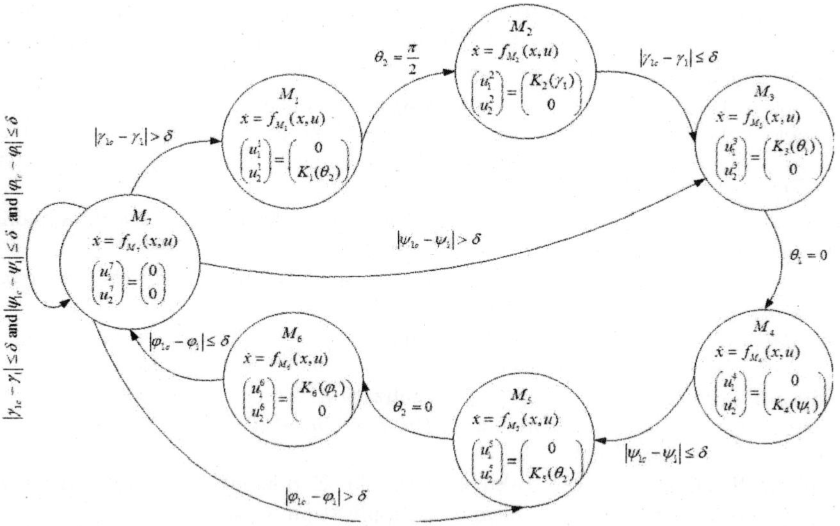

Fig. 3 Evolution of a hybrid control spacecraft system

A computer implementation of the hybrid control strategy can be easily carried out.

4 Conclusions

A feedback hybrid control law is proposed that yields global stabilization of an under-actuated spacecraft with two moving mass actuators to any desired orientation. The feedback control strategy is discontinuous and non-smooth, which are constructed by switching between several feedback functions that are selected to accomplish a sequence of specified spacecraft maneuvers. Each maneuver is accomplished using the one moving mass actuator only via supervisor. In this way attitude dynamic model of spacecraft is transfer to simple form and resulting feedback control law has a very simple structure and easy designed. Future research issues will address on the problem that $H_0 \neq 0$.

References

1. Tsiotras P. and Luo J., Control of underactuated spacecraft with bounded inputs. *Automatica*, 2000, 36:1153-1169.
2. Horri N. M. and Hodgart S., Attitude Stabilization of Underactuated Satellite Using Two Wheels, *IEEE Trans. on Automatic Control*, vol. 6, pp. 2629-2635, 2002.
3. Kolmanovsky I. and McClamroch N. H., Developments in nonholonomic control problem. *IEEE Control System Magzine*, 1995,15(6):20-36.
4. Morinand P. and Samson C., Control fof nonlinear chained systems: From the Routh-Hurwitz stability criterion to time-varying exponential stabilizers, *IEEE Trans. on Automatic Control* , vol 45, no.1, pp. 141-146, Jan. 2000.

5. Closkey R. T. and Murray R. M., Exponential stabilization of drift-less nonlinear control system using homogeneous feedback, *IEEE Trans on Automatic Control*, vol.42, no.5, pp.614-628, May. 1997.
6. Pomet J. B., Explicit design of time-varying stabilizing control laws for a class of controllable system without drift, *Syst. Contr. Lett.*, vol.18, pp.147-158, 1992.
7. Astolfi A., Discontinuous control of nonholonomic systems, *Syst. Contr. Lett.*, vol.27, pp.37-45, 1996.
8. Bloch A. M. and Drakunov S., Stabilization and tracking in the nonholonomic integrator via sliding modes, *Syst. Contr. Lett.*, vol.29, pp.91-99, 1996.
9. Bennani M. K. and Rouchon P., Robust stabilization of flat and chained systems, *in Proc. ECC*, pp. 2642-2646, 1995.
10. Sordalen O. J. and Egeland O., Exponential stabilization of nonholonomic chained systems, *IEEE Trans on Automatic Control*, vol.40, no.1, pp.35-49, Jan. 1995.
11. Morin P. and Samson C., Practical stabilization of driftless systems on Lie groups: The transverse function approach, *IEEE Trans on Automatic Control*, vol.48, no.9, pp.1496-1508, Sep. 2003.
12. Liu K. Z., Dao M. Q. and Takuya Inoue, An Exponentially -Convergent Control Algorithm for Chained Systems and Its Application to Automatic Parking Systems, *IEEE Trans. on Control systems technology*, 14(6):1113-1126, 2006.
13. Kolmanovsky I. and McClamroch N. H., Hybrid feedback laws for a class of cascade nonlinear control system. *IEEE Trans on Automatic Control*, Vol. 41, pp. 1271-1282, 1996.
14. Krishnan H., Reyhanoglu M. and McClamroch N.H., Attitude stabilization of a rigid spacecraft using two control torques: a nonlinear control approach based on the spacecraft attitude dynamics, *Automatica*, vol. 30, no. 6, pp. 1023-1027, 1994.
15. Rafael Fierro, Frank L. Lewis and Andy Lowe, Hybrid Control for a Class of under-actuated Mechanical Systems. *IEEE Trans. on System, Man and Cybernetics-Part A: Systems and Human*, Vol. 29, No. 6, Nov. 1999.

The Gap between Nonlinear Control Theories and Applications in Power Systems

Yuanzhang Sun and Fang Yang

State Key Laboratory of Power Systems. Electrical Engineering Department, Tsinghua University, Beijing 100084, China
yzsun@tsinghua.edu.cn

1 Introduction

Due to the economical pressure and environmental factors, power system has become more vulnerable to disturbances. Multiple contingencies may probably imperils the system into catastrophic outages, finally, result in blackout in large areas. To avoid the tragedy, stability enhancement has become crucial and problematical issue.

The employments of nonlinear control theories greatly promote the developments of dynamic control in power system. Feedback linearization based on differential geometric technique, direct method based on Lyapunov stability theory, nonlinear robust control, adaptive control are all dramatic tools for transient stability control of power system, specific applied to power plant(excitation system and governor), FACTS devices and HVDC systems.

However, despite of the remarkable achievements sofar obtained, control strategies implemented in real power system are still limited. To find the barrier, this paper first recalls the present control strategies and then try to point out the gap between control theories and application in power system.

2 Feedback Linearization Approach

The development in differential geometric theory since 1970s has brought along fruitful results for analyzing and designing nonlinear control systems[1]. As a primary approach, exact linearization via feedback has been a great success in many challenging engineering applications such as power systems. Consider the mathematical model for power systems in synchronous reference frame with n generators, equipped with fast excitation[2],

$$\begin{cases} \dot{E}'_{qi} = -\dfrac{1+(x_{di}-x'_{di})B_{ii}}{T_{d0i}}E'_{qi} \\ \qquad +\dfrac{x_{di}-x'_{di}}{T_{d0i}}\sum\limits_{j=1\neq i}^{n} Y_{ij}E'_{qj}\cos(\delta_{ij}+\alpha_{ij})+\dfrac{1}{T_{d0i}}V_{fi} \\ \dot{\omega}_i = -\dfrac{\omega_0}{H_i}(G_{ii}E'^2_{qi}+E'_{qi}\sum\limits_{j=1\neq i}^{n} Y_{ij}E'_{qj}sin(\delta_{ij}-\alpha_{ij})) \\ \qquad -\dfrac{D_i}{H_i}(\omega_i-\omega_0)+\dfrac{\omega_0}{H_i}P_{mi} \\ \dot{\delta}_i = \omega_i-\omega_0 \qquad i=1,2,\cdots,n \end{cases} \tag{1}$$

it can be rewritten in the form of affine nonlinear systems

$$\dot{X} = f(X) + \sum_{i=1}^{n} g_i(X)u_i \tag{2}$$

where

$X = [E'_{q1}, E'_{q2}, \cdots, E'_{qn}; \omega_1, \omega_2, \cdots, \omega_n; \delta_1, \delta_2, \cdots, \delta_n]^{\mathrm{T}}$, P_{mi}, δ_i and ω_i are mechanical power input, rotor angle and angular speed of the i-th generator. ω_0 is the synchronous angular speed for the synchronous reference frame. x_d and E_q denote the stator winding's self inductive reactance of d axis and idling electrical potential, E'_q is the transient potential behind the transient reactance x'_d with the time constant in the field winding as T_{d0}. And for the network parameters, B_{ii}, G_{ii}, Y_{ij} and α_{ij} represent the self-conductance, self-susceptance of node i, mutual admittance between nodes i and j.

It can be verified that, the system (1) satisfies the conditions for the exact linearization, that is, a mapping $Z = \Phi(X)$ and a state feedback $U(X) = AX + BV$ can be found to transform the system into linear form as following,

$$\begin{cases} \dot{z}_1 = z_{n+1} \\ \cdots\cdots \\ \dot{z}_{2n} = z_{3n} \\ \dot{z}_{2n+1} = \nu_1 \\ \cdots\cdots \\ \dot{z}_{3n} = \nu_n \end{cases} \tag{3}$$

Adopt the procedure in [3], the coordinates transform for linearization can be obtained as

$$\begin{cases} z_i = \delta_i - \delta_{0i} \\ z_{n+i} = \omega_i - \omega_0 \\ z_{2n+i} = \dot{\omega}_i \qquad i = 1, \cdots, n \end{cases} \tag{4}$$

and a simple relation for the control input vector of the exact linearized system can be derived, satisfying

$$V = \begin{bmatrix} \nu_1 \\ \nu_2 \\ \vdots \\ \nu_n \end{bmatrix} = \begin{bmatrix} -\frac{\omega_0}{H_1}\dot{P}_{e1} - \frac{D_1}{H_1}\dot{\omega}_1 \\ -\frac{\omega_0}{H_2}\dot{P}_{e2} - \frac{D_2}{H_2}\dot{\omega}_2 \\ \vdots \\ -\frac{\omega_0}{H_n}\dot{P}_{en} - \frac{D_n}{H_n}\dot{\omega}_n \end{bmatrix} \tag{5}$$

where $P_{ei} = E'_{qi}I_{qi}$ and $\dot{P}_{ei} = \dot{E}'_{qi}\dot{I}_{qi}$. Thus, the excitation control law for each generator is solved,

$$V_{fi} = E_{qi}(1 - T'_{di}\frac{\dot{I}_{qi}}{I_{qi}}) - \frac{D_i T_{d0i}}{\omega_0 I_{qi}}\dot{\omega}_i - \frac{H_i T_{doi}}{\omega_0 I_{qi}}\nu_i \tag{6}$$

where $T'_{di} = \frac{T_{doi}x'_{di}}{x_{di}}$.

Based on the linearized system (3), nonlinear optimal excitation control can be acquired by applying the LQR design method, and the control strategy ν_i is of optimality in the sense of the quasi-quadratic performance index for the i-th generator,

$$J_i = \int_0^\infty (q_1 \Delta\delta_i^2 + q_2 \Delta\omega_i^2 + q_3 \Delta P_{ei}^2 + q_4 \Delta\dot{P}_{ei}^2)\mathrm{d}t \tag{7}$$

The design approach presented above, namely, nonlinear optimal excitation control (NOEC) has been a great foundation in the application of differential geometric theory in power system. People in power system community appreciate several remarkable properties of the control strategy, indeed, of the feedback linearization approach: globally linearization instead of approximate technique based on Taylor series guarantees the transient stability and improves the dynamic responds of the system under large disturbances; the acquired control law in (6) is decentralized or completely decoupled between subsystems, in the sense that, it consists of only the local information on the generator, and has nothing to do with other generators. From practical concerns, it is meaningful for implementation in reality. Besides, the control law is independent of transmission network parameters which implies the robustness and adaptability under structural and parametric changes in the system.

In the light of those characteristics, it is, theoretically, of little difficulty in practical implementation and with satisfactory ability in dealing with dynamic problems in power systems, however, it is not the case in the real system, where still PID control is mostly used. The reasons lie on the following aspects:

1)The perfect characteristics of "decentralized" in multi-machine power system excitation control has specific condition, that is the model of the system be established in the Synchronous Reference Frame. To describe it intuitively, in the system (1) for the generator i, the rotor angle is defined as $\delta_i = \omega_i t - \omega_0 t$, the difference between actual value and a pre-defined rotating axis with speed of ω_0, which determines that, the aim of the excitation control is to assure the angular speed of all the generators be converged to ω_0 and the rotor angles return to the pre-fault value after a disturbance. From the viewpoint of power system, this reveals two problematic items: first, a multi-machine power system model in SRM with n generators is equivalent to a system with $n+1$ generators in which the $(n+1)^{\text{th}}$ one is a virtual node with unlimited capacity that during transient period, its angular speed remains unchanged at ω_0. However, in real power system, it is impossible to find such a ideal node to form the model. Second, for the consideration of transient stability in power system, it is commonly agreed that, a system is said to be stable after a large disturbance, if the difference of rotor angles between any two of generators in the system goes to a constant value. The achievement of decentralized is at the expense of adding a more strict condition to assess the transient stability, which will result in a bigger desired control effort.

In power system transient stability analysis, two reference frames are used: Machine Reference Frame (MRR), choose one generator as reference machine, and Center of Inertia frame (COI)[4], define an equivalent reference angle as the average value of the system weighted by the the inertia of each generator. Establish the model in the MRR and take the nth generator as reference, (1) can be rewritten as,

$$\begin{cases} \dot{E}'_{qi} = & -\dfrac{1+(x_{di}-x'_{di})B_{ii}}{T_{d0i}}E'_{qi} \\ & +\dfrac{x_{di}-x'_{di}}{T_{d0i}}\displaystyle\sum_{j=1,j\neq i}^{n-1} Y_{ij}E'_{qj}cos(\delta_{ij}+\alpha_{ij})+\dfrac{1}{T_{d0i}}V_{fi} \\ \dot{\omega}_i = & -\dfrac{\omega_0}{H_i}(G_{ii}E'^2_{qi}+E'_{qi}\displaystyle\sum_{j=1,j\neq i}^{n} Y_{ij}E'_{qj}sin(\delta_{ij}-\alpha_{ij})) \\ & -\dfrac{D_i}{H_i}(\omega_i-\omega_0)+\dfrac{\omega_0}{H_i}P_{mi} \\ & +\dfrac{D_n}{H_n}(\omega_n-\omega_0)-\dfrac{\omega_0}{H_n}P_{mn} \\ & +\dfrac{\omega_0}{H_n}(G_{nn}E'^2_{qn}+E'_{qn}\displaystyle\sum_{j=1}^{n-1} Y_{nj}E'_{qj}sin(\delta_{nj}-\alpha_{nj})) \\ \dot{\delta}_i = & \omega_i-\omega_n \qquad i=1,2,\cdots,n-1 \end{cases} \tag{8}$$

where all the notion refer to (1). The system in (8) can be verified to satisfy the conditions of exact linearization and following the same procedure, it can be transformed into linear form as (2) via a mapping as

$$\begin{cases} z_i = \delta_i - \delta_{in0} \\ z_{n-1+i} = \omega_i - \omega_n \\ z_{2n-2+i} = \dot{\omega}_i - \dot{\omega}_n \qquad i=1,\cdots,n-1 \end{cases} \tag{9}$$

and the feedback law ν_i satisfies

$$\nu_i = -\frac{\dot{P}_{ei}}{H_i} - \frac{D_i}{H_i}\dot{\omega}_i + \frac{\dot{P}_{en}}{H_n} + \frac{D_n}{H_n}\dot{\omega}_n \tag{10}$$

which implies that, the obtained control law for excitation V_{fi} can not be decentralized. Similarly, when the system is modeled in the COI frame, the state or output variable vector of other generators will be involved in the control law, which cannot be carried out in reality sofar. For one hand, in practice, placement of measure equipments such as PMUs all over the system is not practicable due to the economic concerns; for the other, communication techniques, including synchronized transmission of information in large scale, delay impacts and data loss in network are still under investigated.

2)Linearization approach based on DGT is to use unlimited control output of the controller to cancel highly nonlinearity in the system. Usually, the control law obtained in (7) is up to 10 $\sim$ 15 times the rating value of the excitation output, of which, the maximum limit, determined by the actual capacity of excitation system and isolation tolerance at generator node, is no more than 2 times, which leads to the phenomena that, in severe disturbances, excitation output under input limits is always at its top value. Thus, the effectiveness of the control law under input constraint may not always be assured. To resolve it, [5] proposed a piecewise linear-quadratic control scheme for excitation system concretely to change the matrices Q and R piecewise in different area. Whereas, the physical meaning of the two matrices from practical concerns has not yet been clearly explained. Modification based on engineering experiences may be feasible, but mainstream of the solution relies on the theoretical development in control field.

3)The loss of voltage control during transient periods has been significant in practice. Most researches have come to the consensus of opinion that any stabilizing control must expect changes in the system voltage and the mechanism of stabilization is achieved by change of loads, which caused the voltage variation. The remaining problem has become that, how to keep the generator voltage within safe limits during angle stability stabilization. It has been discovered that, in presence of NOEC, the generator terminal voltage after large disturbances resort to 1.2 $\sim$ 1.3 p.u., which has been far beyond the acceptable range of 1.1 p.u., harmful to the safety of the generator.

In the obtained excitation control law (6), the terminal voltage of generator node is regarded as a measurable variable. Neglecting the resistant of stator windings,

$$E_{qi} = \frac{Q_{ei}x_{di}}{V_{ti}} + V_{ti} \tag{11}$$

where V_{ti} and Q_{ei} are the terminal voltage and reactive power of the ith generator node. The change of the voltage is implicitly included in power flow distribution of the whole system. How to cope with the inequality limits in the algebraic state is still a challenging problem in the implementation of control schemes in power systems.

To relax the restrict, multi-objective control schemes arose as a potential to settle the issue. [6] developed a global control strategy in SMIB system, with the brief idea to design local controllers for stability enhancement and voltage regulation respectively, and by applying a smooth switching function to achieve two objectives. Integrated control of governor and exciter[7] also exhibited some attractive results by choosing the output function as combination of multiple state variables. Nevertheless, multi-objective separation in time domain is not capable of ensuring the safety of voltage all along the stabilizing process which should be strictly satisfied due to physical limits, while integrated control is hard to deal with the zero dynamics in multi-machine systems. As a result, equipments such as fast acting terminal voltage limiter in practice is mostly used to avoid the voltage violation.

3 Nonlinear Control for Uncertainties and Disturbances

Feedback linearization technique based on DGT, relies on the exact model of the system, that is theoretically not capable of robustness with respect to structural and parametric uncertainties. To deal with the widely existent uncertainties in the power system, caused by fault disturbances and load variations, robust control methodologies are required to be employed. Consider an affine nonlinear system described by the following,

$$\begin{cases} \dot{X} = f(X) + g_1(X)W + g_2(X)U \\ Y = h(X) \end{cases} \tag{12}$$

where $X \in \mathbb{R}^n$, $U \in \mathbb{R}^m$, $W \in \mathbb{R}^p$, $Y \in \mathbb{R}^s$ are state, control, disturbance and regulation output vectors, respectively; f, g_1, g_2 and $h(X)$ are smooth vector functions with suitable dimensions, satisfying $f(0) = 0$ and $h(0) = 0$. And a penalty output can be defined as

$$Z(t) = \begin{bmatrix} h(X(t)) \\ 0 \end{bmatrix} + \begin{bmatrix} 0 \\ U(t) \end{bmatrix} \tag{13}$$

The aim of nonlinear robust control for the system (12) is twofold: firstly, to find control strategy which make the close-loop system be asymptotically stable at origin; secondly, the control strategy can make the L_2−gain G_2 from disturbance W to penalty vector Z be less than or equal to a prescribed positive number γ, that is

$$\int_0^{\mathrm{T}} (\gamma^2 \|W\|^2 - \|Z\|^2)dt \geqslant 0, \quad \forall T > 0 \tag{14}$$

To resolve the problem, great contributions have been made: use the results in linear case and recursive procedure avoiding HJI inequalities. Accordingly, nonlinear robust excitation control can be roughly summarized into two major branches, nonlinear H infinite control and nonlinear (adaptive) control via backstepping procedure.

Consider the n−generator system with bounded uncertainties and disturbances, it is conventionally modeled as,

$$\begin{cases} \dot{\delta}_i = \omega_i - \omega_0 \\ \dot{\omega}_i = \dfrac{\omega_0}{H_i}(P_{mi} - P_{ei}) - \dfrac{D_i}{H_i}(\omega_i - \omega_0) + \Delta_{i1} \\ \dot{E}'_{qi} = \dfrac{1}{T'_{d0}}(E_{fi} - E'_{qi} - (X_{di} - X'_{di})I_{di}) + \Delta_{i2} \end{cases} \tag{15}$$

where the notation can refer to (1), Δ_{i1} and Δ_{i2} denote the disturbances. And the ith generator can be represented in the form as,

$$\dot{X}_i = f_i(X) + g_i(X)u_{fi} + q_{i1}w_{i1} + q_{i2}w_{i2} \tag{16}$$

where $X_i = [\delta_i, \omega_i, E'_{qi}]^{\mathrm{T}}$.

For nonlinear H infinite approach reported in literature[2]and [8] , L_2-gain in linear case is precisely equal to the H_∞ norm of the closed loop transfer function, instead of HJI inequality, by solving Riccati inequality, feedback control law can be obtained which asymptotically stabilized the system when $W = 0$, and renders $\|T_{ZW}\| < \gamma$. Apply the feedback linearization approach to (15), following coordinates transforms can be set up,

$$\begin{cases} z_1 = \delta_i - \delta_0 \\ z_2 = L_{fi}h_i(X) = \omega_i - \omega_0 \\ z_3 = L_{fi}^2 h_i(X) = \dfrac{\omega_0}{H_i}\left(P_{mi} - P_{ei} - \dfrac{D_i}{\omega_0}(\omega_i - \omega_0)\right) \end{cases} \tag{17}$$

and the state feedback can be determined as $\nu_i = L_{fi}^3 h_i(X) + L_{g_i} L_{fi}^2 h_i(X) u_i$. Thus, the system (15) is transformed into

$$\begin{cases} \dot{Z} = AZ + B_1\bar{W} + B_2\nu_i \\ y = CZ \end{cases} \tag{18}$$

Therefore, based on linear robust control theory, the control input for the system (18) can be calculated via Riccati inequality,

$$\nu_i^* = -B_2^{\mathrm{T}} P^* Z = -(p_{31}^* z_1 + p_{32}^* z_2 + p_{33}^* z_3) \tag{19}$$

Regarded as a successful extension of DGT, the NREC is also constrained by the limits presented in the previous section.

Except for the linearization related methods, [9] and [10]proposed a nonlinear decentralized disturbance attenuation problem(NDDAP) using recursive design approach without linearization treatment. Enriched with adaptability to unknown parameters, [11] put forward an adaptive excitation control law that possessed the robustness with respect to the external disturbance in the sense of L_2-gain, when the reactance of the generator is unknown.

To summarize the approach, consider the system in (15). The aim of the controller design is to stabilize the system and drive the rotor angle δ_i to a small neighborhood of the desired setting value δ_i^d under the condition that, the damping coefficientD_i, d-axis reactance X_{di} and X'_{di} remain unknown. Thus, a coordination is defined as $x_i = [\delta_i - \delta_i^d, \omega_i - \omega_0, \frac{\omega_0}{M_i}(P_{mi} - P_{ei})]^{\mathrm{T}}$, which can transform the system (15) into the perturbed exact-feedback nonlinear form (20) with $y_i(t) = \delta_i - \delta_i^d$ defined as the output of each subsystem.

$$\begin{cases} \dot{x}_{i1} = x_{i2} \\ \dot{x}_{i2} = x_{i3} + \theta_i^{\mathrm{T}}\varphi_{i1} + d_{i1} \\ \dot{x}_{i3} = \nu_i + \theta_i^{\mathrm{T}}\varphi_{i2} + d_{i2} \\ y_i = x_{i1} \end{cases} \tag{20}$$

Backstepping algorithm is applied using the conventional change of coordinates below,

$$\begin{cases} z_{i1} = x_{i1} \\ z_{i2} = x_{i2} + k_{i1}x_{i1} \\ z_{i3} = x_{i3} - \alpha_i \end{cases} \tag{21}$$

where k_{i1} is a positive constant,α_1 is a function satisfying $\alpha_i \mid_{x_i=0}= 0$. The unknown parameters and disturbances are considered, during the recursive procedure, of which the essence is to construct energy storage function step by step: first to preset an imperfect energy function (22) for the subsystem consisting of the first two functions in (21),

$$V_{i1} = \frac{1}{2}z_{i1}^2 + \frac{1}{2}z_{i2}^2 + \frac{1}{2}\tilde{\theta}_i^{\mathrm{T}}\Gamma_i^{-1}\tilde{\theta}_i + \frac{1}{2\gamma_{i1}}\tilde{\zeta}_{i1}^2 \tag{22}$$

where $\mid d_{i1} \mid\leqslant \zeta_{i1}$ is positive constant bounding the unknown term, with its estimation error $\tilde{\zeta}_{i1} = \hat{\zeta}_{i1} - \zeta_{i1}$, and $\tilde{\theta}_i = \hat{\theta}_i - \theta_i$ denotes the vector of parameter estimation errors. By solving its time derivative, the adaptive laws for parameters and the function of α_i can be determined. Then, extend it into the last sub-equations in (21) yields a Lyapunov function satisfying $\dot{V}_i \leqslant -c_i V_i + \lambda_i$ which implies that, z_i,$\tilde{\theta}_i$,$\tilde{\zeta}_{i1}$ and $\tilde{\zeta}_{i2}$ are uniformly ultimately bounded and the output y_i is regulated to a small neighborhood of zero.

It can be concluded from the two approaches that, affine nonlinear robust control problem has been well settled. However, whether is proper to model the disturbances by a bounded power and voltage term P_{dis} and V_{dis} needs to be further discussed. Changes in system structure and physical parameters after a fault have specific characteristic in system dynamics, errors of parameters, uncertainties during transient period appear in certain parts of the model. Over-simplified expression in the model may lead to unprecise and improper results that restricts the application in reality.

4 Direct Method Based on Lyapunov Theory

Direct method based on Lyapunov theory without necessarily solving differential equations has been a powerful tool to estimate the stability region of power systems after transient dynamics, namely, transient energy function method. Described in a general way, it is to find a energy-like function represented by the system state variables to evaluate the impact of a severe fault onto the system, and estimate whether the system can preserve stability post fault.

Consider a n generator system in MRR, under severe contingency, the dynamics of the system can be decomposed into three time periods.

Pre-fault at steady state:

$$\delta_i = \delta_i(0) - \delta_i^0, \quad \dot{\delta}_i = 0$$

Fault-on period ($0 < t \leqslant t_c$), a fault occurs at $t = 0$, and cleared at t_c:

$$M_i \frac{d^2\delta_i}{dt^2} + D_i \frac{d\delta_i}{dt} = P_{mi}^F - P_{ei}^F$$

with initial states $\delta_i(0) = \delta_i^0$ and $\dot{\delta}_i(0) = 0$.

Post-fault period ($t > t_c$):

$$M_i\frac{d^2\delta_i}{dt^2}+D_i\frac{d\delta_i}{dt}=P_{mi}^{PF}-P_{ei}^{PF}$$

with initial states $\delta_i(t_c)$ and $\dot{\delta}_i(t_c)$.

According to [12], the Aylett-type energy function can be obtained by Energy-Integral Criterion,

$$\begin{aligned}V(\delta,\omega)&=\sum_{i=1}^{n-1}\sum_{j=i+1}^{n}[\frac{1}{2M_T}M_iM_j(\omega_i-\omega_j)^2\\&-\frac{1}{M_T}(P_iM_j-P_jM_i)(\delta_{ij}-\delta_{ij}^s)\\&-E_iE_jB_{ij}(cos\delta_{ij}-cos\delta_{ij}^s)]\\&=V_K(\omega)+V_{P1}(\delta)+V_{P2}(\delta)\end{aligned}\tag{23}$$

where $(\delta^s,0)$ is the equilibrium point in post-fault, and two state switchings occur at $t=0$ and $t=t_c$. In (23), the transient energy consists of three parts, transient kinetic energy in first term, transient potential energy in the second and third terms, representing the part caused by deviation of rotor angle with respect to the equilibrium point and energy stored in the system magnetic field, respectively. It can be verified that, (23) strictly satisfies the conditions of a Lyapunov function, which has been the basis of transient stability assessment, emergency control and preventive control.

However, in the above approach of energy function construction, two assumptions are imposed.

First, in deduction of (23), the shift conductance G_{ij} is ignored. When it is considered in the system, an additional term will be involved

$$V(\delta,\omega)=V_K(\omega)+V_{P1}(\delta)+V_{P2}(\delta)+V_{P3}(\delta)\tag{24}$$

where

$$\begin{aligned}V_{PE3}(\delta)=\frac{1}{M_i}\int_{\delta^s}^{\delta}(\sum_{i=1}^{n-1}\sum_{j=i+1}^{n}(M_j\sum_{k=1}^{n}E_iE_kG_{ik}cos\delta_{ik})\\-M_i(\sum_{k=1,k\neq j}^{n}E_iE_kG_{ik}cos\delta_{ik}))d\delta_{ij}\end{aligned}\tag{25}$$

Actually, the term of (25) belongs to the dissipative item which is related to integral path and the energy function (24) is no longer Lyapunov type. How to properly deal with it needs carefully investigation, since the term(25), practical implying the transmission loss in power system may account for up to 20 percent of the total energy (25)in critical contingencies, which will cause unacceptable errors.

Second, the transient energy function is obtained based on post-fault system, where the post-fault equilibrium point needs to be calculated beforehand. Therefore, when determining the control measures to enlarge the range of stability, the impact of control on the post-fault equilibrium cannot be considered or exactly calculated without iterative procedure. For simplicity, post-fault equilibrium point is commonly supposed to be fixed once the fault (fault-on trajectory)is known, regardless of control implement, which is imprecise and practically not sound.

5 Conclusions

Power system, highly nonlinear in nature, has long been recognized as important field in nonlinear control applications. However, in practice, attractive results can hardly be carried out in real system. In this paper, three major approaches have been reviewed, based on which, the existing problems between theoretical analysis and practical implementation were pointed out from viewpoint of power system.

References

1. A.Isidori, *Nonlinear Control Systems: An introduction*, 3rd Edition, Springer Verlag, 1995.
2. Qiang Lu, Yuanzhang Sun and Shengwei Mei, *Nonlinear Control Systems and Power system Dynamics*, Kluwer Academic Publishers, 2001.
3. Q. Lu, Y. Sun, Z.Xu and T. Mochizuki, Decentralized Nonlinear Optimal Excitation Control. *IEEE Trans. PWRS*, v.11, No.4, pp.1957-1962, 1996.
4. Prabha Kundur, *Power System Stability and Control*, 1st Edition, McGraw-Hill Companies, Inc, 1994.
5. Xie Xiaorong,Qian Hua, and Cui Wenjin, A Design Method of Linear-quadratic Excitation Control Considering Input Constrains. *Power System Technology* vol.24, No.10, 2000.
6. Yi Guo, David J. Hill, and Youyi Wang, Global Transient Stability and Voltage Regulation for Power Systems. *IEEE Trans. PWRS*, vol.16, no.4, 2001
7. Xiaocong Li, Shijie Cheng, Hua Wei and Jia Ma, Multi-Objective Nonlinear Integrated Control for Turbine Generator Unit.*IEEE Proc. Transimission and distribution*, pp. 767-773, 2003.
8. Sun C, and Zhao Z, Design of Nonlinear Robust Excitation Control for Multi-Machine Power Systems. *IEE Proc. Gener. Trans. and Distrib*, vol.143, no.3, pp. 253-257, 1996.
9. Lu Q., Mei S.W., Hu W., Wu F.F., Ni Y.X., and Shen T.L, Nonlinear decentralised disturbance attenuation excitation control via new recursive design for multi-machine power systems. *IEEE Trans. PWRS.*, vol.16, pp. 729-736, 2001.
10. Y.Z.Sun, M.Cao, S.W.Mei, T.L.Shen, and Y.H.Song, Nonliear Disturbance Attenuation Controller for Turbo-generators in Power Systems via Recursive Design", *IEEE Proc. on Control Applications*, pp. 938-943, 2002.
11. Shen Tielong, Mei Shengwei, and Lu Qiang, Adaptive nonlinear excitation control with L2 disturbance attenuation for power systems. *Automatic*, vol.39, pp.81-89, 2003.
12. Aylett P. D., The Energy-Integral Criterion of Tansient Stability Limits of Power Systems. *PTOC. IEE*, vol.105C, 1958.

Part III

Control of Vehicular Systems

New Challenges in Powertrain Control —— Advanced Engine Control System Development Environment

Junichi Kako

Toyota Motor Corporation, Shizuoka-ken, Japan
jun@kako.tec.toyota.co.jp

1 Introduction

The recent control system development requires more sophisticated and complex control strategies and handling more data. It would lead to a continuous and exponential increase of human resources and development time. So, the improvement of the development process and methodologies become urgent issues.

Almost all car manufactures have the activities to realize the V process. In the conventional process, there are a lot of iterative steps. In order to increase the productivity, they should be removed. To accomplish this, the development process will be supported by many CACSD tools and real time simulation technologies. The data and model management tools should be also needed. These tools should be highly integrated and shared among car manufacturers and their suppliers. The verification and the validation of the developed control systems are extremely time-consuming jobs. Toyota is keen to get the technologies for efficient verification and validation methods.

Vehicle and powertrain models play important roles to improve the control performances and the productivity of the control system development processes. Especially rapid modeling is the key to realize the concurrent development environment of powertrain hardware and control software. This is an extension of the V process for software developments. In this paper, the directions to improve Toyota's engine control system development will be described.

In order to realize the above-mentioned efficient development, the concurrent development process between hardware and software should be adopted in place of the traditional development process, i.e., control logic is developed after the completion of the prototype engine.

One of the most important methods for the efficient development is modeling. Many automotive companies and their suppliers carry forward the model-based development (MBD)[1~3]. The model consists of a controller model and a plant model. The controller model expresses the control logic using the bloc diagram and state transition diagram with the Simulink/Stateflow. It also leads to improving the controller performance and shortening the calibration time together with the model-based control (MBC), which means the design of the control logic from the engine model, and for model-based calibration (MBC).

In this paper, we will discuss firstly the concept of the MBD and secondly show an actual example of the concurrent development and the rapid modeling.

2 The Base Concept of MBD

The controller specifications of four cylinder engines have evoluted as described in Fig. 1. The control logic has become more and more complex due to the advanced control logic and high performance ECU for executing it. The control logic can no longer be verified after putting together the engine system and the logic. So it is essential to verify it in each part or step and improve the quality.

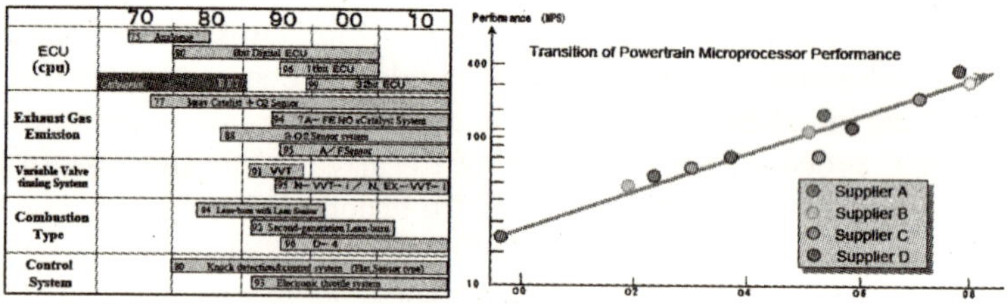

Fig. 1 Controller specifications

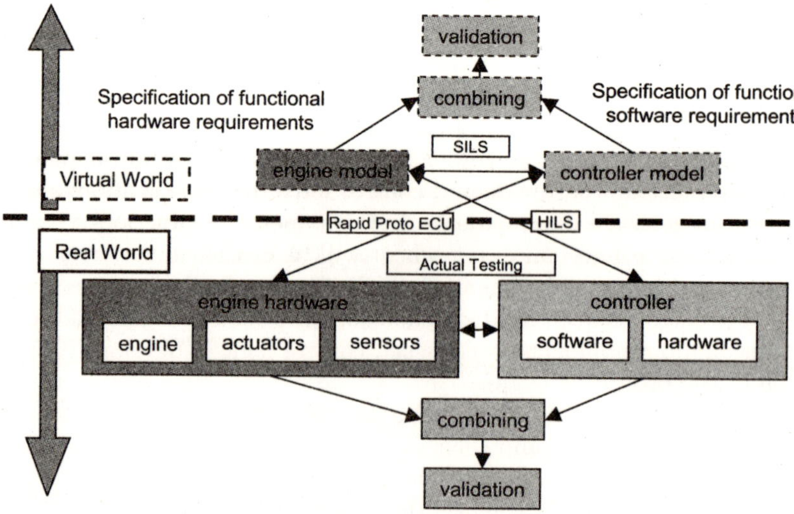

Fig. 2 Controller specifications

Fig. 2 shows the base concept of MBD. The conventional work is mainly in the real world. After the development of both engine and ECU are finalized, the control logic is verified with them. The disadvantage of this developing process is that it needs much time to wait for the completion of the engine and the ECU, or it may need a control logic redesign if the performance is insufficient. In order to avoid the disadvantage, the development in the virtual world is adopted as shown in the figure. One example is the ECU verification with the engine model installed in HILS (hardware-in-the-loop-simulation). Another example is the control logic evaluation with RPE (rapid proto ECU) before the ECU is completed. The controller design and the verification with the models can be used for improving the quality and shortening the development time. It is necessary to change from development in the real world with hardware, to the development in the virtual world with model.

3 Concurrent Development and Rapid Modeling (Modeling Framework)

Fig. 3 shows the development process for the concurrent engineering. The purpose of this process is to start the software development at the same time of the hardware development. When the engine hardware development is started, the engine model is rapidly made using the specifications and the experimental data of the parts. The engine model is used to verify the required performance in the various operating conditions. If the performance is not sufficient, the hardware should be changed and improved in accordance with the result of the simulation. In order to achieve the high quality and the efficient development, the simultaneous development and verification between the hardware and software is important. It means that the rapid modeling is the essential technology in the system design.

In order to realize the rapid modeling, the way how the models are managed functionally is important[4,5]. One of the methods is the modeling framework. It is shown in Fig. 4. It consists of the three items as follows:

a) Model library: all models of the engine parts should be prepared for assembling the engine system model at the same time when the project starts. In the library, the parts models with the various accuracies should be included because the required accuracy depends on the usage.

b) Modeling tool: From the model library, the models of the parts are picked out and combined, and the engine system model is made. The modeling tool should be possible to pick out the parts models, coordinate their inputs and outputs and combine them.

c) Data base: the parts models and the engine system model are used for general purposes. To simulate these models, the specifications should be inputted into the models. Besides that, some parameters should be fitted using the experimental data. The data of the each part that coincides with the part model is rather preferred to the data of the whole engine. The accuracy of the each model can be evaluated before assembling and evaluating the engine system model. The models and the fitted parameters can be used as the substitutes for the test data that the suppliers submit.

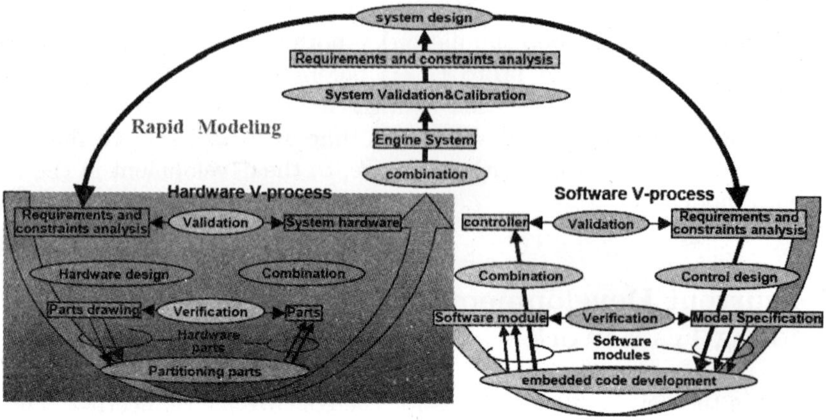

Fig. 3 Concurrent development

Another important process for the rapid modeling is surveying the needs, which means investigating the information of the new sensors and actuators that is carried in the new engine, and storing the models into the library. Based on the concept, the rapid modeling and concurrent development was carried out.

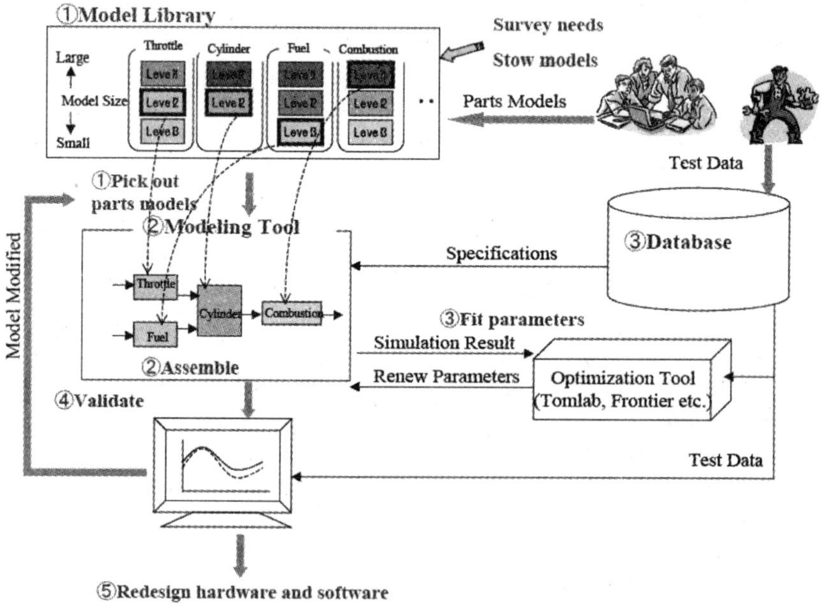

Fig. 4 Concurrent development

4 Constructing the Environment for the Rapid Modeling and its Investigation

The modeling framework and the rapid modeling environment are constructed with the HILS system and examined (Fig. 5).

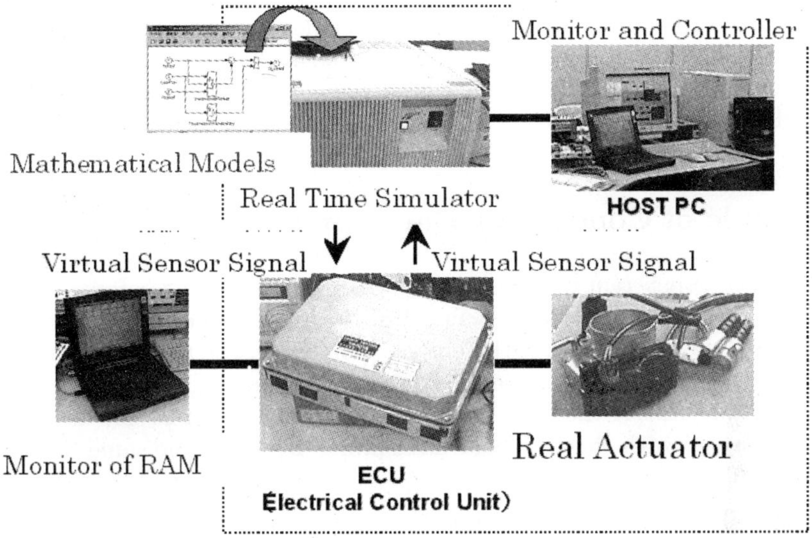

Fig. 5 HILS system

4.1 What Is HILS?

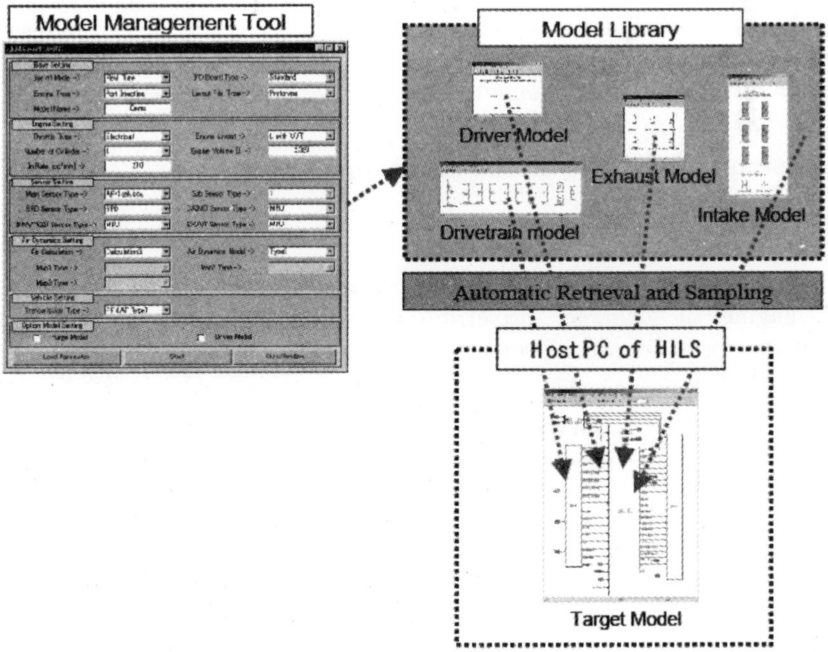

Fig. 6 Automatically assembling function of the parts models

The rapid modeling tool constructed for HILS is shown in Fig. 6. That is named as model management tool. When we input the number of cylinders, sensors and actuators by using the GUI(graphical user interface), the computer detects and picks out the parts models from the model library and also the engine system model is automatically made in the host PC. It can make the engine system model rapidly without artificial errors. A task beforehand is to prepare the model library.

5 Example of Concurrent Development

We examined concurrent development between hardware and software based on the thought of rapid modeling discussed in the previous chapter. We applied it to the actual development of turbo engine. The purpose is to feedback the result of the model simulation (function verification) to the engine hardware design. The important part of the concurrent development is to start the development of control design with this model or a simplified model at the same time.

5.1 Example of Concurrent Development of Turbo Engine

We selected the turbo engine development as the target of the concurrent development. Turbo engine has the problem generally called "turbo lag". To solve that problem, we use the process that can develop hardware and software concurrently and we can choose the best combination between engine part and drivetrain part according to the simulation results. This way we can reduce the variation of trial manufacturing and experimenting with real products, and design the control logic to the simulation model[6] at the same time.

5.2 Construction of The Simulation Model

5.2.1 Whole Construction

We need the total simulation model that contains the whole part of the vehicle such as engine, turbocharger, drivetrain and so on, to improve the vehicle acceleration performance. So we constructed whole vehicle model with engine and drivetrain (Fig. 7).

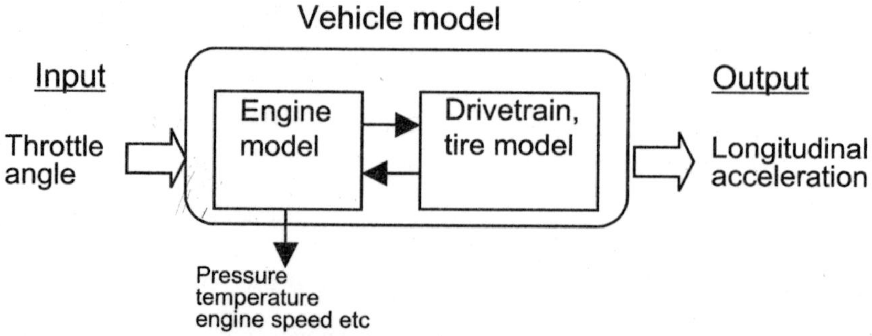

Fig. 7 Configuration of the model

Various simulation tools are used in our company. For example, GT-Power and Boost are used for engine simulation. But these simulations are used for designing hardware and for analyzing phenomena of the engine. Problems arise as below when we use these simulation tools for studies that include the development of engine control:

- We need to request for the software maker, if we want to add new items. (Flexibility).
- Calculation speed is slow if we need the close-loop simulation in examining system performance.
- People who develop (or design) the control logic should know the basic physical equations, but most software is inconvenient for them because inner equations of most package software are hidden.

Because of the reasons as above, we prepare simulation models for this study by ourselves.

5.2.2 Whole Construction

Fig. 8 shows the outline of the engine model. We construct models for each part of the engine and the equations in the models are based on the conservation law of mass and energy.

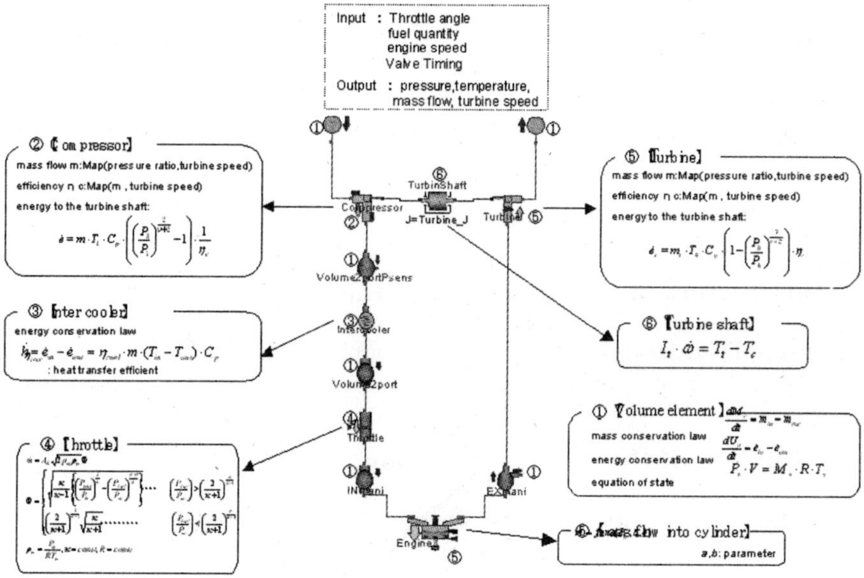

Fig. 8 Engine model with turbocharger (Dymola)

5.2.3 Evaluation of the Engine Model with Turbocharger

A. Steady State

Fig. 9 shows the simulation result of temperature, pressure and mass flow at steady state compared with the measured result. Accuracy of every model is within 10 percent at all calculation points throughout the whole engine operation area.

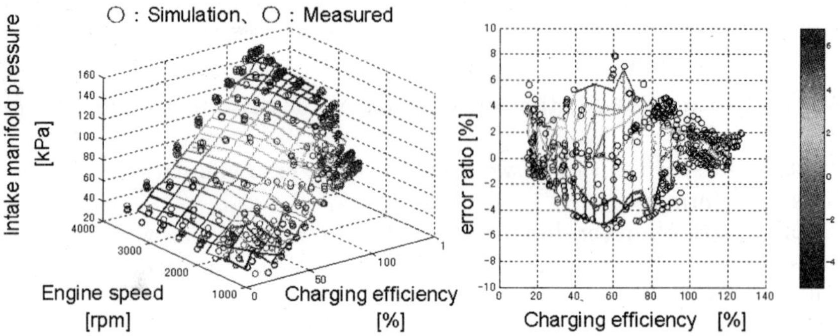

Fig. 9 Verification of the engine system model in the steady state condition

B. Transition State

Fig.10 shows the simulation result at transient condition. The model can simulate the pressure of the inlet pipe, the turbine speed of the turbocharger and so on.

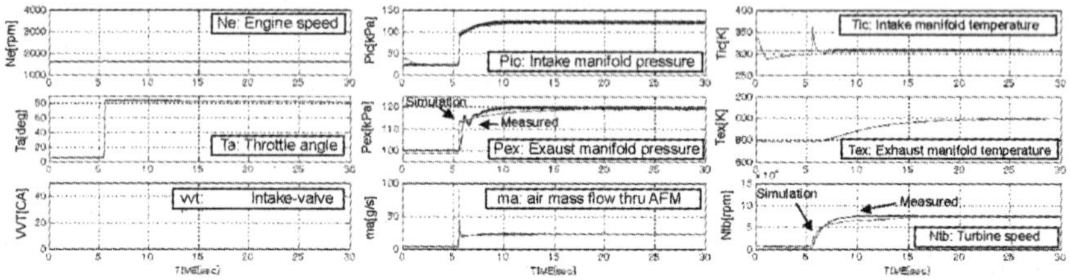

Fig. 10 Verification of the engine system model in the transient

5.2.4 Construction of the Engine-drivetrain Model

We use a simplified model which contains models of torque converter and gear for the drivetrain model, to simulate a longitudinal acceleration of the vehicle.

5.2.5 Evaluation of the Engine-drivetrain Model

Fig. 11 show the simulation result compared with the behavior of the actual vehicle. We compared a measured longitudinal acceleration. The model simulates the real vehicle well.

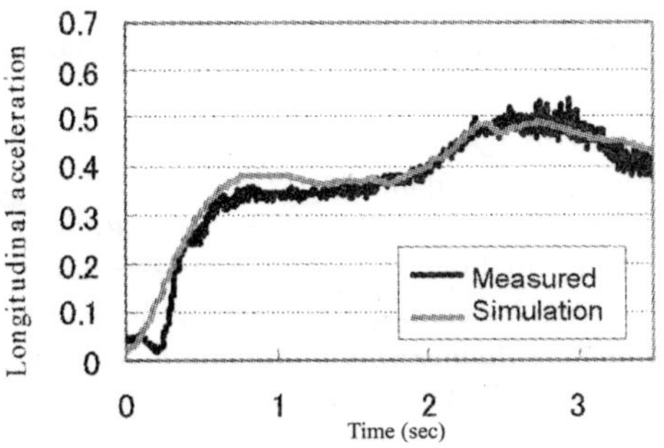

Fig. 11 Accuracy of the model

5.3 Utilization of the Simulation

To improve the acceleration performance, we simulated first the items with largest effect on the acceleration performance among the constituent elements listed below. (effective elements, parameter, item on the acceleration performance)

- engine : intercooler, exhaust gas temperature,· · ·
- turbocharger: turbine size, shaft inertia,· · ·
- drivetrain: torque converter, gear ratio,· · ·

Turbine size, turbine shaft inertia and gear ratio turned out to be effective according to the simulation result that calculates the effect of each item. Fig.12 shows the simulation result of changing the turbine shaft inertia. Fig.13 shows the result of the torque converter. We knew before simulation that acceleration performance was improved if turbine shaft inertia was smaller and torque converter was looser, so we chose the best specification considering other constrains such as durability and manufacturability.

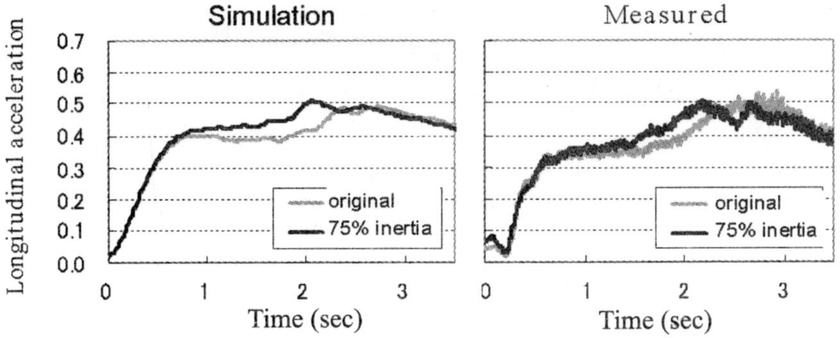

Fig. 12 Influence of the turbine inertia

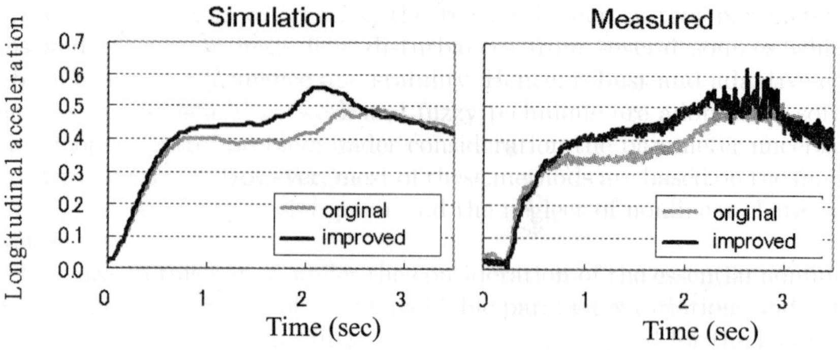

Fig. 13 Influence of the turbine inertia

Next is the study about the turbine size. The line of 1 in Fig. 14 shows the acceleration performance response and the engine power if the turbine capacity is changed when the other parts of the engine and drivetrain are kept constant. The bigger turbine size gives bigger power, but the acceleration performance becomes worse. When we choose appropriate items to acceleration other than turbine capacity, such as the turbine shaft inertia and torque converter,the power is improved to the line of 2 in Fig. 14.

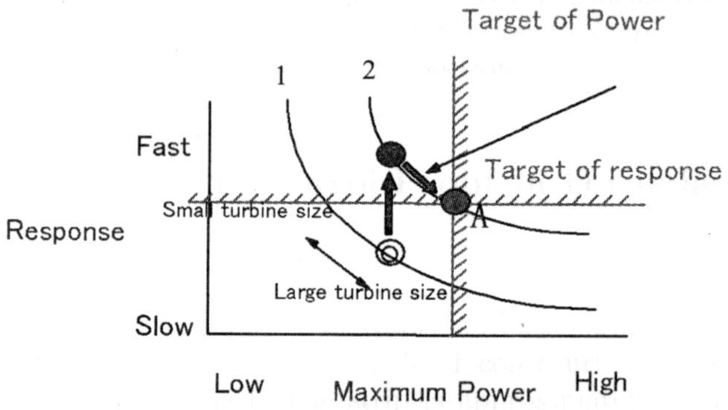

Fig. 14 Turbine capacity vs. acceleration

We select the turbine size that can satisfy both acceleration performance and engine power as result from simulation. As the concrete method, first we estimate the improvement of the acceleration performance by the simulation at the condition to consider the turbine inertia and torque converter, and the next we change the turbine size that satisfy both response and power (point A).

Engine control also has a great influence on acceleration performance, so we used the same model not only for the hardware design but also for the design of engine control, estimating the influence of the exhaust gas temperature, which can be controlled by changing the ignition timing, and so on.

5.4 Result and Problem

By this simulation, we can select the best item without many experimental products. Fig.15 shows that we can achieve the expected performance by comparing longitudinal acceleration between simulation results and real vehicle.

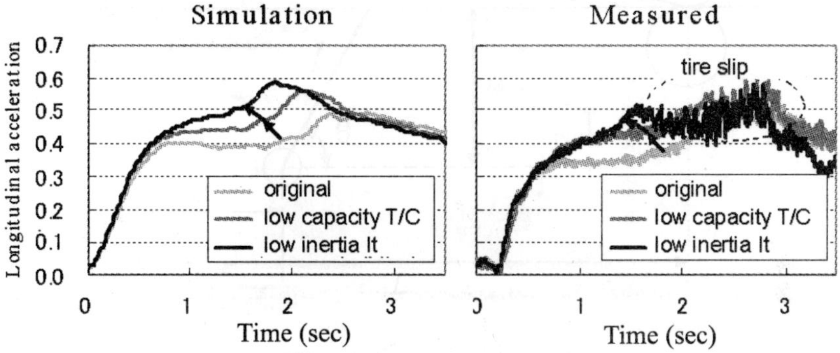

Fig. 15 Measured vs. simulated results on the acceleration

Also we can raise the percentage of completion by simulating various type of control designs on the desk. Problems, which appeared through this study, are listed below:

- We need all parts models like turbocharger and torque converter before starting the development to realize the concurrent development. So we must research in advance what parts models will be needed for the simulation, and we must construct the process of making models timely.
- Although at this study we made an engine model by connecting parts models after checking interfaces like the numbers of I/O and signals of each model well, we must unify the interface of all parts models to connect models at different percentage of completion, so we must match all interfaces among parts models. In other words, if we define the input and the output of each model strictly, we can exchange parts models with suppliers and connect the model easily.

6 Apply Model to Calibration

In the previous section, the modeling framework and the concurrent development are discussed. In this section, the concept of model at the calibration process and an example will be discussed.

6.1 Incremental Modeling

Engine control logic becomes more and more complicated. Reduction of number of calibration points, which has risen to tens of thousands, has become the big challenge. To solve this problem, many research has been done by many companies by using tools like DoE (design of experiment), MBC (model based calibration), or simulation models. The study to increase efficiency of calibration by using models will be reported below.

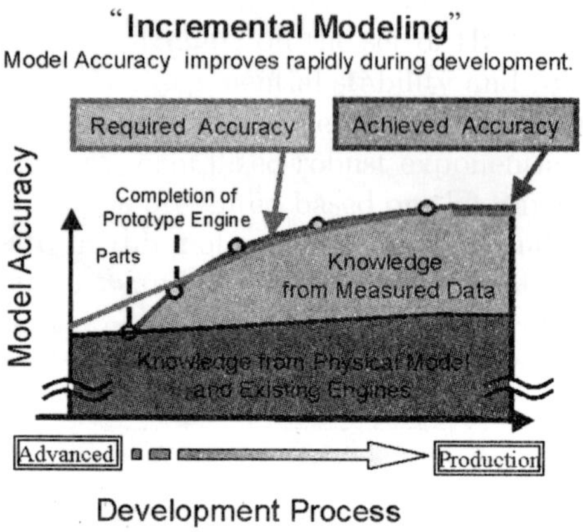

Fig. 16 Concepts of incremental modeling

Fig. 16 shows the model accuracy required from advanced development to mass production development. We don't need models with high accuracy to estimate rough performance of engine at the beginning of the advanced development, but according to the progress to the mass product development, models with high accuracy become important. For example, at the beginning of the development, calibration points are decided by using physical models and database mainly, then after systems are fixed, the model with high accuracy made by measured data is used. In other words, we increase the accuracy of models to the developmental phase and use models appropriate in size and accuracy. It is also effective to combine physical models with statistical models based on the experimental data. Fig.17 shows the concept of how to combine physical models and statistical models. We make a model by superposing the statistical model, which is made by modeling the error between the result of real engine and physical model, on the result of the physical model. If the physical model can express the tendency of real engine, we can approximate the difference by a low level function and reduce the number of measuring points to make the statistical model. To combine physical models with statistical models has the advantage to use experimental design like DoE in reducing the number of measuring points, because the error of one point has big influence on it.

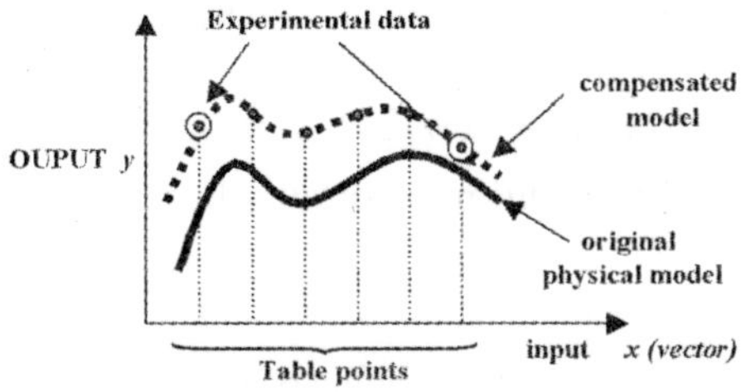

Fig. 17 Concept of error function for indirect calibration

Fig. 18 shows that the combination of physical models and statistical models is very effective to improve accuracy. We show here the example how to construct the model to simulate intake air capacity by using model and some measuring points. Although the accidental error is big in 1 (cylinder model identified by one point) and 2(the statistical model identified by 26 points), we can improve accuracy of model by the combination of 1 and 2, without increasing the number of measuring points so much. Therefore, we use the calibration value made by the physical model at the initial engine testing phase, and we use the more appropriate calibration value made by both physical models and examination data after measuring data more.

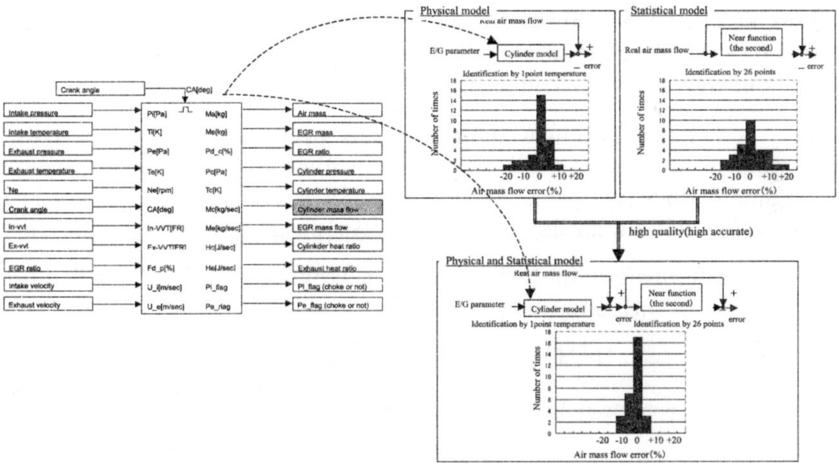

Fig. 18 Results of model based calibration

7 Conclusions

Concurrent development between hardware and software is important improve the quality and to reduce the developmental period. The construction of the rapid modeling is the key technology to accomplish this concurrent development above all. For that purpose we made the concept of the rapid modeling and model framework to realize this. We began with the construction of this mechanism on HILS and proved its effect. Then we applied this rapid modeling tool on HILS to the control and the hardware development of the turbocharger engine. Results are listed up below:

- This rapid modeling method is very effective for the construction of the system model at the early phase of development to improve the quality of both hardware and software.
- Challenges remain such as how to manage parts models and how to unify interface among parts models to apply the rapid modeling to the hardware and software development effectively and timely. Also a system which we can improve the model accuracy according to the development phase is needed.
- For the incremental model, a good result throughout the process from the hardware and software development to calibration was achieved, however more detailed study is required.

8 Closing

The whole automotive industry is trying to change the developing process not only to improve engine control quality but also to shorten the developmental period of engine control system and to reduce the resources for development. Model based development (MBD) based on the control instrument model and the engine model is regarded as the very effective means to realize these purposes.

To make the MBD more effective we should construct a framework to share parts models and system models between car companies and parts suppliers. This includes the construction of a development environment which clarifies the relationship among control, model and experimental data and which establishes the methodology how to simplify the model.

The engine model should be made up of the mixture of mechanical, electrical, thermodynamical, fluidomechanical and chemical information , however there is no modeling tool that can deal with the engine model totally, nor shared guideline for modeling.

References

1. Marco Kunze, et al., Model based Development Environment at Siemens VDO Automotive AG Division Power Train, International Automotive Conference, 2004.
2. Mario Wunsche, et al., Model based development of Cruise Control for Mercedes Benz Trucks, International Automotive Conference, 2004.
3. Yukio Kuroda, The development process of enjine control, A short course teaching materials(No.04-45) of The Japan Society of Mechanical Engineers, 2004 (Japanese).
4. Kenneth R. Butts,et al., A Model Repository for Automotive Embedded Control System Design, Proceedings of DTEC'03 ASME 2003 Design Engineering Technical Conferences and Cpmputers and Information in Engineering Conference.
5. Jason Ghidella, Enterprise-Wide Development of Model-Based Design, Model-Based Design for Control System Conference, MATLAB EXPO, 2004.
6. Martin Muller, et al., Mean Value Modeling of Turbocharged Spark Ignition Engines,SAE Technical Paper No.980784.

Air-Fuel Ratio Balancing Control with Single Sensor for Multi-Cylinder Internal Combustion Engines

Kenji Suzuki, Tielong Shen and Yasuhiko Mutou

Department of Mechanical Engineering, Sophia University, Tokyo, 102-8554, Japan

1 Introduction

In the IC engine with multi-cylinder, the event of combustion occurs sequentially in the cylinders, and due to the uncertainties in air and fuel paths of each cylinder, imbalances of cylinder-to-cylinder and cycle-to-cycle are unavoidable in practice. In order to provide high quality of driving torque generation and reduce emission, balancing control of individual cylinders in the multi-cylinder engine has attracted much attention in the recent years[1~7], and the air-fuel ratio (A/F) control for individual cylinder is one of the challenging issues in the balancing control problems.

A key problem in individual cylinder air-fuel ratio control is the estimation of individual cylinders with a single sensor placed in the gas mixing point. Various approaches to estimation of the A/F of individual cylinders have been proposed in the past years. [1] presented that the intake and exhaust manifold and the sensor were modeled by one order system respectively. Under appropriate geometrical condition on the exhaust runners of the engine, [2] presented an individual A/F estimation method, and in [3] the exhaust gas dynamics was taken into account in the engine model used for individual A/F estimation. [4] estimated the individual A/F by a sliding observer for the dynamics of intake air and fuel. In [5] the individual A/F was obtained by a nonlinear observer for the flows of intake air and the exhaust gas estimated by the exhaust manifold pressure. In addition, there are some papers controlled individual A/F, [1] addressed this problem by utilizing the LQG control theory, [5] applied PI controller and [6] presented an adaptive learning method.

In this chapter, we will focus our attention on the ratio of the fuel mass to the exhaust gas (F/G) for the individual cylinders. Obviously, the ratio is one-to-one mapping of the air-fuel ratio, hence we enable to control the air-fuel ratio via individually control the fuel-gas ratio. Furthermore, we will consider a filtered F/G for each cylinder as controlled output. Our first contribution in this chapter is to provide a linear model for estimation of the output with measurement of the single sensor under an operating condition. Then, an adaptive control law with the estimation will be proposed by applying the adaptive minimum variance control techniques. Finally, some experimental results on a test bench will be demonstrated.

2 Individual F/G Estimation Model

2.1 System Outline

We consider a six-cylinder engine. As shown in Fig. 1, each three cylinders share one exhaust manifold and for each manifold the UEGO (universal exhaust gas oxygen) sensor is placed in the gas mixing points. The injected fuel with the gas determined by the air path is breathed into the cylinders in the intake phase, and after the combustion phase the gas will be exhausted to the exhaust runners. The A/F of individual cylinders is performed in the expansion phase and will be propagated with the gas flow passing through the runners, manifolds and the gas mixing point. In the following, we consider the 2,4,6th cylinders only which share the same exhaust manifold.

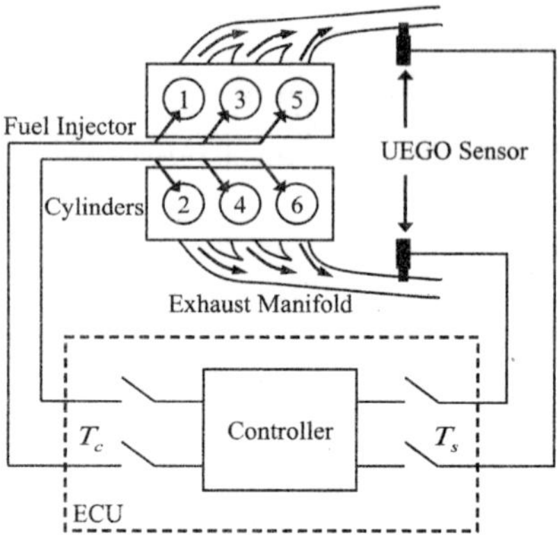

Fig. 1 Schematic representation of A/F control system

Suppose that components of the exhaust gas are fresh air and fuel. Then, if we define the fuel-gas ratio (F/G) as G_f/G_{ex}, where G_f and G_a denote the mass of fuel and the fresh air in the exhaust gas and $G_{ex} = G_a + G_f$, then, it is easy to show that $G_f/G_{ex} = 1/(1+\lambda)$ where $\lambda = G_a/G_f$ denotes the air-fuel ratio. It means that we can obtain the F/G with the sensor measurement of A/F directly. Moreover, in order to normalize G_f/G_{ex}, we redefine F/G as follows,

$$\eta = \frac{15.7}{1+\lambda} \tag{1}$$

Obviously, $\eta = 1$ when λ takes the value 14.7. In order to control the individual F/G of each cylinder, exactly the value of F/G in each exhaust runner at the exhaust phase of the corresponding cylinder, we define a "filtered" output of each cylinder η_{si} as follows,

$$\eta_{si} = G_{sen}(s)\eta_i, \quad i = 2, 4, 6 \tag{2}$$

where

$$G_{sen}(s) = \frac{e^{-\tau_d s}}{\tau_s s + 1} \tag{3}$$

represent sensor dynamics, and define the measurement of the sensor at the gas mixing point as follows

$$\eta_s = G_{sen}(s)\eta \tag{4}$$

where η_i and η denote the F/G of each cylinder and at the mixing point respectively.

As shown in Fig.2, the control system consist of multiple sampling rate, i.e. the control input, fuel injection command, will be delivered once for each cylinder in each cycle, and the estimation of the individual F/G will be provided once too in each cycle by the estimation model. However, the sampling of the sensor at the gas mixing point will provide the values at the BDC of each cylinder in each cycle. In the following, we will show the individual F/G estimation model which provides the estimation of η_{si} based on the sampling data η_s at BDC of each cylinder.

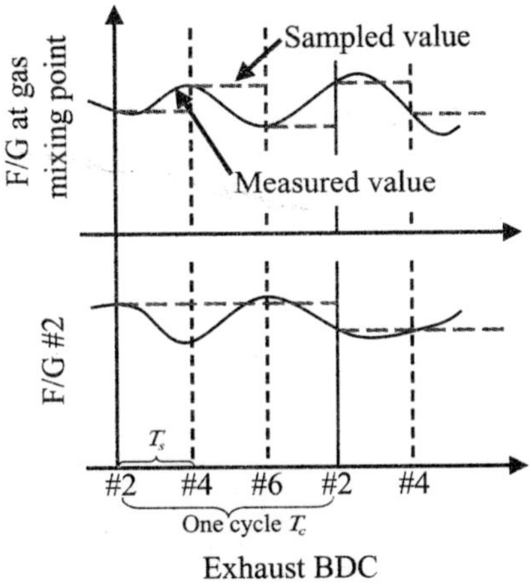

Fig. 2 F/G sampling period

2.2 Estimation Model

After the intake stroke, the A/F will be formed in the combustion and will be propagated to the UEGO sensor. The dynamics of the exhaust gas traveling pass the runners and toward to the gas mixing point, where the sensor is placed, can be represented as

$$\dot{m}_{si} = G_{si}(s)\dot{m}_{ei} \tag{5}$$

$$G_{si}(s) = \frac{1}{\tau_{ei} s + 1}$$

where $\dot{m}_{ei}$ denotes the exhaust gas flow of ith cylinder, $\dot{m}_{si}$ is the exhaust gas flow passing through the gas mixing point.

Suppose that the A/F of each cylinder is constant during one cycle. Then, the fuel mass in the gas flow $\dot{m}_{si}$ is $\eta_i \dot{m}_{si}$. That is exhausted from the ith cylinder passing through the mixing point. Therefore, the F/G of the gas flow passing through the mixing point is given by

$$\eta = \frac{\eta_2 \dot{m}_{s2} + \eta_4 \dot{m}_{s4} + \eta_6 \dot{m}_{s6}}{\dot{m}_{s2} + \dot{m}_{s4} + \dot{m}_{s6}} \tag{6}$$

The sampling period for control loop is $T_c = 4\pi/\omega_e$, where ω_e[rad/sec] is the engine speed, and the sampling period for the sensor is T_s, where $T_s = T_c/3$. For the secondary sampling rate T_s during each cycle, if we set the initial time starting the exhaust phase to be $\tau = 0$, then the gas flow exhausted by ith cylinder passing through the mixing point is represented by

$$\dot{m}_{si}(\tau) = \phi_i(\tau) = \frac{1}{\tau_{ei}} \int_0^{\tau} \mathrm{e}^{-\frac{1}{\tau_{ei}}(\tau - s)} \dot{m}_{ei}(s) ds, \qquad 0 \leqslant \tau \leqslant T_c \tag{7}$$

where $0 \leqslant \tau \leqslant T_c$. As shown in Fig. 3, we assume that after one cycle the gas flow can be ignored from the physical consideration, i.e.

$$\dot{m}_{si}(\tau) = \phi_i(\tau) = 0, \ \forall \tau \geqslant T_c \tag{8}$$

and note that the exhaust event appears sequentially and the time period is T_s. Thus, in the time domain t $(0 \leqslant t < \infty)$, the behavior of the gas flow passing through the mixing point can be represented as a periodic function defined as follow

$$\phi_{ei}(t) = \phi_i(t - (kT_c + (r-1)T_s)), \tag{9}$$
$$t \in [kT_c + (r-1)T_s, (k+1)T_c + (r-1)T_s] \qquad k = 0, 1, \cdots, \infty \qquad r = 1, 2, 3$$

for the ith cylinder.

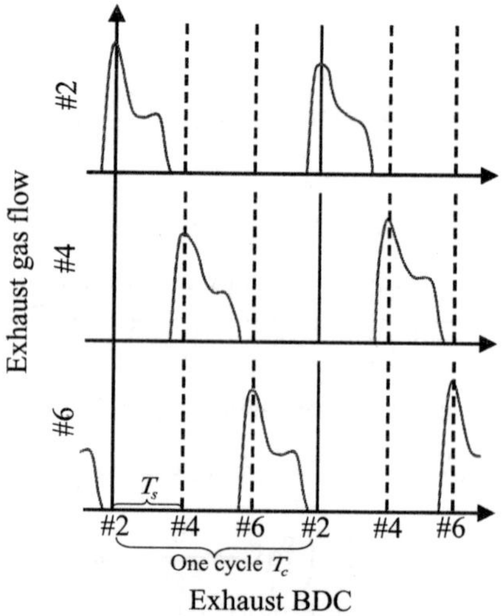

Fig. 3 Individual exhaust gas flow

In the other side, according to (6) we have

$$\eta(t) = \frac{\eta_2\phi_{e2}(t) + \eta_4\phi_{e4}(t) + \eta_6\phi_{e6}(t)}{\phi_{e2}(t) + \phi_{e4}(t) + \phi_{e6}(t)} \tag{10}$$

Therefore, if the timing of BDC of 2th cylinder is chosen as the start time of T_s, we will obtain three sampling data for the $\eta(k)$ at the timing $kT_c, kT_c+T_s, kT_c+2T_s$ in the time domain. We denote the corresponding data as $\eta^{(r)}(k)$ $(r = 1, 2, 3)$. Since $\eta_i(t)$ is constant in the period of each cycle, from (10) we have

$$\begin{aligned}\eta^{(r)}(k) &= \eta(kT + (r-1)T_s)\\ &= \gamma_{r2}(k)\eta_2(k) + \gamma_{r4}(k)\eta_4(k) + \gamma_{r6}(k)\eta_6(k)\end{aligned} \tag{11}$$

where $\gamma_{ri}(k)$ is calculated by

$$\gamma_{ri}(k) = \frac{\phi_{ei}(kT_c + (r-1)T_s)}{\Pi(\phi_{e2}, \phi_{e4}, \phi_{e6})} \tag{12}$$

$$\Pi(\phi_{e2}, \phi_{e4}, \phi_{e6}) = \Sigma_{j=2,4,6}\phi_{ej}(kT_c + (r-1)T_s) \tag{13}$$

Then, if we define the matrix $\Gamma(k)$ as

$$\begin{bmatrix}\eta^{(1)}(k)\\ \eta^{(2)}(k)\\ \eta^{(3)}(k)\end{bmatrix} = \Gamma(k)\begin{bmatrix}\eta_2(k)\\ \eta_4(k)\\ \eta_6(k)\end{bmatrix} \tag{14}$$

and furthermore, if the matrix is invertible, we define the matrix $[\Gamma(k)]^{-1}$ as

$$[\Gamma(k)]^{-1} = \begin{bmatrix}\sigma_{21}(k) & \sigma_{22}(k) & \sigma_{23}(k)\\ \sigma_{41}(k) & \sigma_{42}(k) & \sigma_{43}(k)\\ \sigma_{61}(k) & \sigma_{62}(k) & \sigma_{63}(k)\end{bmatrix} \tag{15}$$

Then, we have

$$\eta_i(k) = \sigma_{i1}(k)\eta^{(1)}(k) + \sigma_{i2}(k)\eta^{(2)}(k) + \sigma_{i3}(k)\eta^{(3)}(k) \tag{16}$$

Moreover, note that under the same operating condition, the $\sigma_{ri}(k)$ is constant, since ϕ_i are periodic functions.

For the transport delay in the sensor, z-transformation of (3) with sampling time T_c obtains the following transform function

$$G_{sen}(z) = \frac{g}{z^m(z-c)} \tag{17}$$

where $g = 1 - e^{-\frac{T_c}{\tau_s}}$, $c = e^{-\frac{T_c}{\tau_s}}$ and for the sake of simplicity, we assume that $\tau_d = mT_c$ but m is unknown. Furthermore, from (2) (4), we obtain

$$z^{-(m+1)}g\eta_i(k) = \eta_{si}(k) - c\eta_{si}(k-1) \tag{18}$$

$$z^{-(m+1)}g\eta(k) = \eta_s(k) - c\eta_s(k-1) \tag{19}$$

According to (16),(18) and (19), we have the following relation involving the sensor dynamics.

$$\eta_{si}(k) = c_i\eta_{si}(k-1) + \Sigma_{r=1}^{3}\sigma_{ir}\eta_s^{(r)}(k) - c\Sigma_{r=1}^{3}\sigma_{ir}\eta_s^{(r)}(k-1) \tag{20}$$

Under the assumption that the operating condition is same for each cycle, the coefficients $\sigma_{ir}(k)$ are constant. Furthermore, we take the error $w_i(k)$ such as modeling uncertainties and measurement noise et al into account in the model, then the model can be rewritten as the following form

$$\eta_{si}(k) = \varphi_i^{\mathrm{T}}(k)\theta_i + w_i(k) \tag{21}$$

with the parameter vector θ_i and the function $\varphi_i(k)$ defined as

$$\theta_i = \begin{bmatrix} c_i \\ \sigma_{i1} \\ \sigma_{i2} \\ \sigma_{i3} \\ -c\sigma_{i1} \\ -c\sigma_{i2} \\ -c\sigma_{i3} \end{bmatrix}, \quad \varphi_i(k) = \begin{bmatrix} \eta_{si}(k-1) \\ \eta_s^{(1)}(k) \\ \eta_s^{(2)}(k) \\ \eta_s^{(3)}(k) \\ \eta_s^{(1)}(k-1) \\ \eta_s^{(2)}(k-1) \\ \eta_s^{(3)}(k-1) \end{bmatrix}$$

According to the model, if the parameter estimation of the model (21) is provided, then we obtain immediately the estimation for the individual F/G as follows:

$$\hat{\eta}_{si}(k) = \varphi_i^{\mathrm{T}}(k)\hat{\theta}_i \tag{22}$$

where $\hat{\eta}_{si}(k)$ is estimated value of $\eta_{si}(k)$ and $\hat{\theta}_i$ is identified value of θ_i.

2.3 Parameter Identification

Thanks to the linear structure on the unknown parameter in the model (21), we can exploit a parameter estimation algorithm to identify the unknown parameter θ_i such as the least-squares method. To do this, we need the measurement of the output of the model η_{si}. However, it is not feasible in the individual F/G control with single sensor. In this section, we will show a result of identification with multiple sensors for measurement of individual η_{si}. It is only for demonstrate the availability and rationality of the proposed model. In the next section, we will propose a control approach with the single sensor.

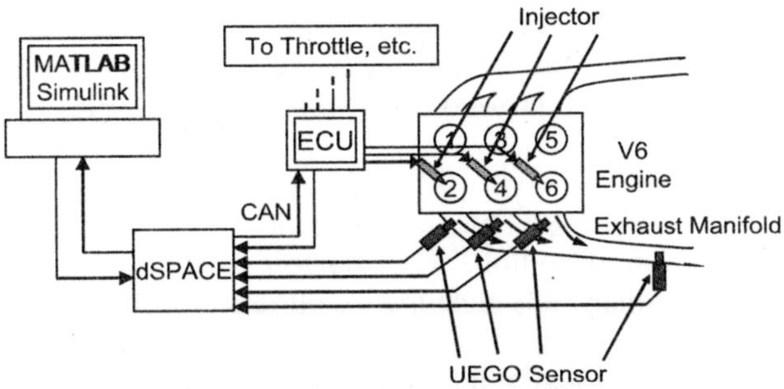

Fig. 4 Experimental facility

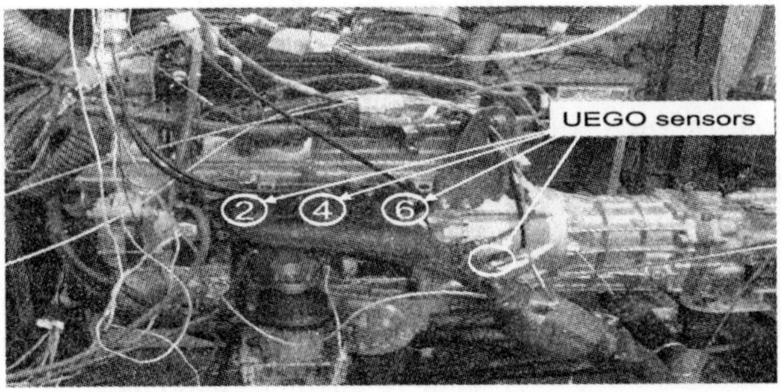

Fig. 5 Engine test bench

The test bench used in this chapter is a V6 DI engine sketched in Fig.4 and Fig.5. The exhaust system is divided into two parts, and the 2,4,6th cylinders share one manifold. The UEGO sensors for measuring the F/G of each cylinder are placed to the corresponding runner near the exhaust valve. In the gas mixing point, another one UEGO sensor for real-time control usually is equipped for sampling the multiple values in each cycle.

The control signals of ECU such as fuel injection, throttle position, spark advance et al. are bypassed by the command from dSPACE via CAN, and the sampling data with UEGO sensors are connected directly to dSPACE where the estimation and the control algorithm will be performed. All experiments are conducted after the engine warm-up and under steady state (Engine speed and load). The $\eta_{si}(k)$ is triggered soon after exhaust valve of ith cylinder opened, and the $\eta_s^{(r)}(k)$ $(r = 1, 2, 3)$ in the mixing point is triggered three times at the BDC of 2,4,6th cylinders in each cycle, respectively.

In order to identify the parameters, we used the data as Fig.6. The fuel injection for each cylinder is changed about 2% during the experiment in order to cause some imbalances of F/G in cycle-to-cycle. The top plot of Fig.6 shows the injection quantities of fuel [mm^3/cycle]. The second, third and forth plots show the F/G of No, 2, 4, 6 cylinder respectively. The plot on bottom shows real-time measurement at the gas mixing point η_s. $\hat{\theta}_i$ are identified to use the fuel injection and the sensed η_{si} according to each cylinder and in the mixing point.

The following recursive least-squares timation (RLS) was used as the method of parameter identification of $\hat{\theta}_i(k)$.

$$\hat{\theta}_i(k) = \hat{\theta}_i(k-1) + K_i(k)\{\eta_{si}(k) - \varphi_i^{\mathrm{T}}(k)\hat{\theta}_i(k-1)\} \tag{23}$$

$$P(k) = \frac{1}{\lambda_{fi}}\{P_i(k-1) - K_i(k)\varphi_i^{\mathrm{T}}(k)P_i(k-1)\} \tag{24}$$

$$K(k) = \frac{P_i(k-1)\varphi_i(k)}{\lambda_{fi} + \varphi_i^{\mathrm{T}}(k)P_i(k-1)\varphi_i(k)} \tag{25}$$

where $\hat{\theta}_i(k)$ is the identified vector of $\theta_i(k)$ and $\lambda_{fi}(0 < \lambda_{fi} \leqslant 1)$ is the forgetting factor.

The estimation results using the identified parameters are shown in Fig. 7. For the same operating condition. Fig. 7 shows affectivity of the estimation model with another experiment where the model (22) with the identified parameters calculates $\hat{\eta}_{si}$ on-line.

Moreover, identification of the parameters was conducted under 9 operating conditions. Some of then are shown in Fig. 8~11. As a result of estimation, variances of $\hat{\eta}_{si}$ estimation error are shown in Table 1.

Table 1 Variances of $\hat{\eta}_{si}$ estimation error $(\times 10^{-5})$

Speed (rpm)	Load (mmHg)	$i = 2$	$i = 4$	$i = 6$
1600	−400	1.331	0.825	0.735
	−300	2.757	2.505	1.971
	−200	2.714	2.694	1.792
2000	−400	2.190	1.594	1.069
	−300	3.140	2.371	2.062
	−200	3.442	3.154	2.535
2400	−400	3.516	2.742	1.339
	−300	5.209	3.415	1.922
	−200	7.990	6.633	3.269

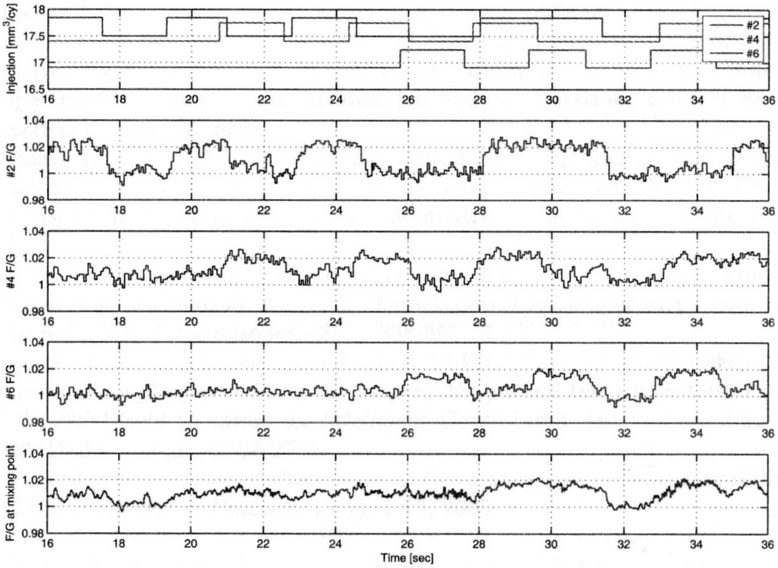

Fig. 6 Data for parameter identification (Engine speed=2000rpm, Load=-400mmHg)

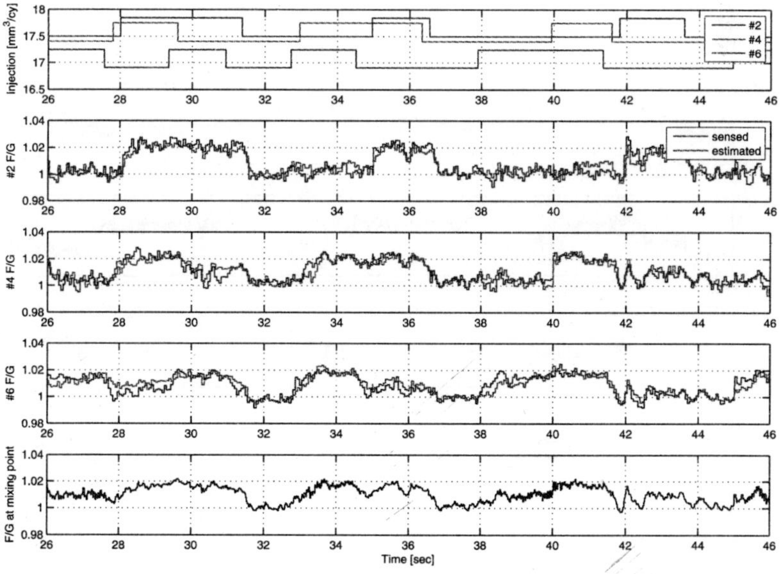

Fig. 7 Individual F/G estimation (Engine speed=2000rpm, Load=-400mmHg)

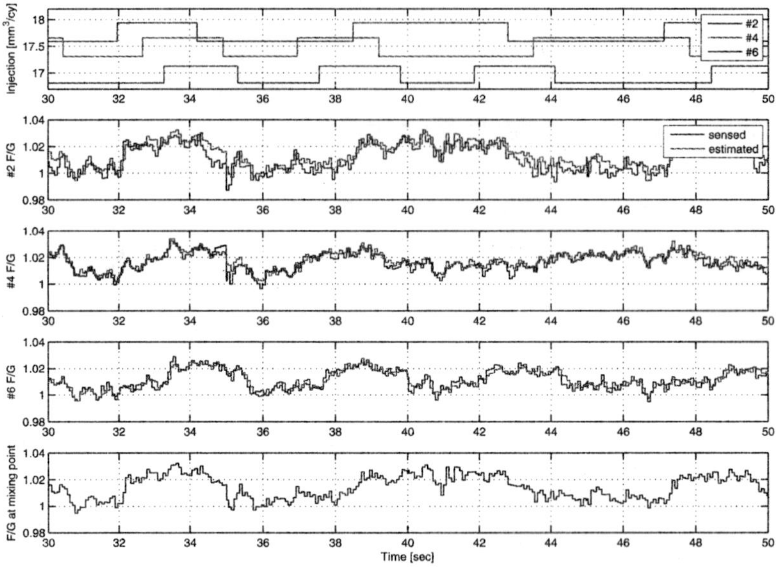

Fig. 8 Individual F/G estimation (Engine speed=1600rpm, Load=-400mmHg)

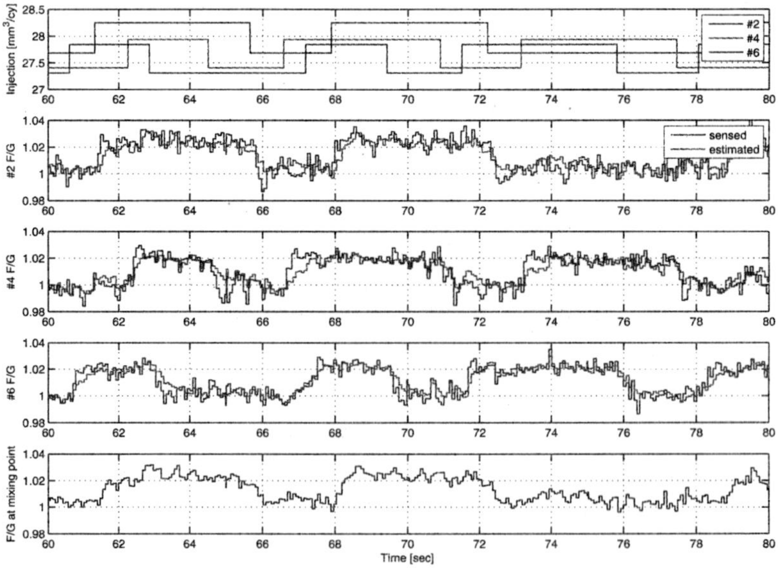

Fig. 9 Individual F/G estimation (Engine speed=1600rpm, Load=-200mmHg)

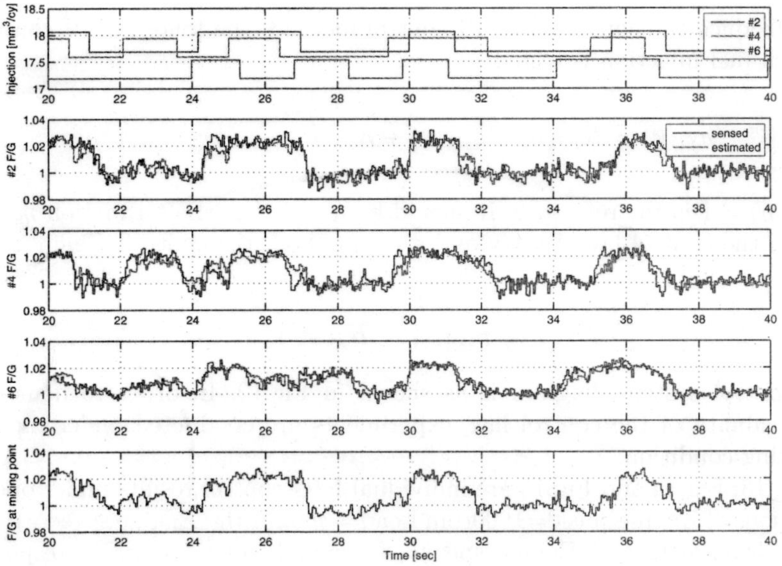

Fig. 10 Individual F/G estimation (Engine speed=2400rpm, Load=-400mmHg)

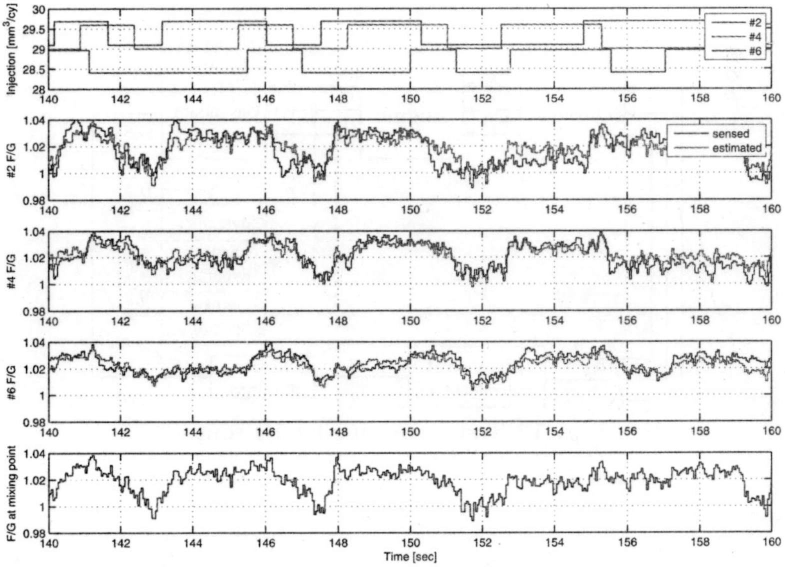

Fig. 11 Individual F/G estimation (Engine speed=2400rpm, Load=-200mmHg)

3 Individual F/G Control by PI Controller

We introduce the conventional PI control method, the following PI control law for each fuel injection is tested:

$$u_{fi}(k) = K_{Pi}(\eta_d - \hat{\eta}_{si}(k)) + K_{Ii} \int_{kT_c - T_c}^{kT_c} (\eta_d - \hat{\eta}_{si}(\tau))\mathrm{d}\tau \tag{26}$$

where $\eta_d = 1$ is the reference. It should be noted that the estimation $\hat{\eta}_{si}$ is also used in the control law. By try and error method, the controller gain is chosen as

$$K_{Pi} = 6, \qquad K_{Ii} = 8 \tag{27}$$

The control system diagram is as shown in Fig.12. In order to demonstrate the feasibility of the control law, experiments are conducted under the steady operating condition.

Fig.13, Fig.14 and Fig.15 are individual F/G control results under operating conditions of Engine speed=1600rpm Load=-400mmHg, Engine speed=1600rpm Load=-300mmHg and Engine speed=2000rpm Load=-400mmHg respectively. In the first half of figures, same mass of fuel were injected to all cylinders by a PI controller using sensed F/G at gas mixing point as feedback. After the individual PI controller activated, each commands of injection is separated and both estimated and measured F/G of each cylinder are converged to 1.

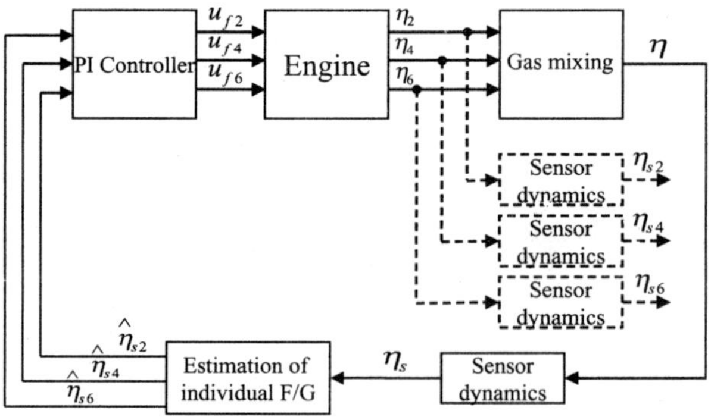

Fig. 12 System outline for PI control

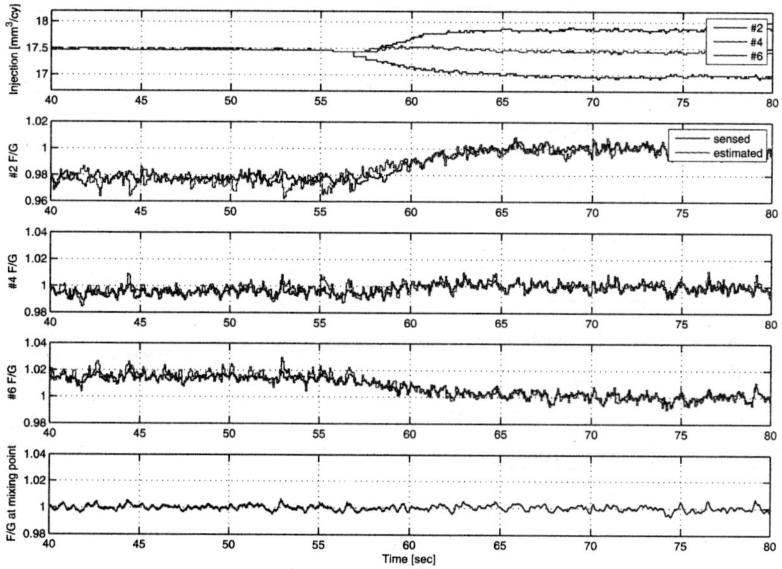

Fig. 13 Individual F/G by PI control(Engine speed=1600rpm, Load=-400mmHg)

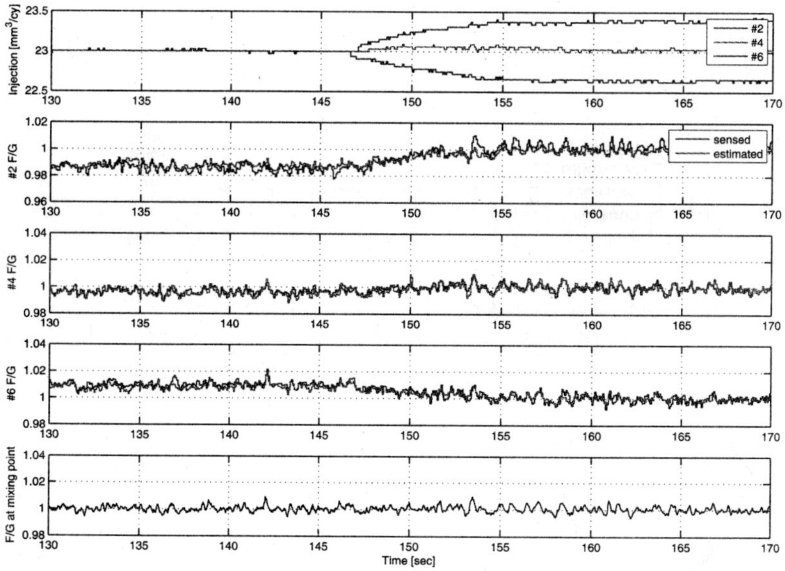

Fig. 14 Individual F/G by PI control(Engine speed=1600rpm, Load=-300mmHg)

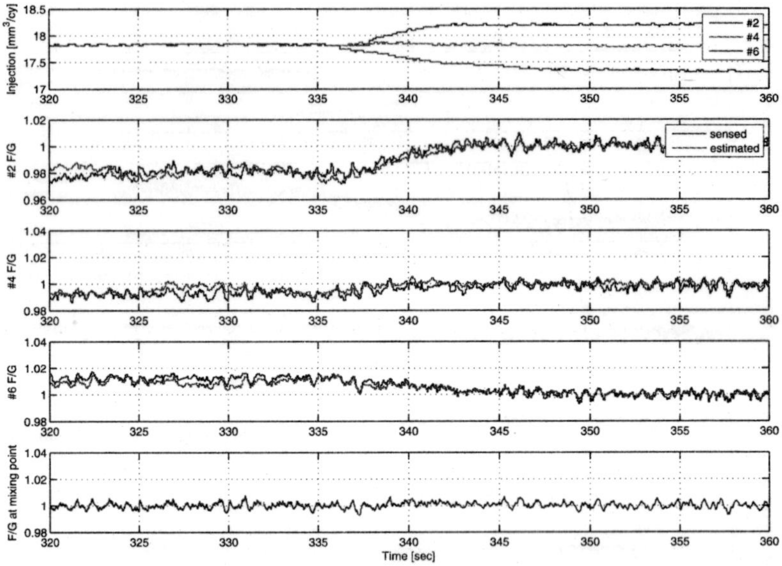

Fig. 15 Individual F/G by PI control(Engine speed=2000rpm, Load=-400mmHg)

4 Individual F/G Control by Self Tuning Regulator

In this section, we construct the adaptive minimum-variance controller based on η_{si} as well as Section 3. The control system diagram is as shown in Fig.16.

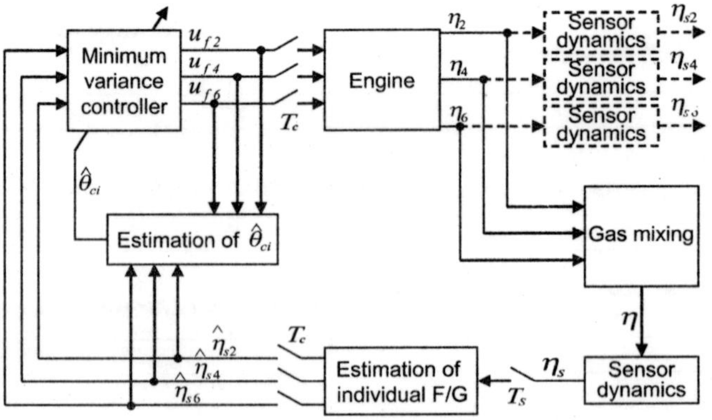

Fig. 16 System outline for STR

4.1 Control Law

We introduce the following index function for the control law

$$J = \min E[\{\eta_{si} - \eta_d\}^2], \qquad i = 2, 4, 6 \tag{28}$$

where $E[\cdot]$ denotes the expectation operator. As is well known, the optimal control law is a solution of minimum variance control problem [8], and it can be easily derived based on the dynamical model from the control input u_{fi}, the fuel injection command, to the controlled output η_{si}. Taking the fuel path dynamics, the delay during the combustion phase and the transfer property of the filter (the virtual sensor), into account, we use the following model for control law design

$$\begin{aligned} A_i(z^{-1})\eta_{si}(k) &= z^{-1}B_i(z^{-1})u_{fi}(k) + C_i(z^{-1})\omega_{ni}(k) \\ A_i(z^{-1}) &= 1 + a_{1i}z^{-1} + a_{2i}z^{-2} \\ B_i(z^{-1}) &= b_{0i} \\ C_i(z^{-1}) &= 1 + c_{1i}z^{-1} + c_{2i}z^{-2} \end{aligned} \tag{29}$$

where $c_{1i} = c_{2i} = 0$ and $\omega_{ni}(k)$ is the white noise including the error in the model. As is well known [8], the solution for the minimum-variance control problem is given as follows

$$u_{fi}(k) = \frac{1}{b_{0i}}\{C_i(z^{-1})\eta_d(k+1) - H_i(z^{-1})\eta_{si}(k) - B_{Ri}(z^{-1})u_{fi}(k)\} \tag{30}$$

where $B_{Ri}(z^{-1}) = B_i(z^{-1})R_i(z^{-1}) - b_0$. The polynomials $R_i(z^{-1}) = 1$ and $H_i(z^{-1}) = -a_{1i} - a_{2i}z^{-1}$ are solution of following equation

$$C_i(z^{-1}) = A_i(z^{-1})R_i(z^{-1}) + z^{-d}H_i(z^{-1}) \tag{31}$$

Finally, from (29), (30) and (31), we obtain

$$u_{fi}(k) = \frac{1}{b_{0i}}\{\eta_d(k+1) + a_{1i}\eta_{si}(k) + a_{2i}\eta_{si}(k-1)\} \tag{32}$$

Since the η_{si} is not directly measurable with a single sensor, in real-time control, $\eta_{si}(k)$ and $\eta_{si}(k-1)$ in the control law (32) will be replaced by the estimation $\hat{\eta}_{si}(k)$ and $\hat{\eta}_{si}(k-1)$ respectively. The latter will be provided by the estimation model proposed in Section 2 with previously given parameters corresponding to the operating mode.

4.2 Experimental Results

In order to demonstrate the feasibility of the control law, experiments are conducted under the steady operating condition. As well as Section 3, Fig.17, Fig.18 and Fig.19 are individual F/G control results under operating conditions of Engine speed=1600rpm Load=-400mHg, Engine speed=1600rpm Load=-300mHg and Engine speed=2000rpm Load=-400mHg respectively. In the first half of figures, same mass of fuel were injected to all cylinders by a PI controller using sensed F/G at gas mixing point as feedback. After the individual STR activated, each commands of injection is separated quickly and both estimated and measured F/G of each cylinder are converged to 1.

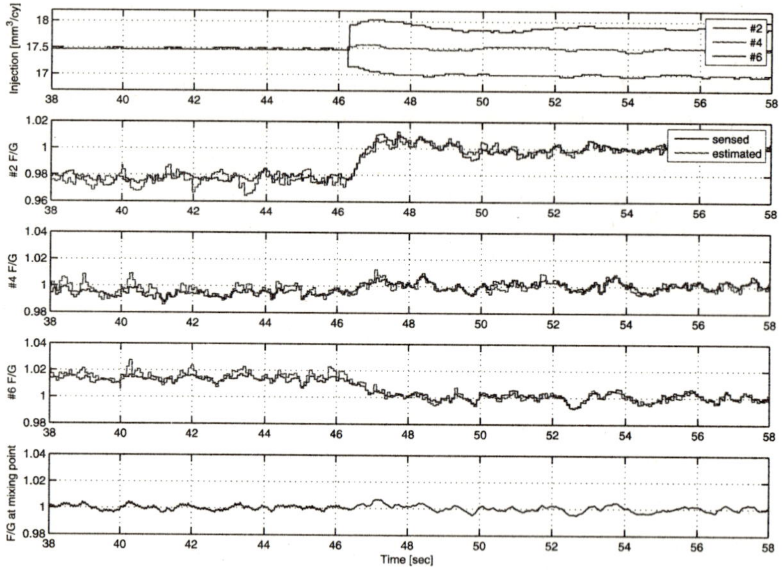

Fig. 17 Individual F/G by STR (Engine speed=1600rpm, Load=-400mmHg)

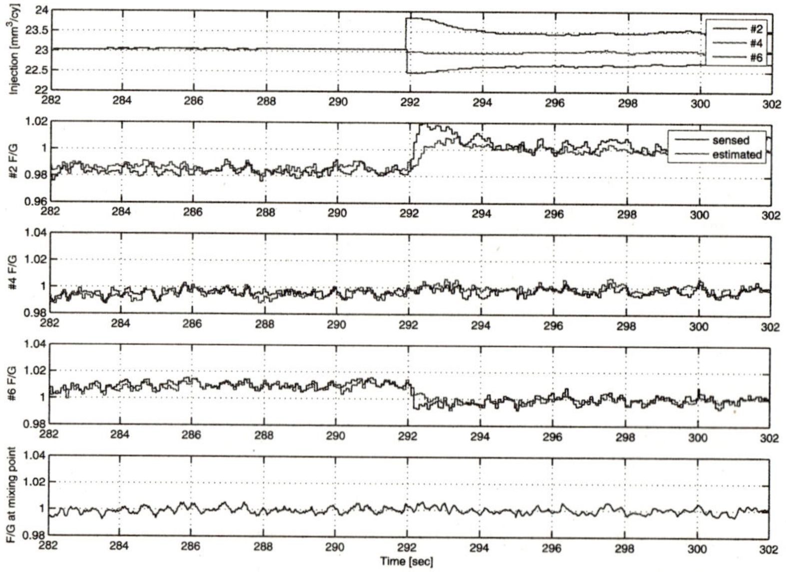

Fig. 18 Individual F/G by STR (Engine speed=1600rpm, Load=-300mmHg)

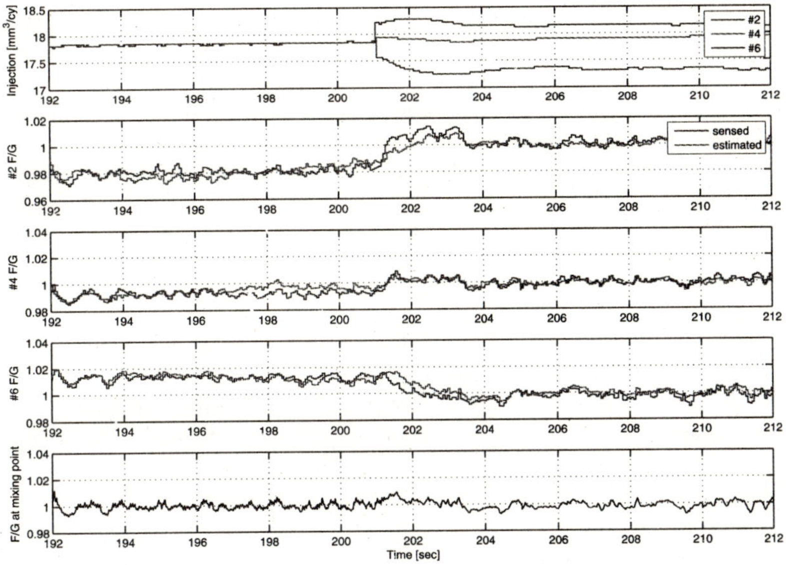

Fig. 19 Individual F/G by STR (Engine speed=2000rpm, Load=-400mmHg)

5 Conclusions

This chapter presented an individual cylinder A/F control approach based on a fuel-gas ratio (F/G) estimation model. Structure of the proposed control systems is of dual-rate sampling, i.e. cycle-based control loop and BDC-based estimation loop. In the secondary sampling rate, it has been shown that the fuel-gas ratio of each cylinder is linearly related to the one of the gas mixing point. Thanks to the linear structure, conventional parameter identification algorithm can be exploited to obtain the parameters of the estimation model under the given operating modes. Maximum and minimum variances of estimation error are 7.990×10^{-5} and 0.735×10^{-5}. With this estimation of individual cylinder, PI controller and adaptive controller are used for each injection channels. The experimental results conducted on a real-scale test bench indicate the performance of the proposed controllers.

Acknowledgement

This work was supported by Toyota Motor Cooperation, Japan.

References

1. Jessy W. Grizzle, Kelvin L. Dobbins, Jeffrey A.Cook, Individual Cylinder Air-Fuel Ratio Control with a Single EGO Sensor, *IEEE Transactions on Vehicular Technology* Vol. 40, No.1, February, 1991.
2. Y. Hasegawa, S. Akazaki, Individual cylinder air-fuel ratio feedback control using an observer, *SAE paper*, no. 940376, 1994.
3. L. Benvenuti, MD. Di Benedetto, S. Di Gennaro and A. Sangiovanni-Vincentelli, Individual cylinder characteristic estimation for a spark injection engine, *Automatica*, vol. 39, no. 7, pp. 1157-1169, 2003.
4. Yaojung Shiao, John J. Moskwa, Model-Based Cylinder-By-Cylinder Air-Fuel Ratio Control For SI Engines Using Sliding Observers, *IEEE International Conference on Control Applications* September 15-18, 1996.
5. Jeff L. Kainz, James C. Smith, Individual Cylinder Fuel Control with a Switching Oxygen Sensor, *SAE paper* no. 990546, 1999.
6. J. Chauvin, G. Corde, P. Moulin, M. Castagne, Cylinder Individual AFR Estimation Based on a Physical Model and Using Kalman Filters, *The FISITA 2004 World Automotive Congress* Barcelona, Spain, May 23-27, 2004.
7. J. Chauvin, N. Petit, P. Rouchon, Six Degrees Crankshaft Individual Air Fuel Ratio Estimation of Diesel Engines for Cylinder Balancing Purpose, *SAE paper* 060013, 2006.
8. Karl Johan Åström, Björn Wittenmark, *ADAPTIVE CONTROL Second Edition*, Addision-Wesley Publishing Conpany, Inc. 1995.
9. James A. Cadzow, *DISCRETE-TIME SYSTEMS An Introduction with Interdisciplinary Applications*, Prentice-Hall, Inc., 1973.
10. J.D. Powell, N.P. Fekete, and C.F. Chang, Observer-based air-fuel ratio control, *IEEE Control Systems*, vol. 18, no. 5, pp. 72-83, 1998.
11. J. Chauvin, G. Corde, P. Moulin, M. Castagne, N. Petit, P. Rouchon, Real-Time Combustion Torque Estimation on a Diesel Engine Test Bench Using Time-Varying Kalman Filtering, *43rd IEEE Conference on Decision and Control* Atlantis, Paradise Island, Bahamas, December 14-17, 2004.
12. P.E. Moraal, J.A. Cook, and J.W.Grizzle, Single-Sensor Individual Cylinder Air-Fuel Ratio Control of an Eight Cylinder Engine with Exhaust Gas Mixing, *Proceedings of the American Control Conference* San Frrancisco, California, June, 1993.
13. K. Suzuki, T. Shen, J. Kako and Y. Oguri, Individual A/F Estimation and Control for Multi-cylinder IC Engines, *Proceedings of SICE-ICASE International Joint Conference* Busan, Korea, Oct 18-21, 2006.
14. K. Suzuki, T. Shen, J. Kako and Y. Oguri, Individual A/F Control with Fuel-Gas Ratio Estimation for Multi-cylinder IC Engines, *Proceedings of the American Control Conference* New York, NY, July 11-13, (To appear), 2007.

A Marshalling Freight Cars in Freight Train Switchyard Using Reinforcement Learning Method

Akira Inoue, Mingcong Deng, Takafumi Harada and Yoichi Hirashima

Graduate School of Natural Science and Technology, Okayama University, 3-1-1, Tsushima-Naka, Okayama, 700-8530, Japan
{inoue, deng}@suri.sys.okayama-u.ac.jp

1 Introduction

Railway transportation is a way of energy saving and demanding environmentally less load with reduced pollution[2]. However, the railroad transportation is less flexible than the highway one because composing the freight trains or loading and unloading containers can execute only at the freight station[4,5]. Some brunch lines are laid in a freight station paralleling a mail line, and the freight train is necessary to stop and load/unload containers on the brunch line and marshalling freight cars into a train according to their destination. Therefore, for reducing the cost of the work, developing efficient freight method is an important problem because the loading, unloading and marshalling operations are complex. That is, it needs complex marshalling operations at a freight train switchyard. There are several researches of train marshalling problems[7~9]. For example, [7] studies a train marshalling method using probabilistic local search and PERT. The research solves this problem by modeling it by PERT and applying probabilistic local search to this model. However, [7] deals with trains and this paper deals with cars composing trains. In general, trains of freight cars arriving to the switching yard are separated and marshaled into other trains according the destinations of the freight cars by controlling switching points in rail tracks. Therefore, more realistic problem is marshalling freight cars needed to be solved.

This paper proposes a new method for marshalling freight cars in trains using reinforcement learning. First, problem setting is given so that the problem of the marshalling freight cars can be solved by using reinforcement learning with multi-agent [3,10]. Then to reduce the number of states, newly proposed are techniques of grouping of cars, unconditional movements of cars, defining target state for each cars and restricted movements of locomotives. Using these techniques, computer simulations show that the problem is solved in reasonably reduced computation time by using single and multi-agent reinforcement learning methods.

2 Freight Marshalling Problems

The objective of this research is to derive an efficient marshalling plan with reinforcement learning for reducing the cost of executing a marshalling work. In this section, firstly, we define a state-action variable. This element is essential to applying reinforcement learning. Also, we describe characteristic constraints of this problem. Secondly, we apply reinforcement learning to this model and update values of state-action sets with a updating expression of Q-learning. Finally, an optimal solution can be acquired by selecting an action whose value is the highest of all.

2.1 Formularization

There are two or more brunch lines in a switchyard and each line brunches off. Freight trains are moved by locomotives. Therefore, we define locomotives as agents and apply reinforcement learning to this problem.

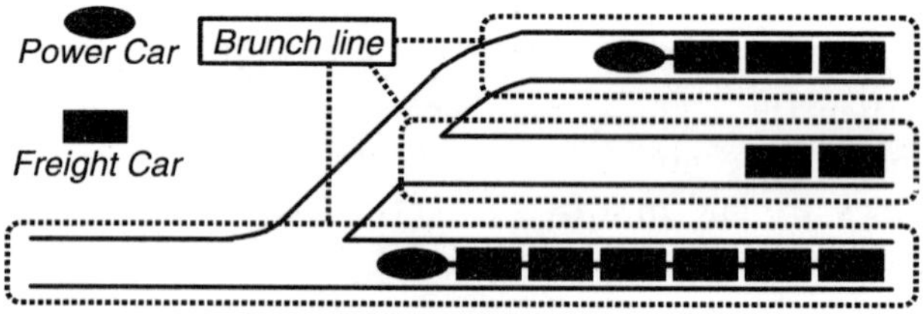

Fig. 1 Freight station yard.

Firstly, we construct state-action space. We assume there are one locomotive and $k-1$ freight cars in a switchyard. And we define a locomotive as $i = k$ and freight cars as $i(1 \leqslant i_k \leqslant k-1)$. The position symbol $i, 1 \leqslant i \leqslant ts$, ($ts$ is the total number of sections in the separated brunch lines) represents each position of cars. State space is represented by $\{(s_1, \cdots, s_k), 1 \leqslant s_k \leqslant f_s, s_i \neq s_j\}$.

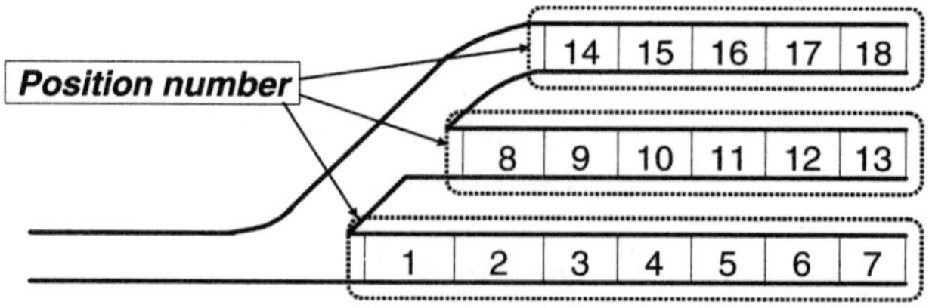

Fig. 2 Partition

Secondly, we deal with action space constructed by actions of locomotives. Actions which locomotives select every time-step are constructed by two kinds of following behaviors:

- Attach a freight car to a locomotive after moving to the line where a freight train is loaded by a locomotive
- Detach a freight car from a locomotive after moving to the line where a freight train is unloaded by a locomotive

An action of locomotives is represented by $a_i = [(l_t, l_g)|1 \leqslant t \leqslant t_l, 1 \leqslant g \leqslant t_l]$ using l_t (the brunch line where a freight car is loaded by a locomotive) and l_g (the brunch line where a freight car is unloaded by a locomotive) as the total number of bruch lines defines t_l and each brunch line is represented by $l_m (m = 1, \cdots, t_l)$. In action phase, agents (locomotives) execute above behaviors in turn.

2.2 Initial and Goal State

In this problem, the positions of freight car and locomotives before marshalling is regarded as the initial state, and the position after marshalling is regarded as the goal state. There are several sets of initial and goal states. For example, we can deal with the work which locomotives move freight trains placing in two or more brunch lines to one brunch lines with dividing groups. On the contrary, we can deal with the work which locomotives move freight trains placing in one brunch line to several brunch lines.

Train's positions of an initial and goal state are represented by the different train symbols. However, same symbols are assigned to freight trains whose goal positions are redundant.

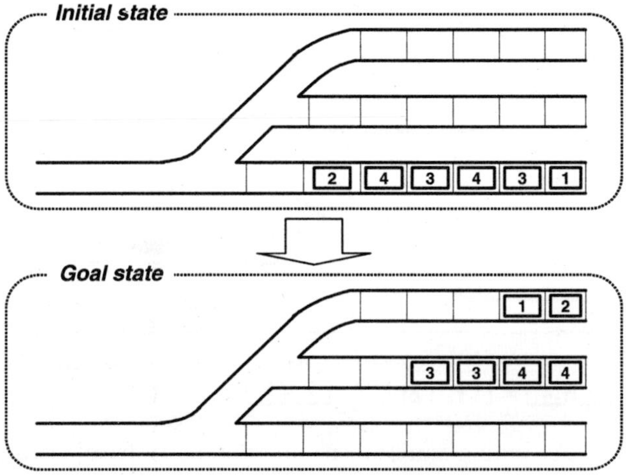

Fig. 3 Initial state and goal state

2.3 Constraints

In the goal state, when freight cars existing side by side have same symbols, these cars are considered as same group. And when freight cars belonging to same group stop side by side, these cars are attached together and move simultaneously. Furthermore, same position symbols are assigned to these cars and the number of states appearing during reinforcement learning can be reduced.

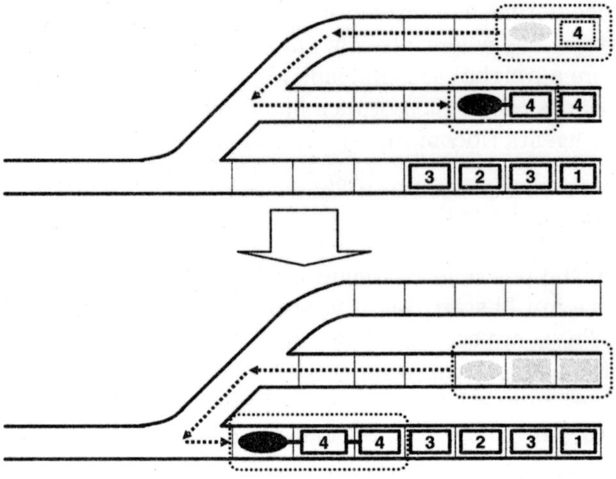

Fig. 4 Attaching and moving freight trains belonging same group

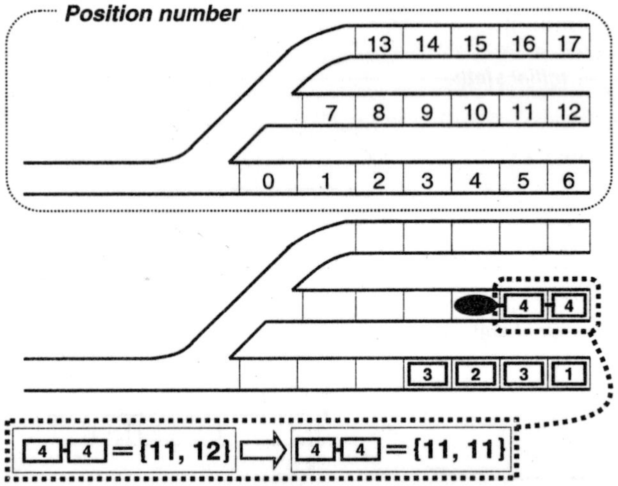

Fig. 5 Assigning same position symbols to freight trains

When there is a freight train which can reach its own goal position with only one transition, a locomotive have to move this train without considering Q-value. We call this constraint the absolute behavior'. Furthermore, when freight trains to which can be applied absolute behaviors exist in same brunch lines side by side, the locomotive move these trains to their goal positions at once.

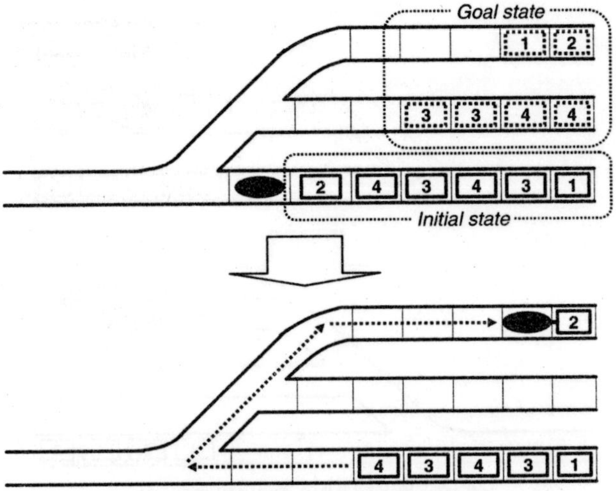

Fig. 6 The absolute behavior

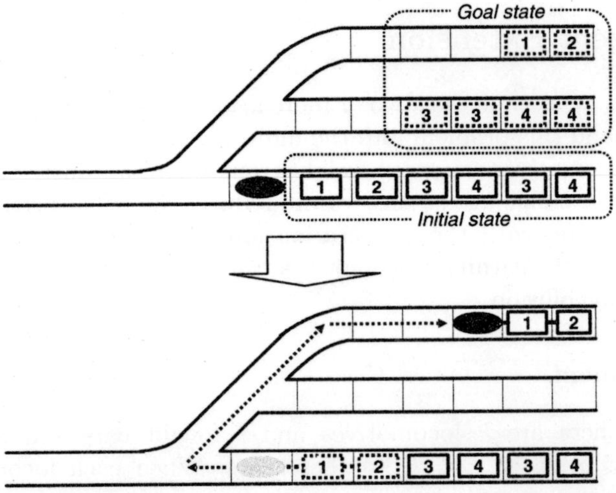

Fig.7 The absolute behavior against two or more freight trains

Agents (locomotives) can acquire reward from environment after all freight trains have reached their own goal positions. However, if we increase trains and brunch lines, the number of states will increase exponentially and learning efficiency is going to reduce greatly. Then we distinguish goal states with each position of freight trains. Once freight trains have reached their own goal position, these trains will never move. However, this rule can be applied to only the freight train whose neighbor train on the right is also applied this one.

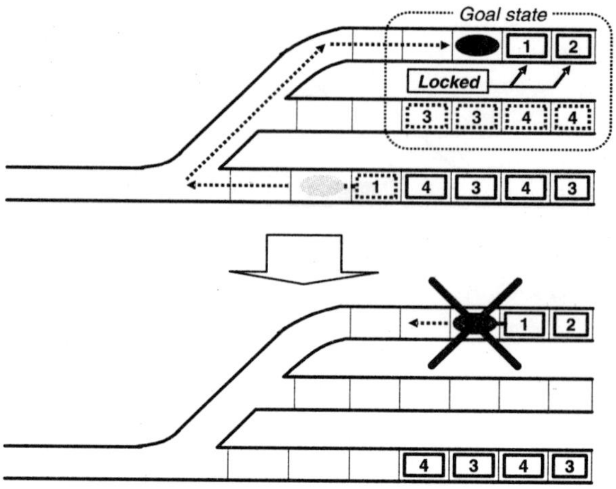

Fig. 8 Locking freight trains

3 Multi-agent Extension

In this section, we assume that two or more agents exist in this problem. In other words, we expand this problem into the multi-agent problem. By this extension, two or more locomotives can move freight trains simultaneously every time-step. Comparing with single-agent, this result reduces the time of the marshalling work. Furthermore, with the cooperation among locomotives given by multi-agent reinforcement learning, locomotives can move on the extremely specified railroad into no collision.

3.1 Environment

We suppose there are k locomotives and l freight cars and assign a symbol $i(1 \leqslant i \leqslant k)(1 \leqslant j \leqslant l)$ to these cars. When each locomotive is represented as lp_m and each freight car as fp_n, state-space is represented as $[(lp_1, lp_2, \cdots, lp_k)(fp_1, fp_2, \cdots, fp_l)|1 \leqslant lp_m \leqslant Ts, 1 \leqslant fp_n \leqslant Ts]$ with the position symbol $p(1 \leqslant Ts)$.

3.2 Interference of Locomotives

In the phase of selecting actions of locomotives, all locomotives select their action simultaneously. In this problem, we previously remove actions occur interference between locomotives. In an above example of Fig.9, one locomotive moves from the top line to the bottom one and the other moves opposite way. In this case, it is obvious that interference between locomotives is occurred. Therefore, this action is previously removed from available actions of locomotives. On the other hand, in a below example of Fig. 9, one locomotive moves from the top line to the middle one and the other moves the middle line to the bottom one. In this case, as we assume the latter locomotive have already moved to the bottom line before the former locomotive move to the middle line, these trains don't interfere. Furthermore, the number of locomotives exists on one brunch line in before and after state transition is defined as one.

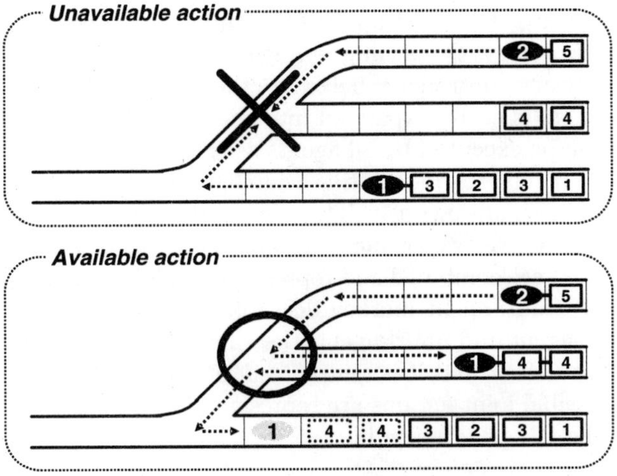

Fig. 9 Constraint of actions

3.3 Additional Actions

Furthermore, we add two following actions to locomotives: "Stop" and "Avoidance". The former action is to stop the locomotive on current place, and the latter is to move from current place to other one without attaching freight trains (Fig.10). When locomotives select these two actions, freight trains don't move at all.

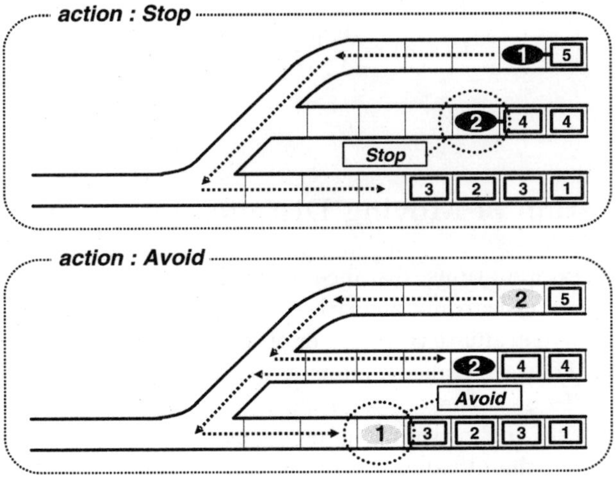

Fig. 10 Stop and avoid action

4 Applying Q-learning

4.1 Multi-agent Q-learning

In this paper, we use the algorithm of Q-learning proposed by Watkins for deriving an optimal policy. Q-learning is a single-agent learning algorithm which assumes that only one controller can execute the action in the environment. However, this algorithm is easily expanded into the multi-agent algorithm when the actions which can be executed by all agents are represented as joint actions[6]. In this problem, we regard the locomotive as an agent and one or more locomotives move freight trains simultaneously. The state and action are defined in previous section. When there are two or more agents in the environment, actions of all agents $(a_1, \cdots, a_k)$ are combined and represented as joint actions a. This method bases on MMDP (muti-agent markov decision process) proposed by [1]. Therefore, both single-agent and multi-agent, the environment of this problem follows discrete and finite MDP and it is guaranteed that the Q-function convergence.

When all possible joint actions are represented as $a = [a_1, \cdots, a_k]$,Q-value is updated with the following formula,

$$Q_{t+1}(s,a) = (1-\alpha_t)Q_t(s,a) + \alpha[r_{t-1} + \gamma \max_a Q_t(s',a)] \tag{1}$$

where $\alpha(0 < \alpha \leqslant 1)$ is a step-size parameter, $\gamma(0 < \gamma \leqslant 1)$ is a discount factor, $\max_a Q_{t-1}(s',a)$ is the maximum Q-value in next state.

4.2 Action Policy

Actions of locomotives are selected by the Boltzmann distribution. In this method, transition probabilities $P(s,a)$ are calculated by

$$P(s,a) = \frac{\exp(Q_{t-1}(s,a)/T)}{\Sigma_u \exp(Q_{t-1}(s,a))} \tag{2}$$

where T is a thermo constant.

5 Consideration of Moving Distance

In freight transfer operations, distance of moving locomotives is not considered in the conventional Q-learning algorithm. Therefore, although we solve railroad transfer problems to evaluate the number of steps, acquired policy is no guarantee of optimal one. Then we consider moving distance of locomotives when solving these problems. To be concrete, the more quickly the acquired transfer plan can achieve the goal, the higher value the model can acquire. In the conventional Q-learning algorithm, the Q-value is updated by (1). Then the Q-value is reduced by constant γ at every transition. On the other hand, in the proposed method, the Q-value is reduced by γ calculated by distance of moving locomotives. When locomotives move the next section, its distance of moving ones defines as 1.

And distance of moving between branch lines also is defined by *weight*. In the proposed method, γ is calculated by the following formula: the longer distance of moving locomotives is, the bigger the Q-value is reduced.

$$\gamma = \frac{l_{max} - l}{l_{max}} \tag{3}$$

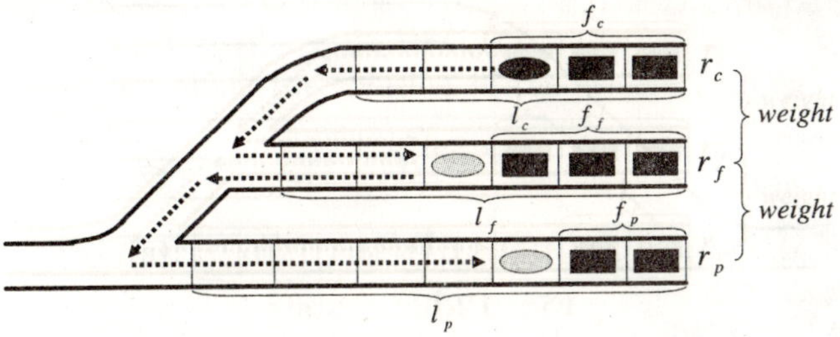

Fig. 11 Calculation of total moving distance

Then distance of moving locomotives is calculated by the following formulas:

- Vertical distance of moving a locomotive

$$dis_v = weight \times (|r_c - r_f| + |r_f - r_p|) \tag{4}$$

- Horizontal distance of moving a locomotive

$$dis_h = (l_c - f_c) + (l_f - f_f) + (l_p - f_p) \tag{5}$$

where *weight* is distance of moving between branch lines, dis_v is vertical distance of moving a locomotive, and dis_h is horizontal distance of moving a locomotive. Therefore, total distance of moving locomotives is calculated by

$$l = dis_v + dis_h. \tag{6}$$

where r_c is the number of the line a locomotive is stopping currently, r_f is the number of the line a freight car loaded by a locomotive is stopping, r_p is the number of the line a freight car unloaded by a locomotive is stopping, f_c is the number of cars existing in the line a locomotive is stopping currently, f_f is the number of cars existing in the line a freight car loaded by a locomotive is stopping, f_p is the number of cars existing in the line a freight car unloaded by a locomotive is stopping, l_c is the maximum number of cars can stop in the line a locomotive is stopping currently, l_f is the maximum number of cars can stop in the line a freight car loaded by a locomotive is stopping, l_p is the maximum number of cars can stop in the line a freight car unloaded by a power car is stopping.

6 Simulation

For confirming the effectiveness of the proposed method, we simulate freight marshalling problem constructed by two or more locomotives, 12 freight trains, 4 brunch lines and 38 sections.

Fig. 12 shows initial state of multi-agent problem. And initial state of single-agent problem is represented by removing the locomotive expressed by 2 from Fig.12. For the Q-learning algorithm, each parameter decides the following value: $\alpha = 0.2$, $\gamma = 0.8$, $r = 10.0$. A thermo constant T is defined as 0.3. In the distance base Q-learning, T is calculated by 11, provided distance of moving neighbor brunch lines defines 3.

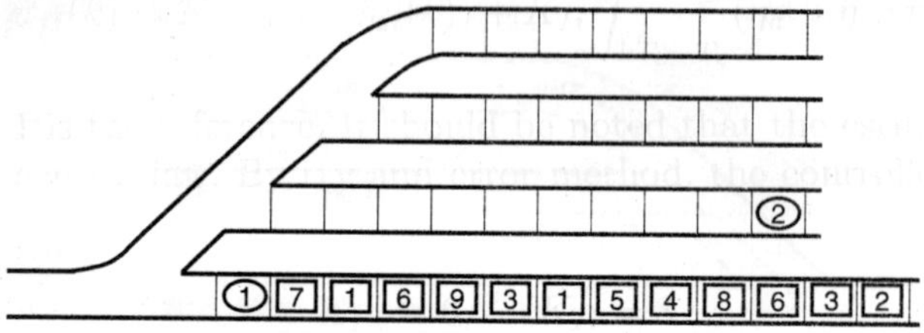

Fig. 12 Initial state

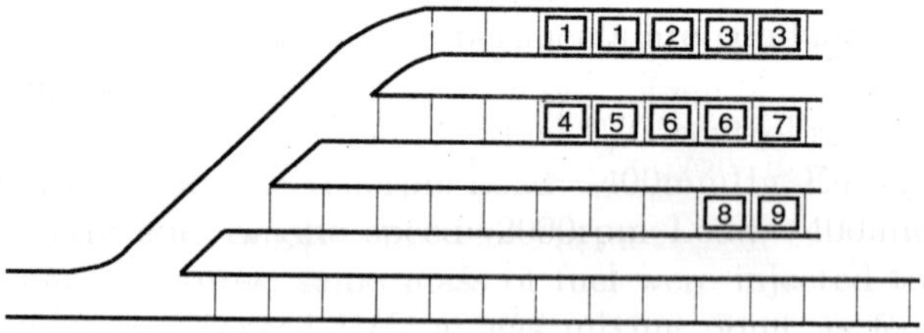

Fig. 13 State of the goal

Fig. 14 shows the result of simulations execute 3000 learning iterations. Fig.15 shows the transition of minimum number of steps in the multi-agent problem. In this figure, the vertical line shows the minimum number of steps and the horizontal line shows the number of iterations. On the other hand, Fig.16 shows the transition of minimum distance in the multi-agent problem. In this figure, the vertical line shows the minimum distance and the horizontal line shows the number of iterations. These results are calculated by the average of 10 independent simulations.

Following these results, to extend the multi-agent problem was able to derive a freight marshalling plan which can move freight trains to these own goal positions quickly. Also, in both single-agent and multi-agent, to consider moving distance of locomotives was able to derive the marshalling plan which can arrive at the goal state shorter.

	Single-agent		Multi-agent	
Considering distance	Yes	No	Yes	No
Minimum steps	19.2	19.8	16.1	16.4
Minimum distance	653	593.3	627.4	585.6

Fig. 14 Result of simulation

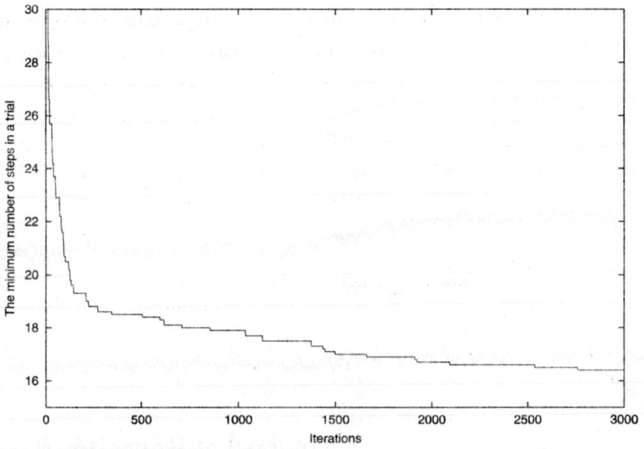

Fig. 15 Minimum number of steps in a trial

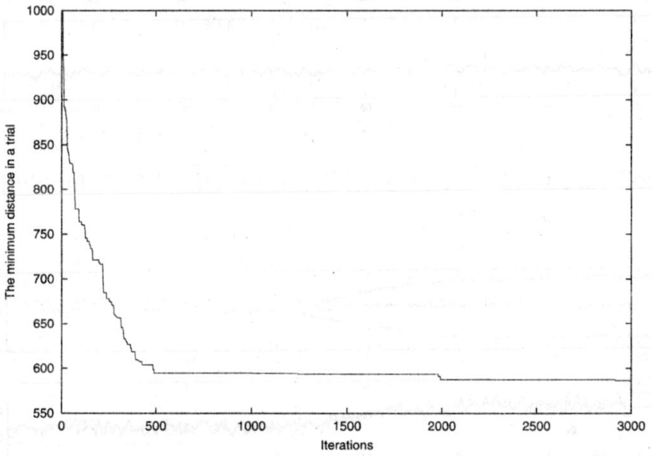

Fig. 16 Minimum distance in a trial

7 Conclusions

In this paper, we proposed a method to solve freight marshalling problems with single-/multi-agent Q-learning which is one of reinforcement learning methodologies. Then, we described constraints which consist of dividing freight cars between groups, absolute behaviors of freight trains and distinguishing goal states with each position of freight trains. Furthermore, we designed the learning model matching peculiar constraints of this problem and the learning algorithm using these constraints as prior information. Results of simulations showed effectiveness of the proposed method.

Acknowledgments

This research is supported by Grant-in-Aid for Scientific Research from Japan Society for the Promotion of Science (Grant No. 16101005). The authors would like to thank the society for the financial support.

References

1. Boutilier, C., Sequential optimality and coordination in multi-agent systems, *Proc. of the Eighteenth International Joint Conference on Artificial Intelligence*, pp.478-485, 1999.
2. Environment Information Plaza: http://kankyo.kkc.or.jp
3. Harada, T., Hirashima, Y., Inoue, A., Deng, M., Ueki, N., Multi-agent reinforcement learning using CMAC -Applying for funter problem-, *Proc. of the 46th Japan Joint Automatic Control Conference*, pp.146-148, 2003.
4. Japan Freight Railway Company: http://www.jrfreight.co.jp
5. Ministry of Land, Infrastructure and Transport Government of Japan: http://www.mlit.go.jp
6. Szer, D., Charpillet, F., Improving coordination with communication in multi-agent reinforcement learning, *Proc. of 16th IEEE International Conference on Tools with Artificial Intelligence*, pp.436-440, 2004.
7. Tomii, N., Zhou, L., Fukumura, N., An algorithm for shunting scheduling problems combining probabilistic local search and PERT, *IEEJ*, vol.119-C, no.3, pp.289-295, 1999.
8. Tomii, N., Zhou L., Development of a daily station shunting scheduling system, *Railway Technical Research Institute Report*, vol. 15, no. 9, pp. 5-10, 2001.
9. Tomii, N., Fukumura, N., NTS, City, Japan, 2005.
10. Watkins, C., Q-learning, *Machine Learning*, Vol.8, pp.279-292, 1992.

Formation Adaptation for Maximum Area Coverage

Tove Gustavi, Xiaoming Hu and Maja Karasalo

Optimization and Systems Theory, Royal Institute of Technology, 100 44 Stockholm, Sweden
{gustavi,hu,karasalo}@math.kth.se

1 Introduction

Formation control of mobile robots is a well studied problem in the literatures, such as [2, 4, 5, 8, 9, 13, 15], and [16]. Much attention has also been paid to formation split and merge and most work use a graph approach for formation switching. For example, in [3] a control graph method is used and in [12] the notion of graph rigidity is used for governing the switch.

In this paper we consider the problem of formation adaptation for maximum area coverage in a clustered environment and with limited information. This problem has many robotic applications such as cleaning, lawn mowing and landmine detection. In order to cover a large field efficiently, the use of multiple robots is essential.

Suppose each agent covers an area of the same size per unit time, then it is obvious that the optimal formation for area coverage is a horizontal line when the area is obstacle free. In many applications a small overlap of explored area is necessary, which motivates a line formation with a tilting angle, see Fig.1.

In order to be cost efficient, it is natural to mix "expensive" agents with "cheap" agents. This implies that some of the agents have very limited communication and sensing capabilities. Thus when the default formation has to split due to, for instance, obstacles, some subformations have to be maintained in order to navigate and cover the area efficiently.

The main contribution of the paper is that instead of using heuristics, we formulate the formation split and merge problem primarily as an optimization problem. Naturally, heuristics is still needed in some scenarios as arbitration. In the model we assume that each agent is nonholonomic and the follower agents have only directional sensors with limited range in terms of navigation. In contrast to switching among formations with different graph structures as is usually the case in the literature, we focus on switching among formations with the same type of graph structure (a line), but with different geometries, such as the length of the line, the orientation of the line, and the relative positions among the lines. In addition, we also provide a feedback formation control to complete the framework.

The paper is organized as follows. In Section 2, we present the problem formulation in detail. In Section 3, an optimization approach is discussed for solving the formation switching problem. In Section 4, a feedback formation control strategy based on limited sensor information is reviewed and in Section 5, some simulation results are given to illustrate our approach.

2 Problem Formulation

We assume we have a set of leader agents $L_i, \quad i = 1, \cdots, m$ which are ranked so that L_i has higher priority that L_{i+1}. Each leader L_i has a set of followers $F_{i,j}, \quad j = 1, \cdots, n$. Denote by Formation i the agents $\{L_i, F_{i,j}, j = 1, \cdots, n\}$. The leaders have greater computational capabilities and greater sensor range than the followers and are able to perform online path planning. We assume the range of the leaders' sensors is greater than $d_i \cdot n$, where d_i is the distance between followers in Formation i, so that L_i has a view of the entire Formation i. Also, we assume the leader agents can broadcast and receive information whereas the followers can only receive. Exchanging information is however costly and should be kept at a minimum. The setup is illustrated in Fig.1.

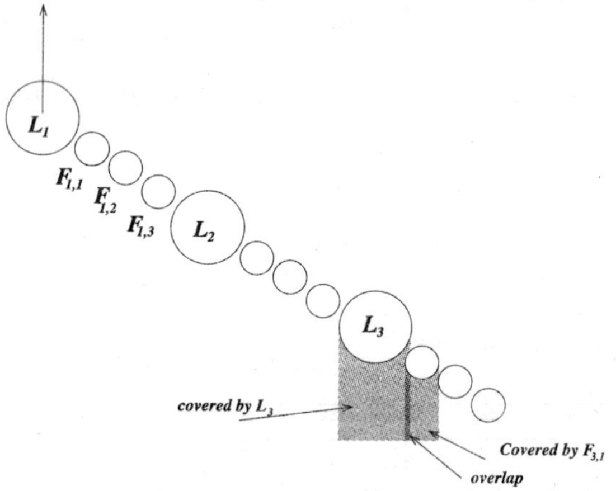

Fig. 1 The default formation with leaders and followers. Overlap is illustrated between L_3 and $F_{3,1}$

At all times, the followers $F_{i,j}$ will track L_i with a specified tracking angle β_i and at a specified inter-agent distance d_i, see Fig. 2. β_i and d_i are broadcasted by L_i. To keep broadcasting at a minimum, a leader will only notify followers if there is a change in the tracking parameters. For this reason, and since encoders might not give an accurate enough position estimate, the followers have to rely completely on noisy data from directional sensors during tracking. A control that achieves this for nonholonomic platforms is presented in Section 4. This control results in a cascaded system, where $F_{i,j+1}$ tracks $F_{i,j}$.

In an obstacle free terrain, the formation will keep together and follow L_1 at the optimal angle β_1 for coverage and overlap. We refer to this as the default formation. During this phase L_i, $i = 2, \cdots, m$, will track L_{i-1} at a distance $d_{L_i} > n \cdot d_{i-1}$ and at angle β_1. This structure prevents the tracking error to grow out of bound for the cascaded system, as there are never more than n agents between any agent and its tracking target, even though the entire formation consists of $m(n+1)$ agents.

While keeping the default formation, no communication is needed between agents, as the tracking parameters are fixed and L_i, $i = 2, \cdots, m$ uses directional range sensors to track L_{i-1}.

When an obstacle is encountered, there are several possible routes of action for the default formation. It can either change the tracking angle for certain subformations to stay together and move around the obstacle or they can split up and regroup after the obstacle. Of course the formation can only divide into m individual formations.

Based on the above discussion, we formulate our problem as follows: A1) Each leader L_i and its followers constitute a team, which should maintain a line formation with an angle $\beta_i \in [0, \pi/2)$ rad, where 0 rad implies a serial formation. This requirement is due to the sensor constraints on the followers (only directional sensors are used) and the partial overlap requirement for area coverage.

A2) Each team is to maximize the coverage of unexplored area. We assume that each leader has the ability to perform local navigation and path planning.

A3) Each agent should avoid obstacles.

A4) Transfer of information between leaders is costly and should be minimized.

A5) The formations should be penalized for unwanted behaviors. The unwanted behaviors are defined by the type of mission and might give rise to some heuristics. For instance we might want to discourage backward movement if the robot is poorly equipped with sensors on the back side.

In the following section we propose an algorithm for coverage of an area with scattered obstacles using a group of m leaders and $n \cdot m$ followers. We use a greedy algorithm that aims to find a locally optimal compromise between maximum coverage and minimum communication under certain constraints on sensors and dynamics. As the optimization is performed locally at each time step this method does not require global knowledge of the environment.

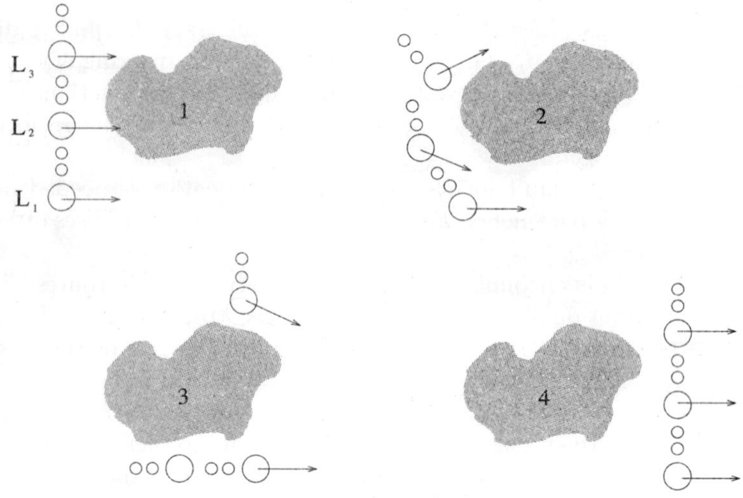

Fig. 2 Split and merge situation (from top left to bottom right). L_1 continues on planned path, while L_2 changes its tracking angle β_2 and L_3 decides to split formation. After the obstacle L_3 strives to reunite with L_1 and L_2 while L_2 in -creases tracking angle to reform the default formation.

3 An optimization Approach to Formation Planning

We base the algorithm for formation planning on receding horizon optimization of a set $\{J_1^t, \cdots, J_m^t\}$ of cost functions under certain constraints. The constraints include limited sensor ranges, nonholonomic constraints on platform movements and obstacles in the terrain.

Consider this as a two level problem. At each time step, t, the high level control computes waypoints for L_i based on optimization of a cost function J_i^t. When a new waypoint is received, L_i uses path planning in order to get there from its current position without loosing its followers. The virtual vehicle approach, investigated in for instance [11] achieves this. We will not go into detail about this lower level waypoint following control here but refer to the literature.

For the high level control the algorithm is hierarchical, so that L_i gets to make a decision before J_{i+1}^t is evaluated. That way, it is up to L_{i+1} to make sure there are no collisions between formations i and $(i+1)$. Followers obey their own leader only at all times and we assume that the tracking distances d and d_L are fixed and equal for all formations.

We will treat this as a mixed integer programming problem. First, we discretize the configuration space by placing a grid on the area. At each iteration, L_i occupies one square in the grid and can move to any adjacent square that is a feasible solution to the local optimization problem in that time step. The variables and parameters of the optimization problem are defined in Table 1.

The aim for each leader L_i is to maximize the total area covered by Formation i, and to stay close to a predefined path, while staying in, or close to, the default formation as much as possible to minimize the need for communication.

Table 1 Variables and parameters of the optimization problem

Parameters	
K	Length of grid in x-direction.
L	Length of grid in y-direction.
d	Tracking distance at lower layer formation (between followers).
d_L	Tracking distance at higher layer formation (between L_i and L_{i+1}).
$f_i(t)$	The planned path for L_i.
$w_{area} > 0$	Weight, reward for area coverage.
$w_{contact} > 0$	Weight, penalty for getting outside the detection range of L_{i-1}'s sensors.
$w_{distance} > 0$	Weight, penalty for distance to desired position relative L_{i-1}.
$w_{still} > 0$	Weight, penalty in order to avoid stalling.
$w_{ref} > 0$	Weight, penalty for distance to reference path $f_i(t)$.
Variables	
p_i^t	Position of L_i at time step t. Position is here defined as a set of indices, (k, l), that defines a square on the grid.
ϕ_i^t	Angle of orientation of L_i at time step t.
β_i^t	Tracking angle of Formation i at time step t.
Functions	
$c_{k,l,i}^t(p_i^t, \phi_i^t, \beta_i^t)$	$= \begin{cases} 0 \text{ if square } (k,l) \text{ is not covered after moving Formation } i \text{ in time step } t. \\ 1 \text{ if square } (k,l) \text{ is covered after moving Formation } i \text{ in time step } t. \end{cases}$
$z(p_i^t, p_{i-1}^t)$	$= \begin{cases} 0 \text{ if } L_i \text{ is within sensor range of } L_{i-1} \\ 1 \text{ else} \end{cases}$
$\hat{p}_i^t(p_i^t, \phi_i^t, \beta_i^t)$	Position for last follower in Formation i at time t.
$b_i^t(p_i^t)$	Integer counting how many time steps L_i has been standing on the same position.
$\sigma^t(p_i^t, \phi_i^t, \beta_i^t)$	Additional and model specific terms, see Section 5. For example, σ^t could include terms for arbitration.
$\mathcal{S}(p_i^{t-1}, \phi_i^{t-1}, \beta_i^{t-1})$	The set of states $(p_i^t, \phi_i^t, \beta_i^t)$ reachable from $(p_i^{t-1}, \phi_i^{t-1}, \beta_i^{t-1})$ in the next time step. The dynamics of L_i define $\mathcal{S}$.
Ψ_i^t	The set of positions not occupied by obstacles or formations with higher priority than Formation i at time t.
$\Xi_i^t(p_i^{t-1}, \phi_i^{t-1}, \beta_i^{t-1})$	Infeasible states for Formation i at time t, due to additional and and model specific constraints.

When the default formation is splitted, information about $c_{k,l,i}^t$ and $\hat{p}_{i-1}^t$ must be communicated between leaders.

The pre-planned paths $f_i(t)$ are defined to obtain optimal coverage of the considered area, assuming that the area is obstacle-free. If additional information is known, for example position or shape of an obstacle, this information can also be included in $f_i(t)$. For a rectangular area the paths would be parallel lines at distances $d_L \sin \beta_1$. The pre-planned paths prevent leaders from moving at random in situations where obstacles and other formations are placed so that none of the feasible solutions to the optimization yields coverage of new area.

We arrive at a set of m mixed integer programming problems. For L_i the equations at time step t are

$$\begin{aligned}\max_{p_i^t, \phi_i^t, \beta_i^t} J_i^t = w_{area} \sum_{\substack{k=1,\cdots,K \\ l=1,\cdots,L}} & c_{k,l,i}^t(p_i^t, \phi_i^t, \beta_i^t) - w_{contact} \cdot z(p_i^t, p_{i-1}^t) \\ & - w_{distance} \cdot |p_i^t - \hat{p}_{i-1}^t| - w_{still} \cdot b_i^t(p_i^t) \\ & - w_{ref} \cdot |p_i^t - f_i(t)| + \sigma^t(p_i^t, \phi_i^t, \beta_i^t) \qquad (1)\end{aligned}$$

$$\begin{aligned}\text{subject to} \quad & (p_i^t, \phi_i^t, \beta_i^t) \in \mathcal{S}(p_i^{t-1}, \phi_i^{t-1}, \beta_i^{t-1}) \qquad (2) \\ & p_i^t \in \Psi_i^t \qquad (3) \\ & (p_i^t, \phi_i^t, \beta_i^t) \notin \Xi_i^t(p_i^{t-1}, \phi_i^{t-1}, \beta_i^{t-1}) \qquad (4)\end{aligned}$$

Recall that the range of the leaders' sensors is greater than $d \cdot n$. Thus L_i can use range sensors to find all obstacles that might affect Formation i. This means that no inter-agent communication is needed for the constraints (2) and (3). The computation of the distance term in the cost function (1) will require communication between L_i and L_{i-1} only when the formation is broken. For L_1 of course the terms $w_{contact} \cdot z(p_i^t, p_{i-1}^t)$ and $w_{distance} \cdot |p_i^t - \hat{p}_{i-1}^t|$ vanish.

As (1) is a mixed integer expression we do not have convex cost functions. Nor can we require the set of feasible solutions to be convex as long as we allow scattered obstacles in the terrain. Note, however, that as long as L_1 keeps moving, conditions for leaders L_2 to L_m will change at each time step. This fact minimizes the risk for getting stuck. Should a leader still end up in a limit cycle we need to use some arbitration, for instance change the weights of the cost function.

To illustrate what is meant by $\mathcal{S}(p_i^t, \phi_i^t, \beta_i^t)$, consider an agent with unicycle dynamics (Eq.(5)). Clearly, using this type of platform for the followers, the formation cannot move sideways. This will limit the feasible moves as shown in Fig.3.

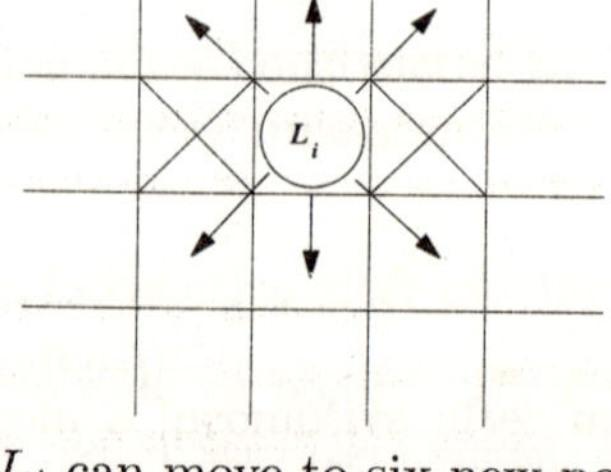

Fig. 3 At each time step, L_i can move to six new positions. Two squares in the grid cannot be reached due to the nonholonomic constraints of the followers

4 Formation Control

In this section we present the cascaded control algorithm used at all times by the followers and by the leaders while in tracking mode. This control has been thoroughly derived and evaluated in for instance [11], both in simulations and experiments under hard conditions. It is globally stable and robust to sensor noise.

Based on the proposed control, a variety of different formations can be obtained by varying tracking angle $\beta_0 \in (-\pi/2, \pi/2)$ and tracking distance d_0.

We assume that the dynamics of each robot can be modeled by

$$\begin{cases} \dot{x} = & v\cos\phi \\ \dot{y} = & v\sin\phi \\ \dot{\phi} = & \omega \end{cases} \tag{5}$$

Here (x, y) are the Cartesian position coordinates of the agent, ϕ its orientation and v and ω its speed and angular velocity.

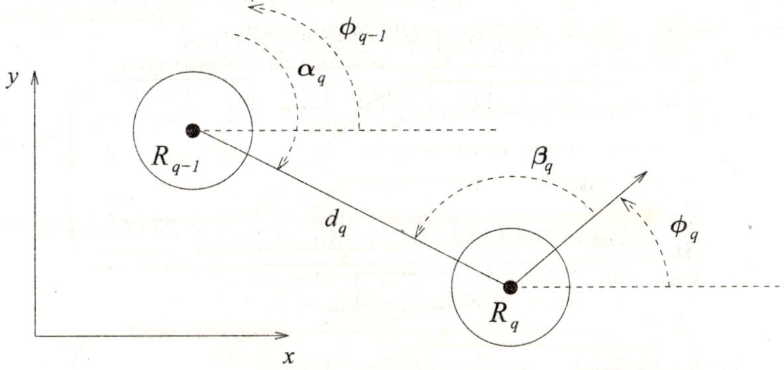

Fig. 4 Notation of angles and distances

In the following discussion of the control we will denote the agents by R_q. Here, R_q is any agent tracking another agent R_{q-1}. Recall that for our setup, the formation has a layered structure where we both have the case where followers track leaders and lower ranked leaders track higher ranked occasionally.

Consider agents R_{q-1} and R_q in Fig.4. Let $\bar{d}_q$ denote then vector between R_q and R_{q-1} and d_q the length of $\bar{d}_q$ (while d_0 is the corresponding desired distance). Defining $\gamma_q = \phi_q - \phi_{q-1}$, let $\alpha_q = \pi - \gamma_q - \beta_q$ be the actual angle from the orientation of R_{q-1} to $\bar{d}_q$ and let β_q be the actual angle from the orientation of R_q to $\bar{d}_q$. Note that the desired formation is defined by $\alpha_q = \pi - \beta_0$, $\beta_q = \beta_0$ and $d = d_0$.

With this notation, the dynamics of the cascaded system is

$$\dot{d}_q = -v_q \cos\beta_q - v_{q-1}\cos\alpha_q \tag{6}$$

$$\dot{\gamma}_q = \omega_q - \omega_{q-1}, \tag{7}$$

$$\dot{\beta}_q = -\omega_q + \frac{v_q}{d_q}\sin\beta_q - \frac{v_{q-1}}{d_q}\sin\alpha_q \tag{8}$$

and the control objective is:

Given $(v_1(t), \omega_1(t))$, find controls $(v_q(t), \omega_q(t))$ such that for all agents R_q

$$\begin{cases} d_q \to d_0 \\ \gamma_q \to 0 \\ \beta_q \to \beta_0 \end{cases} \text{as } t \to \infty, \quad \beta_0 \in \left(-\frac{\pi}{2}, \frac{\pi}{2}\right)$$

The control is finally derived as follows. A reference point (x_0, y_0) is chosen on R_q's axis of orientation at a distance d_0 from the center of R_q. Then

$$\begin{cases} x_0 = x_q + d_0 \cos(\phi_q + \beta_0) \\ y_0 = y_q + d_0 \sin(\phi_q + \beta_0) \end{cases} \tag{9}$$

Note that (x_0, y_0) can be driven arbitrarily close to the leader without causing the angle to target to be undefined and that controlling (x_0, y_0) towards the center of the target, (x_{q-1}, y_{q-1}), means simultaneously controlling the angle of orientation, ϕ_q, so that the relative angle to target, β_i, approaches β_0.

As $t \to \infty$, $(x_0(t), y_0(t))$ converges to $(x_{q-1}(t), y_{q-1}(t))$ with the following control

$$\begin{cases} v_q = \frac{k}{\cos\beta_0}(d_q \cos(\beta_q - \beta_0)) - d_0 + \frac{v_{q-1}}{k}\cos(\gamma_q + \beta_0) \\ \omega_q = \frac{k}{d_0 \cos\beta_0}(d_q \sin\beta_q - d_0 \sin\beta_0 - \frac{v_{q-1}}{k}\sin\gamma_q) \end{cases} \tag{10}$$

Defining $x_e = x_0 - x_{q-1}, y_e = y_0 - y_{q-1}$, we derive

$$\begin{cases} \dot{x}_e = -kx_e \\ \dot{y}_e = -ky_e \end{cases} \tag{11}$$

Thus the control is globally stable.

5 Simulations

Simulations were performed in MATLAB to evaluate the proposed solution to the coverage problem. A formation was set to find a way through a clustered environment. For simplicity, it was assumed that L_1 could move on a straight line through the environment without encountering any obstacles. It was also assumed that the followers could follow their respective leader perfectly with tracking angles 0, $\pi/4$ or $\pi/2$ rad, using for example the control in Section 4, and that each subformation could therefore be modeled as a straight line of a given length. This is a coarse discretization for simulation purposes, for real applications we would have to keep the angle slightly less than $\frac{\pi}{2}$ to obtain the desired overlap between agents. This will also prevent saturation for the proposed control (10).

The optimization problem stated in (1)~(4) is formulated for the general case. When implementing the solution strategy, the term $\sigma^t(p_i^t, \phi_i^t, \beta_i^t)$ in the objective function must be specified and adapted to the present conditions. In the simulations we chose to pay special attention to the nonholonomic motion constraints of the robots. The robots were assumed to be unicycles with a limited maximum speed and angular velocity. Thus, they were not allowed to instantly move sideways relative their orientations (see Fig.3 in Section 3), but needed a certain turning radius unless they stood still during one or more time steps while they rotated. The robots were allowed to reverse, but by adding a penalty term to the objective function it was made more favorable to move in the direction of orientation. A motivation for discouraging reversing is that cheap agents might not have evenly distributed sensors but mainly sensors in the front. For the optimization problem, the constraints related to the nonholonomic model resulted in a decreased number of feasible solutions in each time step.

The leaders were assumed to have better sensors and thereby better knowledge of the surroundings than the followers. In the implementation, the leaders used this information to adapt their speed so that it would be easier for the following formations to keep up.

Two issues were investigated in simulation. Firstly, the advantage of allowing splitting and merging of formations was shown. Secondly, the scalability of the proposed algorithm was tested in a simulation with four subformations.

5.1 Advantages of Splitting and Adaptation

A simulation for the case with two leaders is shown in Fig.5. This will be referred to as Simulation 1. For comparison, a rigid formation of the same length as the default formation in Simulation 1 was set to move through the same environment. This will be referred to as Simulation 2. The result is seen in Fig.6. The considered area is a clustered grid of 390 squares of which 25 are occupied by obstacles. When comparing the two simulations, it is clear that the performance of the splitted formation is much better in this type of environment. When L_1 has reached the end of its path, the robots in Simulation 1 have covered 85% of the obstacle-free area, while the robots in Simulation 2 have only covered 71%. The simulations give a strong motivation for allowing splitting even though the cost for communication increases and the path planning becomes increasingly complicated as we allow more subformations.

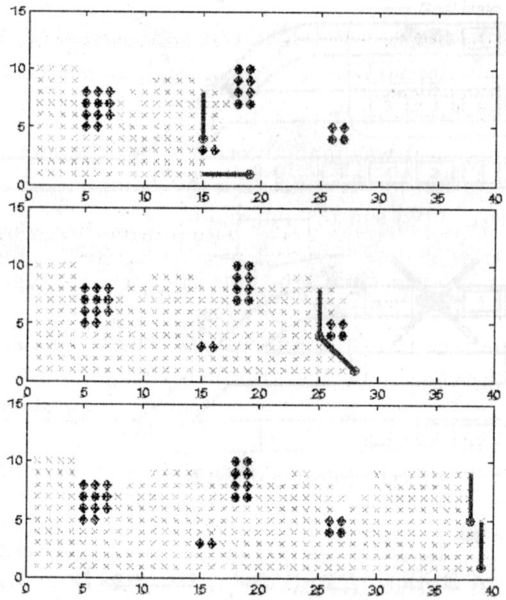

Fig. 5 Two leaders, coverage using split and merge behavior in a clustered environ -ment.The lines represent the formations and the leaders are marked with circles. The black clusters are obstacles and the covered squares are shaded.

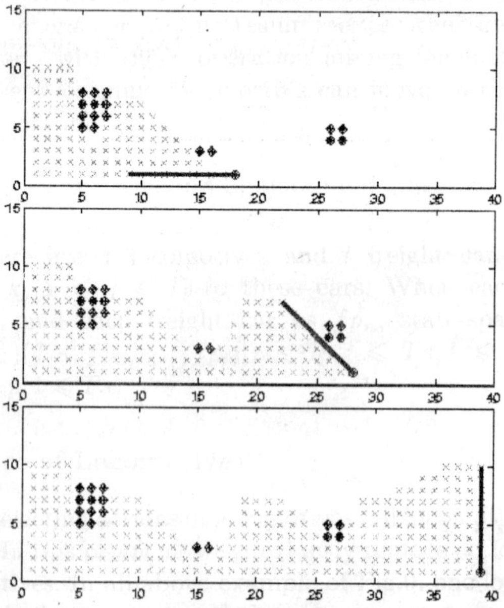

Fig. 6 One leader, coverage with a rigid formation in a clustered environment. The line represents the formation and the leader is marked with a circle. The black clusters are obstacles and the covered squares are shaded.

5.2 Scalability and Adaptation of the Optimization Approach

To illustrate how the split and merge approach can be adapted to suit different tasks a larger simulation with four leaders was performed. As can be seen in Fig.7, the optimization approach works just as well with four leaders as with two, but in order to maintain smooth navigation and vast coverage, more weight had to be put on the term in the objective function that rewards closeness to the reference path. There are however a few gaps in the covered area, especially around obstacles.

For some applications it might be desirable with a more thorough coverage, which can be obtained by instead putting a higher penalty on large distances between formations. This is illustrated in Fig.8. The result is a smaller total covered area but with fewer and smaller gaps.

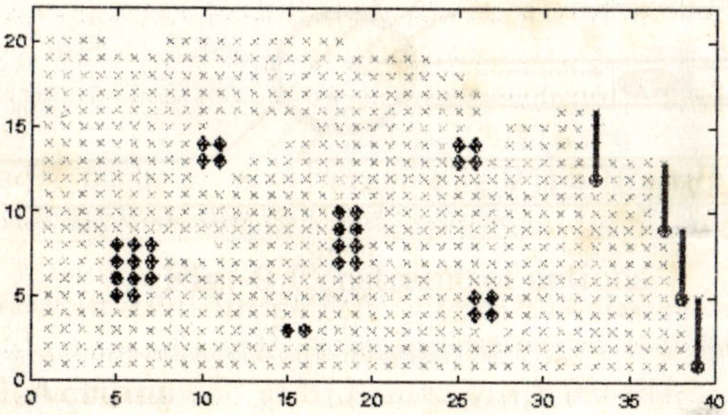

Fig. 7 Four leaders, coverage using split and merge in a clustered environment with high priority on path following

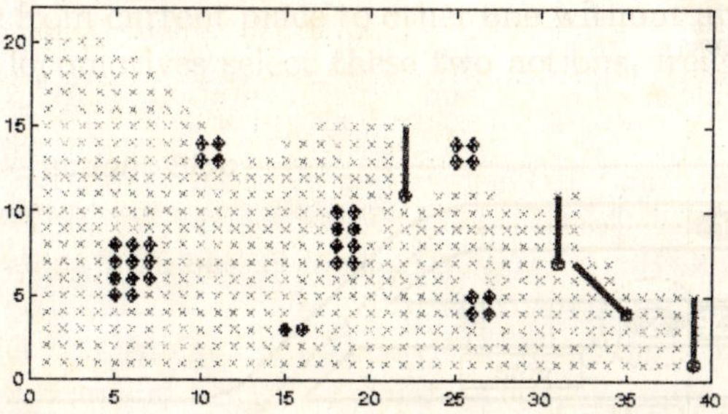

Fig. 8 Four leaders, coverage using split and merge in a clustered environment with high priority on closeness between subformations

6 Conclusions and Future Work

This paper introduces a non-heuristic strategy for merge and split behavior for multi agent formations, motivated by a maximum coverage problem. The formations are assumed to consist of agents with different constraints on sensors and processing capabilities. A local receding horizon optimization algorithm is introduced, which allows for subformations to split up and regroup to maximize coverage while keeping information exchange at a minimum. A globally stable and robust control for tracking is used. Simulation results suggest that this method for online formation adaptation is scalable and significantly improves area coverage compared to a rigid formation control.

References

1. T. Balch and R. Arkin, Behavior-based formation control for multi-robot teams. *IEEE Transaction on Robotics and Automation*, 14(6):926–938, 1998.
2. M. Egerstedt, X. Hu and A. Stotsky, Control of Mobile Platforms Using a Virtual Vehicle Approach, *IEEE Trans. Aut. Control vol. 46* no. 11, 2001.
3. J. Desai, J. Ostrowski, and V. Kumar, Modeling and Control of Formations of Nonholonomic Mobile Robots, *IEEE Transactions on Robotics and Automation, vol. 17*, pp. 905-908, 2001.
4. A. K. Das, R. Fierro, V. Kumar, J. P. Ostrowski, J. Spletzer, and C. J. Taylor, A vision based formation control framework, *IEEE Transactions on Robotics and Automation, vol. 18*, pp. 813-825, 2002.
5. J. Lawton, R. Beard and B. Young, A Decentralized Approach to Formation Manuervers, *IEEE Transactions on Robotics and Automation, vol 19*, pp. 933-941, 2003.
6. P. Ögren, M. Egerstedt and X. Hu, A Control Lyapunov Function Approach to Multi-Agent Coordination, *IEEE trans. Robotics and Automation vol. 18*, 2002.
7. Manuel Mazo Jr., Alberto Speranzon, Karl H. Johansson and Xiaoming Hu, Multi-Robot Tracking of a Moving Object Using Directional Sensors, in Proc. of ICRA 2004.
8. M. Egerstedt and X. Hu, Formation constrained multi-agent control, *IEEE Transactions on Robotics and Automation, vol. 17*, pp. 947-951, 2001.
9. W. Kang, N. Xi, Y. Zhao, J. Tan, and Y. Wang, Formation control of multiple autonomous vehicles: Theory and experimentation, IFAC 15th Triennial World Congress, 2002.
10. X. Hu, D. Fuentes, and T. Gustavi, Sensor-based navigation coordination for mobile robots, in IEEE Conference on Decision and Control, 2003.
11. T. Gustavi and X. Hu, Formation Control for Mobile Robots with Limited Sensor Information, Proc. of ICRA 2005.
12. Resa Olfati-Saber and R. M. Murray, Graph Rigidity and Distributed Formation Stabilization of Multi-Vehicle Systems, in IEEE Conference on Decision and Control, 2002.
13. A. Jadbabaie, J. Lin and A. S. Morse, Coordination of groups of mobile autonomous agents using nearest neighbor rules, *IEEE Trans. Automat. Control 48*, pp 988–1001, 2003.
14. Herbert G. Tanner, George J. Pappas, and Vijay Kumar. Leader-to-formation stability. *IEEE Transactions on Robotics and Automation*, 2004.
15. Rene Vidal, Omid Shakernia, and Shankar Sastry, Formation Control of Nonholonomic Mobile Robots with Omnidirectional Visual Servoing and Motion Segmentation, *Proceedings of ICRA 2003*, pp. 584-589, 2003.
16. Estela Bicho and Sergio Monteiro, Formation control for multiple mobile robots: a non-linear attractor dynamics approach, *Proceedings of IROS 2003*, pp. 2016-2022, 2003.